A Just Transition to a Low Carbon Future in South Africa

EDITED BY

Nqobile Xaba and Saliem Fakir

MAPUNGUBWE
INSTITUTE FOR STRATEGIC REFLECTION (MISTRA)

First published by the Mapungubwe Institute for Strategic Reflection (MISTRA) in 2022

142 Western Service Road
Woodmead
Johannesburg

ISBN 978-1-920690-32-8

Production and design by Jacana Media, 2022
Cover design: Hothouse Specialist Graphic
Text editor: Terry Shakinovsky
Copy editor: Lara Jacob
Proofreader: Megan Mance
Designer: Ryan Layton
Indexer: L-P Content & Creation

Set in Stempel Garamond 7.5/20pt

Please cite this publication as follows:
MISTRA. 2022. Xaba, N. and Fakir, S. (eds) *A Just Transition to a Low Carbon Future in South Africa.* Johannesburg: Mapungubwe Institute for Strategic Reflection

Contents

SECTION 2: SHIFT IN ECONOMIC PARADIGM

SECTION 3: TECHNOLOGY PATHWAYS FOR A JUST TRANSITION

SECTION 4:
SOCIAL FACTORS OF CLIMATE CHANGE AND THE JUST TRANSITION

Preface

THERE IS NOW GLOBAL CONSENSUS that humanity's impact on the earth's ecosystem is significant, and that climate change is an existential consequence of this for flora and fauna alike. Global discourse on mitigation and adaptation has evolved against the backdrop of growing scientific knowledge and all manner of social and geopolitical contestation.

While it has always been acknowledged that global warming will progressively have a negative impact on all humanity, its disastrous impact on the poor is now better appreciated. Yet, depending on how it is handled, the transition to a low-carbon future can itself further worsen the conditions of life for the very same sections of global society that are marginalised.

Strategies and policies on the transition to a low-carbon political economy have thus evolved from technicist, ecological interventions to a broader, transdisciplinary approach. It is in this context that the notion of a just transition has arisen. From its origins within the trade union movement to protect workers' livelihoods, this concept has found resonance among forces advocating for common but differentiated responsibility.

South Africa is in the midst of such debate, made the more urgent also by the COVID-19 pandemic.

This book, A Just Transition to a Low Carbon Future in South Africa, reflects on these issues from a variety of perspectives. It proceeds from the premise that South Africa's economic structure, political economy and broader social relations all come into play in charting the path to a low-carbon society.

Against the backdrop of South Africa's historical path dependency, the authors argue that the country's task resides in more than just reducing carbon emissions. Rather, South Africa should use this opportunity to build a green minerals-energy complex. Extraction of minerals will continue; and South Africa has endowments that are important for green technologies such as Platinum Group Metals, manganese, cobalt and nickel. Unlike in the past, the country must process a large part of these endowments within the country for domestic and global use. The development of the hydrogen economy, for instance, will require bold strategies and practical actions.

In order to place green industrialisation at the centre of the country's transition, policy-makers should facilitate relevant economic activities across South Africa's primary, secondary and tertiary value chains. This implies an industrial strategy that includes ease of entry for firms, as well as focussed skills development.

The authors caution about the danger of powerful forces seeking to subsume low-carbon efforts to the pursuit of large profits and climate diplomacy premised on selfish geopolitical interests. It is important for working people and developing countries to resist any such tendencies. At the same time, all should eschew the warped logic that current carbon-intensive jobs can be preserved at the expense of humanity's future. A just transition requires broad partnerships – with government, investors, workers and communities all part of the effort.

The authors draw attention to the spatial dimension of the just transition, including local government – given the role of municipalities in the energy system and new regulations in this regard – and complementary continental actions in the context of the African Continental Free Trade Area. Practical proposals are made also on interventions required to manage the decarbonisation of electricity generation, particularly in the Mpumalanga province.

Central to all these initiatives is the responsibility to ensure that transition finance is adequate and appropriate. While the focus on coal-gobbling Eskom and the energy sector is understandable, just transition finance should apply to the whole project of green industrialisation; and it should involve local and international commercial and development finance institutions. Critically, hype should not be allowed to substitute for objective analysis of the structure of funding, and of the conditionalities and costs attached to its various components.

This book underlines the fact that the low carbon transition in South Africa has to grapple with complex historical, social, economic, cultural and political factors. The main message is that the transition to a low-carbon society is possible, but it can only succeed if it is just and handled collaboratively.

MISTRA wishes to thank the authors, editors, peer reviewers and coordinators responsible for this volume. Our deepest gratitude goes to those who contribute to the Institute's sustenance, including the Department of Science and Innovation (DSI) for its support for this project.

Joel Netshitenzhe
Executive Director

Acknowledgements

The Mapungubwe Institute for Strategic Reflection (MISTRA) would like to express its gratitude to the project leaders and co-editors of this volume, Nqobile Xaba and Saliem Fakir, who provided oversight of, and editorial contributions to, this book. Thank you also to the project co-ordinator, Anelile Gibixego, for providing valuable support, and to Zamanzima Mazibuko-Makena for her guidance and support. Thanks too to the contributing authors for the time and energy they dedicated to producing these chapters. Appreciation is also extended to the subject specialists who reviewed these chapters and provided valuable comments.

Gratitude goes to MISTRA staff who contributed to the successful completion of this project: the fundraising led by Lorraine Pillay, supported by Magati Nindi-Galenge, operations directorate led by Abba Omar and project management teams led by Xolelwa Kashe-Katiya, supported by Dzunisani Mathonsi and Towela Ng'ambi; Terry Shakinovsky, who copy-edited the book and managed the publication process; Khwezi Mabasa for the support; Professor Susan Booysen for her efforts to ensure that this publication meets the highest standards, and Joel Netshitenzhe for his thorough reading of the manuscript.

Finally, thanks to the Jacana Media publishing team for the design, layout and production of the book.

PROJECT FUNDERS

Intellectual endeavours of this magnitude are not possible without financial resources. The Department of Science and Innovation (DSI) deserve our special thanks for their support of this project.

MISTRA FUNDERS

MISTRA would also like to acknowledge the donors that were not directly involved with this research project but who support the Institute and make its work possible. They include:

Aspen Pharmacare
Anglo American Platinum
Batho Batho Trust
Pareto Ltd
Discovery Central Services
Friedrich-Ebert-Stiftung (FES)
First Rand Foundation
Harith General Partner
Naspers
National Institute for the Humanities and Social Sciences (NIHSS)
National Youth Development Agency (NYDA)
Oppenheimer Memorial Trust (OMT)
Shell South Africa
Simeka Holdings
Standard Bank
Transnet Foundation
Yellowwoods

Contributors

NQOBILE XABA

Nqobile Xaba is a researcher in the Knowledge Economy and Scientific Advancement faculty at the Mapungubwe Institute for Strategic Reflection (MISTRA). Her work focuses on the 'just transition' in South Africa, platinum group metals beneficiation through hydrogen and fuel cell technologies, and broader climate change and environmental issues. Prior to joining MISTRA, she was a lecturer at Tshwane University of Technology. She was previously a doctoral candidate and postdoctoral fellow at the Council for Scientific and Industrial Research focusing on the development of materials for fuel cell electrocatalysts and rechargeable battery applications. She holds a BSc degree in pure and applied chemistry (cum laude) from the University of KwaZulu-Natal, a BSc honours degree in chemistry and an MSc degree in chemical engineering science from the University of the North-West. She received her PhD in chemistry from the University of the Western Cape (UWC).

SALIEM FAKIR

Saliem Fakir is the Executive Director of the African Climate Foundation (ACF). Prior to establishing the ACF, Saliem served as the head of the Policy & Futures Unit of WWF South Africa for 11 years. Saliem has worked as a senior lecturer at the Department of Public Administration and Planning and as an associate director for the Centre for Renewable and Sustainable Energy at Stellenbosch University. Before that, he served as director of the World Conservation Union, South Africa (IUCN-SA) for eight years. Saliem has served on a number of boards and is a prolific writer who contributes regularly to leading South African publications like *Engineering News*, *Business Day* and the *Daily Maverick*.

BUKELWA NZIMANDE

Bukelwa Nzimande is a researcher and Phd candidate at the Power Futures Lab at the University of Cape Town's Graduate School of Business. She has worked as a climate, energy and sustainability professional involved in research, capacity building, project management and policy development processes within private and civil society organisations over the last eight years. Her research focuses on distributed energy resources and power sector transitions, with a special focus on the democratisation of energy in South Africa. She holds an MSc in environmental microbiology from the University of KwaZulu-Natal, during which she took MSc courses in environment and resource management at Vrije Universiteit Amsterdam. Bukelwa is a social and environmental justice advocate who is committed to the pursuit of inclusive and progressive work, presenting contextual and intersectional solutions to the development challenges in society.

HAPPY KHAMBULE

Happy Khambule is an official party delegate to the United Nations Framework Convention on Climate Change (UNFCCC), and negotiates Response Measures for South Africa at international climate change negotiations. He studied law at the University of Johannesburg and was recognised by the British Council as a Global Change-maker and International Climate Champion in 2008 and 2010 respectively. In 2013, he was selected as a *Mail & Guardian* 200 Young South Africans of the year. Currently, he is a non-executive director in Mansa Advisory and a former board member of Fossil Free South Africa. He serves as a board member in EarthLife Africa and serves as an independent non-executive board chairperson of CleanCity South Africa. He also forms part of the inaugural presidential Coordinating Commission on Climate Change and acts as senior political advisor for Greenpeace Africa.

KENNETH CREAMER

Kenneth Creamer is an academic economist based at the University of the Witwatersrand. Creamer has Master's degrees in law (Wits) and financial economics (SOAS, University of London) and a PhD (Wits) for which he was awarded a Gold Medal by the Economic Society of South Africa as South Africa's best PhD in Economics submitted in 2010. In 2020 he completed a certificate course in Leading Economic Growth offered by Harvard Kennedy School. Creamer is an NRF-rated researcher with a range of publications on fiscal policy, monetary policy, open economy macroeconomics, competition policy and labour market policy, published in local and international academic journals and books. In addition to his senior lecturer position at Wits University, Creamer is a member of the management committee of SASSFE, which raises funds for tertiary education students in need of support and provides a platform for inter-generational dialogue. He serves as a director of Creamer Media, publisher of *Engineering News*, *Mining Weekly* and *Polity*. In October 2019, Creamer was appointed by South African President Cyril Ramaphosa to the Presidential Economic Advisory Council for a three-year term. From 2020, he served as a facilitator on economic policy for the OR Tambo School of Leadership.

LUCY BAKER

Lucy Baker is a senior research fellow in the Science Policy Research Unit at the University of Sussex and a visiting associate professor in the DST/NRF/Newton Fund Trilateral Chair in Transformative Innovation, the Fourth Industrial Revolution and Sustainable Development, College of Business and Economics, University of Johannesburg. Lucy is a human geographer with expertise in the political economy of the energy transition; renewable energy policy, finance and technology development; and low-carbon development in the Global South. Her country specialism is on South Africa and she has worked in various countries in Africa, Asia and Latin America throughout her professional and academic career.

JESSE BURTON

Jesse Burton is a researcher in the Energy Systems Research group at the University of Cape Town and a senior associate at global thinktank E3G, where she provides analysis and policy advice on coal transitions globally. She is a specialist in coal and electricity markets, and energy and climate change policy in South Africa. Her research focuses on the challenges and opportunities of the energy transition for coal-dependent countries, including just transition strategies. Jesse holds a BA (Hons) in history from Rhodes University and an MSc in energy studies from the University of Cape Town.

ANDREW MARQUARD

Andrew Marquard is a senior researcher in the Energy Systems Research Group in the Department of Chemical Engineering at the University of Cape Town. Andrew's current research focuses on energy-related climate change mitigation, as well as South African energy policy and governance, and draws on a wide range of skills, including energy analysis and modelling and policy analysis. Andrew holds a BA in African politics (University of Cape Town), an MA in political science (Rhodes University) and a PhD in Energy Studies (University of Cape Town).

PATRICK LEHMANN-GRUBE

Patrick Lehmann-Grube has held various research-related roles focusing on coal transitions in South Africa and renewable energy on the African continent, including being a researcher in the Parliament of South Africa, and a research assistant for the Energy System Research Group. He holds an MSc in Development Studies from LSE, where he focused his research on the political economy of South Africa's energy transition, and a BA from the University of the Western Cape. He is currently working as a programme associate at Climate Strategies.

MARIA NKHONJERA

Maria Nkhonjera is a researcher supporting the energy portfolio at the African Climate Foundation. She has years of research experience, gained as an economist at the Centre for Competition, Regulation and Economic Development, and more recently as a senior research manager at the Centre for Affordable Housing Finance in Africa. Her core areas of work have included trade and regional integration, industrial development, value chains and inclusive finance in Southern and East African markets. Nkhonjera holds a BCom (Honours) in Economics from the University of Johannesburg, and an MCom (Development Theory and Policy) from the University of the Witwatersrand.

ZAMANZIMA MAZIBUKO-MAKENA

Zamanzima Mazibuko-Makena is the senior researcher in the Knowledge Economy and Scientific Advancement Faculty at the Mapungubwe Institute for Strategic Reflection (MISTRA). She obtained her MSc (Med) in pharmaceutics cum laude from the University of the Witwatersrand. Mazibuko-Makena has authored journal articles on nano-enabled drug delivery technologies and the Fourth Industrial Revolution (4IR) and has a pending patent filed with Wits Enterprise for a nano-enabled drug delivery system. Mazibuko-Makena is the editor of and contributing author to the MISTRA volumes *Beyond Imagination: The ethics and applications of nanotechnology and bio-economics in South Africa* and *Epidemics and the Health of African Nations*, and most recently co-edited *Leap 4.0: African Perspectives of the Fourth Industrial Revolution*. Her research interests include healthcare systems in Africa, nanomedicine, systems of innovation, the low-carbon economy and the beneficiation of strategic minerals in South Africa (particularly platinum group metals).

LAUREN HERMANUS

Lauren Hermanus has ten years of experience in sustainable development research and practice. During her career, she has worked in the private and public sectors, academia and with NGOs, focusing on sustainable energy innovation, urban resilience and green economic development. Lauren has an academic background in complexity and systems thinking (MA in Philosophy) and development (MPhil in Development Policy and Practice), and has recently enrolled for her PhD at the University of Cape Town. Through her work and studies, she has demonstrated her particular interest in decentralised development and collaborative, distributed solutions to complex problems.

MALIK DASOO

Malik Dasoo works as a researcher on sustainable agriculture for the African Climate Foundation and has his MSc in International Land and Water Management from Wageningen University specialising in Soil Physics and Land Management. During his upbringing in Johannesburg, and during his BA in Social Science (majoring in Politics and Philosophy from University of Cape Town), Malik served as a committee member in the botanical and zoological student organisation. Malik headed Lintaka Zethu, an outreach project in the Phillipe township, teaching students about the importance of ecology and biodiversity conservation from an African eco-philosophical viewpoint. Malik is also a committee member of the Palestinian Solidarity Forum in Cape Town, as well as the Leftist Students Forum. For the South African Biodiversity Institute, he conducted research on the UN's system of experimental ecosystem accounting (SEEA). He went on to study agri-environmental science in Dublin where he served on the committee of University College Dublin's feminist organisation (UCD for choice).

STANLEY SEMELANE

Stanley Semelane is a senior researcher in Climate Services at the CSIR's Holistic Climate Change Impact Area, where he is responsible for supporting climate change finance as well as the mitigation and adaptation measures in the South African just transition. He has a PhD in Energy Studies, MSc in Engineering and a BCom in Economics. He has previously worked at the Central Energy Fund, the National Energy Regulator of South Africa and as a deputy director responsible for sustainable energy in the Eastern Cape Provincial Government. Dr Semelane led and represented the Eastern Cape government in all national renewable energy initiatives. He was part of the team that initiated the first South African Renewable Energy Independent Power Producer Procurement Programme (REI4P) SMME Support Programme. He contributed to unlocking opportunities for local manufacturing of renewable energy components and SMME development in the renewable energy sector. This was done by ensuring that the government procurement programme incorporates localisation. He is a thought leader in the just energy transition domain and an advocate for an inclusive low carbon economy that will ensure that all South Africans benefit (financially and environmentally) from energy transition. Dr Semelane is currently pursuing his MBA at Henley Business School (University of Reading).

LEBOGANG MULAISI

Lebogang Mulaisi is a Labour Market Policy Coordinator for the Congress of South African Trade Unions (COSATU). Her responsibilities and duties include the coordination and implementation of COSATU labour market policy and the just transition to a low carbon economy. Lebogang has a strong interdisciplinary background in economics, development economics, labour economics and labour law. She has a master's in Development Economics and a postgraduate diploma in labour law. Lebogang Mulaisi is an EXCO and MANCO member at the National Economic Development and Labour Council (NEDLAC) and represents organised labour in the labour market chamber of NEDLAC. She is also a commissioner on the Presidential Climate Change Coordinating Commission (PCCCC).

JACKLYN COCK

Jacklyn Cock has a BA BSocSc (Hons) and PhD from Rhodes University, and has spent sabbaticals at other universities including Columbia, Rutgers and the Princeton Institute for Advanced Studies in the US. She spent five years teaching Development Studies in Botswana and 40 years in the Sociology Department at Wits. She is an Honorary Research Professor at Society, Work and Politics (SWOP), University of the Witwatersand, and has published widely on gender, militarisation and environmental justice, and considers herself an activist-academic.

FATEN AGGAD

Faten Aggad is a consultant and soon to be Senior Climate Diplomacy Advisor at the ACF. Previously, Faten served as senior advisor to the African Union High Representative on relations with the European Union. She worked for several think tanks in Africa and Europe and has acted as a consultant for several international agencies.

ELLEN DAVIES

Ellen Davies is a senior research advisor at the ACF where she oversees the ACF's research team. Prior to this, she oversaw the extractives and nuclear energy portfolios at WWF South Africa. Davies has been working on questions of sustainable economic development for the past ten years and has a keen interest in geopolitics, political economy and gender. She holds BASocSc, LLB, BComHons and MCom degrees.

CHANTAL NAIDOO

Chantal Naidoo is the founder of Rabia Transitions Initiative, which consolidates a 25-plus-year career in various finance contexts (tax, debt capital markets, corporate finance, development and climate finance). Naidoo works at the nexus of transitions, finance and sustainability transitions, advising policymakers, financial actors and civil society in the transition process. She served as a regional advisor for the Green Climate Fund supporting African governments for six and half years to access climate finance and co-designed South Africa's Green Fund. Her policy and academic publications reflect her experiences in South Africa, the rest of Africa and Latin America on financing issues linked to climate and transition processes. She has a doctorate from the University of Sussex, titled 'Transcending the Interregnum: Exploring the role of financial systems in sustainability transition processes'. She is a research fellow at Stellenbosch University and Sussex University, where she guest lectures and supervises Masters and PhD students.

NAJMA MOHAMED

Najma Mohamed is the Policy Director at the Green Economy Coalition, the world's largest movement for green and fair economies. She has a background in climate, environment and sustainable development and has been involved in designing, implementing and profiling green and inclusive approaches to policy and practice. She has worked in academia, civil society and the public sector, at multi-levels and across geographies and economic sectors. Her work centres on building the Coalition's strategic focus on the supply and advocacy of policies, practices and institutions for inclusive green economies, in partnership with its 60-plus members. She works across the major policy themes of green transitions, advancing transformative policies as pathways to systemic change. She studied environmental and geographical sciences at undergraduate and postgraduate level at the University of Cape Town and completed her PhD in environmental ethics and education at Stellenbosch University. She is active in building awareness and communicating on environment, development and climate issues, is engaged in community- and faith-based action for climate and ecological justice, and in 2019 edited a book, *Sustainability Transitions in South Africa*, that explores the country's just transition to a green and just economy.

GAYLOR MONTMASSON-CLAIR

Gaylor Montmasson-Clair is a *Senior Eco*nomist at Trade & Industrial Policy Strategies (TIPS). He leads TIPS's work on sustainable growth. Gaylor is also a research associate at the University of Johannesburg's Centre for Competition, Regulation and Economic Development (CCRED). He holds two master's degrees, respectively in International Affairs from the Institut d'Etudes Politiques (Sciences Po) of Grenoble, France, and in Energy and Environment Economics from the Grenoble Faculty of Economics, France. Gaylor has been working on green economy issues for more than twelve years and has carried extensive research on the transition to an inclusive green economy from a developing country perspective, with a focus on policy frameworks, industrial development, just transition and resource security. Prior to TIPS, Gaylor worked at the French Ministry of Economy and Finance as well as the United Nations Environment Programme (UNEP).

PRESHA RAMSARUP

Presha Ramsarup is the Director of the Centre for Researching Education and Labour, University of the Witwatersrand, Johannesburg. Her PhD focused on a systems approach to change-orientated learning pathways and sustainable development. Her PhD work uncovered systemic insights into the emergence of scarce skill occupational learning pathways. Dr Ramsarup has worked as a practising educator, professional development facilitator and environmental education advisor. She has served as a technical advisor to both provincial and national governments to support the development of environmental and sustainability education within South Africa's education and training transformation process. She has worked as a researcher to produce South Africa's first Environmental Sector Skills Plan and is currently the national coordinator of the National Green Skills Project. Her work is focused on supporting Green Skills development through an employer-led demand project to identify green jobs and researching opportunities to green traditional jobs across sectors. Dr Ramsarup has been a member of EEASA for over twenty years.

Acronyms and abbreviations

AfCFTA	African Continental Free Trade Agreement
ALMPs	Active Labour Market Policies
ASEZ	Atlantis Special Economic Zone
ATR	Autothermal Reforming
AUDA-NEPAD	African Union Development Agency and New Partnership for Africa's Development
B3W	Build Back Better World
BEV	Battery Electric Vehicles
BRI	Belt and Road Initiative
CCUS	Carbon Capture, Utilisation and Storage
CDM	Clean Development Mechanism
CHP	Combined Heat and Power
COP26	Conference of the Parties
COSATU	Congress of South African Trade Unions
CSIR	Council for Scientific and Industrial Research
CSP	Concentrated Solar Power
DBSA	Development Bank of Southern Africa
DEA	Department of Environmental Affairs
DFFE	Department of Forests, Fisheries and Environment
DMFC	Direct Methanol Fuel Cells
DMRE	Department of Mineral Resources and Energy
DTIC	Department of Trade Industry and Competition
DNA	Designated National Authority
DRI	Direct-Reduced Iron
EAF	Energy Availability Factor
EAPP	East African Power Pool
EDI	Electricity Distribution Industry
EGD	European Green Deal
EGSA	Energy Governance of South Africa
EIUG	Energy Intensive Users Group

EPWP	Expanded Public Works Programme
ERA	Energy Regulation Act
ESG	Environmental, Social and Governance
ETS	Emissions Trading System
EU	European Union
FSVs	Fuel Cell Vehicles
GCF	Green Climate Fund
GDP	Gross Domestic Product
GEF	Global Environment Facility
GHG	Greenhouse Gas
GND	Green New Deal
HySA	Hydrogen South Africa
IAP	Invasive Alien Plants
IEA	International Energy Agency
ILO	International Labour Organization
IMCCC	Inter-Ministerial Committee on Climate Change
IPAP	Industrial Policy Action Plan
IPCC	Intergovernmental Panel on Climate Change
IPP	Independent Power Producer
ITSMO	Independent Transmission System and Market Operator
LEDS	Low Emission Development Strategy
LOHCs	Liquid Organic Hydrocarbons
LTMS	Long Term Mitigation Scenarios
MEAs	Membrane Electrode Assemblies
MDGs	Millennium Development Goals
MEC	Minerals Energy Complex
MENA	Middle East and North Africa
MERP	Municipal Energy Resilience Project
NCCC	National Climate Change Committee
NCCRWP	National Climate Change Response White Paper
NDC	Nationally Determined Contribution
NDP	National Development Plan
NEMA	National Environmental Management Act
NERSA	National Energy Regulator of South Africa
NEVA	National Employment Vulnerability Assessment
NPC	National Planning Commission

OECD	Organisation for Economic Co-operation and Development
OECD CSU	Organisation for Economic Co-operation and Development Coal Sector Understanding
P4C	Presidential Climate Change Coordinating Commission
PEMFC	Proton-Exchange Membrane Fuel Cells
PGM	Platinum Group Metals
PV	Photo Voltaic
RED	Regional Electricity Distributors
REFIT	Renewable Energy Feed-In-Tariff
REIPPP	Renewable Independent Power Producer Programme
RERA	Regional Energy Regulators' Association
RMIPPP	Risk Mitigation Independent Power Procurement Programme
SAAP	Southern African Power Pool
SADC	Southern African Development Community
SACREEE	SADC Centre for Renewable Energy and Energy Efficiency
SAFTU	South African Federation of Trade Unions
SALGA	South African Local Government Association
SANBI	South African National Biodiversity Institute
SAREM	South African Renewable Energy Masterplan
SDGs	Sustainable Development Goals
SEZs	Special Economic Zones
SJRP	Sector Jobs Resilience Plans
SLPs	Social and Labour Plans
SMR	Steam Methane Reforming
SSEG	Small-Scale Embedded Generation
TSAM	Toyota South Africa Motors
TVET	Technical and Vocational Education and Training
UNEP	United Nations Environment Programme
ITUC	International Trade Union Confederation
IPBS	Intergovernmental Science-Policy Platform on Biodiversity and Ecosystem Services
UNFCCC	United Nations Framework Convention on Climate Change
WAPP	West African Power Pool
WSSD	World Summit on Sustainable Development
WTO	World Trade Organization

ONE

Introduction

A just transition pathway for South Africa

NQOBILE XABA AND SALIEM FAKIR

INTRODUCTION

CLIMATE CHANGE IS THE DEFINING challenge of the 21st century and the greatest current threat to humanity. As one of the signatories to the United Nations Framework Convention on Climate Change's (UNFCC) Paris Agreement, South Africa recognises the need to decarbonise. The country has adopted a just transition framework and set a path for the low carbon transition as outlined in the National Development Plan (NPC, 2013) and the Integrated Resource Plan (DMRE, 2019). Transition to a low carbon economy is fundamentally an energy transition since three-quarters of global emissions are from the energy sector (IEA, 2021). This is especially significant in the context of South Africa where fossil fuels are significant contributors to economic growth. However, energy transitions do not occur in isolation; they affect people's livelihoods, and this is why notions of 'justice' must be brought to the fore.

In this context, South Africa's Integrated Resource Plan (DMRE, 2019: 15) makes the following appropriate statement:

> The timing of the transition to a low carbon economy must be in a manner that is socially just and sensitive to the potential impacts on jobs and local economies. It is in this context that engagements at global forums such as the G20 refer to 'Energy Transitions' and not 'Energy Transition' as a recognition that countries are different, and their energy transition paths will also be different due to varying local conditions.

The 'just transition' concept was coined by the trade union movement in the 1980s in the United States to describe support for workers who had lost their jobs because of environmental policies (Young, 1998; Ward, 2018). The term emerged from the engagement between a labour movement that was fighting to protect jobs, and an environmental justice movement campaigning against the exposure of black people and other minority groups to environmental pollution. The term 'just transition' was further used to promote green jobs in a collaboration between the International Trade Union Confederation (ITUC), the International Labour Organization (ILO) and the UN Environmental Programme (UNEP) (ILO, 2015). The 'just transition' concept is found in documents such as the Paris Agreement (UN, 2015), the Integrated Resource Plan of South Africa (DMRE, 2019), the National Development Plan of South Africa (NPC, 2013) and the Nationally Determined Contributions (NDCs). Countries that signed the Paris Agreement are obligated to outline and communicate their climate actions in documents known as NDCs.

A just transition to a low carbon economy addresses South Africa's imperatives for social and ecological justice and equity (Sengupta et al., 2019) by reducing reliance on carbon-intensive industries (NPC, 2013). 'Just' refers to fairness in the transition for all the parties involved. It takes into cognisance that the poor and vulnerable are and continue to be disproportionately affected by climate change (NPC, 2013) and could be adversely impacted by the transition itself.

Deliberations on the just transition in South Africa have intensified and will continue to do so for the next few years and decades. Climate change, widening socio-economic inequality, the precarious future of work and emergent approaches to financing arrangements have brought new urgency to the issues.

It therefore remains critical to interrogate how South Africa can ensure a just transition to a low carbon economy. The National Planning Commission (NPC) drafted the '2050 vision and pathways for a just transition to a low carbon, climate resilient economy and society' (NPC, 2019). Social partners agreed that a governing body must be formed to coordinate and oversee the just transition towards a low carbon, inclusive, climate change-resilient economy and society in a jobs summit held in 2018. As a result, the president of South Africa appointed a presidential Climate Change Coordinating Commission (P4C) tasked with advising on South Africa's climate change response (The Presidency, 2020).

The just transition will require concerted planning effort and it is important that critical elements of it are mapped out and understood. The two core questions are: how can South Africa transition to a low carbon society while providing economic opportunities for the most vulnerable? How can key stakeholders ensure a just transition to a low carbon economy in South Africa? In order for the just transition to be realised in South Africa we need to identify key stakeholders and clearly define their roles. We must investigate perspectives that have been marginalised when charting pathways for climate change mitigation and adaptation. Restructuring of the economy for a low carbon future must be a priority, including identifying opportunities in low carbon value chains. It will be necessary also to evaluate how the transition will impact on the means of production and the livelihoods of the marginalised sectors of society and how the most vulnerable communities can be protected from the effects of climate change. In addition, the role of technology in facilitating a just transition must be interrogated. Finally, there is the need to evaluate the regulatory constraints of a just transition and how COVID-19 has affected them. This publication aims to address all the just transition elements described here.

MISTRA's work on the green economy (MISTRA, 2015) provided an opportunity to investigate the path undertaken by South Africa to transition to a low carbon economy. This work examined critical questions about a united global effort on the green economy and engaged decision-makers on matters of global warming. The work was transdisciplinary, but at that point, the just transition framework had not gained the traction it has today, and South Africa was yet to frame its low carbon policies using the notion of just transition. However, various policies on the low carbon economy have since been developed and the concept of just transition has been embraced.

This book aims to broaden the discourse on low carbon transition and explore the opportunities in and impediments to making the transition fair, affordable and socio-economically viable. The core focus of the research is the shift from the traditional economic development pathway that focuses solely on economic growth towards one that also considers the environment and the broader society. It is this nexus that the book aims to explore: the interests of workers are considered; the wellbeing of broader communities is prioritised; equitable growth of the economy is fostered; the environment is preserved; and technologies as enablers of a just, low carbon economy is taken into account. The book provides an analysis of current South African policies and identifies gaps and opportunities for the development of new policies that are critical to a just transition. This introductory chapter discusses the main themes and arguments developed in the publication in various chapters. The aim is not to summarise the authors' arguments but rather to interpret and build on the book's main argument.

THEMES, OVERVIEW OF BOOK CHAPTERS AND THEIR CONTRIBUTIONS

The ability of a society to address climate change is influenced by certain key factors. These are critically explored in this book and will determine whether South Africa can have a just transition to a low carbon future and ultimately achieve net zero emissions. Key factors affecting South Africa's transition and associated policies include job security and skills development; adaptation to advanced technologies and renewable energy; vulnerable communities and climate change; spatial planning; and high carbon emissions.

Key terms are defined and interpreted for consistency, which include 'low carbon transition', 'net zero emissions' and 'decarbonisation'. In this context, low carbon transition is used to denote an 'evolutionary process to reduce carbon dioxide emissions'; it also 'identifies a vision for climate mitigation' (Wimbadi and Djalante, 2020). Net zero emissions refers to the balance between greenhouse gas (GHG) produced and that removed from the atmosphere; this is the point where GHG emissions do not contribute to the planet heating up. Low carbon strategies can be systematic while those for net zero require quantitative targets and systematic changes (Seto et al., 2021). Low carbon strategies can ultimately achieve net zero emissions once associated with quantitative outcomes. Net zero is a highly contentious concept for its underlying assumptions about technology and financialised approaches to carbon markets. For instance, the International Energy Agency's (IEA) net zero pathway relies on carbon capture and storage, a technology that still needs to be developed and is very expensive (IEA, 2021; Layke et al., 2021). Net zero targets and plans must be interrogated and evaluated to check if they truly contribute to net zero emissions. In this book, the term 'low carbon transition' is used as described above, while the term 'net zero' will be used to refer to the 2050 emissions reduction targets. Decarbonisation refers to 'actions or processes to achieve low carbon transition' (Wimbadi and Djalante, 2020). 'Deep decarbonisation' is synonymous with net zero as they both entail systematic changes and reference the 2050 emissions reduction targets (Seto et al., 2021).

This book seeks to develop and contribute to the just transition debate as it unfolds in South Africa by reframing it in the South African context, critically evaluating its elements and providing policy guidelines to enable a 'just', low carbon transition. South Africa is the most unequal society in the world (StatSA, 2019); it also has an unacceptably high unemployment rate, at 34 per cent (StatSA, 2021). Therefore, the transition to a low carbon economy in South Africa must entail addressing the socio-economic challenges the country faces, including inequality, unemployment and poverty. These socio-economic issues frame the chapters in this volume, and are central in the debates brought forward.

Firstly, this book draws attention to the linkages between industrialisation and economic growth. South Africa needs to industrialise to achieve meaningful economic growth. Therefore, green industrialisation must be at the centre of South Africa's low carbon transition in order to achieve economic growth while giving priority to the wellbeing of its citizens. Renewable energy provides a gateway to the formation of new industries, including energy trade across Africa and the globe. Green industrialisation must extend beyond energy alone to include other sectors that have high GHG emissions. Green hydrogen, produced from renewable electricity and electrolysis, has the potential to decarbonise many sectors, including agriculture, chemicals, steel manufacturing and petrochemicals. Green industrial development needs to be supported with transition technologies and critical mineral beneficiation. The transport sector would benefit from green hydrogen-powered fuel cell cars, fuel cell trucks for long-distance transport and electric vehicles. Existing policy frameworks, including South Africa's industrial policy and the African Continental Free Trade Agreement (AfCFTA), should be used as tools to accelerate green industrialisation and green industrial development. A green minerals energy complex (MEC) will emerge as new green industrial sectors are formed, which shift away from the current economy based on the fossil fuel dependent MEC. This new green MEC will be built on renewable technologies and critical minerals.

Secondly, the book emphasises that the low carbon transition needs a people-centred approach in all policies and strategies. The most important stakeholders are the most vulnerable, who will ultimately be disproportionately affected by climate change. All chapters of this book emphasise this in different ways.

Communities that will be affected by the phasing out of coal need to be consulted so that they are part of the solution and their voices are heard. Coalitions for climate justice between civil society organisations have emerged in South Africa. A case in point is the Climate Justice Charter which was submitted in parliament in support of climate justice and a deep just transition (Climate Justice Charter

Movement, 2020). The Charter emerged from the South African Food Sovereignty Campaign and the Cooperative and Policy Alternative Centre campaigns and is informed by inputs from various grassroots communities, organisations and climate activists, as well as people in the media, labour and academia. The systematic alternatives that the Climate Justice Charter proposes emanate from the grassroots inputs, and offers a transformative approach to deep just transition.

Authors in this book emphasise the importance of alliances between labour and climate activists to forge new types of arrangements that would be critical in the just transition. People will inevitably lose jobs during the transition; therefore, skills development will be essential for alternative economic development and to sustain livelihoods in affected areas. This book proposes skills development programmes that look beyond market needs and consider the needs of the individual, including interests, career goals and so on.

The most vulnerable communities will be most in need of a just transition. Just transition finance should not only be about financing climate change mitigation projects, but also about ensuring that those parties affected directly and indirectly have immediate access to finance. Ultimately, just transition finance must ensure adequate, predictable and accessible funding for the most vulnerable and affected. This people-focused approach emphasises that the just transition must be used as a tool to bridge all forms of inequality in South Africa.

Thirdly, the book addresses the gaps between existing policies and strategies that support the just transition in South Africa. The emerging energy system, with an increase in renewable energy capacity, requires structural reform of the energy services sector, especially within municipalities. Low carbon transition plans must extend to local levels and must not only include national, overarching policies that local governments may not be able to implement. The skills and training needed for the low carbon economy requires a fresh approach from all stakeholders involved, as well as caution about the possibility that the energy sector will not be able to make up for jobs losses. Therefore, community involvement in skills planning is important and alternative forms of development should be prioritised in affected areas. The industrial employment and climate policies are all core to the low carbon transition; contributors to the book analyse whether these polices are ambitious enough to be transformative. Overall, all these policies and strategies need to be aligned with the principles of the just transition.

This chapter examines the pivotal themes explored in this publication, namely, the landing of the just transition in South Africa; the shift required in economic paradigm including financing the just transition; social factors of the just transition; and technology as an enabler of the just transition. Authors address these core themes using diverse approaches. The analysis of the literature on the just transition and climate change from government policies draws on books, academic articles and media reports as well as case studies. The book adopts a transdisciplinary approach using frameworks drawn from the social sciences, political science, economics and physical sciences. The chapters feature voices and perspectives from experts in various fields, who have conducted current, inclusive and evidence-based research. The focus is mainly on the South African context but the book also draws on other African and global cases for a broader perspective. The research seeks to pave the way for South Africa to centre the just transition in its policies to ensure that the low carbon economy leaves no one behind.

The landing of the just transition in South Africa

South Africa's transition to a low carbon economy is being conducted through a just transition framework; however, policies and interventions related to climate change were not always framed in this manner. The climate debate has evolved from a limited ecological view to one that considers a broader context, including the effects of climate change on livelihoods and how the vulnerable can be protected. It is important to map and understand how the climate agenda has evolved from a scientific concept and an environmental issue to an economic and social justice issue.

The second chapter by Bukelwa Nzimande and Happy Khambule outlines the science and history of South Africa's transitional path to achieving a low carbon economy. It identifies key underpinning drivers and challenges as these are crucial for devising and implementing inclusive, context-specific solutions. The chapter further presents a case for why an interconnected response to the climate crisis, and associated mitigation and sectoral decarbonisation efforts, should take account of the complex socio-economic linkages that dominate many developing countries and the Global South. South Africa's path to a low carbon future should be designed for the country's context to ensure pragmatic application and success. The authors highlight how the growing understanding of climate change and its associated impacts have influenced South Africa's preliminary response. They outline South Africa's context and progress in developing policy commitments to climate action. Authors also argue that the process of determining South Africa's contribution under the Paris Agreement requires South Africa's leaders to provide ambitious contributions, coupled with decisive and bold actions.

This chapter emphasises how South Africa's commitment towards a low carbon future should be cognisant of and responsive to interconnected environmental, social and economic crises, which converge as key considerations for decision-makers. The COVID-19 pandemic thrust nations into unprecedented conditions, and as countries plan their respective recoveries, numerous possibilities and opportunities exist to refocus the transition. The chapter concludes with an analysis of how South Africa can learn from its history and experience of developing and championing a green recovery, to transition effectively to a more resilient, inclusive, cleaner and low carbon society. The just transition concept has moved from only considering workers to a broader societal approach that seeks to address socio-economic challenges such as inequality and the impact of climate change on the most vulnerable members of society. Identifying the policy areas that will be most impacted by the low carbon economy, and identifying key partnerships, is crucial. Najma Mohamed and Gaylor Montmasson-Clair, in chapter 3, seek to understand how South Africa's just transition vision has been adopted into key policies, namely industrial, employment and climate policies.

Mohamed and Montmasson-Clair develop a normative framework that outlines the various dimensions of a just transition. They then use the framework to assess the alignment of key policies in a just transition in South Africa aimed at a transformative transition. The chapter highlights the importance of stakeholder (particularly civil society) processes to ensure a people-centred just transition in South Africa. The authors argue that in two different framings of the just transition – both a narrow one which prioritises workers and a wider one which also encompasses society – there is a failure to focus on the most vulnerable stakeholders. The framing is cognisant of the fact that not everyone is vulnerable; therefore, in the conceptual framing, no priority is established between stakeholders. Priorities would effectively be place or issue specific. Secondly, the action associated with the just transition is characterised into three dimensions of justice namely procedural, distributive and restorative justice (McCauley and Heffron, 2018; Just Transition Research Collaborative, 2018; Cahill and Allen, 2020).

The authors use case studies of the three key just transition policies (industrial, employment and climate) to interrogate what this looks like in reality. The relevant questions are: who is engaged with, consulted and driving dialogue?; who will pay and who will benefit from transitions?; and how are damages caused by transitions compensated? The chapter concludes by calling for transformative just transition approaches which add depth and meaning to the mantra of 'leaving no one behind'.

A shift in economic paradigm

Transitioning to a low carbon economy requires modification to the current structure of the economy; a shift from a fossil fuel-based economy with energy-intensive industries to a mixed energy system that is energy efficient with diverse energy sources is required. The energy transition must be designed to promote inclusive growth, industrial development and employment creation. The unbundling of South Africa's main electricity supplier, Eskom, needs to be fast-tracked as renewable energy requires Eskom transmission and distribution facilities. Energy planning also directly affects economic growth. The decarbonisation strategy will inevitably involve the decommissioning of coal power plants and grid expansion to accommodate a new clean energy mix and electrification. These changes will have major implications for the structure of the economy. In chapter 4, Kenneth Creamer emphasises that a fundamental change in the South African economic structure is necessary for the just transition. He questions how South Africa's energy transition can be optimally designed to promote inclusive growth, industrial development and employment creation. While doing so, he emphasises that in a well-managed energy transition, with adequate planning for affected workers and communities, trade unions will find it easier to be forward looking and will be less inclined to insist on a worker's right to keep a particular job. The workers' demands can rather be focused on the need for adequate new job opportunities and support for training and new investments. Furthermore, the incorporation of renewable energy into South Africa's energy system to counter the effects of power shortages will simultaneously address the country's energy needs and climate change. The falling costs of renewable energy will foster a new economy based on renewables. However, the economy needs restructuring to allow for renewables to be fully integrated. Creamer argues that there will no longer be any trade-offs where green technology must be adopted even though it costs more. Rather, economic forces will dictate that such technology should be adopted as it costs less.

The amendment of the Electricity Regulation Act 4 of 2006 will allow companies and businesses to procure up to 100MW of electricity. This will be a boost to the economy, which has lost billions of rand due to loadshedding. Easing regulations on independent power generation will ensure energy security and stimulate investment in renewable energy. Independent power producers may produce excess power that must be sold using Eskom transmission and distribution lines, and in turn Eskom can generate revenue. Chapter 4 argues that South Africa needs to transition to a system characterised by less centralised and more distributed electricity generation, which is driven by a combination of self-reinforcing technological changes, decarbonisation objectives and economic forces.

Eskom is an economic liability for South Africa as the country has bailed out the entity year after year. The restructuring of Eskom into generation, transmission and distribution entities could potentially enable the entity to gain access to concessional global Green Finance and make use of such finance to effectively reduce its borrowing costs, as argued by Creamer. Chapter 4 cautions that if the low carbon transition does not occur at an accelerated pace, South Africa risks the imposition of a carbon tax on exports deemed as a 'carbon border adjustment mechanism' by the European Union. Thus, South Africa's competitiveness, and to its export market, could be lost. The chapter concludes that all stakeholders must be forward looking and embrace technological change in a manner that protects those threatened by the low carbon transition. This can be done mainly through retraining, by facilitating new investments and ease of entry for firms, as well as increased competition so that South Africa can move onto a higher productivity, higher wage and higher employment growth path.

In chapter 5, Jesse Burton, Andrew Marquard, Lucy Baker and Patrick Lehmann-Grube analyse the changing structure of the coal industry and the risks to dependent firms and regions reliant on coal for jobs. The chapter focuses on the role of the energy sector and its associated political landscape within what has been termed the minerals energy complex (MEC). This term has been used to characterise South Africa's economy, as it was built on the availability of cheap coal to generate energy. As a result, most industrial activities are quite energy intensive. This was a challenge inherited from the apartheid government; this system needs to be dismantled to make way for a new system that is cognisant of South Africa's carbon footprint. South Africa generates 92 per cent of its electricity and 25 per cent of its liquid fuels from coal (NPC, 2013; Burton et al., 2019). Coal provides 69 per cent of the country's energy supply (DoE, 2019) and coal mining is responsible for 19 per cent of total employment in the mining sector (Minerals Council South Africa, 2018).

This chapter zooms in on the characteristics of South Africa's energy system. It evaluates the significant potential of renewable energy, the Renewable Independent Power Procurement Programme (REIPPP), the growing scramble for gas and the associated risks of carbon lock-in. It also discusses the ongoing controversy around nuclear energy. The chapter explores how technology, market shifts and climate politics are combining to unpack the structure and functioning of the MEC amid tensions around energy and climate policies. Authors argue that emerging trends, both local and global, are slowly dissolving barriers to ambitious mitigation action and have changed the climate policy landscape. Two important factors hinder the pace at which coal is phased out: the first is the political push for gas, despite this being contested by social movements, while the second is unresolved dynamics around nuclear energy. The authors emphasise that unless there is resolution on gas and nuclear, the phasing of coal to pave the way for renewables will be hindered.

In chapter 6, Maria Nkhonjera positions the African Continental Free Trade Agreement (AfCFTA) as a framework to support energy transition and green industrialisation, and considers how South Africa can leverage its capabilities to boost clean energy exports and align with local and continental industrial development goals. The growing renewable and alternative energy sector presents an opportunity for trade globally and within the continent. The AfCFTA is a tool that African countries can utilise to promote intra-Africa trade, industrialisation and a Pan-African approach to addressing the continent's socio-economic needs. Green industries and clean energy are critical for Africa's economic growth as countries on the continent move toward decarbonising. The AfCFTA will unlock markets on the continent for South Africa to trade alternative energy and green industries products. The Agreement will allow for energy market integration, which will foster renewable energy penetration in the region and go beyond existing power pools. Nkhonjera uses the example of the Nordic electricity market to demonstrate the role that AfCFTA can play in energy integration in a Pan-African context. She argues that those involved in South Africa's energy transition and industrialisation agenda need to pay special attention to underlying political economy dynamics, both in terms of entrenched domestic socio-economic structures and South Africa's cooperation with the rest of the continent.

Industrial policy remains important for accelerating energy transition. Therefore, South Africa needs to rethink its industrial policy to reflect the transformative dynamics of a new energy sector. Nkhonjera uses the case of Morocco as an example of a good framework for building linkages between energy and industrial policies. She concludes that South Africa's ability (or inability) to leverage renewable energy to fuel sustainable growth will depend on how well it articulates the link between renewable energy policies and industrial development plans at national, sub-regional and continental levels.

Chantal Naidoo, in chapter 7, provides a critical review of international climate finance and its contribution towards South Africa's aspirations for a just transition towards low emission and climate-resilient development. Broader issues pertaining to the financing of the low carbon transition need to be addressed. Developed countries must finance the transition in developing or underdeveloped countries as the latter groups will be disproportionately affected by climate change that they did not bring about. The year 2021 marked the 26th international climate change conference also known as a Conference of the Parties (COP26); a meeting at which issues around financing the low carbon transition were tabled and addressed. The chapter first considers the origins of climate finance, the impact of COVID-19 on climate finance and potential contributions of climate finance towards a just transition in South Africa. It explores how South Africa engages with such finance and finally reflects on its relevance for the current stage of the climate response. The chapter emphasises that it is timely to re-frame the focus of climate finance on qualitative dimensions, especially as climate interventions remain primarily financed by debt, with access to grants remaining limited or available under conditions that benefit third parties in developed countries.

Naidoo further argues that the Paris Agreement must be used as a potential trigger for reframing how finance engages with climate change as the implementation of climate goals competes with development priorities and socio-economic issues resulting from COVID-19. The chapter argues that the changing dynamics and contexts to which climate finance needs to be applied raise the question of whether climate finance is a dated concept. Naidoo further argues that the dialogues about just transition finance in South Africa are focused on Eskom and Mpumalanga, whereas the entire country is impacted and South Africa's financing of just transitions should extend beyond only energy. South Africa is considering accessing concessional international climate finance to address the Eskom crisis. Naidoo critically evaluates the extent to which climate finance may indeed meet Eskom and South Africa's aspirations for placing the power utility onto a financially, environmentally and socially sustainable pathway. The author concludes that focusing exclusively on the energy sector risks deprioritising sectors that are in urgent need of funding, and that South Africa should work with international climate finance to increase the financing options open to the country.

Technology as enablers for the just transition

The low carbon transition coincides with the fourth industrial revolution and technological innovations that have the potential to nurture decarbonisation across various sectors. According to the IEA, the potential exists for the technology needed for achieving the 2030 emission reduction targets; much of it we already have, while 50 per cent of it requires new technology that is currently in the prototype or demonstration phase (IEA, 2021). Cheap renewable energy technologies will provide the edge needed to reach carbon dioxide emission targets; this will enable the rapid scale up of solar PV and wind by 2030. The IEA estimates that wind and solar energy must be scaled up by four times the 2020 global amount in the next decade, while hydropower and nuclear energy will provide the foundation. Electrification will be a critical tool in reducing emissions as the production of electricity becomes cleaner. Energy storage and conversion technologies are the key to delivering renewable energy and decarbonising the transport sector. Technological advances in battery storage, hydrogen electrolysers, and direct air capture and storage will be critical in reducing emissions in the upcoming decade (2020–2030) (IEA, 2021). Hydrogen and its related technologies will drive many global economies' decarbonisation strategies as these allow for the decarbonisation of many sectors. Reaching net zero is next to impossible without acceleration of hydrogen technologies in the 2020–2030 decade.

Chapter 8, by Nqobile Xaba and Zamanzima Mazibuko-Makena, seeks to evaluate whether hydrogen can enable the South African economy to transition towards a low carbon economy. The key questions are the following: what is the state of the hydrogen and fuel cell technology system? how can the country position itself to fully exploit this transition?; and what opportunities exist to realise a hydrogen economy? The authors use a sustainable transitions framework to provide an analysis across these focus areas and to explore how the hydrogen economy can support a sustainable transition in South Africa. A sustainable transitions framework includes the need for global challenges such as climate change and inequality to be solved with transformative ideas that will bring about changes in the basic systems that provide society with needs such as energy, water and shelter (Wieczorek, 2018). Technological innovations must be able to eradicate energy poverty. Hydrogen and fuel cell technologies present an opportunity for the energy sector to reach rural households and to deliver solutions that are not possible without cheap solar and affordable energy storage. Chapter 8 argues that no investments in hydrogen technologies should be made without careful consideration of whether these technologies are the most appropriate ones for a specific sector; for instance, in the transport sector, batteries may be more suitable than hydrogen-powered fuel cells.

Using green hydrogen to advance the adoption of renewable energy presents a sustainable solution to the climate change crisis and the need to accelerate the low carbon transition. The chapter calls for a compact between stakeholders to help take forward a just transition driven by renewable energy and a hydrogen economy, and moving away from a fossil fuel-dependent economy. Various interventions must be in place for the hydrogen economy in South Africa. Skills training programmes to meet the needs of the hydrogen economy and to create jobs will be critical. Hydrogen export is an emerging area in which South Africa can leverage its vast renewable energy resources and be a key global player. A key to economic growth is the development of a domestic market for key platinum group metals (PGM) and minerals. The chapter emphasises that in order for South Africa to leverage the opportunities provided by the hydrogen economy and renewable energy, the country needs to commit to a systematic, transparent, accountable and enabling policy environment for hydrogen.

Renewable energy requires the decentralisation of the current grid, and digitisation technologies will play a crucial role in this new decentralised grid for the distribution of energy to populations. South Africa's policies on and planning for the just transition focus on the national level and neglect the implementation and planning that will occur at the local level. Lauren Hermanus, in chapter 9, brings to the fore the evolving risks and opportunities for city governments and other local energy governance actors in South Africa's just transition. The incorporation of renewable energy into the current energy system has implications for urban environments and energy governance.

Hermanus proposes just urban transitions as a policy response 'through which a low carbon transition in an urban context is managed to bring about fair and equitable outcomes through representative and inclusive processes' (Hermanus, 2021). Chapter 9 interrogates whether and how socio-technological shifts that are shaping South Africa's urban energy transitions could deepen existing apartheid-legacy inequalities and patterns of exclusion within and between different cities and towns. A multilevel, socio-technical transition framework is used to trace the energy transition as it manifests at the urban scale. The analysis focuses on renewable energy and related technologies. A strong case is made for decentralisation of the energy system in South Africa due to current challenges; however, it remains critically important to interrogate the social aspects and impact of low carbon technologies. The inequality in infrastructure provision that exist between cities, towns and municipalities could potentially perpetuate energy poverty and fail to bridge the widening socio-economic gap. This chapter argues for a multi-scale approach to just transition planning. It calls for a bottom-up, localised, cross-contextual and national approach to defining problems, planning and investing. This approach is needed to facilitate harnessing the benefits and managing the risks of technological innovations. The chapter concludes by calling on all stakeholders to facilitate robust dialogue to debate new possibilities for the control and distribution of political power relating to the electricity system. It also identifies the need to clarify the respective roles of different actors, public and private, to achieve technological and governance integration across scale.

Social and political factors relevant to climate change and the low carbon transition

Transitioning to a low carbon and climate-resilient society requires measures to safeguard populations against the impact of climate change. Social protection systems providing healthcare, income security and social services should be integrated into policy measures and responses that address the challenges arising from the transition for the most vulnerable populations (ILO, 2015). Workers that are dependent on natural resources will be affected as job losses will occur during the transition and workers without the required skills will be displaced. Particularly in South Africa, workers and livelihoods are tied to the high carbon economy (coal mining). Low-income households will be disproportionately affected by a transition to a low carbon economy as their income is reliant on low skilled to non-skilled workers. The transition to a low carbon economy must therefore ensure that all thrive.

In Mpumalanga, where development is centred on coal mining activities, with the advent of energy transition and renewable energy integration, alternative development models must be developed to stimulate economic growth. Chapter 10, by Malik Dasoo and Stanley Semelane, focuses on coal areas, to position and evaluate regenerative agriculture, the repurposing of coal infrastructure and renewable energy as options for Mpumalanga's transition plan. The inevitable retirement of coal plants will result in job losses in Mpumalanga. Coal mining is perceived to be the main employer, but only 69 000 people were employed in the mining sector in Mpumalanga compared to the 86 000 people employed in agriculture (StatsSA, 2020). Dasoo and Semelane ask whether the job losses incurred by the closure and decommissioning of mines can be absorbed by regenerative agriculture. The chapter argues that for regenerative agriculture to be a viable alternative to coal mining in Mpumalanga, it will have to meet the interests of farmers, coal mining-affected communities, the labour sector, government and the private sector. It will also require buy-in from civil society.

The authors further argue that repurposing of coal power plants is a viable option to address environmental sustainability challenges while coal assets are redirected towards a sustainable pathway. Unless proper planning is undertaken, the retirement of coal plants will result in stranded assets. It is therefore critically important for consideration to be given to the retrofitting and re-utilisation of coal assets and associated infrastructure. While repurposing is costly, coal power plants can be repurposed to retain some of their functions thus mitigating against a potentially unjust energy transition.

The chapter makes a case for renewable energy (solar and wind) deployment in Mpumalanga as studies have shown that this region is a great solar energy resource (Semelane et.al., 2021). Stimulation of economic growth in coal phase-out regions requires diverse initiatives, and there is a good case to be made for both regenerative agriculture and decentralised renewable energy.

Labour and social activist groups have an important role to play in the low carbon transition, particularly in coal mining areas such as Mpumalanga, to represent the voices of workers and affected communities. The just transition concept emanated from the labour movement and was introduced by Congress of South African Trade Union's (COSATU) climate change policy in South Africa to protect the rights of workers who would be affected by climate change. Labour maintains that the just transition concept has been stripped of its original transformative content by social powers and that the voices of coal workers and mining communities are not heard, as recounted in chapter 11 by Lebogang Mulaisi and Jacklyn Cock. This chapter uses the lens of the labour movement's framing of a just transition. It contends that the labour movement's commitments to job protection, sustainable investment, comprehensive social security for displaced workers and skills development provide a basis for cooperation between labour and emerging civil society initiatives around climate justice and the established environmental justice movement.

Mulaisi and Cock argue that the transition unfolding is neglecting justice and planning, and that the growing elite's views on the just transition have reduced the concept to mean only a shift to a new energy regime that does not threaten profits. The authors argue further that high structural unemployment, coupled with the lack of a just transition plan that results in actual job creation, creates an environment in which workers and members of the community are unable to comprehend a future without coal. When people are desperate, they will resort to defending and siding with coal mining to protect their livelihoods. The authors call on the labour movement to forge closer connections with other social forces in civil society, particularly the environmental and climate justice organisations and to develop initiatives to better manage the immediate tensions pertaining to the protection of jobs and the reduction of carbon emissions.

Civil society has a role to play in the low carbon transition and there are various organisations that have voiced their concerns over the unfolding low carbon transition in South Africa. South African Nationally Determined Contributions (NDCs) have been contested by various groups who say these contributions are not ambitious enough and do not fall in line with limiting global temperature increases to below 1.5°C. As a result, the NDCs were revised to account for South Africa's fair share of global emissions. Climate activist groups have raised concerns about the updated NDC consultation not being inclusive and accessible to the people who will be most affected by the transition (CER, 2021). The Energy Governance of South Africa (EGSA)[1] network submitted a petition against the current NDCs. Concerns raised are that the proposed emission targets for 2030 are not reflective of South Africa's current fair share of emissions globally (EGSA, 2021). The authors argue that civil society organisations offer ideas which could be building blocks for a just transition, such as climate justice, food sovereignty, a universal basic income grant and energy democracy. However, these ideas are largely inaccessible to grassroot communities. The chapter concludes that labour's conceptual framing of the just transition can provide a basis for a mass coalition for the broader social movement, and that this alliance could create solidarity to achieve a low carbon future in South Africa.

While alliances are being formed between stakeholders for a just transition in South Africa, there is growing geopolitical instability emerging as powerful nations seek new alliances to exert their influence in other regions. The low carbon transition has been politicised and

---

1 A network of over 110 concerned individuals and organisations dedicated to promoting good governance in the energy sector: https://www.egsa.org.za/

used as a power play tool by global powers seeking to maintain their influence in Africa and other developing regions. African countries remain vulnerable to such power dynamics due to the entrenched colonial history that still affects the continent's economies. As a result, Africa remains an extractive economy and lags on development. Chapter 12, by Saliem Fakir, Faten Aggad and Ellen Davis, explores how the superpowers of today are leveraging technology, and in particular green technologies, to exert their soft power influence. The authors argue that we are now witnessing the increasing convergence of global geopolitics and decarbonisation, accompanied by the instrumentalisation of climate diplomacy in geopolitical rivalries. The chapter takes a global overview of the current decarbonisation discourse, reflecting particularly on how China is carving out its dominance in clean energy technology and artificial intelligence ahead of Europe and the United States of America. China has advanced technology, which has enabled it to compete directly with Western multinational and transnational companies for global markets.

The European Green Deal (EGD) seeks to strengthen Europe's future position in the global landscape and to assert the continent's competitiveness in new sectors as it decarbonises and carves new industrial pathways. The authors argue that the EGD does not focus on industrial development in Africa but rather perpetuates precolonial extractivism. The authors caution that the strategic alignment between geopolitics, climate norms, climate finance and climate technologies, which are part of the next wave of the technology revolution, is already upon us. Minerals that are critical in a low carbon transition will be used as pawns for new geopolitical conflicts. The chapter further argues that naïve climate liberalism, which perpetuates the idea of climate internationalism without geopolitical filters, can have dire consequences for countries at the forefront of this new battleground. Technology is the key towards decarbonisation and Africa needs to benefit from the new wave of technology by developing its own industries and not looking to follow other global players.

This chapter points to key strategies for Africa to pursue to lead developments in renewable technology. Firstly, Africa needs to break the long-standing precolonial model of resource extraction. Secondly, the AfCFTA should be used as a tool for regional integration to stimulate investments, green industrialisation and economic growth. The chapter concludes that energy transitions must be framed within a broader developmental model in Africa in order for the climate agenda to succeed on the continent. The authors argue that this will not be accomplished by non-Africans, no matter how committed they may seem. Any development agenda in Africa must have skills development at its core if it is to facilitate economic growth. The just transition framework provides an opportunity to address income inequality by upskilling or reskilling workers in sectors required in the low carbon economy. A capable workforce with the right skills is necessary for an equitable low carbon transition (ILO, 2015). New technologies will require specific skills sets; current and growing skills shortages can limit the rapid deployment of new technologies required to mitigate and adapt to climate change. In chapter 13, Presha Ramsarup and Najma Mohamed draw on cases of multiple skills interventions for sustainable futures to illustrate the interplay between the different interventions and to identify skills needed for a low carbon economy. The authors argue that transitions to low carbon economies are contested and uneven, creating rapidly changing contexts that need a revitalised approach to how skills development can be conceptualised and implemented. The authors further argue that conceptualising skills for a just transition requires a framing that moves beyond the individual. Rather, it requires a framing of skills that involve individuals, organisations and systems to create collectives to drive regime change within the skills ecosystem.

The chapter draws on a particular framework; it situates the skills required within an entire skills ecosystem. Skills are conceptualised within the ecosystem as enabling factors that help create an intersectional framework for skills research in the context of the climate and environment crisis. This framework is then used to analyse local cases to discuss some emerging lessons on the role of skills, and how skills ecosystems can be planned and implemented. The chapter concludes by emphasising that skills development has the potential to drive a transition to just low carbon economies if this development is integrated in a way that promotes transformative change.

CONCLUSION

The low carbon transition in South Africa, framed as the just transition, is currently unfolding and it remains critical to put it in the context of the key socio-economic challenges the country is facing. The just transition framework is a mechanism that is critical to the low carbon transition in South Africa. The just transition framing initially only focused on the needs of the workers. It evolved to a framing that takes cognisance of the needs of the most vulnerable.

This book highlights that the 'just' component of the low carbon just transition needs to be emphasised and critically evaluated to address South Africa's socio-economic challenges. Contributing authors provide a case for the review of current policies and further recommend policy reforms to support and foster a just transition in South Africa. The publication paves a path for new policy discourse in areas including urban transitions, climate finance, hydrogen economy, skills development and green industrial development. It also brings to the fore emerging components of the just transition, such as geopolitical power plays. These elements of the just transition need to be addressed for South Africa to transition to a low carbon future.

REFERENCES

Alternative Information and Development Centre (AIDC). 2016. 'One million climate jobs: Moving South Africa towards a low carbon wage-led and sustainable path'. https://aidc.org.za/download/climate-change/OMCJ-booklet-AIDC-electronic-version.pdf, accessed 5 June 2021.

Burton, J., Marquard, A. and McCall, B. 2019. 'Socio-economic considerations for a Paris Agreement-compatible coal transition in South Africa'. https://www.climate-transparency.org/wp-content/uploads/2019/07/CT-Just-Transition-in-South-Africa.pdf, accessed 5 June 2021.

Cahill, B. and Allen, M.M. 2020. 'Just transition concepts and relevance for climate action: A preliminary framework'. Center for Strategic and International Studies and Climate Investment Funds, Washington DC.

Centre for Environmental Rights (CER). 2021. 'Cabinet urged to adopt more ambitious climate change targets'. https://cer.org.za/news/cabinet-urged-to-adopt-more-ambitious-climate-change-targets, accessed 1 August 2021.

Climate Justice Charter Movement. 2020. 'Climate Justice Charter'. https://www.safsc.org.za/wp-content/uploads/2020/08/Final-Climate-Justice-

Charter_EN_August2020.pdf, accessed 20 October 2021.

Department of Environmental Affairs (DEA). 2018. 'Climate Change Bill'. https://www.environment.gov.za/sites/default/files/legislations/climatechangebill2018_gn41689.pdf, accessed 20 May 2021.

Department of Environmental Affairs (DEA). 2019. 'Draft National Climate Change Adaptation Strategy'. https://cer.org.za/wp-content/uploads/2019/05/DEA-Draft-climate-change-adaptation-strategy.pdf, accessed 20 June 2020.

Department of Energy (DoE). 2019. 'The South African energy sector report: 2019'. Department of Energy, http://www.energy.gov.za/files/media/explained/2019-South-African-Energy-Sector-Report.pdf, accessed 20 October 2020.

Department of Mineral Resources and Energy (DMRE). 2019. 'Integrated Resource Plan (IRP 2019)'. http://www.energy.gov.za/IRP/2019/IRP-2019.pdf, accessed 28 July 2021.

Department of Transport (DoT). 2018. 'Green Transport Strategy: 2018–2050'. https://theicct.org/sites/default/files/Green%20transport%20strategy%202018-2050.pdf, accessed 2 June 2021.

Energy Governance of South Africa (EGSA). 2021. 'Open letter to president and the executive of South Africa: SA's climate change ambition and global pledge'. https://www.egsa.org.za/wp-content/uploads/2021/07/EGSA-letter-on-NDCs-22-July-2021.pdf, accessed 1 August 2021.

Hermanus, L. 2021. 'South Africa's Just Urban Transitions'. https://justurbantransitions.com/wp-content/uploads/2021/03/Just-Urban-Transitions_PolicyNote1.pdf, accessed 20 August 2021.

International Energy Agency (IEA). 2017. 'Digitalisation and energy'. https://www.iea.org/reports/digitalisation-and-energy, accessed 12 May 2021.

International Energy Agency (IEA). 2021. 'Net zero by 2050: A roadmap for the global energy sector'. https://iea.blob.core.windows.net/assets/beceb956-0dcf-4d73-89fe-1310e3046d68/NetZeroby2050-ARoadmapfortheGlobalEnergySector_CORR.pdf, accessed 24 July 2021.

International Labour Organization (ILO). 2015. 'Guidelines for a just transition towards environmentally sustainable economies and societies for all'. http://www.ilo.org/wcmsp5/groups/public/---ed_emp/---emp_ent/documents/publication/wcms_432859.pdf, accessed 12 May 2021.

Intergovernmental Panel on Climate Change (IPCC). 2021. 'Climate change 2021: The physical science basis'. https://www.ipcc.ch/report/ar6/wg1/downloads/report/IPCC_AR6_WGI_SPM.pdf, accessed 10 August 2021.

Intergovernmental Panel on Climate Change (IPCC). 2014. 'Climate change 2014: Synthesis report'. http://ar5-syr.ipcc.ch/ipcc/ipcc/resources/pdf/IPCC_SynthesisReport.pdf, accessed 5 June 2021.

Just Transition Research Collaborative. 2018. 'Mapping just transition(s) to a low-carbon world'. United Nations Research Institute for Social

Development, University of London Institute in Paris and Rosa-Luxemburg-Stiftung.

Layke, J., Jaeger, J., Pastor, K., Levin, K. and Searchinger, T. 2021. '5 things to know about the IEA's roadmap to net zero by 2050'. https://www.wri.org/insights/5-things-know-about-ieas-roadmap-net-zero-2050, accessed 25 October 2021.

Mapungubwe Institute for Strategic Reflection (MISTRA) 2015. *Earth, Wind and Fire: Unpacking the political, economic and security implications of discourse on the Green Economy*. MISTRA: Johannesburg.

McCauley, D. and Heffron, R. 2018. 'Just transition: Integrating climate, energy and environmental justice'. *Energy Policy*, 119: 1–7.

Mgbemene, C.A., Nnaji, C.C. and Nwozor, C. 2016. 'Industrialization and its backlash: focus on climate change and its consequences'. *Journal of Environmental Science and Technology*, 9(4), 301–316.

Minerals Council South Africa. 2018. 'Coal'. https://www.mineralscouncil.org.za/sa-mining/coal, accessed 12 October 2020.

Mooney, C., Dennis, B. and Muyskens, J. 2020. 'Global emissions plunged an unprecedented 17 percent during the coronavirus pandemic'. Washington Post, https://www.washingtonpost.com/climate-environment/2020/05/19/greenhouse-emissions-coronavirus/?arc404=true, accessed 18 May 2021.

National Planning Commission (NPC). 2013. 'National development plan vision 2030'. https://www.gov.za/issues/national-development-plan-2030, accessed 9 June 2021.

National Planning Commission (NPC). 2019. '2050 vision and pathways for a just transition to a low carbon, climate resilient economy and society'. Draft proposal version two, October, Department of Performance Monitoring and Evaluation, Pretoria, https://oneworldgroup.co.za/wp-content/uploads/2019/10/NPC-JT-Vision-and-Pathways-draft-2-final.pdf, accessed 9 June 2021.

Perkins, D.N., Drisse, M.B., Nxele, T. and Sly, P.D. 2014. 'E-waste: A global hazard'. *Annals of Global Health,* 80, 286–295.

The Presidency. 2020. 'Presidential Climate Change Coordinating Commission appointed'. http://www.thepresidency.gov.za/press-statements/presidential-climate-change-coordinating-commission-appointed, accessed 25 July 2021.

PriceWaterhouse Coopers (PwC). 2019. 'Low carbon economy index.' PwC South Africa, https://www.pwc.co.za/en/press-room/low-carbon-economy-index-2019-.html#:~:text=In%20our%20first%20edition%20of,253%20tCO2%2F%24m%20GDP, accessed 18 July 2021.

Purvis, B., Mao, Y. and Robinson, D. 2019. 'Three pillars of sustainability: In search of conceptual origins'. *Sustainability Science,* 14, 681–695.

Sengupta, P., Choudhury, B., Mitra, S. and Agrawal, K. 2019. 'Low carbon economy for sustainable development'. *Encyclopedia of Renewable and*

Sustainable Materials, (3), 551–560.

Seto, K.C., Churkina, G., Hsu, A., Keller, M., Newman, P.W., Qin, B. and Ramaswami, A. 2021. 'From low to net zero carbon cities: The next global agenda'. *Annual Review of Environment and Resources*, (46), 377–415.

Shah, A. 2011. 'Climate change and Global warming introduction'. Global Issues, http://www.globalissues.org/article/233/climate-change-and-global-warming-introduction, accessed 2 June 2021.

Statistics South Africa (StatsSA). 2019. 'Inequality trends in South Africa: A multidimensional diagnostic of inequality'. http://www.statssa.gov.za/publications/Report-03-10-19/Report-03-10-192017.pdf, accessed 12 June 2021.

Statistics South Africa (StatsSA). 2021. 'Quarterly Release Survey Quarter 2: 2021'. http://www.statssa.gov.za/publications/P0211/P02112ndQuarter2021.pdf, accessed 28 August 2021.

Republic of South Africa (RSA), 2021. 'South Africa's First Nationally Determined Contribution under the Paris Agreement'. https://www.environment.gov.za/sites/default/files/reports/draftnationalydeterminedcontributions_2021updated.pdf, accessed 26 May 2021.

United Nations (UN). 2015. 'Paris Agreement'. https://unfccc.int/files/essential_background/convention/application/pdf/english_paris_agreement.pdf, accessed 7 June 2021.

United Nations Environment Programme (UNEP). 2015. 'Sustainable consumption and production: A handbook for policymakers'. https://sustainabledevelopment.un.org/content/documents/1951Sustainable%20Consumption.pdf, accessed 2 July 2021.

Ward, M. 2018. 'Just transitions and the green economy'. Working paper, Centre for Researching Education and Labour, https://www.tips.org.za/just-transition/item/download/2057_bc76ba88cb42a52de05cc12d3288e968, accessed 15 August 2021.

Wieczorek, A.J. 2018. 'Sustainability transitions in developing countries: Major insights and their implications for research and policy'. *Environmental Science & Policy*, 84, 204–216.

Wimbadi, R.W. and Djalante, R. 2020. 'From decarbonization to low carbon development and transition: A systematic literature review of the conceptualization of moving toward net-zero carbon dioxide emission (1995–2019)'. *Journal of Cleaner Production*, 256, 120307–120325.

World Health Organization (WHO). 2014 'Quantitative risk assessment of the effects of climate change on selected causes of death, 2030s and 2050s'. https://apps.who.int/iris/handle/10665/134014, accessed 28 June 2021.

World Bank Group (WBG), 2016. 'Transport Policies for Climate Change: The transformative role transport can play in mitigation and adaptation'. https://openknowledge.worldbank.org/bitstream/handle/10986/24960/Transport0poli0ation0and0adaptation.pdf?sequence=4&isAllowed=y,

accessed 2 August 2021.

World Bank Group (WBG). 2021. 'Climate change action plan 2021-2025 Supporting Green, Resilient, and Inclusive Development'. https://openknowledge.worldbank.org/bitstream/handle/10986/35799/CCAP-2021-25.pdf?sequence=2&isAllowed=y, accessed 5 June 2021.

Young, J. 1998. 'Just transition: A new approach to jobs v. environment'. *Working USA*, 2, 42–48.

SECTION 1

The landing of the just transition in South Africa

TWO

From climate change to a just energy transition

BUKELWA NZIMANDE AND
HAPPY KHAMBULE

INTRODUCTION

WITH INCREASED CERTAINTY about the scientific consensus linking climate change to greenhouse gas (GHG) emissions and global warming, there is growing pressure for countries across the world to act decisively and with urgency. The increasing frequency and greater impact of climate-related events signal imminent runaway climate catastrophe. This necessitates a transition away from carbon- intensive economies to cleaner, low carbon-intensive economies in a manner that is economically and socially sound while addressing this generation's most defining existential threat – climate change. There is a growing and fitting recognition that climate change is not just an environmental issue as earlier perceived and normatively understood. Rather, it is a threat with the certain ability to unravel the very fabric of civilisation and to roll back development milestones, while undermining the future we collectively sought to sow.

In view of this, the chapter aims to outline South Africa's transitional journey towards a low carbon economy. Identifying the key underpinning drivers and challenges is a crucial step towards devising and implementing inclusive, context-specific solutions. Accordingly, this chapter presents a case for why an interconnected climate response, and associated mitigation and sectoral decarbonisation efforts, should deeply consider the complex socio-economic landscapes of developing countries. Considering the influence of high-income countries, those taking South Africa's path to a low carbon future should consider its context, to ensure suitable and pragmatic progress in the transition. This chapter traces South Africa's climate policies and how these have evolved over the years in order to better understand and assess current trends in the country's climate policy environment. It is not a comprehensive review of all climate policies to date; rather it attempts to identify the key policies that have shaped our current ones.

Understanding that the Global South, and Africa specifically, has been identified among the most vulnerable to climate impact, this chapter firstly highlights some of these vulnerabilities. It explores how the growing understanding of climate change and its impacts has influenced South Africa's preliminary response. The chapter details how this response has transformed from one that could be classified as high level and purely scientific to one that is increasingly considering socio-economic contexts. Key drivers for the journey towards a low carbon future are outlined.

Secondly, the chapter pays attention to the targets South Africa has set to decarbonise its economy, highlighting the policy and legislative instruments key to this distinct response. Country context as well as the progress of climate policy are outlined: from the Long-term Mitigation Scenarios (Department of Environment Affairs and Tourism 'LTMS', 2007) which informed the initial Copenhagen pledge to the commitments made in Doha and the eventual ratification of the Paris Agreement. South Africa will need to decide what the country's contribution under the Paris Agreement will be. If it is to deliver ambitious contributions then bold and decisive leadership will be required – a fundamental and necessary step.

Thirdly, this chapter takes the South African mineral energy complex's heavy reliance on coal as a starting point, and how this reliance has given particular shape to its climate action. Any measures towards an inclusive and just transition in South Africa must be founded on a recognition of this reliance. The chapter further emphasises how South Africa's commitment to a low carbon future should be cognisant of and responsive to the interconnected environmental, social and economic crises which converge as key considerations for decision-makers. The importance of an appropriate response directly impacts on the country's development and socio-economic focus, as well as in unifying diverse stakeholders. An appropriate response would also see South Africa further asserting its perceived leadership in the regional and international community.

Finally, in the context of the COVID-19 pandemic, and as countries strategise and implement their respective recoveries, numerous possibilities and opportunities exist to re-start, re-focus and localise the low carbon transition. The chapter concludes with an overview of how South Africa can lean into positive aspects of a green recovery, focusing on building better while transitioning to more resilient, inclusive and just low carbon society.

CLIMATE CHANGE: CAUSE, IMPACT AND LAYERED VULNERABILITIES

Climate change, once an abstract and widely misunderstood phenomenon accompanied by vague circular interpretations of its cause and effects, today unmistakably presents the single greatest threat to most lifeforms on Earth (UN, 2021). Global warming and climate change were once viewed as distant threats. Now they are exerting pressures that challenge the very pillars of present-day societies. Historically, the Earth's heating, and consequent link to anthropogenic greenhouse gas-emitting activities, faced great scepticism. However, the connection between the two is now clearer and more certain, grounded in greater scientific consensus globally (Anderegg, 2010; IPCC, 2015; Cook et al., 2016).

The question of whether climate change is happening has been settled because of the increasing concentration of atmospheric carbon dioxide and other greenhouse gas emissions (IPCC, 2021). A significant number of scholars now agree about the probable linkage of climate trends to human activities over the past century (Cook et al., 2013). With this came the shared recognition that future climate change impacts on humanity, compounded risks and vulnerability are without parameters. The question of whether the climate crisis is real or not is now passé, and has fittingly been replaced by the question of the extent to which climate change is impacting us – the planet, people and future generations who will continue calling this home. How can societies be more prepared and resilient? And an even more fitting, yet greatly challenging, question is: how will societies that have built their economies and socio-political systems around fossil fuel extraction and combustion transition in a just and equitable manner?

As a start, it's appropriate to contextualise the ongoing climate discourse, especially its roots and the progression of its understanding. How has the discourse evolved over time in South Africa and the international community, and which actions have resulted? Before outlining the policy and planning environment in South Africa, it is necessary to highlight the increasing association between climate change and the broader development and sustainability objectives. This association is the basis for an analysis of climate change responses in the developing world.

With global climate action as a backdrop, the Millennium Development Goals (MDGs) (2015) articulated and framed climate change as a development issue threatening poverty eradication, income and security, human rights and wellbeing, and justice. It was envisaged that this wider framing of climate change would allow for the MDGs to be implemented, given that these goals explicitly acknowledged the negative effects of climate change on development, particularly in low-income countries (UN, 2015). The MDGs were subsequently replaced by the UN's 2030 Agenda for Sustainable Development, which summarised the sustainable development objectives in 17 Sustainable Development Goals (SDGs) of 2013. SDG 13 represented the commitment to 'take urgent action to combat climate change' (UN, 2015). This linkage of climate change mitigation and adaptation with broader sustainability and development is a crucial premise. But it has yet to signal and guide more interconnected, less silo-like approaches to addressing even more intricately connected environmental, social and economic justice imperatives.

Further, the Intergovernmental Panel on Climate Change (IPCC) continues to caution that 'business as usual' and unabated greenhouse gas emissions will hasten planet Earth's heating. This will pave a path for accelerated run-away climate devastation, with irreversible ecological impacts and far-reaching social and economic implications (IPCC, 2012). It is this recognition and consensus that has rightfully led to climate change no longer being framed as no longer 'just an environmental problem'.

The Paris Agreement's long-term goal to restrict global warming to below 2°C above pre-industrial levels – below 1.5°C being most preferable – was based on the IPCC's warning that any heating higher than this would result in catastrophic and irreversible impacts. The intergovernmental panel's latest report (IPCC, 2021) further asserts that only urgent and ambitious climate action, paired with consistent mitigation efforts towards net zero emissions by 2050, will likely ensure that this threshold is not exceeded. However, the IPCC now states that the 1.5°C global surface temperature threshold is likely to be exceeded in the early 2030s. The Global South, and Africa more specifically, has been identified as being among the most vulnerable to climate change impacts, which not only presents a new set of challenges but also exacerbates pre-existing ones. The recent IPCC report provides a more detailed analysis of the southern African region. Again, it reiterates what previous assessments have highlighted, namely the increased likelihood of intensified extreme weather events, increased drought, rain, reduced precipitation and warming. These will increase the frequency of drought, which is of concern as the region's warming has always been projected to be twice that of the global rate (IPCC, 2021).

The increased frequency and severity of extreme weather events, such as floods and droughts, will introduce or worsen stresses (DEFF, 2020). Recent flooding events across the country, notably in KwaZulu-Natal, Gauteng and the northern regions of South Africa, and the increased drought periods and associated water shortages and wildfires in the Eastern and Western Cape, are already signalling the extent of previously forecasted challenges. The resultant changes in weather patterns and ecosystems are impacting on the distribution of disease-causing pests, vectors and waterborne diseases such as cholera (Confalonieri et al., 2007). There is a notable connection between increased ambient temperatures and mortality in younger and elderly populations (Kapwata et al., 2018; Scovronick et al., 2018). This is of particular concern considering the number of people across South Africa residing in informal dwellings without heating or cooling systems.

Climate change will also present interlinked food and water security challenges. Shifts in agricultural potential, reduced crops and the loss of livestock resulting from climate change have far-reaching impacts on economic activities, with consequently increased challenges to human wellbeing (Masipa, 2017; Mugambiwa and Tirivangasi, 2017; Kapwata et al., 2018). As it stands, climate change stands to unravel that which holds communities together and to roll back development milestones. Those with low adaptive capacity and more vulnerabilities will be disproportionately impacted (Chersich and Wright, 2019; Ziervogel et al., 2014).

South Africans are increasingly feeling the impacts of the change, rather than just hearing about projections, with the future presenting even more layered challenges. This presents a strong case for wider, concerted and directed climate action in South Africa which places people at the centre of discourse, ideation, decision-making processes and ensuing actions. Despite significant gains in socio-economic development since South Africa's transition to democracy, the nation continues to face the triple challenge of rising unemployment, income inequality and poverty – amid extended periods of national and global economic slumps. As stated in the National Climate Change Response White Paper of 2011, 'climate change is already a measurable reality and along with other developing countries, South Africa is especially vulnerable to its impact' (DEA, 2011: 5). It is one of the world's most unequal countries (StatsSA, 2021) generating $6001.4 of GDP per capita in 2019 with a 32.6 per cent unemployment rate; 55.5 per cent (30.3 million people) of its population living in poverty; and 13.8 million people (25 per cent) experiencing food poverty, all of which raises more concern (World Bank, 2019; World Bank, 2020).

Responses to the climate crisis, particularly mitigation measures, should therefore reflect such complexity, which is common to many developing countries. Further, key consideration should be given to efforts to delink development from capitalist modus operandi such as intensive resource extraction and exploitation of labour, thus bringing justice to the centre. This presents a particularly enormous challenge for South Africa because of its dependence on fossil fuels. Sustainable energy transitions present an opportunity for the country to reduce its carbon footprint and to mitigate the injustices and inequalities of incumbent energy systems rather than further entrenching them (Baker et al., 2014). Those seeking pathways to a transformative development agenda (Wahl, 2019; Sovacool et al., 2020) assert that there is a crucial piece missing from the concept of sustainability in which renewable energy transitions are rooted: they argue that sustainability in its current form does not challenge existing systems of power or privilege, which is a crucial element.

SOUTH AFRICA'S DECARBONISATION JOURNEY

South Africa's GHGs are predominantly emitted from the production and consumption of coal. Consequently, South Africa's key policy and legislative commitments to climate action and to decarbonising its economy are based on reducing this reliance. Coal is used as a fuel source across a variety of sectors as well as in the country's coal-dominated electricity sector. In 2018, 83 per cent of South Africa's total electricity generation capacity was from coal-fired power stations (DMRE, 2019b). Electricity production, therefore, dominates the country's carbon emissions profile. The further facts that the country ranks 12th in the world in carbon intensity and 14th in absolute emissions signals the need to reduce carbon emissions and associated carbon intensity per capita (Carbon Brief, 2018). It is also worth noting that South Africa has through the Low Emission Development Strategy (LEDS) committed to reaching a net zero carbon economy by 2050 (South Africa, 2020).

The country's climate change response is therefore based on this need to decarbonise and transition to greener and more renewable energy technologies. As the country begins its transition away from coal, it needs to concurrently continue its efforts to address the triple challenge, amid the converging global crises. This pathway, if expressed as re-industrialisation, requires more complex decision-making and policy interventions than those made concerning Long Term Mitigation Scenarios (LTMS). Table 2.1 presents key policy decisions manifested in either new legislation or national policy instruments for climate action. What is not highlighted here are the individual areas in which groups were established to provide internal institutional or political momentum, such as the Inter-Ministerial Committee on Climate Change (IMCCC), the National Climate Change Committee (NCCC) or Intergovernmental Committee on Climate Change (IPCC). The manner in which the policy instruments tabled below were established is of significance. However, in no way does this focus mean that the instruments are of greater importance than other interventions. They do, however, signal and reflect the intentions and positions of the decision-makers.

SOUTH AFRICA'S POLICY ENVIRONMENT

The United Nations Framework Convention on Climate Change (UNFCCC) has greatly influenced South Africa's policy environment and consequently resulted in low carbon-inclined development. The impacts of these response measures can be thought of as 'second-order' impacts of responses to climate change – the first-order impact is the reduction of GHG emissions (European Capacity Building Initiative, 2021: 2). Below is a brief introduction to UNFCCC-related instruments and decisions, with examples of connected national responses; these are to facilitate an appreciation of the impact of international policy decisions on South Africa's low carbon journey. There are numerous decisions in international negotiations related to low carbon development and the need to address the impacts, both negative and positive, of climate action. For the purposes of this chapter, the focus will be on the decisions and/or articles that specifically refer

Table 2.1: National policy development between 2004 and 2021 across sectors and in the energy/electricity sector in particular

Period/President	Across Sectors*	Energy/Electricity Sector*
2004–2008 Thabo Mbeki	National Climate Change Policy (NCCP) (South Africa, 2004)	National Energy Act (2008)
2008–2009 Kgalema Motlanthe (Interim)	-	Non-renewable electricity levy (Van der Merwe, 2009)
2009–2014 Jacob Zuma	National Climate Change Response White Paper (NCCRWP) (DEA, 2011)	Integrated Resource Plan 2010 (IRP) (DoE, 2011)
		Energy efficiency in buildings: SANS 204 (SANS, 2011)
	National Development Plan (National Planning Commission, 2011)	Renewable Energy Independent Power Producer Procurement Programme (REIPPPP) (DEA, 2011)
2014–2018 Jacob Zuma	Nationally Determined Contribution (NDC) (South Africa, 2016)	-
2018–2019 Cyril Ramaphosa (Interim)	National Climate Change Bill (DEA, 2018)	Integrated Resource Plan 2018 (IRP) (DMRE, 2019a)
2019–2021 Cyril Ramaphosa	Carbon Tax Act	-
	(Carbon Tax, 2019)	
	Low Emission Development Strategy (LEDS) (South Africa, 2020)	
	Presidential Coordination Committee on Climate Change (PCCCC) (Seale, 2020)	
	Nationally Determined Contribution (NDC) (South Africa, 2021)	

**(Sector-wide emissions: 525 $MtCO_2e$; Energy/Electricity: 401 $MtCO_2e$)*

Source: Author's

to transitions, response measures and/or the addressing of intended or unintended consequences.

With this context, it's important to highlight what is meant by positive and negative impacts. An example is the Renewable Independent Power Producer Programme (REIPPP) in South Africa. (DEA, 2011), an intervention to cut emissions in the electricity sector. Positive impacts, in this case, could include, but are not limited to, increased energy security through the diversification of energy sources backed by the Integrated Resource Plan (IRP), and job creation, orchestrated through strategies such as the New Growth Path 2010. Negative impacts could include the loss of existing fossil fuel-dependant jobs or an increase in gender inequalities where preferential employment or project development is inherently gender biased. Such examples are what necessitate a just transition. The UNFCCC advocates that countries address the negative impacts of low carbon development and climate change responses thus placing it on South Africa's agenda. This is discussed in greater detail in the section below on the domestication of agreements.

On the other hand, 'response measures' refer to the range of actions that countries party to the UNFCCC Congress of the Parties 1 (COP1), Congress of the Parties 3 (COP3) Kyoto Protocol (South African Catholic Bishops' Conference Parliamentary Liaison Office, 2016) and COP21 Paris Agreement should undertake to reduce their greenhouse gas emissions. South Africa is a signatory to all three instruments, having signed the Convention in 1998. In 2002, South Africa signed the Kyoto protocol, which was enforced in 2005.

Since its inception, the UNFCCC has engaged with the international socio-economic impacts of responses to climate change. Clear reference is made to the overlap between trade and response measures in Article 3.5 of the Convention. Article 4.8 of the Convention concerns the implementation of climate change commitments. In the Article, commitments must take full cognisance of concerns of developing country Parties arising from the adverse effects of climate change and/ or the impact of the implementation of response measures. For South Africa, special focus is given to projected climate change vulnerabilities, and an economy highly dependent on the production, processing, export and consumption of fossil fuels. South Africa developed its risk and vulnerability framework, expanded its pollution priority areas – for reporting purposes – to include greenhouse gases (DEA, 2007). The country also developed transition-oriented strategies such as the National Development Plan (NDP) – in part as an attempt to diversify the economy and the energy sector. These were in part guided by the Energy White Paper which speaks to some of the key considerations and Articles expressed in the Convention (DMRE, 1998).

Under the Convention, South Africa also outlines the importance of taking account of the technical and financial needs associated with the proposed low development projects. The country has made progress in this regard: its National Employment Vulnerability Assessment and the Sector Jobs Resilience Plan considers operationalising the provisions of Article 12 of the Convention, while providing key insights into the required transition, and into the impacts of a low carbon trajectory on development agendas.

NEW AGREEMENT AND THE DOMESTICATION OF CLIMATE ACTIONS

In 2012, the Conference of the Parties agreed on an amendment to the Kyoto Protocol (Box 2.1), the Doha Amendment, intended to redress failed attempts to adopt the earlier Copenhagen agreement in 2009. As a result, a second emissions reduction period, from 2013 to 2020, was established for developed countries. In 2015, the Parties finally adopted the Paris Agreement which considers both climate mitigation and adaptation along with any resultant loss and damage. This new ambit came into effect in 2020.

After COP3, further distinctions were made between negative impacts on developing countries. Articles 3(17) and 10(g) jointly pointed to the fact that the trade and competitiveness of developing countries may be affected by decisions made by developed countries undertaking climate action. South Africa would require support and resources to limit this negative impact. Building further capacity and cooperating would be two fundamental elements of this process. Sector Jobs and Vulnerability Plan is a key tool in operationalising the lesser-known obligations of the Kyoto Protocol as well as in providing much-needed data on the impact of a low carbon-oriented development pathway.

Box 2.1: Kyoto Protocol domestication – South Africa

Further domestication of the Kyoto Protocol: The Accord requires countries to cut emissions of carbon dioxide and other greenhouse gases. About 141 countries, accounting for 55 per cent of greenhouse gas emissions, have ratified the treaty, which commits signatories to cutting these emissions by 5.2 per cent by 2012.

A regulation under Section 25 of the National Environmental Management Act establishing a Designated National Authority (DNA) was gazetted on 24 December 2004 by Martinus van Schalkwyk, then Minister of the Department of Environmental Affairs and Tourism. The regulation established the DNA within the Department of Minerals and Energy and provided the DNA with its legal mandate to oversee the Clean Development Mechanism (CDM) in South Africa.

The CDM was established in December 1997 by the Third Conference of Parties to the United Nations Framework Convention on Climate Change (UNFCCC). The CDM allows industrialised countries committed to reducing emissions to meet part of their commitments by investing in projects in developing countries that reduce greenhouse gas emissions while contributing to local sustainable development needs. To allow CDM projects to occur, host countries need to designate national authorities to evaluate and approve the operation of CDM projects in their country. South Africa has established a Designated National Authority to fulfil this function as well as other functions related to the successful implementation of the CDM in South Africa, including the promotion of investment in CDM projects (DoE, 2005).

With the completion of the SDGs in 2015 and the universal adoption of the Paris Agreement, South Africa and other developing countries had to contend with a wider range of obligations under the new climate change policy regime. This included the country being held accountable for any negative impacts from domestic climate action. This is different from the Convention and Kyoto Protocol mandating the reduction of emissions under the Paris Agreement. The Paris Agreement in its adoption text considers response measures and the just transition (UNFCCC, 2015). Article 4(15) normalised the understanding that climate action will present both positive and negative realities; where positive dimensions such as economic diversification must be maximised, negative consequences, such as increasing unemployment in carbon-intensive industries, must be minimised.

Compared to the Kyoto Protocol and the Convention, the Paris Agreement is scant on details of what should be considered when undertaking climate action. However, it presents a requirement for plans and strategies that speak to reducing emissions beyond near terms (Nationally Determined Contributions – NDCs) to long-term plans expressed through LEDS. International obligations and processes have given rise to South Africa's planning processes. When domesticating the Kyoto Protocol, South Africa undertook to legislate to establish the DNA under the National Environmental Management Act (NEMA). Similarly, in 2011 when South Africa held COP17 in Durban, the country approved its National Climate Change Response White Paper (NCCRWP) as the official foundation of national climate change policy. In 2012 climate change became a key element of the NDP, thus providing a national vision (Averchenkova et al., 2019: 4–5). As a result of climate negotiations in Copenhagen held in 2009, South Africa communicated Long Term Mitigation Scenarios (LTMS) pledging a 'Peak, Plateau and Decline' Trajectory. Through the NCCRWP, the LTMS process identified packages of mitigation measures offering strategic options for national mitigation potential (Trollip and Boulle, 2017: 2). In an attempt to implement global climate change commitments, South Africa began to develop climate considerations in other policy instruments, signalling that it was transitioning away from carbon intensity. The IRP of 2010 illustrates this shift: electricity planning was included as a tool in the Energy White Paper and the Electricity Regulation Act of 2006; New Generation Capacity Amendment inserted a carbon constraint for the first time, which was integrated into planning. In 2019 the IRP included carbon tax considerations, and other renewable energy deployment strategies such as small-scale embedded generation. These new developments are in part spurred by the Paris Agreement-inspired NDCs, according to which countries must show successive and progressive climate action. As the IRP of 2010 influenced the NDC of 2015, the subsequent NDC of 2015 greatly influenced the IRP of 2019.

From an international perspective, it's clear that mitigation efforts have played a key role in attempting to address the unfolding climate crisis. With increased mitigation actions, questions about a just transition become more prevalent, including considerations that moving from a particular energy system to another has inherent risks and opportunities. The just transition was first conceptualised in the early to mid-1990s. Throughout that decade, it was conceptualised as mitigating measures and support for workers who risked losing jobs due to stricter environmental protection policies. International union movements provided the guiding framework and narrative of the just transition, and over time the idea of the just transition expanded beyond this initially narrow conceptualisation. The emerging views of the international union movement were that the transition must be just by being deliberately planned and managed to move workers and society into environmentally and socially sustainable operations (Smith, 2017: 2). Such views frame the just transition as opportunity to strengthen labour rights and conditions while creating better chances for decent work and more sustainable jobs. The appreciation of the just transition as an enabler coincided with a growing understanding of the climate crisis. Consequently, the international labour movement began seeking to embed the just transition into international policy regimes with a particular focus on the UNFCCC.

Post 2015, after the adoption of the SDGs and the Paris Agreement, the International Labour Organization (ILO), through a tripartite multilateral negotiation between unions, employers' organisations and government, produced a definitive model for a just transition: 'Guidelines for a just transition towards environmentally sustainable economies and societies for all' (Smith, 2017: 3). These guidelines have proven instructive and have established a set of principles and targets that enable the mainstreaming of the just transition and planning for it. In South Africa, the just transitions lens offers important insights considering the previously mentioned triple challenges of unemployment, inequality and poverty, and the possibilities for inclusive and fair change. Leading up to COP17 in 2011 and the World Summit on Sustainable Development (WSSD) in 2012, the Congress of South African Trade Unions (COSATU) developed a just transition policy (COSATU, 2012). Thereafter, the notion of a just transition has been included in national development plans and policies, as well as commitments related to international climate change responses. As the Paris Agreement places universal obligations on its member countries to undertake mitigation measures, many developing countries, and others that are transitioning, particularly in Eastern Europe, have specifically considered just transitions within their climate response plans. This elevates the just transition from only a labour concern to one of national importance, with direct impacts on development.

When considering the mid-century target of net zero emissions, the scale of changes required and consequences anticipated are immense; this makes it clear that the journey to achieving a low carbon future is non-linear. Global trends and developments in the international policy arena influence not only the possible speed of the transition but also the options available to South Africa for addressing emerging issues. Recently, domestic dynamics in South Africa have begun to necessitate changes and actions, and the country has started to address the just transition in a more institutionalised manner. The immediate response has been a delicate trade-off: legislating for a statutory advisory body to provide a locus for transition discussion, but also doing so in such a manner that it raises the need for an independent, cross-sectoral and multi-disciplinary forum.

In 2019 President Cyril Ramaphosa established a 22-member committee (known as both the P4C, and the PCC or Presidential Climate Change Coordinating Commission) to begin pulling together the concept of the just transition, provide advice on climate change developments such as net zero goals and NDCs while addressing the triple developmental challenges facing South Africa. This is a necessary start in conceptualising and localising the exploration of South Africa's unique, yet very challenging, energy landscape.

PREMISE OF AN INCLUSIVE AND JUST TRANSITION

South Africa's mineral energy complex and its heavy reliance on coal provide a unique character to the country's climate action and how it translates to development and economic strategies. This uniqueness requires that South Africa's responses and commitments to a low carbon future should be cognisant of the country's interconnected environmental, social and economic crises. These converge as key considerations for decision-makers. This is the premise of an inclusive and just transition.

It is important to deeply consider local context and the path traversed thus far when asking: what has been done well and what has been missed that could be beneficial to future work? Additionally, it helps to locate current efforts underway. A clearer picture emerges if one honestly and explicitly reflects on the process, on progress on the ground, and on past or arising challenges. Even more important is explicitly laying out why and how measures should be inclusive, just and well accounted for. Beyond just a call for the planet, re-focusing on how societies are structured and built stands to enrich the engagement with a just transition and yield well-placed solutions. It is also important that this journey is democratic as well as just, brings people closer in all aspects and does not further entrench or replicate past injustices.

Democracy calls for involved and engaged citizens who have a say in the decisions that affect them. The scale and pace of transitions means that they will be a concern for all citizens, and their vulnerabilities cannot be ignored when thinking of broader national development and future sustainability. Wilson (2007: 3) argues that 'sustainable development demands that people participate in the debates and decisions that affect their lives'. Therefore, more focus should be given to participation and communication.

THE COVID-19 PANDEMIC AND RE-EMERGENCE OF GREEN RECOVERIES

The COVID-19 pandemic thrust nations into unprecedented conditions, and it is important that the recovery from the pandemic is inclusive and just for South Africa and the rest of the world. This relates to how countries transition from fossil fuels to renewable energy to achieve net zero emissions by 2050. By focusing on 'building back' better than our former 'normal', we can avoid undermining development goals in a world with carbon and environmental limits. In the face of unprecedented change and grave uncertainty, establishing sustainable, resilient societies should be high on the global agenda, keeping local context as a guide for its localisation.

Some countries are forging ahead with an agenda with this as the essence, most comprehensively expressed in Green New Deal (GND) proposals. The GND was conceptualised and proposed in the United Kingdom in 2008. It detailed a plan of action for addressing climate change. As the name presupposes, the plan was to be green by prioritising the shifting of economies away from fossil fuels towards renewable energy by the following: creating a wider and more inclusive vision beyond energy; eliminating polluting industrial and production activities; working towards social justice imperatives, such as equitable land-ownership, housing and provision of basic services; addressing employment (quality, dignity and security); as well as pursuing racial, gender equity and justice amongst other socio-economic objectives.

Since the GND's origin and formative development in the United Kingdom, its vision and call for action has received increased global attention, first in Europe and North America, then subsequently, a few more countries following suit (see Table 2.2), more strongly during the COVID-19 pandemic. As the pandemic continues to hold its grip on nations across the globe, unsurprisingly the Global South and developing nations are disproportionately impacted, with limited to no socio-economic safeguards. In the context of the pandemic, what is manifest in varied unjust ways is that in this moment of global-scale vulnerability, richer nations are in a better position to recover from economy-wide impacts, leaving the developing and poorer countries behind. This, tied with layered and interconnected losses of livelihoods and increased poverty, amongst other indicators (WHO, 2020), presents a case for why decisive actions and redirection are crucial. Masiya et al. (2021: 2) further assert that the pandemic highlights the crucial role of the state and its institutions in providing strong leadership and unified action, as well as the importance of governments in 'shaping the effectiveness of national responses, strategies and approaches in tackling the crisis'. This further spotlights and raises questions about South Africa's state of perpetual unpreparedness and its lack of action even in the presence of articulate, sound policies and strategies.

Table 2.2 highlights the countries and institutions instrumental in the origins and conceptualisation of the Green New Deal (GND) which emphasises decarbonisation, climate action and strong elements

Table 2.2: Countries and institutions instrumental in the conceptualisation of the Green New Deal emphasising decarbonisation, climate action

Action of Country or Institution	Key Elements
2007 onwards USA: 2010, 2012, 2016, 2019 USA politicians running political campaigns on Green New Deal platforms initiated by the National Green Party (NGP)	A Green New Deal is officially part of the platform of the Green Party of the United States, with most recent developments where a 'nonbinding resolution' was tabled in a Congress sitting. The US Green New Deal includes universal health care and a job guarantee among other social objectives within the GND (US Congress Sitting, 2019).
2008 UK: Green New Deal private member's bill was jointly tabled by the Green New Deal Group in the British Parliament (Green New Deal Group, 2008)	Combined elements of stabilisation in the short term with longer-term restructuring of the financial, taxation and energy systems. Aiming for a drastic reduction of fossil fuels while tackling social issues such as unemployment and equity due to an impoverished financial landscape. It highlights the need for improved policies and directed resources for emissions reduction in combating climate change globally.

Action of Country or Institution	Key Elements
2009 UNEP: The Green Economy Initiative (GEI) Policy Brief (UNEP, 2009a) An Update for the G20 Pittsburgh Summit (UNEP, 2009b)	The Green Economy Initiative aims to create jobs in 'green' industries, thus boosting the world economy and curbing climate change. It highlights the following key areas: clean energy; rural access; sustainable agriculture; sustainable cities including planning, transport and buildings; ecosystem infrastructure; emissions from deforestation and degradation. The UN proposal was for G20 countries to maximise environmental benefits in fiscal stimulus packages rolled out in the wake of the global financial crises.
2009 UNDESA: A Global Green New Deal for Climate, Energy, and Development (UNDESA, 2009)	The Global Green New Deal for Climate, Energy, and Development aims to drive down the cost of renewable energy, increase deployment in developing countries, eradicate poverty, contribute to economic recovery and growth, tackle unemployment and ultimately to counter runaway climate change
2019 EU: European Green Deal presented by European Commission as a set of Policy proposals (European Commission, 2019)	The Green New Deal manifesto 'Democracy in Europe Movement 2025 (DiEM25)' launched a Green New Deal proposal for large investments into transforming Europe's infrastructure and energy across sectors – a recognition of the growing importance of climate change for European industry, trade and politics.
2020 Canada: The Pact for a Green New Deal – A coalition group of 67 organizations, including Indigenous Climate Action; Migrant Workers Alliance for Change; The Leap, and Climate Action Network (MacArthur et al., 2020)	A visionary roadmap to tackling the climate crisis as well as social and economic justice. The Canadian proposal has a strong focus on reparation, justice and upholding the human rights of indigenous peoples. A key message is the importance of inclusion of all and of leaving nobody behind.

of social justice and equity. However, increasingly, more countries and cities across the globe are presenting climate action policies which are congruent with a green recovery. In addition to national and multilateral efforts, cities are increasingly offering support for a GND. In October 2019 the C40 Cities Climate Leadership Group committed to supporting a Global Green New Deal, announcing that there will be determined action from all its 94 cities, with 30 cities having already reached peak emissions, and begun progressing rapidly towards net zero (C40 Cities, 2019). Countries like China and India have not yet announced official plans; however, low carbon and pollution abatement commitments are underway. In 2020, in the wake of its election victory, South Korea's Democratic Party announced its intention to accelerate the adoption of its GND plan, thus making the country the first East Asian one to pledge to reach net zero emissions by 2050.

One result of the GND gaining traction during the pandemic has been increased inquiries about which countries will take bold stands and which will cower behind less ambitious instruments. Further, there have been questions as to how countries' commitments and plans fit into the GND. Perhaps an even more critical question is whether the uptake and implementation of climate-related plans and strategies are collectively aligned in end goals and vision. Are there clear emissions reduction commitments, and do these align with country commitments, socio-political and economic strategies, and the science?

Recent calls for a green recovery – in this current global context – seem to be more ambitious than those formerly articulated. These calls have included the need for a complete change in the tensions between powers, and the institutions that have governed and dominated global economies. The recent focus has also emphasised the need for redress and reparations to less developed countries and communities. The role of government leadership advocated in contemporary versions of the GND sets these new calls apart from earlier versions, which called for free markets and reduced roles for government. More recent proposals advocate for a stronger focus on environmental justice and bring the dominant structural inequalities of present-day economic systems to the fore (Schlosberg, 2013).

These heightened ambitions, however, might not result in immediate positive action, as one would expect. For instance, the United Nations released a report revealing that most COVID-19 recovery stimulus packages were in fact not channelled towards clean energy or key areas affecting basic human needs in society (UNCTAD, 2020). This realistically paints a picture of consistent incongruence between planning and implementation. It also highlights that in the face of adversity and grave disasters or challenges, the pillars of society that were most vulnerable will topple first. This introduces further risk, and makes it a priority of the utmost importance to lay down solid foundations.

The GND's unique focus on decarbonisation, justice and sustainability undoubtedly provides the framework for understanding why a more democratic approach to economic recovery is required. It also offers a basis for delivery of this recovery which is contextual, and carries the fundamental components required for building resilient societies. Socio-economic development driven by aggressively capitalistic and extractive-intense markets and business models has brought us to this point, and will set us on a far worse trajectory. A cleaner, just, low carbon future presents both an opportunity and a challenge: the opportunity to rebuild and redesign systems in more sustainable ways, and the challenge of deconstructing long-standing incumbent systems, powers and ways of being. At stake is a complete rethinking of how nations and states approach their economic and social development.

South Africa is in fact at a crossroads. There is an opportunity for the state to fortify areas that have been exposed as being of greatest vulnerability, while building a solid foundation with the right vision and objectives. Advocating for a transition and a recovery that are both green and just will present unique tensions and struggles. However, if these are for the betterment of all then they are worth fighting for.

REFERENCES

Anderegg, W.R., Prall, J.W., Harold, J. and Schneider, S.H. 2010. 'Expert credibility in climate change,' *Proceedings of the National Academy of Sciences*, 107(27), 12107–12109. doi: 10.1073/pnas.1003187107.

Averchenkova, A., Elizabeth, K., Curran, G. and Curran, P. 2019. 'Governance of climate change policy: A case study of South Africa'. Policy report, https://www.lse.ac.uk/granthaminstitute/wp-content/uploads/2019/06/GRI_Governance-of-climate-change-policy_SA-case-study_policy-report_40pp.pdf, accessed 13 May 2021.

Baker, L., Newell, P. and Phillips, J. 2014. 'The political economy of energy transitions: The case of South Africa'. https://doi.org/10.1080/13563467.2013.849674, accessed 12 May 2021.

Carbon Brief. 15 October 2018. 'The Carbon Brief profile: South Africa'.

https://www.carbonbrief.org/the-carbon-brief-profile-south-africa, accessed 16 June 2021.

Chersich, M.F. and Wright, C.Y. 2019. 'Climate change adaptation in South Africa: A case study on the role of the health sector'. *Globalization and Health*, 15(1), 1–16. https://doi.org/10.1186/s12992-019-0466-x.

Confalonieri, U., Menne, B., Akhtar, R., Ebi, K.L, Hauengue, M., Kovats, R.S., Revich, B. and Woodward, A. 2007. 'Human health', in Parry, M.L., Canziani, O.F., Palutikof, J.P., Van der Linden, P.J. and Hanson, C.E. (eds), *Climate Change 2007: Impacts, adaptation and Vulnerability. Contribution of Working Group II to the Fourth Assessment Report of the Intergovernmental Panel on Climate Change*. Cambridge: Cambridge University Press, pp. 391–431.

Cook, J., Naomi, O., Doran, P.T., Anderegg, W.R.L., Verheggen, B., Maibach, E.W., Carlton J.S., Lewandowsky, S., Skuce, A.G., Green, S.A., Nuccitelli, D., Jacobs, P., Richardson, M., Winkler, B., Painting, R and Rice, K. 2016. 'Consensus on consensus: A synthesis of consensus estimates on human-caused global warming'. *Environmental Research Letters,* 11(4). DOI:10.1088/1748-9326/11/4/048002.

Cook, J., Nuccitelli, D., Green, S.A., Richardson, M., Winkler, B., Painting, R., Way, R., Jacobs, P. and Skuce, A. 2013. 'Quantifying the consensus on anthropogenic global warming in the scientific literature'. *Environmental Research Letters*, 8(2). DOI:10.1088/1748-9326/8/2/024024.

Congress of South African Trade Union (COSATU). 2012. 'A just transition to a low carbon and climate-resilient economy'. https://www.sagreenfund.org.za/wordpress/wp-content/uploads/2017/05/Naledi_A-just-transition-to-a-climate-resilient-economy.pdf, accessed 25 July 2021.

Creamer, M. 2020. " Green hydrogen study intergrating SADC ahead of trillion dollar market emergence'. https://www.engineeringnews.co.za/article/green-hydrogen-study-integrating-sadc-ahead-of-trillion-dollar-market-emergence-2020-09-23, accessed 9 April 2021.

C40 Cities. 2019. 'Mayors announce support for global Green New Deal; recognize global climate emergency'. https://www.c40.org/press_releases/global-gnd, accessed 31 May 2021.

Department of Energy (DoE). 2005 ' Kyoto Protocol to The United Nations Framework Convention On Climate Change'. www.energy.gov.za/files/esources/kyoto/kyoto_overview.html, accessed 25 June 2021.

Department of Energy (DoE). 2011. 'Integrated Resources Plan'. 25 March 2011. http://www.energy.gov.za/IRP/irp%20files/IRP2010_2030_Final_Report_20110325.pdf, accessed 12 October 2021.

Department of Environmental Affairs (DEA). 2011. 'National Climate Change Response White Paper'. www.environment.gov.za/sites/default/files/legislations/national_climatechange_response_whitepaper_0.pdf, accessed 25 June 2021.

Department of Environmental Affairs (DEA). 2017. 'National Climate Change Adaptation Strategy. 2nd draft for public comments'. www.environment.gov.za/sites/default/files/reports/nationalclimate_changeadaptation_strategyforcomment_nccas.pdf, accessed 25 June 2021.

Department of Environmental Affairs (DEA). 2018. 'National Climate Change Bill'. https://www.environment.gov.za/sites/default/files/legislations/climatechangebill2018_gn41689.pdf, accessed 12 October 2021.

Department of Environment Affairs (DEA). 2007. 'Long Term Mitigation Scenarios (LTMS): Scenario Document'. open.uct.ac.za/bitstream/handle/11427/16804/Scenario_Building_Team_Long_Term_Mitigation_2007.pdf?sequence%20=%201, accessed 12 October 2021.

Department of Environment, Forestry and Fisheries (DEFF). 1 April 2020. 'National Climate Risk and Vulnerability (CRV) Assessment Framework summary document'. http://www.csag.uct.ac.za/wp-content/uploads/2020/10/CRV-Assessment-Framework-FINAL-08-May-2020.pdf, accessed 12 June 2021.

Department of Mineral Resources and Energy (DMRE). 2019. 'Integrated Resources Plan'. http://www.energy.gov.za/IRP/2019/IRP-2019.pdf, accessed 12 October 2021.

Department of Mineral Resources and Energy (DMRE). 2019b. 'The South African Energy Sector Report'. www.energy.gov.za/files/media/explained/2019-South-African-Energy-Sector-Report.pdf, accessed 10 June 2021.

Department of minerals and energy (DMRE). 1998. 'White Paper on the Energy Policy of the Republic of South Africa'. https://www.gov.za/sites/default/files/gcis_document/201409/whitepaperenergypolicy19980.pdf, accessed 15 June 2021.

European Capacity Building Initiative. 2021. 'Pocket Guide to Response Measures under the UNFCCC'. ecbi.org/sites/default/files/Pocket%20Guide%20to%20Response%20Measures_1.pdf, accessed 26 June 2021.

European Commission (EU). 2019. 'European Green Deal: Striving to be the first climate-neutral continent'. https://ec.europa.eu/info/strategy/priorities-2019-2024/european-green-deal_en, accessed 22 June 2021.

Green New Deal Group. 2008. 'A Green New Deal: Joined-up policies to solve the triple crunch of the credit crisis, climate change and high oil prices'. New Economics Foundation, https://neweconomics.org/uploads/files/8f737ea195fe56db2f_xbm6ihwb1.pdf, accessed 11 June 2021.

Intergovernmental Panel on Climate Change (IPCC). 2012. 'Managing the risks of extreme events and disasters to advance climate change adaptation Special Report of the Intergovernmental Panel on Climate Change'. Cambridge: Cambridge University Press.

Intergovernmental Panel on Climate Change (IPCC). 2015. 'Synthesis Report: Contribution of Working Groups I, II and III to the Fifth Assessment

Report of the Intergovernmental Panel on Climate Change' (Core Writing Team, Pachauri, R.K. and Meyer, L.A.). IPCC, Geneva.

Intergovernmental Panel on Climate Change (IPCC). 2021. 'Climate change 2021: The physical science basis'. https://www.ipcc.ch/report/ar6/wg1/downloads/report/IPCC_AR6_WGI_SPM_final.pdf, accessed 31 May 2021.

Kapwata, T., Gebreslasie, M.T., Mathee, A. and Wright, C.Y. 2018. 'Current and potential future seasonal trends of indoor dwelling temperature and likely health risks in rural southern Africa'. *International Journal of Environmental Research and Public Health*, 15(5), 952.

Masiya, T., Mandiyanike, D., Molosiwa, D. and Mazenda, A. 2021. 'Southern African responses to the COVID-19 pandemic: A study of Botswana and South Africa'. *Africa's Public Service Delivery and Performance Review*, 9(1), 11. doi: https://doi.org/10.4102/apsdpr.v9i1.497.

MacArthur, J.L., Hoicka, C.E., Castleden, H., Das, R. and Lieu, J. 2020. 'Canada's Green New Deal: Forging the socio-political foundations of climate resilient infrastructure?'. *Energy Research and Social Science*, 65.

Masipa, T.S. 2017. 'The impact of climate change on food security in South Africa: Current realities and challenges ahead'. *Jamba*, 9(1), 1–7.

Mugambiwa, S.S. and Tirivangasi, H.M. 2017. 'Climate change: A threat towards achieving "Sustainable Development Goal number two" (end hunger, achieve food security and improved nutrition and promote sustainable agriculture) in South Africa'. *Journal of Disaster Risk Studies*, 9(1), 1–6.

Republic of South Africa (RSA), 2008. National Energy Act No 34 of 2008. 6 July 2008. www.energy.gov.za/files/policies/NationalEnergyAct_34of2008.pdf, accessed 12 October 2021.

The Presidency. 1998. National Environmental Management Act 107 of 1998. 27 November 1998, https://www.gov.za/sites/default/files/gcis_document/201409/a107-98.pdf, accessed 12 October 2021.

The Presidency. 2005. National Environmental Management and Air Quality Act 2 No. 39 of 2004. 24 February 2005. www.environment.gov.za/sites/default/files/legislations/nema_amendment_act39.pdf, accessed 12 October 2021.

National Planning Commission. 2011. 'National Development Plan'. www.gov.za/sites/default/files/gcis_document/201409/devplan2.pdf, accessed 12 October 2021.

Seale, T. 2020. 'Presidential Climate Change Coordinating Commission appointed'. The Presidency, http://www.thepresidency.gov.za/press-statements/presidential-climate-change-coordinating-commission-appointed, accessed 12 October 2021.

Schlosberg, D. 2013. 'Theorising environmental justice: The expanding sphere of a discourse'. *Environmental Politics*, 22(1), 37–55. doi:

10.1080/09644016.2013.755387.

Scovronick, N., Sera, F., Acquaotta, F., Garzena, D., Fratianni, S., Wright, C.Y. and Gasparrini, A. 2018. 'The association between ambient temperature and mortality in South Africa: A time-series analyses'. *Environmental Research*, 161, 229–35.

Smith, S. 2017. 'Just transition: A report for the OECD'. Just Transition Centre, 2–3, https://www.oecd.org/environment/cc/g20-climate/collapsecontents/Just-Transition-Centre-report-just-transition.pdf, accessed 12 October 2021.

South Africa. 2021. 'South Africa's Nationally Determined Contributions (NDC)'.https://www4.unfccc.int/sites/ndcstaging/PublishedDocuments/South%20Africa%20First/South%20Africa%20updated%20first%20NDC%20September%202021.pdf, accessed 12 October 2021.

South Africa. 2020. 'South Africa's Low Emission Development Strategy 2050'. https://www.dffe.gov.za/sites/default/files/docs/2020lowemission_developmentstrategy.pdf, accessed 25 September 2021.

South Africa. 2016. 'South Africa's Nationally Determined Contributions (NDC)'. https://www4.unfccc.int/sites/ndcstaging/PublishedDocuments/South%20Africa%20First/South%20Africa.pdf, accessed 12 October 2021.

South Africa. 2004. 'A National Climate Change Response Strategy'. unfccc.int/files/meetings/seminar/application/pdf/sem_sup3_south_africa.pdf, accessed 12 October 2021.

South African Catholic Bishops' Conference Parliamentary Liaison Office. 2016. 'South Africa's International Climate Obligations: The Domestication of the Paris Agreement'. http://www.cplo.org.za/wp-content/uploads/2016/02/BP-408-The-Domestication-of-the-Paris-Agreement-June-2016.pdf, accessed 22 June 2021.

South African National Standard (SANS). 2011. 'Energy efficiency in buildings: SANS 204'. www.woodybpower.biz/Sans%20204.pdf, accessed 12 October 2021.

Statistics South Africa (StatsSA). 2021 'How unequal is South Africa'. http://www.statssa.gov.za/?p=12930, accessed 19 June 2021.

Trollip, H. and Boulle, M. 2017. 'Challenges associated with implementing climate change mitigation policy in South Africa'. *Energy Research Centre*, 1–2, https://www.researchgate.net/publication/318394874_Challenges_associated_with_implementing_climate_change_mitigation_policy_in_South_Africa, accessed 24 June 2021.

Sovacool, B.K., Turnheim, B., Hook, A. and Martiskainen, M. 2020. 'Beyond cost and carbon: The multidimensional co-benefits of low carbon transitions in Europe'. *Ecological Economics*, 169.

United Nations (UN). 2021. 'Climate change "Biggest threat modern humans have ever faced", World-renowned naturalist tells Security Council, calls for greater global cooperation'. United Nations Press Release, https://

www.un.org/press/en/2021/sc14445.doc.html, accessed 5 June 2021.

United Nations Conference on Trade and Development (UNCTAD). 2020. 'A comparison of selected stimulus packages in 2008 and 2020: Investing in renewable energy, sustainable agriculture and food security, and gender equality and the empowerment of women for structural economic transformation'. https://unctad.org/system/files/information-document/osg_2020-12-18_StimulusPackages_en.pdf, accessed 25 June 2020.

United Nations (UN). 2015. 'The Millennium Development Goals Report'. https://www.un.org/millenniumgoals/2015_MDG_Report/pdf/MDG%202015%20rev%20(July%201).pdf, accessed 11 June 2021.

United Nations Environment Program (UNEP). 2009a. 'Global Green New Deal: Policy brief. Economics and Trade Branch International Environment House'. UNEP Economics and Trade Branch, https://wedocs.unep.org/bitstream/handle/20.500.11822/7903/A_Global_Green_New_Deal_Policy_Brief.pdf?sequence=3&amp%3BisAllowed=, accessed 17 June 2021.

United Nations Environment Program (UNEP). 2009b. 'Global Green New Deal Policy Brief - Update for the G20 Pittsburgh Summit'. https://wedocs.unep.org/rest/bitstreams/11748/retrieve, accessed 27 June 2021.

United Nations Department of Economic and Social Affairs (UNDESA). 2009. 'A Global Green New Deal for Climate, Energy and Development, Technical Note'. https://sustainabledevelopment.un.org/index.php?page=view&type=400&nr=16&menu=1515, accessed 17 June 2021.

United Nations Framework Convention on Climate Change (UNFCCC) 1992. https://unfccc.int/resource/docs/convkp/conveng.pdf, accessed 4 May 2021.

United Nations Framework Convention on Climate Change (UNFCCC). 2015. 'Paris Agreement: COP21'. https://unfccc.int/resource/docs/2015/cop21/eng/10a01.pdf#page=2, accessed 25 June 2021.

United Nations, 2015. 'Resolution adopted by the General Assembly on 25 September 2015'. https://www.un.org/ga/search/view_doc.asp?symbol=A/RES/70/1&Lang=E, accessed 13 June 2021.

US Congress Sitting. 2019. 'Recognizing the duty of the Federal Government to create a Green New Deal'. 116th, 1st session, https://s3.documentcloud.org/documents/5729033/Green-New-Deal-FINAL.pdf, accessed 26 June 2021.

Van Der Merwe, C. 25 July 2009. 'The levy on non-renewable electricity to become effective July 1'. Engineering News, www.engineeringnews.co.za/article/levy-on-nonrenewable-electricity-to-become-effective-july-1-2009-06-25, accessed 12 October 2021

Wahl, D. C. 2019. 'Sustainability is not enough: We need regenerative cultures'. *Green Planet Blues*, 241–245. https://doi.org/10.4324/9780429322204-25.

World Health Organisation (WHO). 2020. 'COVID-19 Strategic Preparedness and Response Plan: Country Preparedness and Response Status for COVID-19 as of 9 June 2020'. https://www.who.int/docs/default-source/coronaviruse/srp-covid-19-6month.pdf?sfvrsn=a7ac05b1_2&download=true, accessed 20 May 2021.

Wilson, M. 2007.' At the heart of change: The role of communication sustainable development'. *Panos London*, http://panos.org.uk/wp-content/files/ 2011/03/heart_of_change_weby2wvJO.pdf, accessed 8 July 2020.

World Bank. 2019. 'World Bank Data, 'GDP per capita (current US$) – South Africa'. https://data.worldbank.org/indicator/NY.GDP.PCAP.CD?locations=ZA, accessed 19 June 2021.

World Bank. 2020. 'Poverty and Equity Brief Sub-Saharan Africa – South Africa'. https://databank.worldbank.org/data/download/poverty/33EF03BB-9722-4AE2-ABC7-AA2972D68AFE/Global_POVEQ_ZAF.pdf, accessed 19 June 2021.

Ziervogel, G., New, M., Archer van Garderen, E., Midgley, G., Taylor, A., Hamann, R., Stuart-Hill, S., Myers, J. and Warburton, M. 2014. 'Climate change impacts and adaptation in South Africa'. *Wiley Interdisciplinary Reviews: Climate Change*, 5(5), 5–620. https://doi.org/10.1002/wcc.295.

THREE

Applying a normative framework to assess the just transition to a net zero carbon society in South Africa

NAJMA MOHAMED AND GAYLOR MONTMASSON-CLAIR

INTRODUCTION

THE INTERLINKED CRISES of biodiversity and ecosystem loss, climate change and widespread poverty and inequality have created a window of opportunity for radical policy transformations – a moment to question both the purposes and outcomes of development pathways. A plethora of 'green' policies, plans and strategies have emerged, aimed at transitioning development pathways to increased sustainability. These are aligned with the vision of the Paris Agreement on Climate Change, and the broad intent of the Sustainable Development Goals, both of which seek to transform economies and societies to achieve sustainable development.

Concurrently, the need for a just transition has gained prominence in policy circles shaping green transitions. The concept emerged in the 1970s labour movement in the United States to provide workers exposed to toxic chemicals with support to transition away from their hazardous jobs (Just Transition Research Collaborative, 2018). It has since been embraced by the international trade union movement which advocated for its inclusion in the Paris Agreement to secure workers' jobs in the shift to net zero carbon economies. It has now expanded to embrace ambitious social and economic reforms more broadly, encompassing workers as well as vulnerable groups and communities. This whole-of-society scope is illustrated in Figure 3.1. From an initial focus on impacted workers in energy transitions, the just transition agenda is increasingly adopted as a macro-economic and cross-sectoral framing that anchors social justice in policy, planning and investment processes driving green transitions.

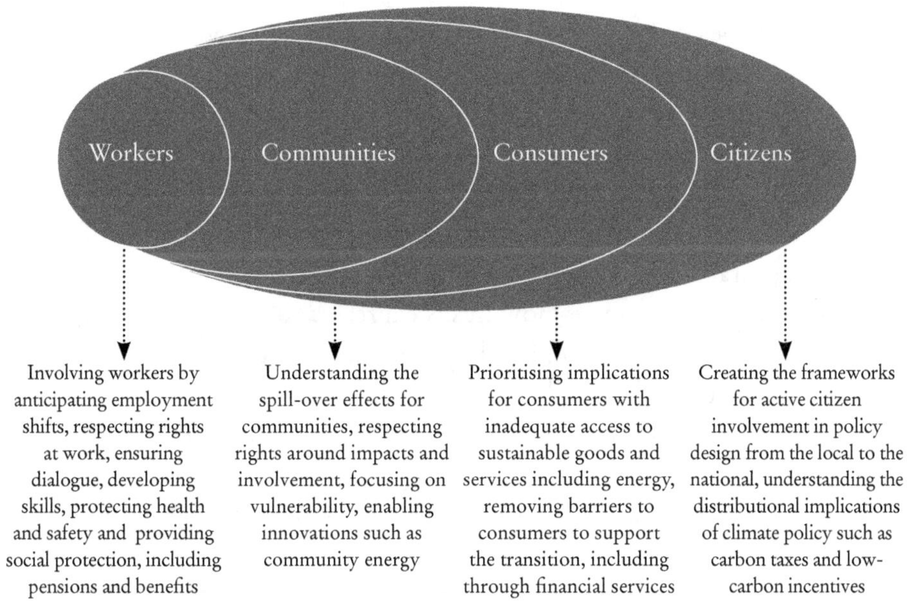

Figure 3.1: The human dimensions of a just transition

Source: Robins et al. (2019: 9).

The concept is now core to the green transition pathways of several countries and regions. Just transition visions, principles and outcomes have been adopted in global, national and subnational policy circles (Just Transition Research Collaborative, 2018). Chile is in the process of developing a 'Strategy for Just Transition' (WRI, 2021a) that protects the rights of the most vulnerable in decarbonising the energy sector. Ireland has worked on formulating a just transition plan for the agricultural sector (Social Justice Ireland, 2020). For small island developing states, like the nations of the Pacific Ocean, a just transition is about strengthening resilience to devastating climate impacts (ILO, 2019). A transition 'deal' in Spain, including early retirement for miners, re-skilling and environmental restoration, brokered through social dialogue processes, has been hailed as a practical illustration of a just transition (Neslen, 2018). In South Africa, the Presidential Climate Commission has spearheaded the development of a just transition framework to foster consensus. Yet, despite the growth in the adoption of a just transition vision, there is mounting concern that the term is being stripped of its meaning and transformational purpose.

This chapter seeks to understand how South Africa's vision of a just transition to an 'environmentally sustainable, climate-change resilient, low-carbon economy and just society' (National Planning Commission, 2012) has made its way into public policy. It first develops and sets out a normative framework that proposes key dimensions of a just transition, and the variants of a just transition that can be discerned. It then assesses how this is expressed in key public policies in South Africa: industrial, employment and climate. Lastly, it draws out insights from these policy processes into how South Africa could maintain the transformative intent of just transitions.

FRAMEWORK FOR A JUST TRANSITION

Conceptualising a framework for a just transition is an important first step towards defining and implementing mechanisms and interventions that would effect a green and inclusive transition. Yet, there is no agreed definition of a just transition (globally or nationally), nor is there a blueprint to use as a reference. In practice, two key variables effectively define the nature of a just transition: its scope of beneficiaries and its ambition of action (Montmasson-Clair, 2021).

Firstly, just transition approaches vary widely in their coverage of beneficiaries. At the one end, a narrow understanding would focus solely on workers directly impacted by a transition. At the other end, some definitions include society as a whole and are arguably too broad. The understanding applied in this chapter extends beyond directly impacted workers to include all vulnerable stakeholders who may be directly and indirectly impacted. This would comprise low-income communities at large, particularly women, the youth and the elderly, as well as small businesses (Robins and Rydge, 2019). However, it also recognises that not everyone in society is vulnerable. Beyond this, at the conceptual level, no specific order of priority between stakeholders is established as priorities would effectively be place- or issue-specific.

Secondly, the degree of ambition for achieving socially just outcomes from climate actions also varies extensively. As illustrated in Figure 3.2, this spread can be categorised according to three equally important dimensions: procedural, distributive and restorative justice (McCauley and Heffron, 2018; Just Transition Research Collaborative, 2018; Cahill and Allen, 2020):

- Procedural justice focuses on identifying the scope of the transition and aims at facilitating an inclusive process;
- Distributive justice deals with the distribution of risks and responsibilities, and focuses on addressing the direct impacts resulting from the transition process; and
- Restorative justice considers damages against individuals, communities and the environment, with the goal of rectifying or ameliorating historical damages.

A just transition, at its core, requires a recognition of the need for reform and transformation to address the roots of climate, inequality and ecological crises. Yet, in some cases, stakeholders aim to maintain the status quo, by protecting industries (such as fossil fuels) and resisting the changes needed to address the damaging social and ecological outcomes of the existing socio-economic system. Such approaches are not consistent with a just transition.

Moving from status quo, three key variants of a just transition can be identified. They vary in ambition, ranging from managerial reform to structural reform, to transformation (Montmasson-Clair, 2021). Efforts to broaden just transition ambition – from visions to plans to financing strategies, from affected workers to a whole-of-society approach, from energy to cross-sectoral analyses – are increasingly visible. The variants of a just transition, outlined below, are used in subsequent sections to assess how South Africa fares with its just transition ambition.

The first variant of just transition ambition only achieves managerial reform. This version of a just transition does not envision changes to the economic model and the balance of power, but does seek to foster greater equity and justice within the existing system. In addition, the fact that the existing regime generates rising inequality, and that existing labour standards are ill-adapted to secure workers' health and wellbeing, is accepted. Vulnerability at the level of the labour market is also recognised. The focus is on dealing with direct impacts on workers. Other vulnerable stakeholders are, however, not included.

The next variant of ambition targets structural reform. Like managerial reform, the structural inequalities and injustices that are produced by the existing economic system are acknowledged. However, unlike managerial reform, the structural reform agenda aims to address (at least to some extent) the roots of inequities. Solutions are not solely produced via market forces or techno-economic innovations – modified governance structures as well as democratic participation, decision-making and ownership are core to this variant. As such, achieving structural reform departs from top-down processes and promotes a bottom-up approach, driven by the agency of affected groups (workers and citizens).

The most ambitious variant of a just transition targets transformation. This implies an overhaul of the existing economic, social and political system considered responsible for the interlinked sustainability and inequality crises. It involves the dismantling and reconfiguration of existing systems, a change in the rules and modes of governance and the promotion of alternative development pathways. This approach is rooted in bottom-up, grassroots democracy; high social/public ownership; strong social protection; community-level resilience; and inter- and intra-generational solidarity.

Procedural justice

A key underlying assumption in just transition discussions is that a just outcome can only emerge out of an inclusive process. Indeed, in the shift from brown to green economies, 'inclusion' is not a nice-to-have: it should be core to achieve procedural justice (Mohamed, 2020). A just transition should focus on facilitating an inclusive decision-making and implementation process, paying particular attention to enabling and empowering vulnerable stakeholders.

Overall, participatory justice calls for ongoing, rather than ad hoc, public engagement. Processes at the community as well as firm level should provide the platform for meaningful, long-term engagement, enabling trust building, capacity development, experience learning and co-creation. Any meaningful process should be continuous, to ensure joint monitoring of implementation and, if needed, course correction. The participation process itself should foster inclusion

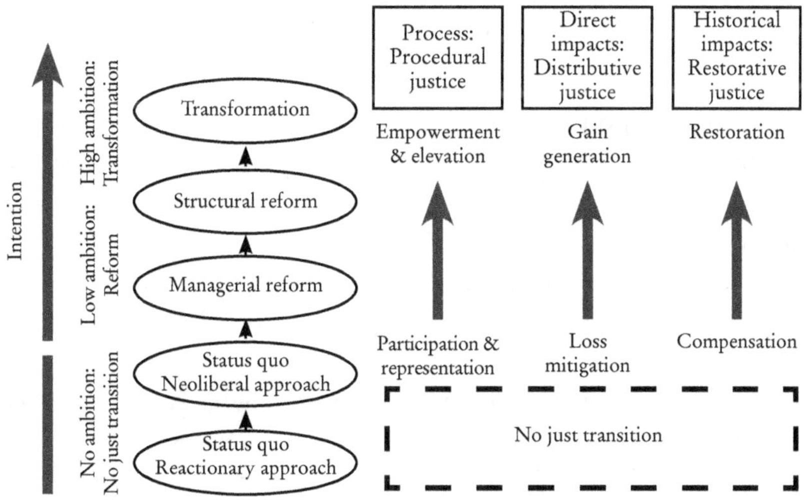

Figure 3.2: Dimensions of a just transition and degrees of ambition

Source: Montmasson-Clair (2021: 8)

and recognise the need to engage marginalised and excluded voices. All stakeholders should be provided the opportunity and resources to participate meaningfully. Participation and access to information should be transparent, equal and unrestricted, so that decisions can be informed by evidence, rather than opinions. All parties should have the opportunity and resources to collect and bring forward evidence.

A spectrum of procedural systems that enable participation, from direct to representative democracy, exists. To enact participatory justice, all available avenues that enable social inclusion should reinforce each other. A central difficulty is always to balance the power of organised constituencies and the desire for participatory and open procedures with the need to bring in expertise to test diagnostics and proposals against evidence, and to identify the resources necessary for action (Makgetla, 2019). A multiplicity of platforms is fundamental to build trust between both stakeholders and in the transition process itself.

Distributive justice

Achieving distributive justice hinges on addressing the direct negative impacts associated with the transition (such as loss of economic activity, employment and livelihood). It relies on harnessing a set of (generally) existing policy tools to lessen or mitigate adverse impacts as well as generate counter-balancing positive forces. Very often, these are focused on the world of work but should in fact be about equitable access to the opportunities arising from transitions as well as managing the impact on affected workers and industries. It is also about ensuring that all stakeholders benefit from new 'green' technologies, through direct access and/or indirect benefits. Over and beyond access, distributional justice, through the promotion of the social ownership of productive assets, aims to have a net positive effect on impacted communities.

A country-specific mix of 'macroeconomic, industrial, sectoral and labour policy' (ILO, 2015) reforms is critical and necessary to achieve distributional justice. For instance, labour market policy, in South Africa and elsewhere, has been identified as critical to foster green and decent work, and harness the employment creation potential of transitions. It combines both active labour market policies (ALMPs), such as income support programmes, reskilling and small business support, with passive labour market policies that impact labour market conditions (Carter et al., 2019). Yet, labour market policies are necessary but insufficient to achieve distributive justice. They need to be complemented by sectoral and industrial policy to drive or support the emergence of new economic opportunities (UNCTAD, 2016) as well as strong social protection interventions, especially to provide safety nets beyond workers. Plans and strategies, centred on greening key sectors (such as energy, transport, manufacturing, construction and agriculture) should be socially just and concretise the distributional dimensions of a just transition.

Restorative justice

Restorative justice represents the truly transformative potential of a just transition, extending beyond process and direct, short-term impacts to address long-term historical dynamics.

It fosters socio-economic empowerment of vulnerable stakeholders, notably improving access to modern housing and associated services (energy, water, sanitation). It is also forward-looking, ensuring that intergenerational justice is taken into consideration (including through more equitable ownership), and that the rights of future generations to a healthy planet and society is prioritised.

Advancing socio-cultural restoration is a critical complement to progress on socio-economic empowerment and also acknowledges the historical marginalisation of vulnerable stakeholders. This restoration can notably be implemented by enforcing non-predatory use of the land, recognising local rights and ownership, as well as the validity of local and indigenous culture, heritage, knowledge and practice (Montmasson-Clair, 2015b). Access to and quality of community services (health, education, safety) is another core component of empowerment (Walton, 2012).

Last but not least, restorative justice involves environmental restoration. This is evident in the case of land (mine) rehabilitation, but also extends to air and water. Frontline communities have in most cases suffered the negative consequences associated with decades (if not centuries) of natural resource extraction and/or industrial pollution.

Besides the destruction of the natural environment and associated climate impacts, these impacts have had dramatic spillovers on the health of frontline communities.

APPLYING THE NORMATIVE JUST TRANSITION FRAMEWORK TO KEY POLICY PROCESSES IN SOUTH AFRICA

The ILO (2015) set out a policy framework for a just transition, which acknowledges that a country-specific mix of policies is needed to integrate a just transition into the national climate and development agendas. South Africa has been at the forefront of nations and regions that have sought to adopt a just transition approach with over a decade of institutional support, dialogue, policy and planning processes in place. What does this look like in reality? Who is engaged, consulted and driving dialogue? Who will reap the benefits and who will bear the costs? These questions are explored through the lens of three case studies, on industrial, employment and climate policy.

Case study on industrial policy

Industrial policy is a core component of an ambitious just transition framework. It is also fundamental to reverse the pattern of premature de-industrialisation witnessed in South Africa (Andreoni and Tregenna, 2018). In essence, industrial policy is a balancing act, between maximising the benefits of the transition, minimising the risks associated with not transitioning and mitigating short-term trade-offs and threats. This requires a careful alignment of industrial policy with the inclusive green economy paradigm to support green industrial development within a just transition. Ultimately, this requires a shift to green and inclusive industrial policy (Montmasson-Clair, 2015a; Montmasson-Clair and Chigumira, 2020; Nilsson et al., 2021). South Africa's industrial policy displays foundational 'green shoots' but is yet to be an ambitious green industrial policy.

Procedural justice

Historically, the development of industrial policy in South Africa has been a top-down process, led primarily by the government, in consultation with select social partners. Effectively, the degree of stakeholder engagement has varied vastly from one industry to the next, with a strong focus on so-called 'strategic industries', such as the automotive value chain. In most cases, though, engagement has appeared to be more reactive than proactive. The degree of engagement on green industrial development has also depended on the political agenda, as discussions around a carbon tax illustrated. Stakeholders (be it business, labour unions or civil society) have often expressed reservations on both the process and content of the tax, tabling concerns that their proposals were not considered meaningfully in its formulation. Moreover, pro-active attempts at creating a social compact in favour of an inclusive and green industrial transition, such as the Green Economy Accord and the Decent Work Country Programme, have failed to deliver on their promises, despite generating agreements approved by social partners (Montmasson-Clair, 2017). This contrasts somewhat with the management of industrial relations through bargaining councils and strong trade unions, which has delivered important social advances for workers (ILO, 2010).

Since 2019, a more inclusive approach in the development of industrial policy has been initiated under the leadership of the Presidency and the Department of Trade, Industry and Competition (DTIC). The master plan approach provides a more inclusive platform for pro-active, forward-looking planning and implementation (Levin and Makgetla, 2019). Led by national government, the process involves the co-creation of sector-specific plans by stakeholders, primarily industry and trade unions. This is a key departure from the previous approach. Industrial Policy Action Plans developed by the then-Department of Trade and Industry (dti) from 2007 to 2018 did not involve such co-development, nor were plans discussed at the country's established social dialogue forum, the National Economic Development and Labour Council (NEDLAC). While an important step in the right direction, master plans do not yet reflect an ambitious approach to procedural justice, particularly due to the lack of involvement of affected communities and society as a whole.

Distributive justice

Industrial policy is central to achieving distributive justice. Numerous policy measures have been implemented in South Africa to foster the transition to an inclusive and green industrial development (Montmasson-Clair and Chigumira, 2020).

About a fifth of South Africa's R&D expenditure in 2016/2017 was directed towards green activities (Montmasson-Clair et al., 2019). Likewise, 16 per cent of the funding from South Africa's Industrial Development Corporation targeted 'green industries' over the 2008–2017 period and 7 per cent of the DTIC's Black Industrialist Support programme assisted clean technologies and energy over the 2015–2018 period (Montmasson-Clair and Chigumira, 2020). Infrastructure development has, to some extent, also positively contributed to green industrial development, through the extension of rail and public transport. Furthermore, some of the country's special economic zones (SEZs) have aspects supporting the transition to a green economy, such as the greentech manufacturing hub of the Atlantis SEZ, and the move towards eco-industrial parks. Procurement requirements (such as local content targets and requirements) and fiscal rules (such as deductions for 'green' investments) have, likewise, been used with some success in South Africa to promote the transition to a green economy, essentially in the energy sector. Regulations (both command-and-control and pricing) have been utilised to support behaviour change, with some progress achieved for plastic bags, electric filament lamps and recycling. Master plans are also under development to actively promote some key 'green industries', such as renewable energy, and water and sanitation.

Overall, industrial policy tools remain to be meaningfully harnessed for supporting green industrial development (Altenburg and Assmann, 2017; Nilsson et al., 2021). In South Africa, only a small fraction of industrial policy targets the transition to green industrial development and much more can be done to fully utilise the power of industrial policy to foster an inclusive and green transition. In many cases, South Africa's industrial policy still promotes an economic development model that counteracts the transition to a green economy. The example of the envisaged Musina-Makhado SEZ, in Limpopo, which would include numerous industrial, steel and ferrochrome facilities, fed by a coal-fired power plant, exemplifies this point. In addition, the amount of support directed at unsustainable activities remains particularly high. Based on International Monetary Fund data, direct fossil fuels subsidies amounted to 2.0 per cent of gross domestic product in 2017, rising to 13.6 per cent when the cost of externalities is included.

Restorative justice

South Africa's industrial policy has yet to be meaningfully aligned with the imperative of a just transition, particularly to break the historical pattern of injustice.

On the one hand, industrial policy has been a key avenue to address inequality in the South African society. Although imperfect, regulations on Broad-Based Black Economic Empowerment (B-BBEE), which set sectoral targets in terms of empowerment of, ownership by and control by previously disadvantaged South Africans, have made some inroads in addressing inequality (Makgetla, 2021). In addition, several initiatives, such as the Black Industrialist Support programme, and agencies, such as the Small Enterprise Development Agency and the Small Enterprise Finance Agency, have been actively supporting the diversification of the economy.

On the other hand, the longstanding promotion of an extractive and polluting industrial development model is at the root of the very problems which restorative justice must address. South Africa's industrial policy is rooted in the minerals energy complex, i.e. energy-intensive industrial activities underpinned by mineral extraction and abundant, cheap coal-based electricity (Fine and Rustomjee, 1996). For the most part, the country is yet to meaningfully move to a more sustainable development paradigm (Mohamed, 2019).

Case study on employment policy

Socio-economic transitions affect employment in different ways, depending on the prevailing conditions and dynamics of the labour market. In the last decade, there has been a drumbeat around the potential of low carbon transitions to create jobs (ILO, 2018; IRENA, 2020). Notwithstanding the promise of the creation of 'green jobs' in new industries, such as renewable energy, public transport and eco-agriculture, most existing jobs are likely to be either transformed or substituted for similar but hopefully more sustainable jobs. And some jobs will be lost in carbon-intensive industries. A national employment vulnerability assessment (Makgetla et al., 2020), and a complementary assessment of job opportunities arising from a green transition, affirm that a just transition in South Africa must address the grave unemployment challenge facing the country.

South Africa has a vision of a 'just transition to a resource-efficient, low-carbon and pro-employment growth path' (DEA, 2011: 7). Despite gains in economic development since its democratic transition, the country has faced persistent high unemployment (43.2 per cent in mid-2021, using the expanded definition, which includes discouraged job-seekers). While few countries have enacted employment policy and legislation aimed at greening employment, South Africa has a mixed approach, centred on social dialogue and has increasingly integrated labour issues into sectoral laws and policies.

Procedural justice

South Africa has had an 'extended, critical engagement with just transition, including a range of assessments, social dialogues and policies' and was among the handful of countries to mention a just transition in its climate change commitments in 2015 (WRI, 2021b). It has experienced growing dialogue and strengthened capacity on the labour market implications of low carbon transitions, including 'green jobs' and 'green skills' assessments and mapping, employment vulnerability analyses and social dialogue processes. These have put the country on course to implement a wide range of labour market policies that support a just, inclusive transition.

For the last decade, policy assessments and ongoing multi-stakeholder social dialogues have focused on the analysis and promotion of green jobs. In 2014, a national dialogue provided a platform for discussing and (collaboratively) refining government approaches to promoting green employment. Green jobs training and capacity development programmes, and an increasing focus on green skills anticipation and research ensued, at macro-economic and sectoral levels. By 2020, another iteration of the national green jobs dialogues fully addressed ALMPs, in particular skills development and entrepreneurship support, as core to employment policy reform. The National Planning Commission's (NPC) 'Social Partner Dialogue for a Just Transition' (NPC, 2019), identified the need to plan for job losses and job absorption as part of a just transition. National-level analysis and dialogue have supported the development of a job-rich transition (Makgetla et al., 2020). Labour market analysis has increasingly embraced a just transition approach, exemplified in the National Employment Vulnerability Assessment (NEVA) and associated Sector Jobs Resilience Plans (SJRPs) for stakeholders vulnerable to climate change-related impacts (Makgetla et al., 2020). Social dialogue, particularly at sectoral, firm and sub-national level, now needs to take this further.

Social dialogue has been supported by an array of green job assessments, to identify and quantify existing green jobs and to project how effective policies and investment programmes can be in providing new job opportunities. In 2011, a national report (Maia et al., 2011) presented an assessment of the potential for creating green jobs in key sectors in South Africa. While the study has played a central role in showing the anticipated net direct green jobs creation, it paid scant regard to not only the challenges and enabling conditions required to realise these projected jobs, but also to how these would be measured in future. This has been partly addressed through studies on green jobs in renewable energy, natural resource management, food systems and through specific initiatives, notably the Expanded Public Works Programme (EPWP) discussed below (Mohamed, 2017). Civil society-led research, such as the 1 Million Climate Jobs campaign, complements this analysis (AIDC, 2016). However, there is very little reliable and on-going reporting on green jobs creation in South Africa.

Distributive justice

Public employment programmes, which were identified as one of the key labour market policies for scale-up by the NPC (2019), have created a significant amount of work opportunities that could be classified as green jobs. They have also featured prominently in social dialogue on green employment policy in South Africa.

The EPWP is the country's long-standing and cross-sectoral public employment programme, which delivers multiple outcomes: employment, social protection (income) and the provision of assets and services. The programme covers all spheres of government and state-owned enterprises, and partners with civil society through non-governmental organisations, aiming to draw significant numbers of unemployed people into productive work accompanied by training. The EPWP has made a weighty contribution to creating work opportunities, and has a targeted focus on youth, women and persons with disabilities. It remains a key mechanism for poverty alleviation and income provision, and has played a central role in the country's developmental journey by offering social protection for the most vulnerable, while promoting environmental sustainability and climate resilience. The programme has contributed substantively to the country's green employment ambition: about 13 per cent of all work opportunities created by the EPWP are deemed 'green jobs' (Mohamed, 2017), primarily through the programmes focused on environmental outcomes.

The EPWP is instrumental to achieving social protection in South Africa. It can also make a key contribution to the employment shifts envisaged as South Africa transitions to a climate-resilient development pathway. The EPWP is among the key strategies of the country's post-pandemic reconstruction and recovery plan (The Presidency, 2020). Its focus on women and youth assists in addressing the gendered and generational dimension of unemployment. The programme has been identified as one of the key ALMPs that needs to be expanded to achieve a just transition (NPC, 2019), ensuring that job opportunities from the transition are distributed equitably. Some examples of possible sectoral extension for the EPWP (Mohamed, 2017) include renewable energy and energy efficiency; sustainable water management; transport (eco-mobility); construction (green buildings and sustainable infrastructure); waste managements and climate-smart agriculture. These provide a key lever to balance interventions between climate mitigation and adaptation.

The decent work dimension of the EPWP, however, begs consideration. Remuneration levels in the programme are not in line with minimum wage levels, and there has been limited success in supporting workers to enter the labour market so that the state becomes 'an employer of last resort'.

Restorative justice

While green transitions are resulting in the creation of new employment, there is no guarantee that these jobs will be created in areas or among those most in need of employment, or that they will be decent jobs. Well-informed employment policies (supported by diagnostics and assessment) can help anticipate the labour market challenges and opportunities of moving toward a green economy. However, they often assume that workers are fully mobile between jobs and locations, that there are sufficient workers equipped with the required skills to take up new jobs, that decent work criteria are prioritised or that workers can, in fact, access opportunities to upgrade or reskill to keep their existing job.

The lack of social protection has been magnified during the COVID-19 pandemic and labour policy instruments, such as universal basic income grants or wage subsidies, have been back on the table globally. This reflects the growing recognition that income protection should be fundamental in planning for resilient societies and communities.

Neither employment policy in general nor green jobs diagnosis and planning processes have yielded the granularity required to achieve restorative justice and to fundamentally address the greening of work. South Africa's climate policy has begun to take this further through its focus on employment vulnerability and job resilience planning.

Case study on climate policy

Climate policy has been central to crafting an enabling framework for a just transition in South Africa. The country's climate policy processes have been developed through an inclusive process, including social dialogue with business, government, unions and civil society. It is lauded globally as one of the 'few countries that have conducted national-level, ongoing social dialogue to develop a vision for a just transition' (WRI, 2021b). South Africa has played a leading role globally in placing a just transition as a central goal of climate policy.

Yet, due to its dependence on coal, it is one of the most carbon-intensive economies. Linked largely to its colonial and apartheid history, South Africa is also among the most unequal societies, not only in terms of income but also access to opportunities and essential services, stressing once more the need for a just transition.

Procedural justice

Several milestones along the climate policy process highlight the centrality of a just transition and the application of a procedural justice approach to climate policy formulation. South Africa's first stakeholder-driven National Climate Change Response Strategy in 2004 identified the country's vulnerability to climate change, as well as key issues and problems related to climate policy. This was followed up by the development of the Long-Term Mitigation Scenarios (between 2006 and 2007) and the 2013 Long-Term Adaptation Scenarios. These were both developed through facilitated stakeholder processes and technical analysis, the twin-formula that has been applied consistently in formulating climate policy. In 2011, the South African government approved its National Climate Change Response White Paper. This outlines a vision for an effective climate change response and the long-term just transition to a climate-resilient and lower-carbon economy and society, setting the tone for a decade of climate policy.

Two policy processes structured around social dialogue and engagement are particularly noteworthy for their attention to social inclusion – in both process and outcome – namely the inclusion of a just transition in the 2012 National Development Plan (NDP) and the establishment of a Presidential Climate Commission in 2020. The formulation of Chapter 5 of the NDP ('Ensuring environmental sustainability and an equitable transition to a low-carbon economy') involved extensive engagement with a broad range of stakeholders, including focused discussions with individual stakeholder groups, culminating in a vision and key principles of a just transition. There was broad consensus on the challenges and trade-offs in implementing South Africa's climate policy, and in 2018–2019, the NPC initiated a further step, a facilitated consensus-building stakeholder engagement process to develop options for a just, climate-resilient and equitable future for South Africa (NPC, 2019).

Taking on the reins for steering this vision, and chaired by the president of South Africa, the Presidential Climate Commission is rooted in social dialogue. It emanates from the Presidential Jobs Summit, held in October 2018, when social partners agreed that a statutory body be formed to coordinate and oversee the just transition. The Commission has the mandate to advise on South Africa's climate change response; provide independent monitoring; review emissions reduction; and adaptation goals and drive the engagement of key stakeholders. It seeks to facilitate a common understanding of a just transition and formulate a national just transition framework. The Commission epitomises a commitment to social dialogue, with representatives from government, business organisations, labour, academia, civil society, research institutions and traditional leadership.

These government-led social dialogue processes have been complemented by a wide range of civil society processes. Civil society coalitions and alliances have called for deepening just transitions by addressing structural economic reform. The Climate Justice Coalition is made up of an array of members working on justice issues. It seeks to foster 'a transformative climate justice agenda' and advocates for a 'vision of climate justice which advances environmental, energy, gender, racial, immigrant, climate and economic justice together' (Climate Justice Coalition, 2021). This intersectional lens also characterises the work of the Climate Justice Charter, a movement for a people-centred and society-driven just transition with 'democratic, transformative and just solutions' (SAFSC, 2021). These platforms for democratic participation and citizen ownership are central to social dialogue for a just transition, and should be integrated in inclusive policy processes, from diagnosis and design to monitoring and impact analysis – in cities, communities and companies.

Distributional justice

Climate policy has deepened its analysis and application of a just transition approach, outlining the climate change-related impacts on vulnerable groups in the NEVA, and developing SJRPs that seek to protect vulnerable groups that may lose their jobs or livelihoods because of climate change impacts. In-depth assessments and proposals for five value chains identified as particularly vulnerable in the near future, namely coal, metals, petroleum-based transport, agriculture and tourism, were developed in 2020. These stressed the need for a multi-pronged response encompassing the three dimensions of transitional justice (Makgetla et al., 2020).

For the coal value chain, five key interventions were put forward (Patel et al., 2020). The first relates to allocating responsibility for driving the development and implementation of a resilience plan. It is vital that responsibility is clearly vested in an agency that is able to monitor impacts on the coal value chain as well as implementation itself. This function would need to be dynamic and responsive, given the current uncertainty in the coal value chain. It would also have to mobilise resources and stakeholder inputs at community level. A second intervention is to improve the effectiveness of existing Social and Labour Plans (SLPs), which are a prerequisite for acquiring mining and production rights. In their current form, evidence indicates that SLPs have not delivered on their intended purpose of developing opportunities for workers and communities post-mining. Critically, the SLPs need to be more accountable to workers and coal towns that are affected by mine downsizing and closure. Third, the coal towns need to have additional support in developing plans to diversify their economies away from coal over the longer run. Industrial policy would here play a critical role in developing new economic activities. Fourth, ALMPs have to be strengthened and adjusted to serve potential future downsizing in coal. Linked to this, a fifth proposal relates to strengthening income support and social protection for workers and communities, including through an extension of public employment schemes.

Restorative justice

As South Africa's just transition deepens, reparations to 'stranded' workers and communities for historical and ongoing damages are needed. Accordingly, options to finance just transition plans and strategies need to consider reparations. Place-based just transition strategies have highlighted the need for contextualised approaches that prioritise local and regional economic development.

For example, the Mpumalanga province, which accounts for more than 80 per cent of coal production and the bulk of South Africa's coal-fired power production, has emerged as a testbed for a just transition approach. The provincial government has established a Green Cluster Agency – engagement at the intersection of government, business and academia, to unlock opportunities in the green economy. Many other economic opportunities are also contemplated, notably in manufacturing, agriculture and tourism. Furthermore, tensions between the expansion of the mining industry and the development of other economic activities across the province (such as agriculture and tourism) will have to be resolved. Significant efforts are also required to rehabilitate the environment (land, air, water) as well as address the inequalities in terms of access to housing and associated services (energy, water) and economic opportunities more broadly.

Much of the restorative dimension of just transitions will come to life in places such as Mpumalanga's coalfields. The planning frameworks, partnerships, dialogue mechanisms and policies for a just transition need to be tried and tested on the ground. They must be pitted against the structural barriers that they will inevitably face. They must deliver the lessons needed to craft employment-rich, equitable and inclusive low carbon pathways. The lessons emerging from Mpumalanga will be critical as just transition frameworks are increasingly implemented in regions, sectors, firms and communities.

ADVANCING A COHERENT AND COORDINATED JUST TRANSITION POLICY FRAMEWORK

South Africa has put in place a political and policy vision for a just transition to a low carbon economy, which features prominently in the long-term development vision and is an integral part of the country's national climate change response strategy. Changing the trajectory of the political and economic system, rooted in carbon dependence, is a herculean task. Close to 90 per cent of the country's electricity mix is derived from fossil fuels, while soaring unemployment and inequality compound the context. Climate action still rests largely on mitigation actions, although both public and private sector stakeholders have increasingly put emphasis on climate adaptation. So, does South Africa make the grade in its ambition for a just transition? It's a pass, but with a very narrow margin.

South Africa's vision of a just transition advanced in this chapter is broad-based, extending beyond directly impacted workers and communities to include all vulnerable stakeholders likely to be affected by transitions. In terms of the variants of a just transition, South Africa sits somewhere between low and high ambition, between reform and transformation (see Figure 3.1).

However, from the analysis undertaken above, the policy agenda is mostly at the level of managerial reform and sits at the lower end of the ambition spectrum. South Africa's just transition variant aims to foster greater equity and justice and recognises vulnerability at the level of the labour market, likely a consequence of the strong voice of trade unions in social dialogue processes. However, it does not yet address the roots of vulnerabilities and resultant inequalities, nor does it consider meaningfully reviving democratic participation, decision-making and ownership, which are core aspects of a structural reform approach to just transitions. The transformation of existing economic, social and political systems considered to be responsible for the multiple crises has increasingly become a rallying point of civil society alliances demanding a deep and transformative transition.

The policy framework that shapes the enabling environment for just transition largely reflects this managerialist approach. Industrial policy has only recently taken on board more participatory policymaking processes, even though green and inclusive industrial development is key to achieve the distributional dimensions of a just transition. And despite 'green shoots', it remains to be meaningfully aligned with the tenets of a just transition. There has been much dialogue, diagnosis and some planning for a job-rich transition, but not nearly enough policy reforms to achieve a pro-employment pathway. While public employment programmes create green jobs and offer a measure of social protection to vulnerable and unemployed workers, they cannot drive the country's efforts to green the labour market. A much deeper transformation is necessary. Climate policy has been built on a rich tradition of participatory policymaking and has made inroads into the distributional dimensions of a just transition by virtue of necessity. As climate change impacts hit harder and faster than anticipated, climate vulnerable regions (like Africa) will have to face the challenge of applying restorative just transitions in the decades to come. This is yet to be internalised by climate policy. Key insights emerge from the analysis that provide some direction for achieving a more transformative approach to just transitions.

The policy processes discussed in the previous section, when viewed through a just transition lens, have shown strong recognition and support for procedural justice, but insufficient enactment at the local level. This commitment to social dialogue should evolve from engagement with civil society representatives, for the most part at national level, towards a societally driven dialogue at multiple levels (notably in firms, cities and communities). This requires not only recognising and including multiple voices, but also activating citizen (and worker) agency to engage throughout the policy cycle – from problem identification and diagnosis through to policy monitoring and review. Just transitions without inclusion are both unjust and risky – but with policies and institutions that foster inclusion, participation and citizen agency, the essential foundations for a sustainable, enduring and transformative transition could be established.

Just transitions must address the needs of the most vulnerable – affected workers, urban and rural poor, women and youth – to ensure that the benefits of transitions are accessible to everyone and that transition risks are borne equitably. Some headway has been made in this regard, notably in identifying the impacts of climate change on employment and in the efforts to develop resilience plans. A deeper application of the distributional dimension of a just transition would require applying the right policy mix – taking into consideration the availability of policy tools such as industrial, social protection, skills and labour market policies. There is no 'one size fits all' and a low carbon transition will impact sectors, industries and places differently. Policies that address this dimension should consider the specific conditions to identify negative impacts (direct and indirect) associated with the transition as well as the responsibilities for bearing the costs of the transition. The work underway as of August 2021, to take forward the SJRPs as well as develop both a just transition framework and a just transition finance roadmap for South Africa, is a welcome step in this direction.

South Africa has a rich tradition in restorative justice, given the reparations that were needed to craft a post-apartheid society. This dimension contains the truly transformative nature of any just transition. Restorative justice extends beyond process and direct, short-term impacts to include long-term historical dynamics and pathways. It adopts a rights-based approach to development, with the intent of improving the access of vulnerable stakeholders to healthy and safe environments, upholding universal economic and social rights, and safeguarding and protecting equitable access to and ownership of assets. It is about development models and imaginaries that rethink the relationship between people and nature, and between people and the state. It seeks to redefine the relationship between the state and citizens, based on the welfare of all people. It leads to a just, new and inspiring social contract that spurs the transformation of economies and societies to fight poverty and inequality, halt climate change and address environmental breakdown. This dimension is championed by the civil society movement in South Africa.

Operating at the nexus of social, environmental and climate justice, civil society is holding power to account, highlighting the need for government and business to meaningful embrace their role in effecting restorative justice. Civil action, on the streets, in bargaining councils and in the courtrooms, has put South Africa's just transition ambition to the test – and won some battles.

CONCLUSION

Just transitions towards sustainability, in which the equity and wellbeing of all South Africans and the environmental sustainability of the country's valuable natural systems is prioritised, need to be commensurate with the scale of the challenge. They should deepen and pick up pace. And they must shift from managerialist approaches towards structural and transformative just transition ones, which add meaning to the mantra of 'leaving no one behind'.

The COVID-19 pandemic has unmasked (once more) the full extent of the inequalities between and within countries, and reinforced the need to carve a safe and just space for all of humankind. It has opened, in some places, the political moment to question the purpose of our economies. It is possible to build societies and economies that are more just, equal and inclusive; are better integrated with nature; offer social protection for all and that are more informed by science, but only if we act now. A just transition is imperative to achieve the policy frameworks and processes that will deliver development pathways leading to a fair and sustainable world.

REFERENCES

Altenburg, T., & Assmann, C. (eds) (2017). 'Green Industrial Policy. Concept, Policies, Country Experiences'. Geneva, Bonn: UN Environment; German Development Institute / Deutsches Institut für Entwicklungspolitk (DIE). https://www.unido.org/sites/default/files/files/2017-12/green_industrial_policy_book.pdf, accessed 12 May 2021.

Alternative Information and Development Centre (AIDC). 2016. 'One Million Climate Jobs: Moving South Africa Forward on a Low-Carbon, Wage-led and Sustainable Path'. https://aidc.org.za/download/climate-change/OMCJ-booklet-AIDC-electronic-version.pdf, accessed 13 October 2021.

Andreoni, A. and Tregenna, F. 2018. 'Stuck in the middle: Premature deindustrialisation and industrial policy'. Centre for Competition, Regulation and Economic Development, Johannesburg.

Cahill, B. and Allen, M.M. 2020. 'Just transition concepts and relevance for climate action: A preliminary framework'. Center for Strategic and International Studies and Climate Investment Funds, Wasjington DC.

Carter, B., Roelen, K., Enfield, S. and Avis, W. 2019. *Social Protection Topic Guide, revised edition*. Brighton: Institute of Development Studies.

Climate Justice Coalition. 2021. 'The Climate Justice Coalition'. 350 Africa, https://350africa.org/the-climate-justice-coalition/, accessed 6 August 2021.

Department of Environmental Affairs (DEA). 2011. 'National Strategy for Sustainable Development and Action Plan(NSSD 1)'. https://www.dffe.gov.za/sites/default/files/docs/sustainabledevelopment_actionplan_strategy.pdf, accessed 5 August 2021.

Fine, B. and Rustomjee, Z. 1996. *The Political Economy of South Africa: From minerals energy complex to industrialisation*. London: C. Hurst & Co. Publishers.

International Labour Organisation (ILO). 2019. *Future of Work for Climate Resilience in the Pacific Islands*. Asia Pacific, Fiji: International Labour Organisation.

International Labour Organisation (ILO). 2018. *Greening with Jobs. World Employment and Social Outlook 2018*. Geneva: International Labour Office.

International Labour Organisation (ILO). 2015. *Guidelines for a just transition towards environmentally sustainable economies and societies for all*. Geneva: International Labour Office.

International Labour Organisation (ILO). 2010. 'Skills for Green Jobs in South Africa'. International Labour Office, Geneva.

International Renewable Energy Agency (IRENA). 2020. *Renewable Energy and Jobs – Annual Review*. Abu Dhabi: International Renewable Energy Agency. https://www.irena.org/-/media/Files/IRENA/Agency/Publication/2020/Sep/IRENA_RE_Jobs_2020.pdf, accessed 8 August 2021.

Just Transition Research Collaborative. 2018. 'Mapping just transition(s) to a low-carbon world'. United Nations Research Institute for Social Development, University of London Institute in Paris and Rosa-Luxemburg-Stiftung.

Levin, S. and Makgetla, N. 2019. 'Master Plans and industrial policy'. Trade & Industrial Policy Strategies, https://www.tips.org.za/policy-briefs/item/download/1768_1d434c179a454f535ed615ad3002c3fb, accessed 3 July 2021.

Maia, J., Giordano, T., Kelder, N., Bardien, G., Bodibe, M. et al. 2011. 'Green Jobs: An Estimate of the Direct Employment Potential of a Greening South African Economy'. Industrial Development Corporation, Development Bank of Southern Africa and Trade and Industrial Policy Strategies, http://www.tips.org.za/files/green_jobs_-_an_estimate_of_the_direct_employment_potential_of_a_greening_south_african_economy.pdf, accessed 13 May 2021.

Makgetla, N. 2021. *The Impacts and Outcomes of BBBEE: A Preliminary Assessment*. Pretoria: Trade and Industrial Policy Strategies. https://www.tips.org.za/research-archive/trade-and-industry/economic-regulation/item/download/1999_7b2101d4b51883615939c16bbc55086b, accessed 24 May 2021.

Makgetla, N. 2019. 'Draft – Learning for the SJRPs from International and Local Debates and Experience'. Department of Environmental Affairs and Economic Development Department, Pretoria.

Makgetla, N., Maseko, N., Montmasson-Clair, G. and Patel, M. 2020. 'The SJRP Toolbox: Summary for Policy Makers'. Trade and Industrial Policy Strategies, https://www.tips.org.za/images/TIPS_for_DEFF-dtic_-_SJRP_-_Summary_for_Policy_Makers_May_2020.pdf, accessed 3 June 2021.

McCauley, D. and Heffron, R. 2018. 'Just transition: Integrating climate, energy and environmental justice'. *Energy Policy,* 119: 1–7.

Mohamed, N. 2020. *Inclusion Matters. Policy insights and lessons from the Green Economy Coalition's national dialogues.* London: Green Economy Coalition.

Mohamed, N. 2019. *Sustainability Transitions in South Africa.* Oxon and New York: Routledge.

Mohamed, N. 2017. 'Developing a green jobs roadmap for the Expanded Public Works Programme'. Unpublished report, International Labour Organization.

Montmasson-Clair, G. 2021. *A Policy Toolbox for Just Transitions.* Pretoria: Trade & Industrial Policy Strategies. https://www.tips.org.za/research-archive/sustainable-growth/green-economy-2/item/download/2116_c86ef5202ab47b375a61f0aa1b1e0e43.

Montmasson-Clair, G. 2017. *Governance for South Africa's Sustainability Transition: A Critical Review.* Pretoria and London: Trade & Industrial Policy Strategies and Green Economy Coalition. https://www.tips.org.za/research-archive/sustainable-growth/green-economy-coalition/item/download/1541_e8697e3d5e67332854b18f53418bda36.

Montmasson-Clair, G. 2015a. 'The two shall become one: Overcoming the stalemate between industrial and climate change policies'. Pretoria: Trade and Industrial Policy Strategies. https://www.tips.org.za/policy-briefs/item/download/1059_27131fcab6ea69f6f359df9e21026ef8, accessed 24 May 2021.

Montmasson-Clair, G. 2015b. *The Interplay between Mining and Green Economy: An energy lens.* Grenoble: Pierre Mendès-France University.

Montmasson-Clair, G. and Chigumira, M. 2020. 'Green Economy Policy Review of South Africa's Industrial Policy Framework'. United Nations Environment Programme, Department of Environment, Forestries and Fisheries, Department of Trade, Industry and Competition, and Department of Science and Innovation, https://www.tips.org.za/research-archive/sustainable-growth/green-economy/item/download/1897_f6c6556328e791a627b30f86cd28e739, accessed 14 April 2021.

Montmasson-Clair, G., Mudombi, S. and Ryan, G. 2019. 'Measurement of green economy research and development 2010/11-2016/17'. Trade & Industrial Policy Strategies and Department of Science and Technology, https://www.tips.org.za/research-archive/sustainable-growth/green-economy/item/download/1873_be4c8af5d4e9c88afb0fa567e6e51ee1, accessed 5 May 2021.

National Planning Commission (NPC). 2012. *National Development Plan 2030: Our Future – Make It Work.* Pretoria: National Planning Commission.

National Planning Commission (NPC). 2019. 'Draft Proposal – Version Two

2050 Vision and Pathways for a Just Transition to a low carbon, climate resilient economy and society'. https://oneworldgroup.co.za/wp-content/uploads/2019/10/NPC-JT-Vision-and-Pathways-draft-2-final.pdf, accessed 6 August 2021.

Neslen, A. 26 October 2018. 'Spain to close most coal mines in €250 million deal'. *The Guardian*, https://www.theguardian.com/environment/2018/oct/26/spain-to-close-most-coal-mines-after-striking-250m-deal, accessed 6 August 2021.

Nilsson L.J., Bauer, F., Åhman, M., Andersson, F.N.G., Bataille, C. et al. 2021. 'An industrial policy framework for transforming energy and emissions intensive industries towards zero emissions'. Climate Policy, 21(8), 1053–1065.

Patel, M., Makgetla, N., Maseko, N. and Montmasson-Clair, G. 2020. 'Sector Jobs Resilience Plan: Coal Value Chain'. Department of Environmental Affairs, Department of Trade, Industry and Competition, and Trade and Industrial Policy Strategies, https://www.tips.org.za/research-archive/sustainable-growth/green-economy-2/item/3986-sector-jobs-resilience-plan-coal-value-chain, accessed 3 August 2021.

Robins, N and Rydge, J. 2019. 'Why a just transition is crucial for effective climate action'. https://www.unpri.org/download?ac=7092, accessed 12 April 2021.

Robins, N., Gouldson, A., Irwin, W. and Sudmant, A. 2019. 'Investing in a just transition in the UK: How investors can integrate social impact and place-based financing into climate strategies'. Grantham Research Institute on Climate Change and the Environment, London.

Social Justice Ireland. 2020. 'A just transition for farmers'. https://www.socialjustice.ie/content/policy-issues/just-transition-farmers, accessed 6 August 2021.

South African Food Sovereignty Campaign (SAFSC). 2021. 'Climate Justice Charter'. https://www.safsc.org.za/climate-justice-charter/, accessed 6 August 2021.

The Presidency. 2020. 'Building a New Economy: Highlights of the Reconstruction and Recovery Plan'. https://www.gov.za/sites/default/files/gcis_document/202010/building-new-economy-highlights-reconstruction-and-recovery-plan.pdf, accessed 13 October 2021.

United Nations Conference on Trade and Development (UNCTAD). 2016. 'Virtual Institute Teaching Material on Structural Transformation and Industrial Policy'. https://vi.unctad.org/stind/indpolfull.pdf, accessed 7 August 2021.

Walton, O. 2012. 'Evidence for the development impact of inclusive service delivery'. GSDRC Helpdesk Research Report, Governance and Social Development Resource Centre, University of Birmingham.

World Resources Institute (WRI). 2021a. 'Chile: Incorporating a just transition into Chile's Nationally Determined Contribution'. https://www.wri.org/

just-transitions/chile, accessed 6 August 2021.
World Resources Institute (WRI). 2021b. 'South Africa: Strong foundations for a just transition'. https://www.wri.org/just-transitions/south-africa, accessed 6 August 2021.

SECTION 2

Shift in economic paradigm

FOUR

Shaping a new economic growth model for South Africa

The role of a well-managed energy transition

Kenneth Creamer

OVERVIEW

A key current question about economic policy is how South Africa's energy transition can be optimally designed to promote inclusive growth, industrial development and employment creation. To answer this question effectively, it is necessary to have a clear understanding of the objectives, strengths and weaknesses of South Africa's current policy frameworks. These include policy on the restructuring of Eskom and the wider electricity sector; relevant regulatory policies; electricity-planning instruments, such as the Integrated Resources Plan (IRP), as well as industrial policy; export promotion strategies; minerals exploration; minerals beneficiation; green hydrogen policy and other interventions to maximise growth and create employment multipliers.

Historically, the apartheid growth model was built on two pillars. Firstly, the dispossession, oppression and super-exploitation of the black majority. Secondly, the promotion of industrial development, based in large part on the use of the country's extensive coal reserves, to provide low-cost and abundant electricity to drive mining, industry, commerce and finance.

As a result, democratic South Africa has inherited a racially fractured, unequal and highly carbon-intensive economy. Furthermore, the democratic period has seen a lack of investment in electricity infrastructure, resulting in an electricity shortage. This deficit is proving to be a binding constraint on investment, growth and employment creation.

There are both threats and opportunities for South Africa as the country embarks on an energy transition towards a low carbon future. Appropriate government policy, supported by forward-looking social compacting by labour, business, communities and government, has the potential to manage and minimise the threats which the energy transition poses, and also to maximise the opportunities.

A NEW GROWTH MODEL FOR SOUTH AFRICA

A pertinent set of questions for a democratic South Africa, struggling to overcome its exclusionary and fractured legacy, would include: where is economic growth going to come from?; how can economic inclusion be fostered?; what strategies are required to accelerate the rate of employment creation?; and how can the energy transition best be designed to promote economic growth and job creation?

The answers must surely, at least in part, lie within the new investments, new industries and new products and services that will come into being as a result of the country's decarbonising energy transition. This transition, if well designed and managed, can be inclusive and fundamentally transformative of the livelihoods of millions of people in South Africa. It will, in addition, necessarily stimulate other related transitions – for example, in the mobility and urban planning sectors.

According to South Africa's Council for Scientific and Industrial

Research (CSIR), the country's energy transition can be managed to substantively strengthen the fundamentals of South Africa's economic growth model (CSIR, 2019), facilitating the following:

- net increase in employment;
- reduced carbon emissions and reduced water consumption;
- creation of new industries such as renewables and electric vehicles;
- restore the competitive advantage of low-cost electricity;
- enable exports of hydrogen and clean synthetic fuels;
- support universal access to electricity;
- increase flexibility of the economy to respond to changes in growth and energy demand; and
- increase electricity security.

A well-known insight of economic theory is that sustained rising living standards can only be achieved if economies experience a combination of increased investment in capital machinery together with technological improvements. Growth models, such as those of Solow (1956) and Swan (1956), show that it is because of the diminishing marginal returns on capital that technological advances are required to ensure that increases in productivity and living standards can be sustained.

On the other hand, such models do not provide insight into the dynamics of how productivity gains are shared over time between capital and labour, or who will be the winners and losers as technologies change and growth drivers shift. To better understand the conditional nature of such dynamics, supply-side models based in the labour market (as per Layard et al., 2005) provide helpful insights. As indicated in Figure 4.1, where the wage-setting curve represents the supply side of the labour market and the price-setting curve the demand side, the introduction of new technology is initially likely to lead to an increase in unemployment as a number of workers at 'B' are displaced from their existing jobs. During this phase, incumbent workers in old-technology firms face the risk of losing their jobs.

Due to the fact that output per worker has risen as a result of the impact of the productivity gains of the new technology, the potential for higher profits incentivises new firms to enter the market. If the entry of new firms is relatively easy, the economy will move from 'B' to 'C' – pushing up employment levels and ultimately wages at 'D'. While the increase in employment may or may not benefit workers in old-technology firms who have lost their jobs, the overall level of employment at 'C' and 'D' is higher than before the introduction of the new technology. If, on the other hand, new firm entry is difficult and there are supply-side barriers and rigidities, the economy may get stuck at 'B' for a prolonged period. If this occurs, the net effect of the new technology will be reduced employment levels and falling real wages.

It is vitally important that these potential dynamics are fully

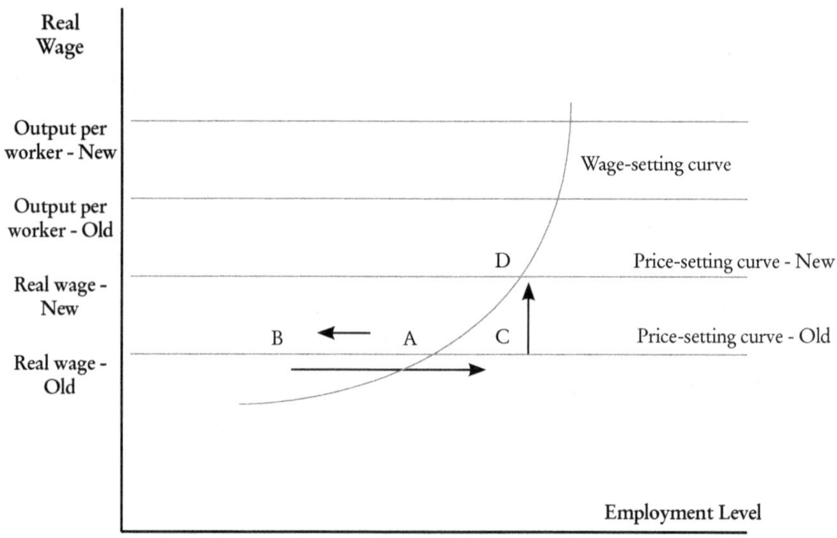

At A: New technology shifts up output per worker and the price setting curve
A to B: New technology leads to fall in employment level
B to C: High profits encourages new firms to enter
C to D: Higher employment leads to higher real wage
At D: If correct supportive conditions prevail, such as easy entry for firms and appropriate skilling of labour, then the overall effect of the new technology is an increased overall employment level and higher real wages

Figure 4.1: Conditions for technology to result in increased employment and higher wages

Source: Adapted from The Core Team *(2019), Figure 16.9b.*

understood in designing policies for South Africa's energy transition. Essentially, both sides of the argument have theoretical support; it can be shown in theory that technological changes will result in more employment and higher wages, just as it can be shown that technological change will result in job losses and lower wages. The outcome achieved will be conditional; it depends on how the supply-side of the economy actually responds to the technological change. Overall, the introduction of new technology will mean that there will be winners and losers, but whether the net effect, at an aggregate level, will be positive or negative depends on how dynamic the economy is in its responses. In the language of Joseph Schumpeter's 'perennial gale of creative destruction' (Schumpeter, 1942: 82–83): will the implementation of new technology create more firms than it destroys and create more jobs than it destroys?

This is not an inevitable process. Rather, it depends crucially on the institutions and government policies that guide the introduction of new technologies. Legal frameworks, public policy and the practices of trade union and employer organisations will all determine the direction and the extent to which changes in technology impact on employment and wage levels. If public resources are mobilised in order to re-skill workers, if public utilities are able to re-purpose ageing plants and provide new employment opportunities, then the risks to incumbent workers and affected communities will be ameliorated. If policy frameworks operate efficiently to ensure that new firms are able to gain licenses to begin deploying the new technologies and speedily commence their operations, then the net effect may be increased employment levels and rising real wages. If such contingencies do not occur, then there is a real risk that losers will outnumber winners and that the net effect of the technology shift will be negative.

As technologies change, a supportive policy framework, buy-in from social partners in labour, business and government, as well as a clear 'just transition' programme will assist in promoting an inclusive, higher-employment, higher-wage outcome. For example, as old technologies cease to operate and new technologies come on-stream, there should be the resourcing of supportive programmes for re-training, reallocation and job-matching for affected personnel.

There should also be investment in new forms of productive activity for affected regions. Ideally, workers released from failing firms and technologies should be able to move quickly to better ones.

In the context of a well-managed energy transition, with adequate planning for affected workers and communities, trade unions will find it easier to be forward looking and will be less inclined to insist on a worker's right to keep a particular job. Rather, demands can focus on the need for adequate new job opportunities and for support for training and new investments. If trade unions and government policies are backward looking and seek to protect the status quo, this will slow the rate of diffusion of new technologies and slow the rate at which South Africa will be able to put in place a new economic growth model: one based on a transition to low-cost, low carbon electricity and all the related investment, export and employment linkages that hinge on such a transition.

GLOBAL CONTEXT OF ENERGY TRANSITION

The global problem of environmental damage due to rapid industrialisation over the past two centuries has gained increasing recognition in recent decades. The impact of rising greenhouse gases, in particular carbon dioxide, and its link to global warming and climate change has come to be scientifically well established. The August 2021 report of the United Nation's Intergovernmental Panel on Climate Change (IPCC, 2021) has shown conclusively that human drivers have contributed to rising global temperatures.

The IPCC report found 'multiple lines of evidence' of climate change, based not only on computer models, but also on detailed data of ongoing physical events. The report stated that climate change is already 'affecting every inhabited region across the globe, with human influence contributing to many observed changes in weather and climate extremes' (IPCC, 2021: 12).

Over a decade ago, in reports such as *The Economics of Climate: The Stern Review* (Stern, 2006), the emphasis was on the costs and constraints associated with changing the patterns of economic development to abate and mitigate environmental damage. As Kemal

Dervis (2021) describes it, 'Policymakers would therefore have to consider a trade-off between more economic output in the near term and the damage caused by global warming in the longer term'.

Due to technological change in recent years, in particular the falling price of renewable sources of electricity, the transition towards decarbonised green energy has come to be regarded as an opportunity rather than a constraint. As with all technological change, there will be winners and losers, but in the aggregate the new technologies will mean that it costs less to build renewable energy systems than traditional carbon-emitting energy systems. This means that there is no longer a trade-off where green technology must be adopted even though it costs more; rather, economic forces will dictate that such technology should be adopted as it costs less. To coin a phrase, rather than what former US Vice President, Al Gore, described as *An Inconvenient Truth* of climate change (Gore, 2006), the emerging 'Convenient Truth' is that the fact that wind and solar are the lowest cost sources of electricity means that there is a direct alignment between low cost production and decarbonisation – there is no longer a trade-off, where in order to achieve one, you need to have less of the other.

As Dervis (2021) describes it:

> This new framing reflects the tremendous rate of technological change, which the old narrative had largely assumed to be constant or at least exogenous. Green innovation is now not only rapid but also endogenous. The cost of producing renewable energy from solar and wind, and of battery storage to solve the intermittency problem, has already declined substantially… The new, optimistic story … [includes] climate measures that are embedded in a vision of global growth and a profit-enhancing technological wave... Many countries are already deploying these green technologies, but continued innovation (and therefore cost reduction) crucially hinges on more and stronger policy incentives. The recent systemically important commitments by the United States and China to become carbon neutral by 2050 and 2060, respectively, promise and anchor just such incentives. And such pledges are becoming more credible as more countries

complement them with shorter-term commitments contained in 10–15-year action plans.

South Africa is one of the many countries participating in this global process. In terms of South Africa's proposed updated Nationally Determined Contributions (NDC) (South African Government, 2021), prepared for the upcoming 26th Conference of the Parties (COP26) as required by parties to the United Nation's Framework Convention on Climate Change, South Africa is committing to the reduction of its greenhouse gas emissions. The NDC has been updated and calls continue to be made on South Africa to be more ambitious in this regard, both to be more effective in helping to assist in the slowing down of rising global temperatures, and potentially, in the country's own direct interest, to gain access to global grants and concessionary green finance offered as incentives to accelerate decarbonisation interventions and to ensure untrammelled entry of South African goods into export markets in countries that introduce carbon-related barriers.

As outlined in the NDC (South African Government, 2021: 15):

> South Africa has updated its NDC target ranges taking into account our status as a developing county, our national circumstances and common but differentiated responsibility and respective capability, and the long-term temperature goal, as specified in the Paris Agreement's Article 2, in the light of the latest science.

Many countries have pledged that in future they aim to achieve net carbon neutrality, in the sense that they will remove as much carbon dioxide and other gases from the atmosphere as they put into the atmosphere each year. In August 2021, Germany had pledged net carbon neutrality by 2045, the United States by 2050 and China by 2060. Although there are calls for South Africa to transition to a net zero emission economy by 2050, the focus until mid-2020 had been to set targets or give commitments to reduce the amount of carbon dioxide and other gases that it produces. It is likely that pressure will continue to mount on South Africa and other countries to make commitments to net carbon neutrality at some time in the future.

MAPPING SOUTH AFRICA'S ENERGY TRANSITION

To gain deeper insight into the risks and opportunities of the electricity crisis and the energy transition that South Africa is currently facing, it is useful to highlight certain key facts and trends about South Africa's electricity situation.

- South Africa's electricity production fell by around four per cent from 2010 to 2019 from a total production of 249TWh in 2010 to 239TWh in 2019 (Figure 4.2). If the unusual year of 2020 is included, impacted on by the COVID-19 pandemic and related lockdown on a wide range of economic activities, electricity production fell by 8.8 per cent from 2010 to 2020, to a total of 227TWh in 2020.

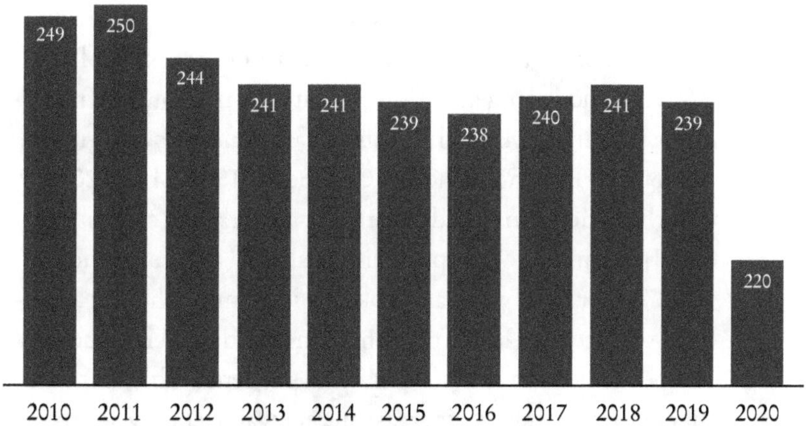

Figure 4.2: South Africa's declining electricity production (TWh per year)

Source: Adapted from Calitz and Wright (2021: 16)

Table 4.1: South Africa's Integrated Resource Plan 2019

	Coal	Coal*	Nuclear	Hydro	Storage
Current Base	37149		1860	2100	2912
2019	2155	-2373			
2020	1433	-557			
2021	1433	-1403			
2022	7111	-844			513
2023	750	-555			
2024			Extension life of Koeberg		
2025					
2026		-1219			
2027	750	-847			
2028		-475			1575
2029		-1694			
2030		-1050		2500	
Total installed capacity by 2030 (MW)	33364		1860	4600	5000
% Total installed capacity	43		2.36	5.84	6.35
% Annual energy contribution	58.8		4.5	8.4	1.2

* *Decommissioning*

Source: IRP (2019: 42)

- The electricity generation mix that powers the South African economy is in transition, with coal to be largely replaced by wind and solar generation capacity. As per South Africa's Department of Mineral Resources and Energy's Integrated Resources Plan published in October 2019 (DMRE, 2019), South Africa's installed electricity generation capacity in 2018 comprised 71.3 per cent coal, 3.5 per cent nuclear and 7.2 per cent wind and solar. It is planned that by 2030 coal will account for 43 per cent of installed capacity, nuclear 2.4 per cent and wind and solar 33.8 per cent (Table 4.1). It is likely that the relative increase in renewable energy sources, like wind and solar, will be even greater than that envisaged in IRP 2019. This is because, inter alia, power stations have

Table 4.1: South Africa's Integrated Resource Plan 2019 (contd)

	PV	Wind	CSP	Diesel & Gas	Other**
Current Base	1474	1980	300	3830	499
2019		244	300		2019 to 2002 allocation needed by shortage of capacity and energy gap
2020	114	300			
2021	300	818			
2022	1400	1600			
2023	1000	1600			500
2024		1600		1000	500
2025		1600			500
2026		1600			500
2027		1600		2000	500
2028	1000	1600			500
2029	1000	1600			500
2030	1000	1600			500
Total installed capacity by 2030 (MW)	8288	17742	600	6380	
% Total installed capacity	10.52	22.53	0.76	8.1	
% Annual energy contribution	6.3	17.8	0.5	1.3	

*** Distributed energy, Cogen, Biomass, Landfill*

Source: IRP (2019: 42)

performed below expectations and assumptions regarding the availability of Eskom plant have proved invalid, as well as the fact that the falling costs of wind and solar technology will lead to an expansion of embedded, or distributed, generation by firms.[1]

- The rise of renewable energy is being driven by the fact that wind and solar technologies offer the lowest cost of new electricity generation capacity. According to Eskom (Eskom, 2021), at 2020 prices the levelised cost of energy for new energy investments was 4.1 US cents/kWh for

[1] The mix in installed capacity is a distinct metric from the contribution of different technologies to overall energy production, which was at the following ratios in 2020: coal 83.5 per cent, nuclear 5.2 per cent and wind and solar 10.5 per cent.

Table 4.2: Comparative costs of building new generation capacity

Technology	Levelised cost of energy	Capital cost	Build time	Eskom position
PV	4,1 US$¢/kWh	825 US$¢/kWh	18 to 24 months	Identified potential sites to retrofit PV to capitalise on existing infrastructure and available resources
Wind	5,4 US$¢/kWh	1450 US$¢/kWh	24 to 36 months	Leverage sites for wind, with environmental authorisations to capitalise on existing infrastructure and available resources
Gas	7,3 US$¢/kWh	1250 US$¢/kWh	24 to 60 months	Intend to use gas as means to enable renewables, thereby supporting the transition
Nuclear	19,8 US$¢/kWh	12500 US$¢/kWh	12 to 15 years	Supports governments plans to roll out nuclear, will be unable to build due to inadequate balance sheet
New Coal	15,9 US$¢/kWh	62250 US$¢/kWh	10 to 12 years	Will own and operate current coal fleet till end of life, will focus on repurposing sites to be decommissioned with renewables. No new coal projects by Eskom

Source: Eskom (2021b: 5)

solar PV; 5.4 US cents/kWh for wind; 7.3 US cents/kWh for gas; 15.9 US cents/kWh for coal and 19.8 US cents/kWh for nuclear. Wind and solar PV technologies also entail shorter building time and less capital expenditure than investments for electricity generation based on gas, nuclear and coal technologies (Table 4.2).

- Even though wind and solar power are inherently variable, depending on wind and sun, these generation technologies work together with a mix of other electricity sources, particularly flexible gas and battery storage, to meet demand requirements (Bischof-Niemz and Creamer 2019).
- The replacement of coal by renewable energy sources also advances South Africa's global commitments to advancing decarbonisation in one of the world's highest carbon-intensive economies.

- South Africa's constrained and unreliable electricity supply has resulted in load shedding which has imposed significant economic costs estimated at between R59 billion and R118 billion in 2019.[2]
- South Africa's electricity supply utility, Eskom, is in a debt trap which means that the government has had to inject fiscal resources to enable the company to meet its cost and interest repayment obligations. In 2021 government plans to transfer R56 billion to Eskom with future transfers expected of between R23 billion and R32 billion per year from 2022 to 2026.

Various interventions need to be undertaken in order to improve energy security, promote economic investment, employment and growth, facilitate a just energy transition and restructure Eskom. It is instructive to assess these interventions with the aim of addressing South Africa's electricity crisis, as well as the country's broader socio-economic crisis.

ALLOWING FOR LARGER EMBEDDED, OR DISTRIBUTED, POWER INVESTMENTS BY FIRMS

Government's amendment of Schedule 2 of the Electricity Regulation Act of 2006 will provide for licensing exemption for electricity generation projects of up to 100MW. The positive aspect of lifting the licensing exemption to 100MW, up from the previous 1MW exemption, is that the impact of the reform will be much larger in terms of likely investment in generation capacity and in terms of wider economic impact.

It is estimated that if the easing of regulations leads to the investment in 5 000MW of additional electricity generation capacity by firms, this will boost South Africa's GDP by 0.5 per cent, will result in

[2] For example, load shedding in 2019 took place for a total of 530 hours and resulted in the shedding of 1352GWh of energy at an estimated cost to the economy of R59–118 billion (Calitz and Wright, 2020).

R75–85 billion in additional investment, and will create 12 000 to 16 000 direct jobs (Operation Vulindlela, 2021).

Allowing mines, farms, factories and commercial operations to instal their own electricity generation capacity will ensure greater energy security for these operations and will likely also lead to lower costs and decarbonisation. An enabling environment that allows firms to wheel electricity over the grid and sell electricity to unrelated parties will also allow for a range of new commercial possibilities. For example, economies of scale may dictate that a firm builds a bigger plant than it needs and then it can sell excess power to other firms. It could also supply three of its own operations from one of its sites where it has space to build its embedded generation plant. In both these cases, companies would require permission to link to the grid and would have to pay wheeling costs to Eskom's transmission entity or the municipality. Of course, there will also be scenarios where firms just use their generation capacity for their own needs as a substitute for or supplement to power supplied by Eskom or the municipality, in order to lower their electricity costs.

The expanded investment in embedded, or distributed, power, which is planned for in the IRP 2019, will have many advantages.

Firstly, research shows that such investments could add about 5 000MW of generation capacity in a five-year period (Steyn and Renaud 2021). Secondly, such investment will be from firms' own balance sheets rather than from the fiscus or from Eskom. Thirdly, paradoxically, even though Eskom will forego revenue as a result of firms producing their own electricity, Eskom supports the reform as it will save money for Eskom if it means reduced resorting to expensive diesel fuel sources to try and keep South Africa's lights on. Fourthly, increased investment in distributed power sources is in line with the broader transition taking place in the sector. This wider transformation will be facilitated by Eskom's restructuring, as Eskom's transmission entity (Gridco) will charge firms for transmitting (or wheeling) power over the network if they wish to send electricity to their own operations on other sites, or if they wish to sell electricity to unrelated parties. Fifthly, the local employment and investment multipliers that will result from enabling firms to invest in their own electricity-generating plant are significant. Sixthly, it is a decentralised solution, which entails cutting through red tape and can happen comparatively quickly in small steps that add up, rather than waiting for longer-running, utility-scale procurement processes.

UPDATING THE INTEGRATED RESOURCES PLAN AND ACCELERATING INVESTMENT IN WIND AND SOLAR CAPACITY

The Integrated Resources Plan (IRP) 2019 is the key electricity policy planning instrument of government. The IRP is managed by the Department of Mineral Resources and Energy (DMRE). It is an instrument which aims to predict South Africa's future electricity demand and map out plans for the country's future investments in electricity.

This has been a highly contested policy area; for example, technology choices which should have favoured a mix of least-cost, carbon-reducing technologies have continued to be roiled by crosswinds of vested interests, state capture and corruption and as geo-political factors. These forces have argued variously in favour of nuclear, coal, gas or renewable technologies.

To be effective, the IRP needs to be utilised as a technical planning instrument – with any policy deviations from least-cost technologies being strictly limited and being explained by explicit reasons. Furthermore, the IRP should be regularly re-calibrated and updated as relative technology costs change and as supply-and-demand trends and assumptions require adjustment. For example, one of the reasons that IRP 2019 needs to be updated is that it assumes that Eskom plants will have an energy availability factor (EAF) rising from around 67 per cent in 2019 to 75.5 per cent by 2030. However, due to the delays and poor performance of Eskom's new Medupi and Kusile plants as well as deterioration of the utility's ageing fleet, performance is below this expected EAF, resulting in an ongoing electricity supply gap. A recalibrated IRP would allow the government to plan to accelerate the procurement of increased electricity capacity, as well as consider relevant reforms such as reducing red tape for non-utility scale, embedded (also known as distributed) electricity investments by private entities. The consequence of allowing a supply gap to continue is a shortage of electricity that results in ongoing load shedding and lost investment, jobs and growth potential.

Another reason that the IRP should be regularly reviewed and recalibrated is so that delays and adjustments to lead times in bringing onstream new capacity can be factored into planning processes. Otherwise, delays will be hard-baked into the planning process, extending the period of the electricity supply gap and imposing significant costs on the wider economy.

REAFFIRMING CORRUPTION-FREE BIDDING PROCESSES RUN BY THE INDEPENDENT POWER PRODUCER OFFICE

Based on the IRP's plans for electricity capacity investments, bid windows are opened inviting entities to bid for the right to build the required capacity. South Africa's Independent Power Producer (IPP) Procurement Programme Offices then selects the most competitive bids to build the required technology.

It would be fatal to the process if corruption were to be allowed to take root in the electricity procurement process. This is why recent allegations, from a losing bidder, of corruption and political interference in the IPP office's selection of powerships (specially modified craft that can burn gas or heavy fuel oil to generate electricity) as part of the government's emergency Risk Mitigation Independent Power Procurement Programme (RMIPPP) are most disturbing and need to be fully investigated.[3] The independence and good governance of the

[3] There has been much criticism of the design of the RMIPPP. Put together in haste in response to South Africa's severe bout of load shedding in December 2019, the RMIPPP specified the need for dispatchable power during peak hours. The specification was more conducive to the use of gas and diesel, or renewable sources linked to large battery storage. This design specification is likely to saddle South Africa with about 2 000MW of high-cost electricity for many years to come, which could have been obviated if the programme had been better designed to meet emergency requirements by allowing for lower-cost, more systemically integrated solutions.

IPP office must be reaffirmed if the IRP procurement processes that are currently underway are not to be fatally undermined at tremendous cost to South Africa.

COMMITTING TO AN ACCELERATED DECARBONISATION TARGET TO ASSIST IN ALLEVIATING ESKOM DEBT AND TO FUND A JUST TRANSITION

Electricity production is no longer a natural monopoly, in which marginal costs fall as a result of the scales of production. Rather, system-wide electricity is more cost-effectively produced by smaller, distributed generation units – typically variable wind and solar, supported by readily dispatchable electricity sources, such as batteries and gas.

If Eskom is to be fit for purpose as part of the country's transition to a system characterised by less centralised, and more distributed, electricity generation will need to be restructured into three entities, namely a generation entity, a transmission entity and a distribution entity. This transition will be driven by a combination of self-reinforcing technological changes, decarbonisation objectives and economic forces.

The Eskom generation entity is likely for some time to be the largest supplier of electricity in South Africa, though it will be joined by a growing number of privately owned electricity generation entities. Electricity from various sources will be supplied into a single national grid run by the Eskom transmission entity, referred to as the Independent Transmission System and Market Operator (ITSMO). The ITSMO will manage the grid and serve as an intermediary contracting with public and private entities generating electricity, as well as with those running consumer-facing distribution systems, a large part of which is likely to be Eskom's distribution entity.

Eskom (transmission) will be required to invest in the maintenance and extension of the national grid network. To connect the best acreage for wind and solar generation to the grid, some R188 billion will need to be invested over the next 10–15 years to build close to 8 000km of new transmission lines by 2030.

Eskom (distribution) will be required to invest in distribution networks, as well as battery and other storage facilities to better manage fluctuations in supply caused by the increasing proportion of variable generation capacity.

Eskom's current debt level of over R400 billion is unsustainable, in that ongoing high interest payment obligations undermine the liquidity and financial viability of the entity. As part of the wider planned restructuring of Eskom, the potential exists for Eskom and South Africa's national government, working in close coordination, to gain access to concessional global green finance and to use such concessional finance to reduce Eskom's borrowing costs.

Using such concessional arrangements, certain Eskom-related refinancing could be undertaken that would allow for future lower, concessional interest payments. These would be on condition that a carbon reduction roadmap, including the closure or repurposing of old coal power stations, is achieved by Eskom and, relatedly, by South Africa more broadly.

Eskom has identified its coal-fired Komati Power Station, which commenced operation in 1961, as a flagship site for demonstrating how the just energy transition could be managed in a way that ameliorates the potentially negative impact on affected workers and communities. It is envisaged that as Komati's last coal-fired unit is shut down in 2022, a repurposing programme will kick in, which will include the following elements: the repowering of the power station; the building of the renewable energy capacity of the power station's land; and the creation of local manufacturing opportunities. All of these interventions would have positive benefits for the Komati community who would otherwise only face the consequences of the plant closure. Another advantage to such repurposing is that existing power plants – like Komati Power Station – are already linked to the national electricity grid, which will save time and costs for the project. An example of the kind of manufacturing activity that could be housed at repurposed Eskom plants could be that related to the building of microgrid components – including solar panels and battery components. These could be deployed so as to provide access to electricity to the 13 per cent of

South African households that are off-grid and have not historically been serviced via the national grid.

Eskom's Just Energy Transition Transaction should be regarded as a first step towards the country mobilising concessional funds on a larger scale. A ramping-up of the process could be operationalised through government-to-government, or sovereign-to-sovereign, international financial support. South Africa could be granted access to concessional finance, for example through significantly reduced interest payments over 25 years as the country achieves its decarbonisation milestones. This would involve agreeing on a $/t price for decarbonisation that would be realised as South Africa accelerates its decarbonisation against the IRP 2019 baseline. In such a scenario, the South African government would not be required to raise debt outside of its normal borrowings programme, but would use the agreed $/t savings to reduce the interest rate on those borrowings to highly concessional levels. Such a transaction would create the fiscal space required to partly recapitalise the unbundled Eskom units and to set up a Just Transition Fund to support workers and communities affected by the early retirement of coal.

The mobilisation of finance at scale would be necessary to financially stabilise a restructured Eskom and to capitalise on the massive investments that would be required if South Africa is to achieve its just energy transition objectives. Resources are also required to assist workers and communities who would be negatively affected by the transition. This would help to unlock the process and increase the likelihood of putting the country onto a higher employment, higher wage trajectory. If the transition is approached without such resources in hand it is likely that it will fail, as it will provoke great resistance and will not be capable of operating at a large enough scale to allow the energy transition to be able to serve as a catalyst for wider economic growth and employment creation.

Significant potential exists in South Africa's body politic to mobilise support for plans to better manage and reduce Eskom's debt. Government, business, labour and community representatives, via a Nedlac process, agreed to the following, as outlined in their Framework Agreement for a Social Compact on Supporting Eskom for Inclusive

Growth, released by December 2020 (Nedlac, 2020):

> [2.8.2] There is a need for a strategy to reduce Eskom's debt level … [2.8.3] social partners are committed jointly to mobilising adequate financial resources for Eskom. The precise financing mechanisms will be evaluated considering all options available.

UPSTREAM AND DOWNSTREAM LINKAGES FOR JOB CREATION

The programme to restore electricity security in South Africa together with the ongoing energy transition has the potential to stimulate large-scale investment in the country's electricity generation, transmission and distribution infrastructure. Such investment will need to be maintained for many years to come. The overall developmental objective of the energy transition should be to restore economic growth and employment creation through the restoration of reliable and widespread access to competitively priced, low carbon electricity. The transition should also take advantage of all potential backward, forward and lateral linkages that such an investment programme would entail.

Eskom estimates that expanded wind and solar capacities during construction, operations and manufacturing activities from 2022 to 2030 have the potential to create about 38 000 direct jobs, 11 600 indirect jobs and 192 000 induced jobs. Added to this is the significant job creation and manufacturing potential that would result from the related construction of 8 000km of electricity transmission lines by 2030 (Eskom, 2021). This needs to be set against the estimated decline of 22 700 coal mining jobs and 6 200 coal-fired power station jobs from 2020 to 2040 as IRP 2019 is implemented (Tyler et al., 2021).

There are significant new upstream and downstream industrialisation opportunities for South Africa. Upstream opportunities would include the need for investment in the manufacture of solar panels, wind towers and turbines, flexible gas plants, transmission infrastructure, large-scale battery installations and other components. Research has indicated that 'the manufacturing, construction, services and sales sectors experience the highest gross employment gains during the construction and operations phases of adding new renewable energy capacities to the power mix' (IASS/CSIR, 2019: 14).

Supportive and well-designed industrial policy will help to maximise localisation, employment, and race and gender transformation objectives. Careful sequencing and realistic programme design are very important so as not to undermine this vision. The debacle whereby the RMIPPP's local content requirements for solar panels had to be subsequently removed due to the absence of local supply capacity serves to undermine this localisation vision. Furthermore, such mismanagement is likely to result in legal challenges from those companies that decided not to bid due to local content criteria which they could not meet. They will argue they were unfairly disadvantaged as local content criteria were subsequently withdrawn but only after bidding had been closed and winning bidders had been announced.

Tragically, a number of local wind turbine tower manufacturing plants and solar panel manufacturing facilities have been shut down in South Africa in recent years due to delays and stops and starts in procurement.[4] To succeed in maximising industrial policy and employment benefits, there needs to be certainty and credibility in the management of the country's energy transition.

Government is in the process of developing an instrument known as the South African Renewable Energy Masterplan (SAREM), to position the country as a 'globally significant' producer of inputs used in renewable-energy plants. The masterplan will cons ider a matrix of value chains with priority to be given to those primary materials, components and subcomponents used in the manufacture and assembly of renewable technologies including solar photovoltaic,

[4] In April 2019, uncertainty in the renewable energy sector in South Africa led to job losses in Nelson Mandela Bay. A wind turbine tower manufacturer, DCD Wind Towers, closed its factory in the Coega Industrial Development Zone (IDZ) after failing to find an equity investment partner. DCD ran into trouble in 2016 when no new orders were placed due to the planned gap in wind farm expansions. The Industrial Development Corporation took an 80 per cent stake in DCD Wind Towers but that did not generate renewed interest. The manufacturing facility was forced to close its doors and retrench its 110 employees (Fekisi, 2019).

wind and battery storage (Creamer, T, 2021a).

Interestingly, the energy transition also presents growth opportunities for the mining sector. The energy transition is projected to be metals intensive. For example, the global growth in solar power is projected to double the demand for metals like aluminium, copper and zinc by 2040. An important linkage for South Africa would be to promote mining exploration in South Africa and Africa more widely to increase market share in the provision of these critical minerals.

Once South Africa has invested in a significant renewable energy base, downstream opportunities would include a wide range of new activities including those linked to the world's mobility transition, such as electric vehicles, green hydrogen and green jet fuel.

A draft Green Paper on electric vehicle production has been developed by the South African government based on the insight that it is important that South Africa does not simply become a market for electric vehicles produced elsewhere in the world, relegating the country's car manufacturing to internal combustion engines (Venter, 2021). It is also regarded as vital that South Africa maintains the local industry's capacity to export to key markets, such as the European Union (EU) and the UK, both of which have set new targets and deadlines to reduce the number of fossil fuel-reliant vehicles on their roads (Venter, 2021).

The domestic market for electric vehicles in South Africa remains nascent with very few units sold each year, but it is projected as a growth area linked to global development in the years ahead. Significant electric vehicle charging infrastructure would need to be developed as a pre-condition for the massification of South Africa's electric car market. The electrification of public transport systems, such as taxis and buses, would require specific plans, interventions and related incentives.

RISKS ASSOCIATED WITH SOUTH AFRICA'S CARBON-INTENSIVE INDUSTRIAL BASE

If decarbonisation of South Africa's electricity base does not happen at an acceptable pace and scale, the risks to investment and trade are significant. For example, Amazon recently invested in South Africa strictly on condition that all its electricity requirements would be served by renewable energy sources. The project will see 28 GWh of solar energy wheeled via Eskom's grid from a solar farm in the Northern Cape to Amazon's facilities each year (Liedtke, 2020).

Research has indicated that South Africa's export of greenhouse gas (GHG) emissions are closely linked to the country's export profile. As such (Montmasson-Clair, 2020; 21):

> China captures the largest share of South Africa's exported GHG emissions, followed by the EU, India, the USA and Japan. At a sectoral level, South Africa's exported GHG emissions are concentrated on the mining value chain exports. Basic metals, mining and quarrying products accounted for more than half of exported GHG emissions (53 per cent) in 2015. Motor vehicles, utility services, chemicals and chemical products, and machinery and equipment followed.

A risk is that if South Africa does not begin substantially to reduce the country's carbon intensity then our trading partners will begin to erect tariff and non-tariff barriers, which will have the effect of curbing exports and reducing South Africa's international competitiveness. The European Union (EU) is taking the lead in this matter as the body has proposed 'a carbon border adjustment mechanism' as a tool to scale up the EU's climate ambitions. Essentially, this would entail the imposition of a carbon tax on South Africa's goods, such as cars and fruit, intended for export into the EU (Oharenko, 2021). It is not clear, however, at this stage, whether such practices will be found to be acceptable under World Trade Organization (WTO) rules, and what positions will be taken on the matter by other powerful geopolitical decision-makers, such as the US, China, Japan and the AU.

On the positive side, there may be emerging opportunities for South Africa to gain export advantage through the creation of new products such as the so-called 'green iron' for export to international steelmakers seeking to transition away from the use of carbon-intensive coking coal in the production of the basic material. Should green iron technologies, such as hydrogen direct-reduced iron (HDRI), be proven to be commercially viable over the coming decade, dedicated renewable energy plants could be developed to produce green hydrogen through a process known as electrolysis, which uses electricity to split water into hydrogen and oxygen. The hydrogen could then be used to convert South African iron ore into HDRI and be used by international steelmakers with net zero emission commitments to produce carbon-free steel.

The production of green iron in South Africa for export to the EU could have substantial financial and economic benefits for both South Africa and Europe, as it will reduce the overall cost of EU decarbonisation, while making its steel industry more competitive. Furthermore, ArcelorMittal South Africa's mothballed Saldanha steel plant, on the West Coast, includes a direct reduced iron plant that could be modified to be supplied with green hydrogen. 'This would provide a new business model for a plant that was unable to compete with cheap Chinese steel supply, and would be synergistic with the Saldanha port, now reconfigured for green hydrogen and power fuels production and export' (Creamer, 2021b).

In another initiative, mining company Anglo American has signed a memorandum of understanding with German steel product manufacturer Salzgitter Flachstahl to collaborate on decarbonising the steelmaking industry. 'The companies will conduct research into feed materials, including iron-ore pellets and lump iron-ores, that are suitable for use in direct reduction steelmaking – based on natural gas and hydrogen – which is a less carbon-intensive production method compared with conventional blast furnaces' (Arnoldi, 2021).

It would be prudent for South Africa to fully appreciate the linkage between the decarbonisation of the country's energy profile and its export competitiveness. As Montmasson-Clair (2020: 27) has suggested:

> This situation calls for decisive action to reduce the carbon intensity of the South African economy as well as diversify the structure of exports to low(er)-carbon products. This is essential to maintain South Africa's competitiveness and market access going forward. Despite some progress (for instance, in grid

decarbonisation and energy efficiency efforts), much more is required to reduce South Africa's vulnerability to climate change regulations and to set the country on a sustainable pathway.

CONCLUSION

In response to global warming, worldwide policy is shifting towards low carbon energy. This, coupled with the need for investment in new electricity infrastructure in South Africa (in the context of low carbon renewable energy sources being the lowest-cost source of new capacity), means that South Africa has the opportunity to embark on a deep-rooted and extensive energy transition. This transition has the potential to change the economy – and to drive growth, employment and inclusion.

Along with this opportunity, there are threats of dislocations and losses for those in coal-producing areas and for those working in the coal sector's value chain. These threats need to be managed and ameliorated for the energy transition to be inclusive and just. Social compacting should be viewed as an important instrument to mitigate the negative impacts of the overall net positive energy transition.

For such social compacting to be effective, each social partner has a particular role to play. Government needs to provide a clear and rational set of policy frameworks to guide the South African economy through a just energy transition. With the exception of the national grid, in most instances, it is not necessary for the state to own all the elements of the electricity system to achieve desirable public policy objectives. Rather, these objectives can best be achieved via appropriate legislative, regulatory, restructuring and coordination mechanisms. Government also needs to be effective in providing wide access to appropriate skills, especially for young people, as well as in sustaining an environment of safety, security, public health and social cohesion.

Worker, community and business representatives engaged in social compacting for a just energy transition need to be forward looking and to embrace technological change in a manner that protects those who are threatened by the change. They can do this mainly through retraining, the facilitation of new investments and by allowing ease of firm entry and increased competition, so that South Africa can move onto a higher productivity, higher wage and higher employment growth path.

REFERENCES

Arnoldi, M. 4 August 2021. 'Anglo partners with German firm to decarbonise steelmaking'. Engineering News, https://www.engineeringnews.co.za/article/anglo-partners-with-german-firm-to-decarbonise-steelmaking-2021-08-04, accessed 5 August 2021.

Bischof-Niemz, T. and Creamer, T. 2019. *South Africa's Energy Transition.* Johannesburg: Routledge.

Calitz, J. and Wright, J. 2021. *Statistics of Utility-scale Power Generation in South Africa in 2020*. Pretoria: CSIR Energy Centre. https://researchspace.csir.co.za/dspace/handle/10204/11865, accessed 15 June 2021.

Calitz, J. and Wright, J. 2020. *Setting Up for the 2020s: Addressing South Africa's electricity crisis and getting ready for the next decade.* Pretoria: CSIR Energy Centre. https://researchspace.csir.co.za/dspace/handle/10204/11282, accessed 12 June 2021.

Creamer, T. 8 June 2021a. 'Masterplan to position South Africa as "globally significant" renewables manufacturer'. *Engineering News*, https://www.engineeringnews.co.za/article/masterplan-to-position-south-africa-as-globally-significant-renewables-manufacturer-2021-06-08, accessed 10 June 2021.

Creamer, T. 5 June 2021b. 'New research shows South Africa well-placed to export "green iron" to EU'. *Engineering News*, https://www.engineeringnews.co.za/article/new-research-shows-south-africa-well-placed-to-export-green-iron-to-eu-2021-06-04, accessed 5 June 2021.

Council for Scientific and Industrial Research (CSIR). 2019. 'CSIR Presentation to the Portfolio Committee on Mineral Resources and Energy'. https://www.csir.co.za/sites/default/files/Documents/CSIR%20Portfolio%20Committee%20on%20Mineral%20resources%20and%20Energy2019.pdf, accessed 3 October 2021.

Department of Mineral Resources and Energy (DMRE). 2019. 'Integrated Resource Plan 2019'. http://www.energy.gov.za/IRP/2019/IRP-2019.pdf, accessed 5 July 2021

Dervis, K. 4 June 2021. 'The New Climate Narrative'. Project Syndicate, https://www.project-syndicate.org/commentary/green-transition-is-growth-opportunity-not-economic-burden-by-kemal-dervis-2021-06, accessed 12 June 2021. The Presidency, 2006. Electricity Regulation Act 4 of 2006. https://www.gov.za/sites/default/files/gcis_document/201409/a4-060.pdf, accessed 24 May 2021.

Eskom. 2021. 'Just Energy Transition (JET) Plans', presented to the Presidential Climate Commission, 30 July 2021, https://www.climatecommission.org.za/programs, accessed 5 October 2021.

Fekisi, L. 2019. 'Uncertainty over renewable energy results in job losses at turbine company'. *SABC News*, https://www.sabcnews.com/sabcnews/uncertainty-over-renewable-energy-results-in-job-losses-at-wind-turbine-company/, accessed 7 June 2021.

Gore, A., 2006. *An Inconvenient Truth: The planetary emergency of global warming and what we can do about it*. Pennsylvania: Rodale. Council for Scientific Research/Institute for Advanced Sustainability Studies (IASS/CSIR). 2019. Future skills and job creation through renewable energy in South Africa. Assessing the co-benefits of decarbonising the power sector. Potsdam/Pretoria: IASS/CSIR.

Intergovernmental Panel on Climate Change (IPCC). 2021. 'Climate Change 2021: The Physical Science Basis'. https://wwedw.ipcc.ch/report/ar6/wg1/, accessed 10 December 2020.

Layard, R., Nickell, S. and Jackman, R. 2005. *Unemployment, Macroeconomic Performance and the Labour Market*. Oxford: Oxford University Press.

Liedtke, S. 10 December 2020. 'Flagship project set to demonstrate flexibility, convenience of procuring independent power'. *Engineering News*, https://www.engineeringnews.co.za/article/flagship-project-set-to-demonstrate-flexibility-convenience-of-procuring-independent-power-2020-12-10, accessed 10 December 2020.

Liedtke, S. 11 August 2021. 'South Africa needs to commit to transitioning to net-zero by 2050 – report'. *Engineering News*, https://www.engineeringnews.co.za/article/south-africa-needs-to-commit-to-transitioning-to-net-zero-by-2050-report-2021-08-11, accessed 12 August 2021

Mining Weekly. 10 August 2021. 'Base metals to profit from solar demand'. *Mining Weekly*, https://www.miningweekly.com/article/base-metals-to-profit-from-solar-demand-2021-08-10, accessed 10 August 2021

Montmasson-Clair, G. 2020. 'The global climate change regime and its impacts on South Africa's trade and competitiveness: A data note on South Africa's exports'. *Trade & Industrial Policy Strategies*, https://www.tips.org.za/images/TIPS_data_note_The_global_climate_change_regime_and_its_impacts_on_SAs_trade_and_compettitiveness_August_2020.pdf, accessed 15 August 2021.

National Economic Development and Labour Council (Nedlac). 2020. 'Framework agreement for a social compact on supporting Eskom for inclusive growth'. https://nedlac.org.za/wp-content/uploads/2021/03/Signed-Framework-Agreement-for-a-social-compact-on-supporting-Eskom.pdf, accessed 20 July 2021.

Oharenko, Y . 17 May 2021. 'An EU carbon border adjustment mechanism: Can it make global trade greener while respecting WTO rules?'.

International Institute for Sustainable Development (IISD), https://sdg.iisd.org/commentary/guest-articles/an-eu-carbon-border-adjustment-mechanism-can-it-make-global-trade-greener-while-respecting-wto-rules/, accessed 28 May 2021.

Operation Vulindlela. 2021. 'Supporting the implementation of priority structural reforms', Presentation to the Presidential Climate Commission (PCC), 30 July 2021.

Schumpeter, J. 1942. *Capitalism, Socialism and Democracy*. London: Routledge.

Solow, R. 1956. 'A contribution to the theory of economic growth'. *Quarterly Journal of Economics*, 70(1), 65–94.

South African Government. 2021. 'South Africa's First Nationally Determined Contribution under the Paris Agreement'. https://www.environment.gov.za/sites/default/files/docs/southafricasINDCupdated2021sept.pdf, accessed 10 July 2021.

Stern, N. 2006. *The Economics of Climate Change: The Stern Review*. London: HM Treasury.

Steyn, G. and Renaud, C. 2021. 'Survey Results: Scoping Interest in South African Distributed Energy Generation Sector'. Briefing Note (No. 2021/01), Meridian Economics, Cape Town.

Swan, T. 1956. 'Economic growth and capital accumulation'. *Economic Record*, 32(2), 334–361.

The Core Team. 2017. *The Economy: Economics for a changing world*. Oxford: Oxford University Press.

Tyler, E., Renaud, C. and Mgoduso, L. 9 March 2021. 'Financial support needs for Mpumalanga's economic transition: Scoping study'. Slide Presentation, Meridian Economics, Cape Town. https://meridianeconomics.co.za/wp-content/uploads/2021/03/Financial-support-needs-for-MP-Just-Transition_final_2.pdf, accessed 21 August 2021.

Venter, I. 28 May 2021, 'Draft Green Paper on electric vehicle production out for public comment'. *Engineering News*, https://www.engineeringnews.co.za/article/dtic-publishes-draft-green-paper-on-electric-vehicle-production-2021-05-28, accessed 10 June 2021.

FIVE

From MEC to net zero

The role of the energy sector in the just transition

Jesse Burton, Lucy Baker, Andrew Marquard and Patrick Lehmann-Grube

INTRODUCTION

South Africa finds itself in a rapidly changing global context from a climate change and energy perspective. Climate change has moved from a distant threat to a daily reality, both globally and locally. At the same time, the world's focus on climate change for the last three decades is, alongside processes of technological innovation and declining costs of renewable energy, leading to widespread changes in energy systems globally. The increasing urgency of the global climate problem is leading to international pressure on all countries to act faster. Measures towards this include long-term net zero greenhouse gas (GHG) emissions commitments by almost all major global economies (covering a large share of both global gross domestic product (GDP) and emissions)[1]; enhanced short-term action; and potentially punitive trade regimes for persistent high emitters which may render South African exports based on coal-fired electricity uncompetitive in the medium to long term. Coupled with this is focused international pressure to exit coal, the most carbon-intensive fossil fuel, including financial exclusions for new coal infrastructure and pressure on corporations to disclose their exposure to investments in fossil fuels. These pressures will be brought to bear on both South Africa's domestic consumption of coal and its coal exports, still a key source of foreign exchange and jobs.

Current policies are nonetheless still insufficient to achieve the temperature goals of the Paris Agreement, namely, to limit warming to well below 2°C and pursue efforts to limit it to 1.5°C (IPCC 2018; UNEP, 2020; IEA, 2020). Key elements of the international regime remain out of sync with the growing impetus described above, notably the necessary financial support (in terms of total quantum and form) from developed to developing countries (OECD, 2021a; Colenbrander et al., 2021). Nonetheless, and despite the failures of high-income countries to meet the financial commitments made under the United Nations Framework Convention on Climate Change (UNFCCC) in Copenhagen in 2009, South Africa's domestic policy landscape is not untouched by the aforementioned global trends.

The declining economics of coal power, air pollution legislation, negative impacts on people's health, and national and international climate policy ambitions all point to a shifting energy future for South Africa. In particular, the financial sector's exclusion of coal has had an impact on new plants, on mining investment and on the debt-raising capacities of the state-owned electricity utility, Eskom. Excellent renewable energy resources and global technology trends have made wind and solar energy technologies the cheapest options for new power generation in South Africa (Bischof-Niemz and Fourie, 2016; Arndt et al., 2019). Yet, the state continues to pursue costly new coal and nuclear plants and is targeting gas extraction and use (DMRE, 2019).

[1] Net zero emissions refers to a balancing of anthropogenic sources of greenhouse gas (or carbon dioxide) emissions and sinks.

These global and domestic trends are already having noticeable effects on new generation capacity. Factors and initiatives affected include the economic viability of new coal plants; higher climate ambition in South Africa's recently updated Nationally Determined Contribution (NDC) for 2030; a 'soft commitment' in the long-term strategy to net zero carbon emissions by 2050, and the proliferation of emerging processes, strategies, frameworks and plans at national, provincial and sectoral level with a stated commitment towards a just transition. This is in addition to a potential Eskom-focused country funding deal discussed in the build-up to the 2021 United Nations Climate Change Conference (COP 26) (De Ruyter, 2021).

The structure of South Africa's economy has been characterised by its minerals energy complex (MEC) – a system of accumulation that has shaped the country's energy-, capital- and carbon-intensive economy. Indeed, due to the historical development of its energy system and economic structure, South Africa is the most coal dependent economy in the G20 (Climate Transparency, 2021a) (Figure 5.1).

In 2020, coal supplied 74 per cent of primary energy in South Africa. It is used as an input into Sasol's coal-to-liquids process to produce around 20–25 per cent of liquid fuels and as feedstock for the petrochemicals sector. It is also used directly in industries such as steel and cement; is one of the country's largest exports; and is also used by households which lack affordable access to modern energy services

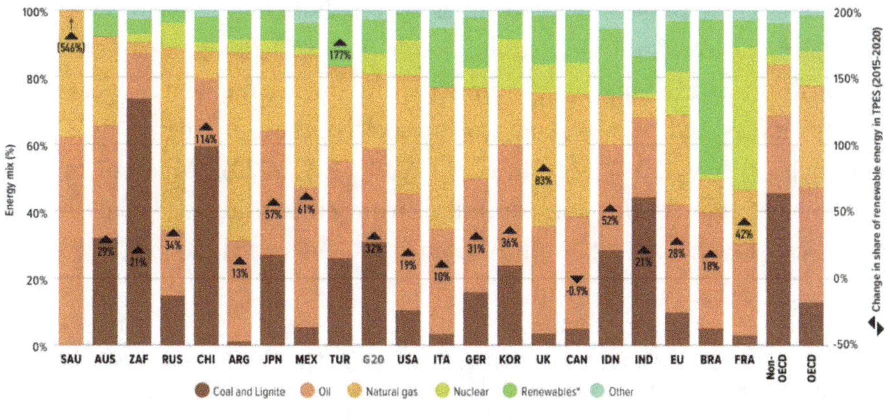

Figure 5.1: Energy mix in G20 countries, 2020

Source: Climate Transparency (2021a: 8)

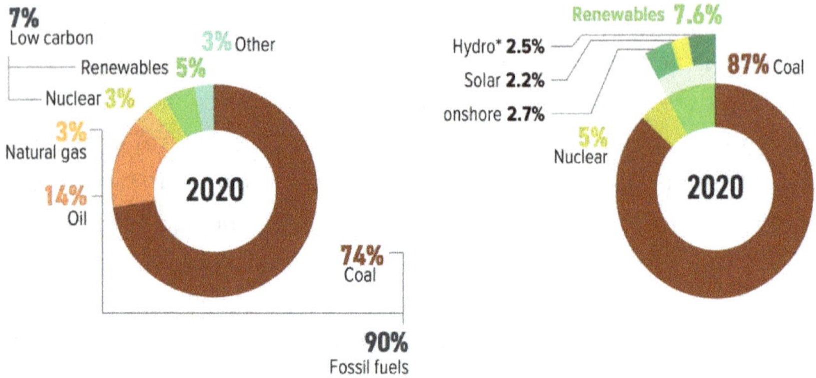

Figure 5.2: Total primary energy supply (left) and share of electricity production (right), 2020[2]

Source: Climate Transparency (2021b)

(Burton et al., 2018a). In 2020 in the power sector, coal accounted for 83 per cent of electricity production; nuclear for 5 per cent; diesel for 0.9 per cent, and wind and solar are negligible at 5 per cent, despite the intentions of scale shown in Figure 5.2 (Burton et al., 2018a; Calitz and Wright, 2021; Climate Transparency 2021b).

The transition to a net zero emissions economy and society will require a considerably faster renewable energy roll-out; multiple changes in technology and in practices in demand sectors; a limited role for gas; and the phase-out of coal. All of these will require a fundamental restructuring of the South African energy system and economy, which goes beyond 'least cost' infrastructure futures. An accelerated transition will require South Africa to almost completely transform its existing energy infrastructure during the next 30 years, from mines and power plants to internal combustion engine (ICE) vehicles (IPCC, 2018; McCall et al., 2019; IEA, 2020).[3] Much of the design of this existing infrastructure, from coal-to-liquids plants to the very low density of South African cities and spatial inequalities, is

[2] Hydro includes pumped storage.

[3] There are currently several net zero emissions studies being undertaken for South Africa by different research and business groups, for which economy-wide published results are not yet available. However, preliminary results show that transformation of supply and demand sectors will be necessary, consistent with international analyses that show deep structural transformation across all sectors.

linked to the history of apartheid, and within that, the MEC.

The country now finds itself roughly mid-way between the end of apartheid and the target for ending fossil fuel use and achieving zero emissions. This, in a context in which energy and climate policy have largely co-existed uneasily and in tension, with climate policy having had limited effects on the 'powerful and resistant' electricity sector thus far (Tyler and Hochstetler, 2021), and an overall energy policy that is fragmented and lurches from crisis to crisis.[4] In this context, attempts at mitigation have often had a small (emissions wise) but significant (institutional) impact. Emissions reduction targets have, until now, been lax enough to have limited impact on generation choices in the national electricity plan, the Integrated Resource Plan (IRP) for Electricity, or in other sectors, where mitigation ambition has been far down a list of more pressing infrastructural or institutional priorities.

South Africa must now pursue a fundamental restructuring of its power, liquid fuels and industrial sectors, while addressing the persistent development challenges created by apartheid-era energy and industrial policies. With this in mind, this chapter outlines the structural trends and key political dynamics in some of the country's key energy sub-sectors over the past 15 years. The chapter covers the changing structure of the country's coal industry and the implications of its rapid phase-out; the renewable energy procurement programme and the challenges it has faced; and the on-going political pursuit of new nuclear energy and the growing dash for gas. We also describe the climate policy trajectory over the past decade. In conclusion, we argue that new climate targets for 2030 herald a potential new policy trajectory for the country, enabled by technology and market shifts and global and national climate politics, which are combining with structural changes in the MEC to ease tensions between energy and climate policy. However, achieving net zero emissions implies an even greater transformation beyond the supply sectors covered here.

---

[4] For example, despite the Energy Act of 2003, there is still no Integrated Energy Plan or process that can assess holistically the future of the energy sector and interactions between sub-sectors; electricity supply is insecure; there is no liquid fuels planning to address refinery futures and clean fuels investment; and household energy poverty remains an issue with affordability of key concern.

There is a long tradition of linking climate ambition to social consequences in South Africa (DEA, 2011; NPC, 2013; Burton et al., 2019), where just transition has been a key element in climate policy since 2011 and is high on the political agenda in current climate policy processes. This chapter will not repeat this history nor the considerable analysis on jobs, socio-economic consequences and stakeholder positions, but rather examine dynamics in the energy sector and implications for transition in key sub-sectors.

THE HISTORY OF ENERGY AND INDUSTRIAL POLICY IN SOUTH AFRICA: THE MINERALS ENERGY COMPLEX

The MEC refers to South Africa's evolving system of accumulation over much of the last century, characterised by the relationship between the country's mining, minerals beneficiation and electricity sectors (Fine and Rustomjee, 1996). A supply of cheap black labour, secured through racist labour policies, has been central to the MEC (Heintz, 2010: 270), alongside the establishment of state-owned enterprises such as Eskom, Iscor and Sasol, which played a key role in the country's industrial development. As the state-owned electricity utility, Eskom has been a crucial actor, providing historically cheap electricity via historically cheap coal to the same mining and minerals industry that supplied it from the country's substantial coal reserves (Christie, 1984). At the core of the MEC lay the primary economic relations defined by the use of coal for electricity generation and liquid fuels, with that very same coal provided by many of the largest consumers of electricity, who required it for their energy-intensive mining and mineral beneficiation operations. The structure and interlinkages were essentially a sophisticated hedging strategy by business around pricing that hinged on Eskom, while the coal contracts parcelled out by the state supported the development of new mining capital.

The MEC was enabled by an apartheid state that prioritised mining and mineral beneficiation, intertwined with strong financial institutions (Mohamed, 2016). The construction of new coal-fired power plants by Eskom in the 1970s and 1980s resulted in a huge increase in generation capacity. In parallel, Sasol also expanded its operations in the early 1980s, creating the conditions for the country's current heavy reliance on coal. By the 1980s, the MEC had developed into more complex relationships between mining, Eskom, beneficiation of minerals, crude oil and coal-based petrochemicals industries and financial institutions (Marquard, 2006: 67).

In the 1990s and early 2000s, the socio-economic structure of the MEC remained largely in place despite the transition to democracy (Marquard, 2006). The transition brought an end to explicitly racialised labour policies, and included new Black Economic Empowerment (BEE) legislation aimed at changing ownership patterns within the economy. While national policy was also influenced by broader international developments of the time, Eskom largely avoided the trend of electricity sector liberalisation, despite attempts by some national political factions to do so in the early 2000s (Baker et al., 2015). The major mining firms (dominated by Anglo American Corporation and Gencor) internationalised: Gencor becoming BHP Billiton and later South32, with Anglo listing in London. Due to these changes the structure of South Africa's economy has become marked by increasing financialisation, deindustrialisation and the decreasing relevance of the mining industry (Mohamed, 2016; Mbazima, 2020).

Core features of the MEC remained largely intact for the first 15 years of South Africa's democracy, supported by state subsidies, access to cheap energy, infrastructural path dependencies and a generally favourable policy environment (Baker, 2015; Burton et al., 2018b). The result was that, in 2011, coal still accounted for 93 per cent of electricity generation and 30 per cent of liquid fuels. During that time, 80 per cent of coal was mined by five coal companies, who were either part of the original MEC mining conglomerates or spin-offs from them: Anglo American, Exxaro, Sasol, BHP Billiton and Xstrata (Eberhard, 2011), though over the last decade these ownership patterns have changed dramatically. These conglomerates also continue to form part of the Energy Intensive Users Group (EIUG), a group of companies that to today consume over 40 per cent of South Africa's electricity (EIUG, 2021) and strongly advocated for expanded coal and nuclear in the earlier IRP processes. Since 2010, however, the relatively stable core of the MEC, which survived the transition to democracy largely intact, has begun to unwind.

FRAGMENTATION AND FRACTURE: THE NASCENT DISINTEGRATION OF THE MEC

The fragmentation of the MEC has been driven by and is a result of several intersecting dynamics. In the electricity sector, these have included a financial, management and supply-side crisis within Eskom; the introduction of legislation for the procurement of electricity from independent power producers (IPPs) and declining costs in renewable energy technologies (Baker and Burton, 2018). Also included is the fracturing of Eskom's coal supply, and more recently, the divestment or demerger of major mining companies from the country as thermal coal becomes increasingly untouchable for investors, leading to a fundamental change in the coal mining industry. This has not (yet) however had a serious effect on emissions reductions or existing coal dependence but could impact on the pace and costs of rapid decarbonisation; in turn, the closure of coal mines and coal-fired power plants will have differing degrees of impact depending on choices made now about re-investment in mining, new fossil fuel plants and just transition planning (or lack thereof).

THE END OF NEW COAL-FIRED POWER

Proposed coal plants have faced economic, financial, legal and regulatory hurdles. There are multiple (at least ten) independent studies showing that new coal-fired power is not competitive in South Africa, and is not built in future power system studies unless forced into the modelling (Merven et al., 2021a). Economic cost has played an important role here: new coal plants will, if built, require significant funding from consumers. Two proposed coal plants, Thabametsi and Khanyisa, were projected to add costs of R19.8–28 billion if built (Ireland and Burton, 2018). Similarly, the 1.5GW of new coal proposed in the IRP would, if built, cost R23–28 billion more than alternatives. In light of new climate targets, this is even higher – if the capacity is built and new mitigation targets are met in 2030, the additional costs would total R74–109 billion versus alternatives (Merven et al., 2021a).

Financing for new coal-fired power has become increasingly difficult internationally, with 148 banks and insurers and 32 asset managers having coal exclusions in place (IEEFA, 2021), including major multilateral development banks. Public finance restrictions have been in place for export credit agencies since 2016 through the Organisation for Economic Co-operation and Development (OECD) Coal Sector Understanding (CSU), which limited the type of plants and size of units that can receive export credit support. The OECD CSU was updated in October 2021 to ban support for new and existing unabated coal plants (OECD, 2021b). The ban will apply to new coal-fired power without operational carbon capture, utilisation and storage (CCUS) and to existing coal-fired power plants, unless the purpose of the equipment supplied is pollution or carbon dioxide (CO_2) abatement and such equipment does not extend the useful lifetime or capacity of the plant, or is used for retrofitting for CCUS.

Local commercial banks have gradually withdrawn their support for new coal plants since 2018, some in line with OECD CSU rules. Updates on financing policies have tightened the internal lending guidelines for all banks, with FirstRand and Nedbank entirely excluding new coal plants, and have introduced new coal mining exclusions (Table 5.1). Alongside international withdrawal by, for example, equity investors in Thabametsi, the financing of new coal seems very unlikely in South Africa going forward. However, neither the Development Bank of South Africa nor the Industrial Development Corporation explicitly exclude investment in new coal infrastructure.

As well as the declining economics of new coal-fired power, new coal plants have also faced sustained opposition from civil society, including through licensing processes and regulatory and legal instruments. Civil society groups have tracked and opposed air pollution, water use and generation licenses for various proposed plants, and have pursued court proceedings against the Thabametsi plant on the grounds of climate change (this action was successful in requiring that new plants be assessed for climate impacts).

The pipeline of proposed projects has consequently shrunk

considerably – from 6GW planned in the IRP 2010 and seven plants totalling around 5GW pursuing licenses in 2015, to only 1.5GW of new capacity included in IRP 2019 and almost no plants pursuing licenses, barring the 1.2–3.5GW[5] Chinese-backed plant in the Musina-Makhado Special Economic Zone in Limpopo.

Table 5.1: Fossil fuel exclusions by major commercial banks in South Africa.

Bank	Coal power	Coal mining	Oil and gas
ABSA	2020: No financing, if alternatives available. Enhanced due diligence; including OECD guidelines	2020: Enhanced due diligence for new projects; expansion projects for existing facilities subject to the Equator Principles	2021: Key policy document expected end of 2021
FirstRand	2021: No funding for new-build coal plants	2026: No new direct project finance to new thermal coal mines	2021: Enhanced due diligence
Investec	2020: New build with advanced technology, higher quality thermal and strong socio-economic motivation; Existing funding subject to extra criteria	2020: Only finance new coal mining transactions or expansion with comprehensive socio-economic motivation, processed through special senior risk forums and approved by senior executive	2020: Funding available for baseload power with lower emissions than coal 2021: No new utility scale/embedded oil-fired generation* 2030: Limited financing for new gas-fired generation* 2035: No new financing for oil production
Nedbank	2021: No funding of new coal plants	2021: No funding of thermal coal mines outside of South Africa 2025: No project finance to new thermal coal mines	2021: No direct financing of oil or gas exploration projects
Standard Bank	2019: Enhanced due diligence; including OECD guidelines	2020: Thermal coal mining transactions designated as high risk require enhanced due diligence	2020: Transactions designated as high risk require enhanced due diligence.

** Exceptions possible if gas or oil is used as a backup supply for renewable energy*

Source: Authors' analysis

[5] Project documents for the plant differ regarding its size.

FROM STABILITY TO CRISIS: ESKOM COAL SUPPLY AND MINING

As the new coal pipeline has shrunk, and Eskom coal plants approach the ends of their lives, questions of how to ensure that closures are fair and just have risen to the fore. Since there are more jobs in coal mining (approximately 90 000) than in Eskom generation plants (approximately 12 000), and coal mining is a heavy contributor to local economies in Mpumalanga (Makgetla and Patel, 2021), the structure and dynamics of the coal mining sector are becoming increasingly important for the planning and implementation of a just transition. There is a high risk of stranded assets, of political lock-in and uncoordinated closures leading to higher economic and social costs of a phase-out. Furthermore, much of the current public discussions on the just transition are focused on Eskom's coal-fired power plants and the potential for them to be repowered or repurposed as part of a global financing deal. However, risks in the mining sector are potentially much greater because poorly managed mine closures will have far greater impacts on livelihoods through, for instance, mismanaged social closure and risks related to land degradation and air and water pollution; potential just transition projects with high social ambitions may be in other sectors (Lowitt, 2021). Major shifts in ownership, supply-side dynamics and expectations about the sector into the future are thus of importance in planning a rapid phase-out of coal in line with the Paris Agreement goals.

South Africa's coal-mining sector was historically dominated by a small number of large companies that emerged out of an apartheid-era process of building South African mining capital, and diversified into or out of other types of mining and subsequently, in the 1990s, out of South Africa. BEE deals and overseas listings meant that by mid-2000s, the coal mining sector was dominated by Anglo American, Exxaro (built from Anglo and Iscor assets), Sasol, BHP Billiton (whose roots came from Afrikaner capital, namely Gencor) and Xstrata (Eberhard, 2011). The ownership and profiles of mining have changed significantly in the past decade, partly due to ownership changes amongst the major mining houses in response to post-apartheid economic transformation imperatives.

Historically, Eskom's plants were designed for and co-located next to major mines to minimise transport costs, with most coal moved via conveyor. The coal was sold on two types of long-term contracts to match the lives of power stations, initially designed to be 30 years: cost-plus and fixed price contracts (Burton and Winkler, 2014; Burton et al., 2018). In the former, the tied mines were co-financed by Eskom who paid all operational costs. Eskom secured access to the coal resource but bore expenditure risks (with some planning oversight) and closure liabilities. In fixed-price contracts, companies would export higher-grade coal and supply intermediate grade product to Eskom at marginal cost. This resulted in very low prices. Company returns were supported from higher value exports, and low grade coal that could not be sold for export was used by Eskom (Burton and Winkler, 2014).

However, Eskom has increasingly purchased coal on short- and medium-term contracts, rising from around 2 million tonnes per annum (Mtpa) in 2000 to 56 Mtpa in 2020 (Eskom, 2020). Eskom now buys 47 per cent of its coal on a short/medium fixed price contract. The increase in short-term contracting was driven by the need for Eskom to supplement its long-term coal supply agreements to ensure security of supply and to meet economic transformation objectives by opening up the industry to new players (Figure 5.3).

Between 1999 and 2017, coal costs rose 300 per cent in real terms. Eskom coal costs in 2021 translate into 42c/kWh on (Eskom, 2021). The general average upward price trend masks high divergence in contract types. For example, in 2020, cost plus contracts accounted for 29 per cent of value and 28 per cent of volume (R19.3 billion and 33Mt), averaging R578/tonne. Fixed-price contracts account for 17 per cent value and 25 per cent volume (R11.3 billion and 30Mt), averaging R380/tonne. But short/medium-term contracts account for 54 per cent of value and only 47 per cent of volumes (R35.9 billion and 56Mt), averaging R641/tonne (Eskom, 2020).

Over the past decade, cost-plus contract prices have risen significantly as Eskom did not re-invest in mines, leading to declining volumes (and hence higher unit prices). One of the main reasons that Eskom has not made the necessary investments is because it is

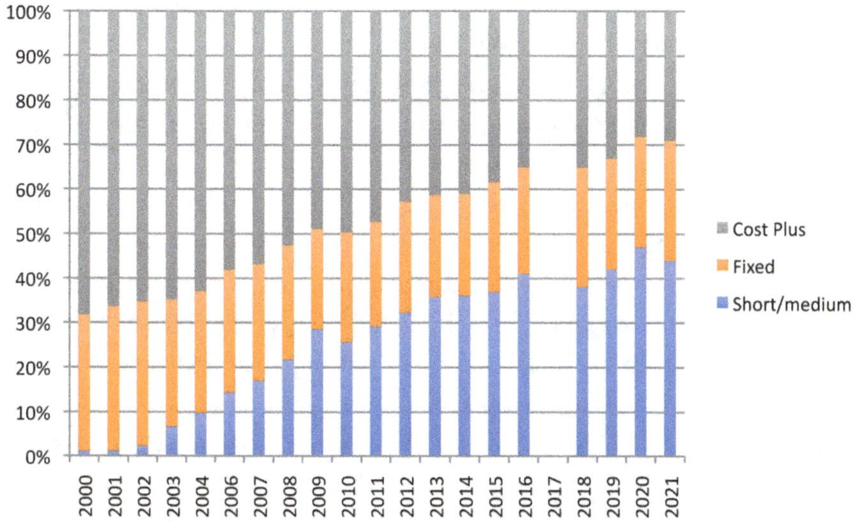

Figure 5.3: Eskom's share of coal contract volumes by contract type, 2000–2021 (2017 data not available)

Source: Burton et al. (2018); Eskom (2018, 2019, 2020, 2021)

highly capital constrained (Eskom, 2015: 49). However the failure to recapitalise old mines or timeously negotiate new cost-plus contracts, e.g. at the Kusile coal-fired power plant, was also a result of economic policy direction and state directives (including an instruction from government that Eskom could not invest in cost-plus coal mines) (Dentons, 2015; Steyn et al., 2017). Eskom's diversification of its coal supply aimed to enhance BEE in the coal sector through what was termed their 'Emerging Miner Strategy', which included a requirement that suppliers must be 50 per cent plus 1 black-owned – higher than the relevant legislation and a crucial sticking point in the development of new resources such as the Kusile co-located mine (New Largo) by major mining houses such as Anglo (Steyn et al., 2017). One effect of the lack of investment was to raise the cost of coal from cost-plus mines, making alternative supply options appear more attractive (Steyn et al., 2017).

In 2015 – the last time that a comprehensive list of Eskom suppliers was made public – the contract data suggested that as much as 50 per cent of the delivered cost of short-term contracts had been transport related (Burton et al., 2018a). A large driver has been the growth in coal trucking, which grew from 14 per cent of coal volumes in 2007 to 30 per cent by 2015, to serve the growth in short term contracts from mines that are not co-located (Burton and Winkler, 2014; Steyn et al., 2017).

The developments described above have resulted in a switch to small mining companies (from established mining houses) and, notably, towards coal transport companies, who have in turn acted to defend their interest in coal trucking and oppose the roll out of new renewables which they claimed were putting their industry at risk (Burton et al., 2018a). Coal transporters are now a large part of the just transition question. Hermanus and Montmasson-Clair (2021) note that there are around 15 000 transport-related jobs, spilt between Transnet Freight Rail (an estimated 12 000 people directly depending on the domestic and export coal lines), the Richards Bay Coal Terminal (532 people in 2014) and coal trucking (about 200 trucking small businesses employing 2 000 to 4 000 people in 2018). Makgetla and Patel (2021) note the important role of coal for income for freight transport, accounting for 20 per cent of Transnet revenue in 2019 and 6 per cent of the total payload (by weight) for road freight in the late 2010s.

Eskom's new, board-approved coal procurement strategy favours a return to long-term, conveyor-delivered contracts and investment in cost-plus mines (at Kendal, Kriel, Majuba, Matla and Tutuka stations) (Eskom, 2019, 2020). However, a 50-year lifetime for coal plants, as laid out in the IRP 2019, is between 5–20 years longer than Paris-compatible scenarios would suggest for the coal fleet (Burton et al., 2018a; McCall et al., 2019; Roff et al., 2020), especially since the potential for rapid mitigation action is overwhelmingly concentrated in the power sector and in the phase-out of coal-fired power plants.

Coal contracting/re-investment needs to consider the long-term electricity planning choices that will be made in a future carbon-constrained world and in light of new climate targets, to avoid Eskom committing to further coal contracts. Capital expansion plans that aim to meet the IRP's coal demand will overestimate the production requirements that will materialise. The nature of Eskom's coal contracts externalises much of this production risk onto the utility, since Eskom is either liable for all mining costs in cost-plus mines or has defined contractual volumes in fixed-term, take-or-pay coal contracts.

From a heavily concentrated sector, Eskom's top ten suppliers have changed dramatically over the last ten years. Xstrata merged with Glencore in 2012 and Glencore remains a major player, along with Exxaro and Sasol. Anglo American no longer mines coal in South Africa, having sold its Eskom-related assets to Seriti in 2018 and demerged its remaining mines into JSE-listed Thungela Resources in 2021. BHP Billiton spun out its South African operations into South32 in 2015, and in turn South32 sold its thermal coal assets to Seriti in June 2021 (now called Seriti Power). Eskom now buys most of its coal from major BEE miners and a plethora of smaller junior mines, illustrating the successful economic transformation of ownership that the sector has achieved.

Major suppliers are supplemented from smaller, mostly private players with small- or medium-sized collieries supplying a few million tonnes per year from relatively shorter-lived assets. The short life of mines means r educed risk of early mine closures as plants close, but does make coordination of worker transition and rehabilitation and social closure more complicated to coordinate and manage. It also points to the need for alternative sectors in the region to absorb workers who would have found work in new mines. The many junior mining companies also have fewer resources to manage social and environmental closure processes.

Furthermore, the future of the industry is not as rosy as such economic transformation trends would suggest. Some of these sales have required cash injections from the sellers to make them viable, including both South32 and Anglo (Mackay, 2021). And major miners are planning for a gradual phase down of the sector. Exxaro has publicly stated that the company will not invest in further greenfield expansion after their under-construction Belfast mine is completed and are pursuing a strategy to diversify their role in the energy sector, including in renewable energy. Glencore have indicated that they will target the managed decline of their South African assets (Glencore, 2020; Cohen, 2019), with only small resources remaining undeveloped. Sasol, which supplies its own coal, completed a capital expansion plan over the last 10 years for long-term production, and is unlikely to require further production increases to meet demand for its liquid fuels/chemicals processes. Sasol has also announced a reduction from 40Mtpa to 31Mtpa in coal use to 2030, no new coal mine investments, and a 2050 net zero target (Sasol, 2021). Several other coal companies are exploring just transition projects as part of their mine closure and rehabilitation obligations.

The questions for coal mining include: how quickly will it be phased out?; how will the socio-economic impacts of that process be managed effectively to ensure a just transition for workers and communities?; how will reduced lifetimes impact on company revenues and the ability to close mines responsibly?; how can unnecessarily costly lock-ins through coal contracting be avoided?; and how to assess the implications of net zero for emerging mining companies – many of whom are believed to have connections to the African National Congress (ANC)? (Hanto et al., forthcoming). A final and key element is that – while the share of export revenues has fallen in recent years – exports still account for almost half of coal sector revenues. High prices in the short term may mask the structural transformation of demand globally, which is projected to stagnate or decline (IEA, 2020). Currently, potential export risks for capital, labour or communities in coal mining are masked by domestic policy choices, but a rapid collapse in global markets could result in significant and fast collapse in export markets that is not being planned for.

EMERGENCE OF THE RENEWABLE ENERGY INDEPENDENT POWER PRODUCERS PROCUREMENT PROGRAMME

The 2007/08 supply-side crisis in South Africa's electricity sector marked a major turning point for the MEC. The causes of this crisis are complex but include a successful post-apartheid domestic electrification programme and a commodities boom which increased electricity demand. Other contributing factors were failed attempts to liberalise the power sector, which resulted in delays to the construction of new generation capacity (Baker et al., 2020). Consequently demand began to outpace supply, and Eskom implemented what has since become a multi-year loadshedding strategy to maintain system integrity. This culminated in power cuts for around 10 per cent of 2020 despite reduced demand from the COVID-19 lockdowns and economic collapse (Calitz and Wright, 2021). Walsh et al. (2020) estimate that loadshedding cost the South African economy nearly R35 billion in the years between 2007 and 2019 – the authors note that this translates into around a 5 per cent contraction in real quarter on quarter GDP growth (albeit over 12 years), roughly equivalent to the impact the 2008/09 financial crisis had on GDP growth. Their estimate excludes 2020's loadshedding, higher by far than any preceding years.

In addition to the coal dynamics discussed above, Eskom's operational crisis has been accompanied by a financial crisis due to cost and time overruns at the Medupi and Kusile coal-fired power plants, corruption and unpaid debts from municipal distributors who purchase electricity from Eskom. In parallel, high tariff increases have still been insufficient to recover all costs, whether legitimately incurred or not. The result is that as of September 2021, Eskom has around R150–200 billion of 'unserviceable debt' on its books (De Ruyter, 2021).

Partly in response to the electricity supply-side crisis, the National Energy Regulator of South Africa (NERSA) began developing the Renewable Energy Feed-In-Tariff (REFIT) in 2008. However, REFIT was soon abandoned and replaced with the Renewable Energy Independent Power Producers Procurement Programme (REIPPPP) (Montmasson-Clair and Ryan, 2014; Baker and Burton, 2018). The REIPPPP follows a competitive, market-based framework under which IPPs submit a bid with a price per unit below a set cap at which they will sell electricity to the grid over the project lifetime, subject to inflation-linked increases. The project that meets the qualifying criteria at the lowest price wins the bid, with some criteria related to socio-economic and local economic development indicators (Baker et al., 2021).

The emergence of REIPPPP was not informed solely by the electricity crisis but was also an attempt to circumvent Eskom and its coal orientation. Liberalisation of the electricity sector had briefly been considered in the late 1990s and early 2000s. However, after much contestation and pushback from Eskom and trade unions, plans for the unbundling, restructuring and privatisation of Eskom were brought to a halt in 2004 (Baker and Burton, 2018). The global recognition of climate change mitigation was also a significant driver.

The REIPPPP was officially launched in August 2011 (Eberhard and Naude, 2017) and is based on a competitive tendering process, organised around bidding windows, of which there have been five and a half for the large utility-scale renewable energy Independent Power Producers (IPPs), and two for the small project renewable IPPs. As of September 2020, four and half bidding processes have been completed with a total of 92 individual projects, contracted to supply Eskom with 6.4GW of electricity (DMRE, 2020) (of which approximately 5GW are connected). The fifth bidding window closed in August 2021.

In the decade since the introduction of REIPPPP, the cost of renewable energy generation has declined considerably, driven by global trends in improved technology, increasing investment and growing economies of scale (IEA, 2020). In South Africa as well as other countries, electricity generation from renewable energy projects is often cheaper than electricity generated from recently constructed coal-fired power plants (Bischof-Niemz and Fourie, 2016). In South Africa this has meant that renewable electricity is the least-cost option for the power system going forward, supplemented by flexible capacity such as pumped storage, batteries and gas (Merven et al., 2021a). South Africa's excellent renewable resources and these global cost trends mean that all independent analysis of the country's future power system, by the Council for Scientific and Industrial Research, National Business Initiative and the University of Cape Town, shows the viability of a renewables-dominated system, supplemented by flexible, dispatchable capacity (Merven et al., 2021a).

In the power sector, electricity planning processes under the IRP and the REIPPPP have become a site of political conflict over technology options and the associated institutional structure of their roll out. This is in addition to a conflict between those who benefit from different technologies, ownership models and state participation (Baker et al., 2021). On top of this, issues around grid access and employment outcomes (number, quality and location of jobs) persist.

Renewable energy from IPPs have been a small but significant change to Eskom's monopoly control, as well as a technological and institutional break with the centralised, state-owned and coal-based electricity sector of the past. However, instead of supporting renewable energy technologies, former president Jacob Zuma and members of his cabinet instead pushed for more nuclear energy in South Africa's electricity system (Baker et al., 2020). In more recent months, Eskom has proposed using retiring coal sites for new renewable energy, as part of a concessional climate deal. Whether or not this includes private sector partners, it is an opportunity for enhanced state participation in renewable generation.

2030 CLIMATE TARGETS REDEFINE SOUTH AFRICA'S POLICY TRAJECTORY

Climate change mitigation policy over the past decade has undergone a dramatic shift. Before 2010, the key challenge of mitigation was developing policies capable of addressing the cost gap between a high emissions 'business as usual' future (epitomised in South Africa by cheap coal), and a more expensive low emissions future. By 2020, however, even in South Africa with its vast and cheap coal reserves, the economics of mitigation have changed profoundly, and a low-carbon future is now cheaper than a high-carbon one. The key policy challenge now is about the speed of the transition.

South Africa's climate policy was established formally with the 2011 National Climate Change Response White Paper (DEA, 2011), finalised in the same year that the country hosted the United Nations Framework Convention on Climate Change (UNFCCC) Conference of the Parties (COP 17) in Durban. The policy framework was built on a decade or so of policy development nationally, as well as on the country's long-standing participation in the UNFCCC. The policy framework for climate change mitigation gave policy recognition to the balance, which needed to be struck between national development priorities and South Africa's obligation to contribute to global efforts to address climate change. The policy was built around a long-term 'national emissions benchmark trajectory range' for national GHG emissions from 2011 to 2050, which set targets that peaked in 2025, remained stable on a 'plateau' up to 2035 and declined to 2050. The range was, in turn, built on a combination of South Africa's GHG emissions target communicated at COP 15 in Copenhagen (and formalised a year later in the aftermath of COP 16), and the Long-Term Mitigation Scenarios (LTMS) process of 2006–08. The breadth of the range (between 2025 and 2035, from 398–614Mt CO_2-eq) represented an accommodation by government of stakeholders with diametrically opposed views on mitigation.

The White Paper in 2011 was accompanied by the country's first IRP later that year (DoE, 2011). Both documents were concluded under the political pressure of South Africa hosting COP 17 in Durban at the end of 2011. The IRP was the first South African electricity plan that contained a GHG emissions constraint. It resulted in a large-scale renewable energy plan, and the most concrete mitigation policy implemented in South Africa to date. The White Paper was followed in 2012 by the National Development Plan (NPC, 2013), which contained a chapter on low carbon development, and provided an enduring narrative for decarbonisation. Aside from the IRP and the REIPPPP discussed above, three key pillars of climate mitigation policy in South Africa – the carbon tax, the carbon budget system and sectoral emissions targets – took around a decade to operationalise, as did the GHG emissions reporting system.

Obligatory reporting of GHG emissions by large emitters was only successfully implemented recently; the Carbon Tax Act was only finalised in 2019, after a decade of consultation; the Climate Change Bill, which provides the legal basis for allocation of carbon budgets to large emitters, and the development of sectoral emissions targets, still awaits parliamentary approval. The long delays in implementation are arguably a result of both institutional limitations, including an asymmetry of information, and effective resistance by large emitters, including many of the coal mining companies and energy-intensive users discussed above. The mitigation component of South Africa's first NDC (communicated as its 'Intended Nationally Determined Contribution' or INDC in 2015, and becoming South Africa's first NDC in 2016 on ratification) was merely a restatement of the 2011 mitigation policy framework (the 2025 and 2030 target ranges were extracted from the GHG emissions benchmark range in the White Paper). South Africa's commitment to these targets also strengthened the case for implementation.

The NDC targets were updated in 2020/21 in the context of several years of low economic growth and severe COVID-19 GDP impacts, the Eskom crisis, the cost of alternative options, and the international dynamics described above. The result was a revised target range for 2025 of 398–510Mt and for 2030 of 350–420 $MtCO_2$-eq (Marquard et al., 2021).

This new range incorporates emissions outcomes consistent with existing policy (e.g., the IRP 2019). However, meeting the lower end of the range also implies the need for significantly enhanced implementation of mitigation policy (e.g., energy efficiency, the green transport strategy) and a significantly faster roll out of wind and solar than currently envisaged in the IRP – around 15GW above IRP this decade at least, and possibly more if demand is higher than expected. It also implies using coal plants at lower levels and faster retirement of coal plants, which impacts on the need for new coal supply (Merven et al., 2021a).

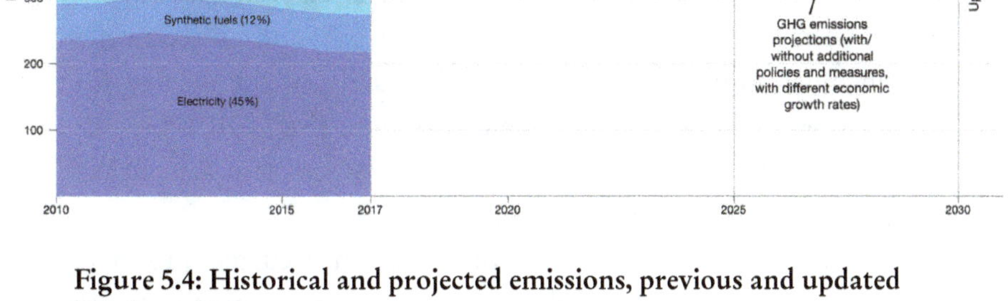

Figure 5.4: Historical and projected emissions, previous and updated NDC targets

Source: Author's own

UNRESOLVED DYNAMICS: THE RESURGENCE OF NUCLEAR?

The centralised nature of nuclear technology is such that it would serve the interests of a state controlled monopoly electricity system, as compared to renewable energy which has more dispersed infrastructure, even at the utility-scale. In addition, ownership of renewable energy is dominated by international, private sector companies (Baker and Burton, 2018).

The political dynamics surrounding South Africa's potential nuclear energy programme have been present for some years. At all times, this potential programme has remained highly controversial and untransparent. A potential 9.6GW state-driven nuclear fleet was long considered a legacy project for former South African president Jacob Zuma, which he supported throughout his time in office, until his departure in early 2018. During this time, Eskom, backed by the presidency, seemed set to pursue the programme, despite clear evidence from independent analyses showing that building the fleet would lead to higher electricity costs and negative economic impacts for South Africa (ERC, 2015). Russia's state-owned nuclear company, Rosatom, was seen as the main contender to build this fleet.

Various steps were taken during Zuma's time in office to try and push through the nuclear programme (Baker et al., 2020). Such moves saw significant opposition from civil society, including a case brought by civil society organisations Earthlife Africa Johannesburg and the South African Faith Communities Environment Institute (SAFCEI) in late April 2017. Ruling on this case, the Western Cape High Court judged that the intergovernmental agreements on nuclear cooperation that had been signed in 2014 between South Africa and five countries were unconstitutional and unlawful, particularly in the case of the agreement signed between Eskom and Rosatom (Fig, 2017). Despite this ruling, the government subsequently announced that the nuclear procurement programme would start afresh.

In late January 2018, shortly before taking office, current president Cyril Ramaphosa announced at the World Economic Forum that South Africa did not have the financial capacity or the need for additional nuclear power and would therefore abandon plans to build nuclear plants (Baker et al., 2020). The finalisation of a new IRP in October 2019 appeared to reflect this commitment and nuclear did not form part of the final IRP.

However, the possibility of a nuclear programme has resurfaced in recent months. While there is no allocation for nuclear in the IRP 2019, Decision 8 had still left open this possibility, stating that the Department of Mineral Resources and Energy (DMRE) should '[c]ommence preparations for a nuclear build programme to the extent of 2 500MW at a pace and scale that the country can afford because it is a no-regret option in the long term' (DMRE, 2019: 48). The DMRE approach seemed to take on some of the many public criticisms levelled at the procurement of a nuclear fleet, including long lead times and lack of flexibility, by commencing procurement now for much less capacity (than the 9.6GW fleet) and only for post-2030. Nonetheless, independent analysis shows that the proposed 2 500MW of nuclear will cost more than a wind and solar-dominated system, regardless of even ambitious climate targets (Merven et al., 2021b; Wright and Calitz, 2021).

In August 2021 the DMRE announced plans to put out a tender for 2.5GW of nuclear power, stating that it had gained approval from NERSA for this move (DMRE, 2021). NERSA's approval was, however, subject to 'suspensive conditions', which include an update/ extension of the IRP to post-2030 to provide evidence for the need for nuclear power. It also indicated that the capacity would be state-owned, either by Eskom or another organ of state (NERSA, 2021).

The DMRE has in part justified such a move with the claim that the decommissioning of 24GW of coal-fired power post-2030 could introduce instabilities to the national electricity grid. The political return to the potential construction of a nuclear fleet has caused alarm and concern in the renewable energy industry and among environmental organisations. They see this step by the DMRE as a political move to thwart the further construction of renewable energy, rather than a decision with any technical justification (Carnie, 2021).

UNRESOLVED DYNAMICS: THE DASH FOR GAS

Following general acceptance of the gradual demise of coal in South Africa, there is currently a new and strong political and industry push for new gas extraction and use. At the time of writing in September 2021, there is a pipeline of at least 24GW of natural gas plants and approximately 25 projects currently pursuing licenses in South Africa (CER, 2021), including related infrastructure (e.g., storage facilities, liquefied natural gas infrastructure and floating plants). This is significantly higher than at the peak of expected new coal capacity and includes Eskom's proposed plant at Richard's Bay, plus others aiming for the gas IPP and emergency power procurement programmes.

However, gas proposals are not limited to the power sector given that gas is also viewed as a potential mitigation option for South Africa's second largest emitter, Sasol, at its coal to liquids plant and associated downstream petrochemical industries, and as an option for other industrial users. Sasol has proposed to reduce its coal consumption by 9Mt by 2030 and to increase its use of gas as an industrial feedstock (Sasol, 2021). In government, the gas industry potential is tied to the as-yet-unproven opportunities associated with domestic extraction, including offshore gas and fracking, as well as with regional links to Mozambique. An opaque gas masterplan process is underway, led by the DMRE.

One of the challenges is that there is divergence of views about gas use in global climate pathways, and between global pathways and local energy analyses. Unlike coal, which is rapidly phased out in all global analyses, including both 2C and 1.5C compatible scenarios (i.e., more or less ambitious scenarios that meet the goals of the Paris Agreement), there is divergence of views around the possible future of gas. At a global level, gas use even grows in some well-below 2C scenarios (though not 1.5C scenarios) (IPCC, 2018). This has brought global equity issues to the fore, as resource-rich developing countries argue that they have the right to extract and use their potential oil and gas resources given their development challenges and low responsibility for historical emissions. However, such arguments frequently ignore the economic and environmental risks of new gas extraction, beyond the climate change impacts, and overestimate the benefits (Cust and Mihalyi, 2017). The key question is thus whether gas as a 'transitional fuel' to support coal phase-out is possible without incurring stranded assets and increased carbon lock-in in the long term (NBI, 2021).

There is wide agreement between national power system studies that the total volume of gas needed to complement a higher renewables system is relatively low. National power studies suggest an uptake of gas capacity but limited dispatching of the capacity, i.e. gas plants are built but are little used in annual terms (Roff et al., 2020; Merven et al., 2021a; NBI, 2021), especially in the medium term.

In general, however, technical analysis needs to consider both real-world commercial limitations and political realities. The term 'gamechanger' is frequently bandied about in discussions of gas potential in South Africa, including in the President's State of the Nation Address in 2019 and by Minister of Mineral Resources and Energy Gwede Mantashe (Hamilton, 2021). Associated government entities have also promoted gas (e.g., the Petroleum Association of South Africa and officials in the DMRE), while the gas industry and its consultants have quickly appropriated the language of 'just transition' to argue that a gas-led phase-out of coal can protect workers and communities and that gas forms part of a net zero emissions pathway for South Africa (Masangane, 2021; Xabadiya and Manyaga, 2021; Ebrahim, 2020; Shell, 2021; ESI, 2021; Swart, 2021).

Strong political interest in gas as well as industry pressure for new infrastructure needs to be balanced by economic and environmental realities and risks. The timing of new gas infrastructure, and the length and flexibility of fuel contracts are important for avoiding unnecessary and expensive lock-in. In the longer-term, alongside flexible contracts and avoiding expensive, state-supported infrastructure, the technical need for new gas use will be tempered by new technology developments, especially in green hydrogen, and in other long-duration storage opportunities. Current political and diplomatic interest in green hydrogen for national and export use may offer an alternative to gas in the medium to long term, and green hydrogen will be key for both power sector flexibility and decarbonising industrial sectors that lack alternative options, notably liquid fuels/chemicals and steel (IEA, 2020).

CONCLUSION

As this chapter has discussed, until recently, national mitigation targets had comfortable limits that required relatively little political attention to be paid to the energy sector, and the power sector in particular. For many years, South Africa's coal-dependent and carbon-intensive economy, built through state intervention over many years and characterised by its MEC, was long able to resist or to at least hinder climate action. However, as we have explored, multiple trends at both global and domestic levels have recently resulted in an unlocking of barriers to ambitious climate mitigation action, and to the potential for a fundamentally altered climate policy landscape. With this in mind, we now offer the following four conclusions.

First, while some core elements of the coal sector persisted in the post-apartheid era, important fundamental shifts took place in terms of ownership and economics. Beyond this, the more recent shift away from the construction of new, coal-fired power plants and investment therein, and the emergence of increasingly cheap, privately owned renewables, has enabled far greater levels of climate ambition to be contemplated. The new NDC targets have opened up the possibility of a globally funded country deal that could support Eskom's transition away from coal. The just transition within the coal value chain as it starts to decline is now at the top of the political agenda, highlighting the need to address the socio-economic future of the Mpumalanga region where most of the coal extraction is currently concentrated. The pace of phase-out, and how it is managed, are key to the livelihoods of those most affected.

Second, the gradual demise of South Africa's coal industry and the emergence of new climate institutions and policies mark a turning point. The newly approved NDC thus symbolises a new period of climate policy, where reaching the ambitious NDC target now requires implementation across government and policy spheres, but especially in the power sector. Political questions around technology choices in that sector point to a potential re-formation of the MEC around gas-based infrastructure, or a fundamentally altered political economy of energy focused on renewables.

Third, South Africa's energy sector now sits at a crossroads. The structure of its MEC, which historically has been based on a dependence on cheap coal and cheap labour for cheap electricity for an economy based on mining and minerals beneficiation, has now unravelled. Coal and electricity are no longer cheap and many of the institutions and strong interlinkages between them – which used to control this system of accumulation – no longer have the same level of political and economic power. Such institutions have started to redefine, disintegrate and/or diversify. Coal still retains a stronghold over the economy and electricity supply, and Eskom still has a continued monopoly in this space. Despite this, pressures from climate change mitigation targets and the emergence of an economically viable renewable energy sector are pointing to a fundamental change in relationships between natural resources, technologies and the country's political, economic and social institutions.

How these relationships may continue to evolve, and the implications they will have for any just and low carbon transition, however so defined, is currently unclear. A utility-scale renewable energy sector has gained a foothold, though it may not necessarily bring about the creation of the hoped-for skills and jobs that are central priorities for a just transition. Despite this, potential challenges are posed by a persistently problematic and still possible nuclear fleet, and an increasingly organised gas industry with industrial and political backing from inside and outside government. While technical analysis shows that nuclear does not feature in the power sector even in climate policy scenarios (though this may change as net zero analyses are finalised), the DMRE is pursuing new state-backed nuclear plants.

Finally, the gas industry has been noticeably absent from the key narratives of South Africa's energy sector and particularly its electricity sector to date; it is only in recent years that gas has been declared by multiple constituencies as a 'game changer'. The fact that it is being promoted as a significant option for the power sector (rather than merely as a balancing option), that it will contribute to the just transition and that it forms part of a net zero emissions pathway for the country is highly significant, particularly in the absence of studies and analyses that provide evidence for such claims. In this sense, it would seem that the future struggles of South Africa's energy sector lie as much in the fields of narrative and discourse, as in what is technologically and economically optimal. Independent voices, for instance from civil society and academia, therefore have an important role to play in investigating such claims. The current state of tension and uncertainty that we have described is a further illustration of the realities of any just transition which, rather than being an ordered sequence of events based on technically optimal scenarios, is a messy, conflict-ridden process of winners and losers, influenced by power and politics.

REFERENCES

Arndt, C., Arent, D., Hartley, F., Merven, B. and Mondal, A. 2019. 'Faster than you think: Renewable energy and developing countries'. *Annual Review of Resource Economics*, https://www.annualreviews.org/doi/abs/10.1146/annurev-resource-100518-093759, accessed 25 October 2021.

Ashman, S., Fine, B. and Newman, S. 2013. 'Systems of accumulation and the evolving South African MEC', in Fine, B., Saraswati, J. and Tavasci, D. (eds), *Beyond the Developmental State: Industrial Policy into the Twenty first Century*. London: Pluto Press, 245–267.

Baker, L., Hook, A. and Sovacool, B.K. 2021. 'Power struggles: Governing renewable electricity in a time of technological disruption'. *Geoforum*, 118, 93–105.

Baker, L., Burton, J. and Trollip, H. 2020. 'The energy politics of South Africa', in Hancock, K. and Allison, J.E. (eds), *The Oxford Handbook of Energy Politics*. DOI: 10.1093/oxfordhb/9780190861360.013.25.

Baker, L. and Burton, J. 2018. 'The politics of procurement and the low-carbon transition in South Africa', in Goldthau, A., Keating M. F. and Kuzemko, C. (eds), *Handbook of the International Political Economy of Energy and Natural Resources*. Cheltenham, Gloucester: Edward Elgar Publishing Limited, 91–106.

Baker, L., Burton, J., Godinho, C. and Trollip, G. 2015. 'The political economy of decarbonisation: Exploring the dynamics of South Africa's electricity sector'. https://www.africaportal.org/publications/the-political-economy-of-decarbonisation-exploring-the-dynamics-of-south-africas-electricity-sector/, accessed 5 October 2021.

Baker, L. 2015. 'Renewable energy in South Africa's minerals-energy complex: A "low carbon" transition?'. *Review of African Political Economy*, 42(144), 245–261.

Bischof-Niemz, T. and Fourie, R. 2016. 'Cost of new power generators in

South Africa: Comparative analysis based on recent IPP announcements'. Council for Scientific and Industrial Research, https://www.ee.co.za/wp-content/uploads/2016/10/New_Power_Generators_RSA-CSIR-14Oct2016.pdf, accessed 21 August 2021.

Burton, J., Marquard, A. and McCall, B. 2019. 'Socio-economic considerations for a Paris Agreement-compatible coal transition in South Africa'. Energy Research Centre, University of Cape Town, South Africa. https://www.climate-transparency.org/wp-content/uploads/2019/07/CT-Just-Transition-in-South-Africa.pdf, accessed 12 October 2021.

Burton, J., Caetano, T. and McCall, B. 2018a. *Coal Transitions in South Africa. Understanding the Implications of a 2oC-Compatible Coal Phase-out Plan for South Africa*. ERC, IDDRI, Climate Strategies. https://www.iddri.org/sites/default/files/PDF/Publications/Catalogue%20Iddri/Rapport/20180609_ReportCoal_SouthAfrica.pdf, accessed 12 July 2021.

Burton, J., Lott, T. and Rennkamp, B. 2018b. 'Sustaining carbon lock-in: Fossil fuel subsidies in South Africa', in Van Asselt, H. and Skovgaard, J. (eds), *Politics of Fossil Fuel Subsidies and Their Reform*. Cambridge: Cambridge University Press.

Burton, J. and Winkler, H. 2014. 'South Africa's planned coal infrastructure expansion: Drivers, dynamics and impacts on greenhouse gas emissions'. Energy Research Centre, University of Cape Town.

Calitz, J. and Wright, J. 2021. 'Statistics of utility-scale power generation in South Africa in 2020. Council for Scientific and Industrial Research, https://cisp.cachefly.net/assets/articles/attachments/84839_calitzwrightmarch2021.pdf, accessed 9 October 2021.

Carnie, T. 1 September 2021. 'Going nuclear: Mantashe's big push to build South Africa's second nuke power station under fire'. *Daily Maverick*, https://www.dailymaverick.co.za/article/2021-09-01-going-nuclear-mantashes-big-push-to-build-south-africas-second-nuke-power-station-under-fire/, accessed 25 September 2021.

Centre for Environmental Rights (CER). 2021. Personal communication.

Christie, R. 1984. *Electricity, Industry, and Class in South Africa*. Oxford: Macmillan.

Climate Transparency 2021a. 'Climate Transparency: Comparing G20 climate action towards net zero 2021'. https://www.climate-transparency.org/wp-content/uploads/2021/10/CT2021-Highlights-Report.pdf, accessed 10 August 2021.

Climate Transparency 2021b. 'Climate Transparency: Comparing G20 climate action towards net zero: South Africa 2021'. https://www.climate-transparency.org/wp-content/uploads/2021/10/CT2021SouthAfrica.pdf#page=8, accessed 15 August 2021.

Cohen, T. 28 Feb 2019. 'Glencore's watershed on coal.' Business Live, https://www.businesslive.co.za/fm/money-and-investing/2019-02-28-glencoreswatershed-on-coal/, accessed 3 September 2021.

Colenbrander, S., Cao, Y., Pettinotti, L. and Quevedo, A. 2021. 'A fair share of climate finance? Apportioning responsibility for the $100 billion climate finance goal'. ODI Working Paper, ODI, London, https://odi.org/en/publications/a-fair-share-of-climate-finance-apportioning-responsibility-for-the-100-billion-climate-finance-goal/, accessed 2 September 2021.

Cust, J. and Mihalyi, D. 2017. 'Evidence for a presource curse?: Oil discoveries, elevated expectations, and growth disappointments'. Policy Research Working Paper No. 8140. World Bank, https://openknowledge.worldbank.org/handle/10986/27643, accessed 12 September 2021.

Dentons. 2015. 'REPORT: in respect of the investigation in to the status of the business and challenges experienced by Eskom, instituted by the board of Eskom Holdings (SOC) Ltd in terms of a resolution passed on 11 March 2015'. https://serve.mg.co.za/content/documents/2017/02/09/150702dentonseskomlow-resocr.pdf, accessed 5 October 2021.

Department of Energy (DoE). 2011. 'Integrated Resource Plan for Electricity (IRP), 2010– 2030'. Government Gazette no. 34263 (6 May 2011), http://www.energy.gov.za/IRP/2019/IRP-2019.pdf, accessed 23 September 2021.

Department of Environmental Affairs (DEA). 2011. 'National Climate Change Response White Paper'. https://www.gov.za/sites/default/files/gcis_document/201409/nationalclimatechangeresponsewhitepaper0.pdf, accessed 12 October 2021.

Department of Mineral Resources and Energy (DMRE). 26 August 2021. 'NERSA concurrence with the Section 34 determination for 2 500mw of new nuclear generation capacity'. http://www.energy.gov.za/files/media/pr/2021/NERSA-Concurrence-with-The-Section34Determination-for-2500mw-New-Nuclear-Generation-Capacity.pdf, accessed 4 October 2021.

Department of Minerals Resources and Energy (DMRE). 2020. 'Independent Power Producers Procurement Programme (IPPPP): An Overview as at 31 March 2020'. https://www.ipp-projects.co.za/Publications/GetPublicationFile?fileid=35cc2033-94b4-ea11-950b-2c59e59ac9cd&fileName=20200604_IPP%20Office%20Q4%20Overview%202019-20.PDF, accessed 12 October 2021.

Department of Mineral Resources and Energy (DMRE). 2019. 'Integrated Resource Plan (IRP 2019)'. http://www.energy.gov.za/IRP/2019/IRP-2019.pdf, accessed 12 August 2021.

De Ruyter, A. 2021 'Eskom's Just Energy Transition (JET) Plans'. Presentation to the Presidential Climate Commission, 30 July. https://a9322a19-efe3-4459-9a6c-ab806fededa3.filesusr.com/ugd/1eb85a_a580234ae5704025855a495d9de565cd.pdf, accessed 12 October 2021.

Eberhard, A. 2011. 'The future of South African coal: Market, investment, and policy challenges'. *Program on Energy and Sustainable Development.*

https://fsi-live.s3.us-west-1.amazonaws.com/s3fs-public/WP_100_Eberhard_Future_of_South_African_Coal.pdf, accessed 4 October 2021.

Eberhard, A. and Naude, R. 2017. 'The South African Renewable Energy IPP Procurement Programme: Review, lessons learned & proposals to reduce transaction costs'. UCT Graduate School of Business Report. https://www.gsb.uct.ac.za/files/EberhardNaude_REIPPPPReview_2017_1_1.pdf, accessed 5 October 2021.

Ebrahim, A. Oct 2020. 'Gas-to-power: A bright future for South Africa?'. Africa International Investors, https://www.africaia.com/insights/gas-to-power-a-bright-future-for-south-africa, accessed 21 October 2021.

Energy Intensive Users Group (EIUG). 2021. https://eiug.org.za/, accessed 12 October 2021.

Energy Research Centre (ERC). 2015. 'South Africa's proposed nuclear build plan: an analysis of the potential socioeconomic risks'. http://www.epse.uct.ac.za/sites/default/files/image_tool/images/363/ESRG/Publications/2015_ERC-Nuclear_build_plan_Technical_report.pdf, accessed 15 August 2021.

ESI. 8 June 2021. 'South Africa braces for the gas revolution'. *ESI Africa*, https://www.esi-africa.com/industry-sectors/generation/south-africa-braces-for-the-gas-revolution/, accessed 9 June 2021

Eskom Integrated Reports 2021, 2020, 2019, 2018, 2017, 2016. https://www.eskom.co.za/investors/integrated-results/, accessed 12 October 2021.

Fig, D. 2017. 'Court ruling on Zuma's nuclear deal is a marker of South Africa's political health', *Mail & Guardian*, 29 April. https://mg.co.za/article/2017-04-29-court-ruling-on-zumas-nuclear-deal-is-a-marker-of-south-africas-political-health/, accessed 18 August 2021.

Fine, B. and Rustomjee, Z. 1996. *The Political Economy of South Africa: From minerals energy complex to industrialisation*. Boulder: Westview Press.

Glencore. 2020. 'Pathway to net zero'. Climate Report 2020, https://www.glencore.com/dam/jcr:c1e7faf7-1928-4251-819e-aa8918be42ba/2020-climate-report.pdf, accessed 15 May 2021.

Hamilton, G. 2021. 'Economic impacts of offshore oil and gas on South Africa'. https://thegreenconnection.org.za/wp-content/uploads/2021/10/Economic-impacts-of-offshore-oil-and-gas-on-South-Africa.12042021-1.pdf, accessed 12 May 2021.

Hanto, J., Krawielicki, J., Schroth, A., Oei, P. and Burton, J. (2022). 'The political economy of energy and climate policy in South Africa', in Jakob, M. and Steckel, J. (eds), *Political Economy of Coal: Obstacles to clean energy transitions*. Routledge: Abingdon and New York: Routledge.

Heintz, J. 2010. 'The social structure of accumulation in South Africa', in McDonough, T., Reich, M. and Kotz, D.M. (eds), *Contemporary Capitalism and its Crises: Social structure of accumulation theory for the 21st century*. Cambridge: Cambridge University Press, 267–285.

Hermanus, L. and Montmasson-Clair, G. 2021. 'Making sense of jobs in South Africa's just energy transition: Managing the impact of a coal transition on employment'. https://www.tips.org.za/policy-briefs/item/4111-making-sense-of-jobs-in-south-africa-s-just-energy-transition-managing-the-impact-of-a-coal-transition-on-employment, accessed 20 October 2021.

Institute for Energy Economics and Financial Analysis (IEEFA). 2021. 'Finance is leaving thermal coal'. https://ieefa.org/finance-leaving-thermal-coal/#1596145653395-89446f18-be8d1269-34c9, accessed 20 October 2021.

International Energy Agency (IEA). 2020. 'World Energy Outlook 2020'. https://www.iea.org/reports/world-energy-outlook-2020, accessed 23 August 2021.

Intergovernmental Panel on Climate Change (IPCC). 2018. 'Global warming of 1.5°C. An IPCC Special Report on the impacts of global warming of 1.5°C above pre-industrial levels and related global greenhouse gas emission pathways, in the context of strengthening the global response to the threat of climate change, sustainable development, and efforts to eradicate poverty'. [V. Masson-Delmotte, P. Zhai, H. O. Pörtner, D. Roberts, J. Skea, P.R. Shukla, A. Pirani, W. Moufouma-Okia, C. Péan, R. Pidcock, S. Connors, J. B. R. Matthews, Y. Chen, X. Zhou, M. I. Gomis, E. Lonnoy, T. Maycock, M. Tignor, T. Waterfield (eds)] https://www.ipcc.ch/sr15/, accessed 4 October 2021.

Ireland, G. and Burton, J 2018. 'An assessment of new coal plants in South Africa's electricity future: The cost, emissions, and supply security implications of the coal IPP programme'. Energy Research Centre, University of Cape Town, Cape Town.

Kretzman, S. 2021. 'How an inattentive Eskom board allowed Guptas to buy a mine using taxpayers' money.' *Daily Maverick*, https://www.dailymaverick.co.za/article/2021-02-11-how-an-inattentive-eskom-board-allowed-guptas-to-buy-a-mine-using-taxpayers-money/, accessed 12 August 2021.

Lowitt, S. 2021. 'Toward a contribution to a just transition finance roadmap in South Africa'. Trade and Industrial Policy Strategies. https://www.tips.org.za/research-archive/sustainable-growth/green-economy-2/item/4178-toward-a-contribution-to-a-just-transition-finance-roadmap-in-south-africa, accessed 20 October 2021.

Makgetla, N. and Patel, M. 2021. 'The coal value chain'. Trade & Industrial Policy Strategies, https://www.tips.org.za/research-archive/trade-and-industry/item/4161-the-coal-value-chain-in-south-africa, accessed 12 August 2021.

Marquard, A. 2006. 'The Origins and Development of South African Energy Policy'. University of Cape Town.

Marquard, A., Hartley, F., Merven, B., Burton, J., Hughes, A. et al. 2021.

'Technical analysis to support the update of South Africa's First NDC's mitigation target ranges'. University of Cape Town Report, https://zivahub.uct.ac.za/articles/report/Technical_Analysis_to_support_the_update_of_South_Africa_s_First_NDC_s_mitigation_target_ranges_UCT_2021_/16691950, accessed 2 August 2021.

Masangane, P. 5 September 2021. 'SA's road to net zero emissions will be via gas'. *Business Day*, https://www.businesslive.co.za/amp/bd/opinion/2021-09-05-phindile-masangane-sas-road-to-net-zero-emissions-will-be-via-gas/, accessed 6 September 2021.

Mbazima, N. 2020. 'Reviving a declining mining industry'. *Viewpoints*, 9, 1–7. https://media.africaportal.org/documents/viewpoints-reviving-a-declining-mining-industry-norman-mbazima.pdf, accessed 6 September 2021.

McCall, B., Burton, J., Marquard, A., Hartley, F., Ahjum, F., Ireland, G. and Merven, B. 2019. 'Least-cost integrated resource planning and cost-optimal climate change mitigation policy: Alternatives for the South African electricity system'. Energy Research Centre, University of Cape Town, Cape Town.

McKay D. 1 April 2021. 'South32 overhauls thermal coal sale to Seriti with $250m cash and finance injection'. *Miningmx*, https://www.miningmx.com/news/energy/45757-south32-overhauls-thermal-coal-sale-to-seriti-with-250m-cash-and-finance-injection/, accessed 1 April 2021.

Merven, B., Burton, J. and Lehmann-Grube, P. 2021a. 'Assessment of new coal generation capacity targets in South Africa's 2019 Integrated Resource Plan for Electricity'. Energy Systems Research Group, University of Cape Town.

Merven, B., Schers, J., Burton, J., McCall, B., Marquard, A. and Bergh, C. 5 February 2021b. 'Comments for the National Energy Regulator of South Africa on the Ministerial Determination on the procurement of 2500 MW new generation capacity from nuclear'. Energy Systems Research Group, http://www.epse.uct.ac.za/sites/default/files/image_tool/images/363/ESRG/Publications/2021_ESRG_Comments%20for%20NERSA%20on%20the%20procurement%20of%202500%20MW%20new%20generation%20capacity%20from%20nuclear_AcknFixed.pdf, accessed 4 April 2021.

Mohamed, S. 2016. 'Financialization of the South African economy'. *Development*, 59(1), 137–142.

Montmasson-Clair, G. and Ryan, G. 2014. 'Lessons from South Africa's renewable energy regulatory and procurement experience'. *Journal of Economic and Financial Sciences*, 7(4), 507–526.

Moolman, S. 2019. '2019 update: Eskom tariff increases vs inflation since 1988 (with projections to 2022)'. *Power Optimal*, https://www.poweroptimal.com/2019-update-eskom-tariff-increases-vs-inflation-since-1988-with-projections-to-2022/, accessed 20 September 2021.

National Planning Commission (NPC). 2013. 'NDP 2030: Our future, make it work'. https://nationalplanningcommission.files.wordpress.com/2015/02/ndp-2030-our-future-make-it-work_0.pdf, accessed 10 October 2015.

National Energy Regulator of South Africa (NERSA). 3 September 2021. 'NERSA's concurrence with the ministerial determination on the procurement of 2 500MW generation capacity from nuclear technology'. https://g2z2c7d2.stackpathcdn.com/wp-content/uploads/2021/09/Media-Statement-NERSAs-concurrence-with-the-ministerial-determination-on-the-procurement-of-2-500MW-generation-capacity-from-Nuclear-technology.pdf, accessed 5 September 2021.

National Business Initiative (NBI) 2021. 'Decarbonising South Africa's power system'. Report from Just Transition and Climate Pathways Study for South Africa, https://www.nbi.org.za/climate-pathways-and-a-just-transition-for-south-africa/#reports, accessed 11 August 2021.

Organisation for Economic Co-operation and Development (OECD). 2021a. 'Climate finance provided and mobilised by developed countries: Aggregate trends updated with 2019 data, climate finance and the USD 100 billion goal'. https://doi.org/10.1787/03590fb7-en, accessed 15 October 2021.

Organisation for Economic Co-operation and Development (OECD). 2021b. 'Agreement reached at OECD to end export credit support for unabated coal-fired power plants'. https://www.oecd.org/newsroom/agreement-reached-at-oecd-to-end-export-credit-support-for-unabated-coal-fired-power-plants.htm, accessed 25 October 2021.

Presidential Climate Commission (PCC). 2021. 'Recommendations on South Africa's draft updated Nationally Determined Contribution'. https://www.climatecommission.org.za/ndc, accessed 10 October 2021.

Roff, A., Steyn, G., Tyler, E., Renaud, C., Brand, R. and Burton, J. 2020. 'A vital ambition: Determining the cost of additional CO2 emission mitigation in the South African electricity system'. *Meridian Economics*, https://meridianeconomics.co.za/wp-content/uploads/2020/07/Ambition.pdf, accessed 9 October 2021.

Sasol. 2021. 'Climate Change Report 2021'. https://www.sasol.com/sites/default/files/financial_reports/Sasol%20Climate%20Change%20Report_2021_22Sep21.pdf, accessed 10 October 2021.

Shell. 2 July 2021. 'Gas works in partnership with renewables'. Business Live, https://www.businesslive.co.za/fm/fm-fox/2021-07-02-native-natural-gas-will-be-a-critical-component-of-sas-energy-transition/, accessed 2 July 2021.

Steyn, G., Burton, J. and Steenkamp, M. 2017. 'Eskom's financial crisis and the viability of coal-fired power in South Africa: Implications for Kusile and the older coal-fired power stations'. *Meridian Economics*, https://meridianeconomics.co.za/wp-content/uploads/2017/11/CoalGen-Report_FinalDoc_ForUpload-1.pdf, accessed 4 July 2021.

Swart, J. 2021. 'Gas-fired power is a no-brainer'. *Business Live*, https://www.businesslive.co.za/bd/opinion/2021-07-05-jurie-swart-gas-fired-power-is-a-no-brainer/, accessed 15 October 2021.

Tyler, E. and Hochstetler, K. 2021. 'Institutionalising decarbonisation in South Africa: Navigating climate mitigation and socio-economic transformation'. *Environmental Politics*, DOI: 10.1080/09644016.2021.1947635.

United Nations Environment Programme (UNEP). 2020. 'Emissions Gap Report 2020'. https://wedocs.unep.org/xmlui/bitstream/handle/20.500.11822/34426/EGR20.pdf?sequence=1&isAllowed=y, accessed 21 October 2021.

Walsh, K., Theron, R., Seedat, A. and Reeders, C. 2020. 'Estimating the economic cost of load shedding in South Africa'. *Nova Economics*, https://www.nersa.org.za/wp-content/uploads/2021/09/Appendix-C_Estimating-the-Economic-Cost-of-Load-Shedding-in-South-Africa-Report.pdf, accessed 12 September 2021

Wright, J.G. and Calitz, J.R. 2020. 'Systems analysis to support increasingly ambitious CO_2 emissions scenarios in the South African electricity system'. Council for Scientific and Industrial Research.

Wright, J.G. and Calitz, J.R. 26 February 2021. 'CSIR Response: Consultation Paper on concurrence with the Ministerial Determination on the procurement of 2 500MW generation capacity from nuclear'. CSIR Research space, https://researchspace.csir.co.za/dspace/bitstream/handle/10204/11795/WrightCalitz_Feb2021.pdf?sequence=3&isAllowed=y, accessed 25 September 2021.

Xabadiya, A. and Manyaga, S. 26 August 2021. 'SA needs an energy mix'. *Business Live*, https://www.businesslive.co.za/fm/opinion/on-my-mind/2021-08-26-avuyile-xabadiya-and-shonisani-manyaga-sa-needs-an-energy-mix/, accessed 26 August 2021.

SIX

Green industrial development under the African Continental Free Trade Area (AfCFTA)

Positioning South Africa's renewable energy manufacturing

MARIA NKHONJERA

INTRODUCTION

HISTORICALLY, SOUTH AFRICA'S PATTERN of industrial development has been heavily dependent on coal-based, energy-intensive industries. This presents a challenge for transitioning away from a non-renewable resource economy. South Africa's energy policy has undergone substantial revisions over the years and the launch of the Renewable Energy Independent Power Producer Procurement Programme (REIPPPP) in 2011 was viewed as a catalyst for energy diversification and clean energy supplies (DoE, 2015: 21). At the core of enabling and scaling South Africa's energy transition is its industrial development strategy. This strategy integrates renewable energy and industrial policies. It was given impetus in the Industrial Policy Action Plan (IPAP) (DTIC, 2018). Subsequently, the development of the South African Renewable Energy Masterplan (SAREM) (Green Cape, 2020) was aimed at unlocking growth and industrialisation in priority sectors. Central to the green industrialisation agenda is that energy-intensive manufacturing sectors in South Africa, including renewables manufacturing, should have alternative, decarbonised energy sources. South Africa has vast untapped potential, leaving a strategic opportunity for active renewables energy industrialisation as part of a broader integration of regional energy markets.

This chapter provides an overview of South Africa's renewable energy programmes, policies and outcomes to date and, within the framework of the African Continental Free Trade Area (AfCFTA), considers how South Africa can leverage its capabilities to boost clean energy exports and align with local and continental industrial development goals. It specifically analyses the ways in which the just transition debate will influence South Africa's broader industrial policy agenda and how key policy instruments for industrialisation will be located within the scope of a single continental market. Finally, the chapter uses this evidence and draws on international experience to examine the industrial positioning and policy remediation South Africa needs to adopt to unlock a just transition in support of the new climate agenda. The chapter argues that South Africa's energy transition and industrialisation agenda needs to pay special attention to underlying political economy dynamics, both in terms of entrenched domestic socio-economic and market structures, as well as its cooperation with the rest of the continent. Any attempt at real transformation will need to capture the deep and complex social, political and economic context within which the energy transition is unfolding.

To unpack this, the chapter is structured as follows: section 2 reviews South Africa's renewable energy policy landscape; section 3 makes the case for energy transitions as a green industrial development agenda; section 4 discusses AfCFTA as a pathway to industrialisation, highlighting the opportunities for energy market integration and an industrial policy framework that would accelerate the energy transition; and section 5 concludes with policy implications and areas for further research.

RENEWABLE ENERGY POLICY LANDSCAPE – A LACK OF POLITICAL WILL?

South Africa's electricity market (the largest in Africa) is heavily dependent on low-cost coal and a vertically integrated state-owned power utility (Eskom), which has faced financial, structural and operational challenges over several years (Semelane et al., 2020). With Eskom accounting for more than 90 per cent of power generation capacity and combined economic and environmental pressures to support a just energy transition, South Africa is committed to decarbonising its energy system and progressively diversifying its energy mix. This has been guided by various key policies driven by South Africa's Department of Mineral Resources and Energy (DMRE), Department of Trade Industry and Competition (DTIC) and the Department of Environmental Affairs (DEA).

The South African government acknowledged the importance of alternative and more efficient energy sources as far back as 1998, as articulated in the White Paper on Energy Policy (DMRE, 1998: 25). The White Paper on Renewable Energy (DMRE, 2003: 2) provides the framework for the government's plans to support greater deployment of renewable energy, and industries based on deployment and renewable energy, establishing key policy priorities and locating the policy within a national and international context of development and climate imperatives.

A critical component of South Africa's energy policy is the Integrated Resource Plan (IRP) – first adopted in 2010, with the most recent gazetted in 2019. The IRP 'is an electricity infrastructure development plan based on least-cost electricity supply and demand balance' (DMRE, 2019: 8). Based on various technology targets, the IRP, therefore, considers various objectives of the national government, including the availability of affordable electricity; reducing greenhouse gas (GHG) emissions; diversification of electricity sources and links to domestic industries and jobs. The IRP 2019 is at the centre of diversifying South Africa's electricity mix and off-grid power generation systems, through solar, wind and concentrated solar power (CSP) (with storage). The Plan envisages commissioning additional utility-scale renewable capacity: approximately 20 gigawatts (GW) of solar photovoltaic (PV) and wind technology, in addition to the decommissioning of 11GW of coal power plants by 2030 (DMRE, 2019: 10–44; Yelland, 2020).

Building on the IRP, the National Climate Change Response White Paper (NCCRP), passed in 2011, consists of both a Renewable Energy Flagship Programme and Energy Efficiency Flagship Programme (DEA, 2012: 31–32). In support of creating new pathways for a sustainable energy system, the National Development Plan which closely aligns with the Sustainable Development Goals (SDGs) has set a target to phase out 35GW of coal capacity (83 per cent of the current operating capacity) by 2030 (Tena, 2021).

Between the period that the first renewable energy policy was promulgated, and the IRP was updated (IRP 2019), technology options have rapidly evolved and have given rise to new low-cost business models for energy generation (Power Futures South Africa, 2019: 2). In 2011, South Africa adopted the REIPPPP as part of its strategy to implement the IRP's clean energy vision (Nomjana, 2020). Accordingly, it recognised its dual role in restructuring both the power sector and the broader economy. By encouraging independent power producers (IPPs) to bid to generate grid connected renewable energy, the REIPPPP expects over 17GW of its electricity to be derived from renewables (27 per cent of the energy mix) (see Table 6.1). The country also still has existing coal investments that are in a build and test phase.

The Council for Scientific and Industrial Research (CSIR) reports approximately 30 000 jobs created and upwards of R200 billion of private investment directed into projects under the renewable procurement programme. A further R19 billion has been used to fund specific socio-economic development outcomes (Calitz and Wright, 2019: 4). Despite this, the programme has been met by continued resistance from labour unions associated with coal mining industries. Their concerns are largely concentrated on the socio-economic implications of the phase-out of coal (i.e., on the risk of being left behind). The Congress of South African Trade Unions (COSATU) argues that 'local content requirement targets are too lenient, and impressive job creation (difficult to verify) has to be contextualized

Table 6.1: IRP's targeted energy mix, 2030

	Current (GW)	Total installed by 2030 (GW)
Coal	29.13	33.85
Nuclear	1.86	1.86
Hydro	2.19	4.93
Solar PV	1.47	7.95
Wind	1.98	11.44
Concentrated Solar Power (CSP)	0.3	0.6
Gas/diesel	3.84	11.9
Other (co-generation, biomass, landfill)	0.5	0.5
Total (GW)	**41.27**	**73.03**

Source: Adapted from Anthony (2018: 8).

by the tendency to inflate numbers based on temporary, low-value, and/or low-skilled jobs' (Grant et al., 2019: 8). These remarks, made in relation to the Atlantis Special Economic Zone (ASEZ), are suggestive of the tensions that exist between stakeholders impacted by the energy transition, particularly the conundrum of how to build trust with disconnected communities. Moreover, it reflects the high levels of components, parts and materials that are imported, which effectively limit upstream supply opportunities and employment.

The experience of independent power producers suggests that on the one hand the availability of cost-competitive international suppliers, particularly for solar components, hampers the ability of foreign investors to meet localisation targets (Kaziboni and Stern, 2021: 29). On the other hand, the flexibility of local content requirements, as contained in the REIPPPP, 'leaves project developers with the decision to assign local content, which creates ambiguity along the value chain, especially upstream' (Kaziboni and Stern, 2021: 32). Localisation requirements have also been less focused on high-value components, with a greater orientation towards local sourcing of construction services (Grant et al., 2019: 8; Kaziboni and Stern, 2019: 29). The combination of an obscure local content policy and one that does not necessarily prioritise higher value content limits industrial policy linkages, and the REIPPPP's potential as a lever for building local manufacturing capacity in the renewable energy value chain. Local content requirements cannot be developed in isolation of other critical factors; rather they need to target viable markets with stable and potential growth for renewables manufacturing (Bazilian, et al. 2020: 9). This is critical for nascent but more complex industrial components such as wind turbines and solar inverters, which need the support of complementary industrial, trade and procurement policies.

Efforts to unbundle and restructure South Africa's centralised power system still need to be fast tracked, as these efforts are integral for unlocking the potential of independent power producers (IPP's) (Slater, 2021; Baker et al., 2014: 813) and facilitating a more diversified, competitive power generation sector. Furthermore, regulatory and technical barriers as well as prohibitive bidding processes have put the effective implementation of the REIPPPP at risk (Eberhard and Naude, 2017: 38). Others have argued, simply, that South Africa's energy and electricity policy requires far more proactive leadership and implementation to allow domestic, industrial and agricultural sectors to generate their own power (Yelland, 2020). Grant et al. (2019: 65) note that working with strategic interests within Eskom itself is central to increasing the utility's willingness to sign and honour purchasing power agreements.

South Africa's energy transition is underway and the REIPPPP has catalysed a shift in the energy market. A number of the barriers identified in the 2003 White Paper, for example, have been overcome by the declining cost of renewable technologies, and an increasing appetite for financing green economy solutions. The government's move to increase the embedded generation threshold for unlicensed power from 1 megawatt (MW) to 100MW will benefit power generation capacity outside of the national grid (Merten, 2021). The higher threshold will facilitate economies of scale and enhanced competitiveness. These are, in turn, expected to encourage a lot more investment into embedded generation projects, which are urgently needed to reduce demand on Eskom and ease power outages. This does, however, raise concerns around the capacity of Eskom Transmission to manage the variability of renewable power supply together with inflexible coal-fired plants (Baigrie, 2021). To address infrastructure requirements, Eskom has planned capital expenditure on transmission for the 2021 to 2030 period, including expanding capacity and strengthening networks (R86.9 billion) and refurbishing existing assets (R18.8 billion) (Schepper, 2020: 140).

South Africa's energy transition is not happening with the speed and urgency that it deserves. The energy landscape has yet to be transformed and the complexity of such an endeavour requires sufficient political will to accelerate the implementation of existing policies. The shift to renewable energy in South Africa is not unfolding as part of an active just transition policy agenda but is more of a reaction to the electricity crisis, including with the 100MW concession that has been made. It comes at a time when Eskom is experiencing persistent power outages, which is squeezing economic activity and growth. The South African state needs a more proactive approach to the renewable energy transition as part of a deeper just transition.

Grant et al. (2019: 8) posit that 'the focus of the [REIPPPP] programme is on the lowest cost rather than total economic benefit', suggesting the need to look beyond energy policy and build clear linkages with sustainable industrialisation and employment strategies. The development of SAREM, led by the DTIC, is a step in this direction (see below). While still in its early phases of development, it complements the IRP by identifying prospects for catalytic growth, industrialisation and job creation in the energy sector through the coordination of multiple stakeholders (government, industry, labour, civil society and academia) (Green Cape, 2020: 1–2). As this chapter shows, the 'complex politics' of energy transitions can be overcome by a coordinated set of policy objectives, targets and instruments that are integrated into a broad-based agenda for industrialisation.

Energy transitions as a green industrial development agenda

United Nations Economic Commission for Africa (UNECA, 2016: 24) describes a complex set of economic, social and environmental dimensions as a precondition for inclusive structural transformation (i.e., moving to more complex and higher value productive activities). South Africa, underpinned by uneven and exclusionary growth, and a scourge of unemployment, has largely failed to deliver meaningful structural change (Bell et al., 2018: 15). The value added by the manufacturing sector in South Africa to the gross domestic product (GDP) is relatively low (12 per cent in 2019), when compared to other upper middle-income countries (Figure 6.1). This is true across several macroeconomic indicators. The political economy of South Africa's industrial policy choices has shaped its (lack of) transformation pattern and coincides with poor economic diversification and patterns of premature industrialisation (Andreoni and Tregenna, 2018: 3). In the South African context, therefore, a green industrialisation agenda provides an impetus for an alternative model of development – one that generates sustainable employment and inclusive socio-economic outcomes.

Deploying renewable or clean energy is the foundation of a vision for green industrialisation (Altenburg and Assmann, 2017: 7), not merely from the perspective of meeting South Africa's environmental targets but also for triggering industrial development objectives. In South Africa, energy production and use (driven largely by coal) contribute 80 per cent to overall GHG emissions, of which 50 per cent is emitted from electricity alone (DMRE, 2019: 8).

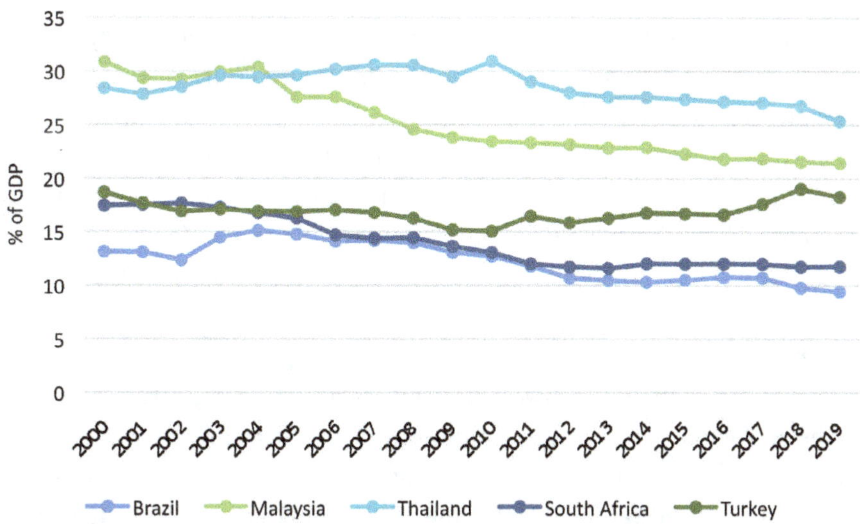

Figure 6.1: Manufacturing value add (% of GDP) in selected comparator countries, 2000–2019

Source: World Bank (2020).

South Africa's industrial sectors are the most energy intensive. A particularly significant amount of energy is consumed in industrial sectors linked to the production of energy-intensive commodities, including iron and steel, chemicals and petrochemicals, mining and quarrying and non-ferrous metals (Ratshomo and Nembahe, 2019: 24), which have historically benefitted from unsustainably cheap coal-based energy (Bell et al., 2018: 51). These resource-intensive sectors are not labour absorbing and have consequently locked South Africa on to an industrial path that is focused on energy and capital, and not labour. Today, energy unequivocally accounts for the highest cost of production, resulting in an uncompetitive cost base for industry.

South Africa's energy insecurity reinforces the need to fundamentally transform towards a low carbon pathway that delivers jobs, economic growth and social benefits. Promoting the development and adoption of renewable energy technologies is essential for building a new economic system (Söderholm, 2020: 1), which differs structurally from South Africa's carbon-intensive and coal-driven industrial economy.

As fossil fuel industries, infrastructure, rents and legacies reach the end of their historical cycles, energy should be a pivot for South Africa's industrial development strategies. The benefits derived from a shift from fossil fuel energy sources to renewable energy support the creation of new industrial value chains, and radically reconfigure existing mining and industrial complexes. The case for advancing the energy transition with renewable technologies is based on energy efficiency, reliability and increasing evidence of dramatic declines in the cost of key renewable energy sources (Mathews, 2015; IRENA, 2021: 28). The availability of cost-effective clean energy solutions will be a catalyst for supporting South Africa's industries, expanding productive capacity and increasing (cost) competitiveness.

Aligning industrial growth strategies with the energy transition requires the integration of green initiatives into strategic value chains (Ighbor, 2016), which have the potential to expand manufacturing capacity, create decent 'green jobs' and reduce the country's dependence on fossil fuels. The energy transition thus builds a new energy economy and system that becomes a mechanism for value creation, providing economic and society-wide benefits (Blumenschein et al., 2017: 7).

THE AFRICAN CONTINENTAL FREE TRADE AREA: A PATHWAY TO GREEN INDUSTRIALISATION

The energy transition and green industrialisation can be supported and promoted within the context of various frameworks. The African Continental Free Trade Area (AfCFTA) holds the promise for catalysing intra-Africa trade (by up to 60 per cent), creating a continental investment hub and a Pan-African approach to addressing the continent's socio-economic needs. In its current form, the AfCFTA also boosts prospects for environmental sustainability at scale. The free trade area should not be considered purely as the trade policy that it fundamentally is; rather, its scope means that it extends to become a mechanism that drives economic diversification and facilitates transformative industrialisation on the continent (Mkhabela, 2021). This includes the potential for energy exports and the development and expansion of renewable energy corridors.

Nearly half of Africa's population (approximately 600 million people) lack access to electricity (AfDB, 2019: 3) – and if energy is viewed as the engine of economic growth, this reality is costing the continent significantly. As the AfCFTA is progressively implemented, promoting green industries and clean energy will become an imperative for South Africa's growth. With primary energy demand expected to rise along with Africa's burgeoning urban population (driven largely by North Africa, Nigeria and South Africa) (IEA, 2019: 49), there is ground for prioritising energy generation from alternative sources.

Energy access for productive use is similarly low and constrained by electricity disruptions and technical losses. This could continue to constrain South Africa and the continent's industrial development ambitions. In about 60 per cent of African countries, fossil fuels and minerals make up more than a third of the export basket, and account for 80 per cent of the region's GDP (IEA, 2019: 171). This demonstrates both the continent's commodity dependence and its failure to capitalise on its resources. Cleaner, more efficient and affordable energy is fundamental for shaping an inclusive and sustainable development agenda on a continent plagued by unreliable power networks, high energy costs and low productive capacity.

The exponential growth of renewable energy will create demand for mineral resources and the manufacturing of clean energy technologies, such as platinum and chromium in South Africa, and cobalt, which is abundant in the Democratic Republic of Congo (IEA, 2019: 175). Trade in these strategic materials will be central for driving energy transitions, energy storage capacity and the manufacturing potential that this can generate at a local and continental level. Clean energy demand will further support the continent's insertion into global value chains.

The benefits of the AfCFTA will be dependent on creating conditions for enabling infrastructure and policies that support regional energy cooperation and create shared value within the broader framework of Africa's industrialisation.

Energy market integration

Increasing electricity cooperation and trade through regional power systems are well understood to be channels through which South Africa can take advantage of economies of scale, and increase renewable energy penetration in the region (Economic Consulting Associates, 2009). Although power pools have been established across the continent, they have often proved difficult to coordinate. Existing regional energy integration efforts and power pools have largely been constrained by insufficient infrastructure investment, and a lack of policy coordination and harmonisation of regulatory frameworks (Adeniran et al., 2021). In addition, the high capital costs of transmission interconnections across borders 'require strong co-ordination among two or more governments' and the perceived risks have often discouraged investments (IEA, 2019: 61).

Cross-border cooperation and trade across Africa's regional power pools, including the Southern African Power Pool (SAAP), which South Africa participates in, remain low and largely dominated by bilateral agreements (IEA, 2019: 60). There is a legacy of a political preference for bilateral, rather than regional, agreements (Medinilla et al., 2019: 3). In the 2019/20 financial year, energy traded in the bilateral market made up 78.6 per cent of energy traded in the SAAP, with the remainder traded on the competitive market (SAPP, 2020: 7). Given South Africa's dominance, the SAPP's generation mix is largely coal based (83 per cent), with an additional 14 per cent from hydro and only 2 per cent from solar. Tanzania, Malawi and Angola are all non-operating members of the SAPP due to transmission constraints. The SAPP is assessing the potential for renewables in the SAPP network, as well as regulatory, institutional and infrastructure gaps necessary for further integration (SAPP, 2020: 22). There are various interconnections under construction within southern African countries, but also with the East African Power Pool (EAPP). Similar efforts are underway to build the regulatory capacity and the transmission infrastructure in the SAAP and EAPP, to wheel power across borders in East Africa (IEA, 2019: 60).

Box 6.1: The Nordic Example

The Nordic electricity market (comprising Norway, Denmark, Sweden, Finland and Iceland) is cited as having a well-established tradition of cooperation and trade between national electricity systems. Established in 1993, the success of the Nordic electricity market rests on a strong political mandate, high levels of renewable energy integration, regional planning and operational transmission infrastructure (Flatabo et al., 2003). The Nordic countries succeeded in finding ways to complement their energy resources and technologies but, more importantly, they developed a coherent and integrated framework for electricity integration. This formed the basis for a common market structure (consisting of one market operator and five system operators with a regulatory agency). The Nordic market also demonstrates the possibilities of further integration with adjacent regional markets, given its proximity to a pan-European electricity market.

Lessons can also be drawn from the African continent. Since the 1970s, the Cahora Bassa project on the Zambezi River has demonstrated the levels of cooperation, political commitment and shared objectives required between Mozambique and South Africa. The availability of cheap power reduced pressure on South Africa's coal-fired plants and water resources, while positioning Mozambique as an electricity exporter in the largest hydropower facility in southern Africa (Economic Consulting Associates, 2009: 1–4). Similarly, mega hydroelectric, Grand Inga project, has the potential of 42 000MW of generating capacity, and is an opportunity for the Democratic Republic of the Congo to increase access to clean renewable energy and to support local economic activity, but also to supply markets across sub-Saharan Africa. Grand Inga has become a key project for several regional organisations including the African Union, Southern African Development Community (SADC), EAAP and Eskom. The project has also illustrated the challenges of achieving a just transition, and the need to balance socio-economic development objectives that directly impact local communities, with wider regional imperatives (Benoit, 2021).

The potential for regional energy integration within the AfCFTA provides an avenue for overcoming some of these bottlenecks. A single, larger market (of 1.3 billion consumers) provides greater incentive for private sector finance into the renewables market – strengthening the energy sector and interconnection of power systems, pooling of resources and increasing cross-border power trade. There is a strong economic case for cross-border interconnected 'green' grids that allow countries to tap into diverse sources of power (IEA, 2019: 61) through which areas with rich renewable energy resources and high generating capacity can connect to areas of high demand (ESI Africa, 2020). The option to deploy renewable energy solutions at a small scale allows energy-importing countries to exploit their natural resource endowment to generate sufficient low-cost energy locally, while exporting excess capacity (Govender, 2020).

This pan-continental sentiment is shared by the African Union Development Agency and New Partnership for Africa's Development (AUDA-NEPAD), who are developing an African power systems masterplan for generation and transmission. The masterplan aligns with the aspirations of AfCFTA to create a single electricity market that integrates all five power pools to create one of the world's largest continent-wide energy networks. This approach to creating a renewable energy corridor will require the integration of transport networks, ICT infrastructure and myriad industries. It will also require governments to institutionalise their planning processes and put appropriate policy frameworks in place.

Regional energy integration is attractive for a country like South Africa, with relatively advanced industrial structures and technological capabilities on the continent. South Africa's export basket shows its dependence on mineral and agricultural-based products (Figure 6.2). Mineral fuels (dominated by coal, petroleum oils and electrical energy) are also significant in South Africa's export composition. South Africa accounted for 27 per cent of intra-Africa trade in 2019 (Tralac, 2019: 2) and was the leading exporter of electrical energy. The opening up of markets and the potential for regional economies of scale create unique opportunities to promote renewable energy production and to foster a pro-export environment through which South Africa can trade in alternative energy products (such as solar, wind, hydrogen, geothermal and hydropower).

Regional integration further provides a more competitive energy landscape, which could create incentives to divert resources from unproductive fossil fuels to more competitively priced energy sources – accelerating the energy transition (Adeniran and Onyekwena, 2020: 8).

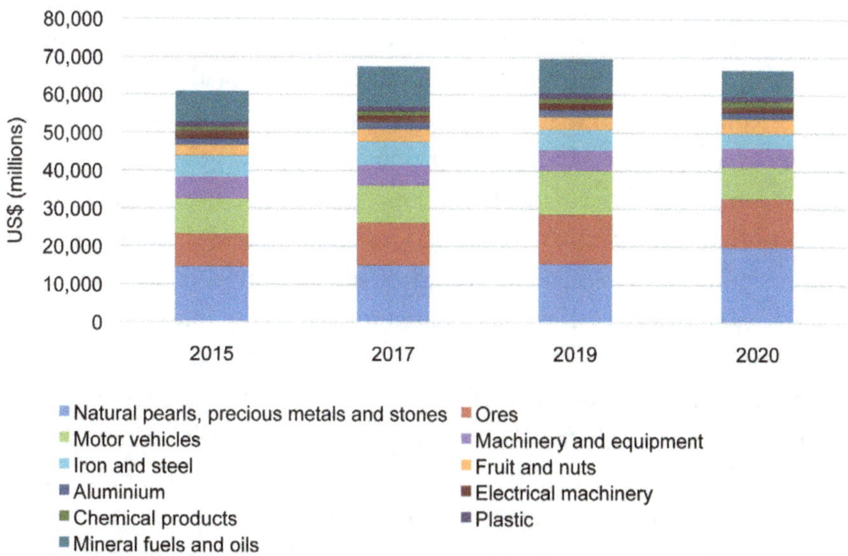

Figure 6.2: South Africa top exports, US$ millions

Source: ITC Trademap (2021)

Other dimensions of regional integration, including the free movement of people and capital, would be critical for enabling collaboration, and enhancing skills and knowledge across markets and specifically building capacity to adapt green technologies and innovations.

Many warn against AfCFTA not being a panacea for the continent's development challenges; if not underpinned by 'developmental regionalism that supports structural transformation and industrialisation' (Zalk, 2021), its success will be minimal. Any consideration of energy integration within a single continental market, and the benefits that could follow for South Africa, must take account of the politics to date of regional economic communities and market integration. At a SADC level, efforts to broaden regional integration through value chains and free trade have often been impeded by a lack of concrete actions and implementation at a regional level. South Africa has often pursued its short-term national interests (e.g., not agreeing to purchase electricity from Botswana's power plant Mmamabula), over the benefits of scale and scope associated with regional markets (Nkhonjera and Roberts, 2020: 153).

Of Africa's five power pools, the North African Power Pool (COMELEC) and SAPP are more advanced, while the West African Power Pool (WAPP) and EAAP are relatively underdeveloped. The lack of a historical champion that could lead regional cooperation seems to have played a significant role in constraining the progress of the West and East African power pools (Medinilla et al., 2019: 25). South Africa's political and hegemonic power has been central to regional trade integration to date and was similarly critical in initiating and sustaining the SAPP. The record of integration in many regions shows hegemons are viewed as essential for sustaining integration and power pooling.

As an economic hub and leading player in intra-Africa trade, South Africa will be crucial for building consensus around a unified and diversified African market (Komane, 2020). In pursuit of new value chains, manufacturing growth and renewable energy infrastructure, the South African government and industry alike will need to show political leadership and commitment to the AfCFTA – the benefits of which should, in principle, accrue to the region as a whole. South Africa would need to ensure that existing bilateral and multilateral agreements that dominate regional power trade do not serve to undermine the AfCFTA. 'With properly altered industrial policy, South Africa could lead the climate sensitive development discourse in Africa' (Komane, 2020), and this would facilitate South Africa's national and regional interests beyond the SADC level. As the AfCFTA gains political momentum, if South Africa pursues integration into a regional energy economy, it will need to consider the interdependencies between its own industrialisation and those of other (particularly smaller) African member states. Efforts to accelerate sustainable energy development and build stronger regional linkages should go beyond attracting private sector investment in renewables to supporting mutual cooperation in energy trade (e.g., through the integration of power grids), enabling regional infrastructure and knowledge diffusion (UNECA, 2020).

As well as individual nations, energy producers and national utilities are key participants and 'political champions' of power pools (Medinilla et al., 2019: 67). This plays into the politics of power production. The scope of South Africa's role in the SAAP has been reduced because of its domestic energy crisis and governance challenges. Despite Eskom's proposed capital expenditure over the next few years, the extent to which the utility can effectively orient itself as a 'champion' in the sub-region and continent could still be constrained by its liquidity position. Furthermore, with attempts to decentralise power, SADC is seeking to encourage and identify other key states to champion integration (in partnership with South Africa) (Louw-Vaudran, 2019: 2). Regional cooperation efforts would need to work around and within the politics of energy production, transmission and distribution in the context of Eskom and regional utilities more broadly. South Africa will have to clearly balance the trade-offs and complexities around meeting its own domestic needs, with feeding and tapping into regional markets.

Rethinking industrial policy to accelerate an energy transition

Industrial policy has for over a decade been a mechanism for allocating resources to priority sectors and enhancing labour capacity to alter the structure of South Africa's economy. Various iterations of the IPAP have focused on the development of strategic industries and sectors which enable the transition to high levels of value addition. This has included agro-processing, mineral beneficiation, automotive and 'green' industries. Despite the design and implementation of various policies, the post-apartheid state has largely failed to develop active industrial policy (Tregenna et al, 2021: 12) and has rather set the country on a path of deindustrialisation. South Africa's experience draws attention to the political economy dynamics underpinned by its historic system of accumulation (Ashman et al., 2013: 247). It further highlights the challenges of developing a coherent industrial strategy, which must entail a suite of policy instruments including productive capabilities, finance, technology and trade.

Global energy transition pathways and decarbonisation strategies have seen a combination of government-led policies and market-based approaches, with direct incentives offered to the private sector. Despite different models reflecting country-specific historical approaches (as in the case of China), there is sufficient evidence to suggest that deliberate government policy instruments are effective (Dell'Aquila et al., 2020: 248–249). Although in principle the strategic importance of South Africa's energy sector has meant it has always been supported by government intervention, existing industrial policies require revision. The role of the state in the energy sector is arguably even more legitimate in the context of climate change (Bordoff, 2021). South Africa's political economy and entrenched economic structures require that industrial policies (and not just market forces) support the transition to a green economy (Montmasson-Clair, 2020).

South Africa's strategy for green industries seeks to reverse its historic dependence on fossil fuels for energy, and simultaneously reduce GHG emissions (DTIC, 2018: 41). The IPAP recognises the potentially crippling impact this could have for industrial development and trade. It also recognises the opportunities for renewable energy generation. Efforts are underway, with the support of the Industrial Development Corporation (IDC) to fund energy-efficient industrial projects, and partnerships with local universities to support research and development of advanced materials in solar PV have also been established. Such collaborative efforts will continue to be essential for identifying the best applications for South Africa's mineral resources. Within its industrial policy, South

Africa identifies the value of mineral beneficiation for industrialisation, and strategic opportunity for South Africa in the hydrogen economy and energy storage technology – in lieu of energy efficiency and carbon reduction strategies (DTIC, 2018: 39).

While IPAP is not sufficiently aligned with a global economy that is increasingly decarbonising, the SAREM, along with a number of other industry-specific masterplans under development, provide new impetus for a medium- to long-term industrial strategy and action plan for South Africa (EE Publishers, 2020). Its emphasis on fostering a climate of collaboration that extends across ministries, the private sector, labour and communities is critical for breaking down silos, developing a multi-stakeholder plan of action and evidence-based policies for renewable energy. The masterplan addresses the importance of driving sustainable investment in renewable energy, identifying employment and opportunities for skills development and deepening industrial development. It recognises the renewable energy industry as central to not only rebuilding the economy but supporting catalytic growth through sector-wide linkages. The plan, along with policies to support it, will be crucial for developing capacity and investment in local manufacturing and for broader climate change objectives (Creamer, 2021a).

SAREM is also being developed within the broader context of South Africa's just transition and its shift away from coal to renewables, which should ensure that coal mining regions and communities are empowered with quality jobs and investments, generated in consultation with civil society, labour unions and industry players. This collaborative, bottom-up, iterative learning process is a different institutional configuration of industrial policy, one that is critical for a more sustainable growth path (Rodrik, 2020: 192). According to Aiginger and Rodrik (2020: 19), 'the contemporary conception and practice of industrial policy is much less about top-down incentives and much more about establishing a sustained collaboration between the public and private sectors around issues of productivity and social goals'. Moreover, the debate on industrial policy has evolved to consider how ecological impacts intersect with production systems.

The emphasis on employment is critical. Given the current context and stage of South Africa's (under)development, industrial policy will need to focus heavily on producing a sufficient number of jobs – productive and decent jobs. While the country has managed to build productive, export-oriented industries that are globally competitive, these have been concentrated amongst a small elite. The co-existence of high-value manufacturing jobs and low-skilled, informal jobs is a dualistic and entrenched structure within the economy (Rodrik and Sabel, 2019: 5). This dualism, which new technologies could aggravate, often exists with high levels of inequality, exclusion, and spatial and social segregation. Concerns about the environment and labour are central to shaping industrial policy in the context of disruptive political and technological change. This makes the hard and soft conditionalities of job creation critical, together with new priorities such as shifting from fossil fuel use or the development of green technologies for various sectors. Rodrik and Sabel (2019: 3) propose policies focused on upskilling all sections of the labour force, increasing productivity levels of existing jobs and supporting the creation of new jobs and firms.

With local content requirements that support supplier industries, the masterplan could position South Africa as a globally competitive producer of inputs required in renewable energy plants. This would include a value chain of critical mineral resource-based materials and components used to manufacture and assemble renewable energy technologies, such as solar PV, wind and battery storage (Creamer, 2021b). The industry could leverage productive capabilities developed in metal and mining industries, as well as synthetic fuels and chemicals, to exploit these opportunities. Multiplier effects could in turn support the country's broader industrialisation and employment drive (including ancillary and service-related jobs). SADC's green hydrogen initiative, as well as Sasol's repurposing of its facilities to drive large-scale green hydrogen capacity are both an opportunities to decarbonise key local energy intensive sectors, including transport and steel (Creamer, 2020; Sasol, 2021). This forms part of greening energy and capital intensive production processes in secondary industries, which is a critical element of structural transformation. The capability advantages that South Africa enjoys in aerospace (through Denel), can similarly be repurposed for renewable energy manufacturing. Leveraging special economic zones also has the potential to unlock the market and establish export-oriented hubs for clean hydrogen.

The ASEZ formally designated in 2018 is an example of a novel industrial policy aimed at leapfrogging to a production regime that supports the development of green technologies and economic activities (Grant et al., 2019: 4). A number of strategies have been implemented in the ASEZ, as a Special Greentech Economic Zone, aimed at getting it established as a manufacturing and supplier hub of renewable technology components (including inverter parts, aluminium structures, wind tower, PV, green building materials and electrical component manufacturers) (Green Cape, 2019: 9). This includes seeking foreign investment for these targeted products and services. Importantly, a key driver of this initiative was profoundly political, with the Western Cape government demonstrating its political will to support a structural transition to a greener economy (Grant et al., 2019: 5).

The special economic zone (SEZ) has attracted about R700 million in investments and created over 300 direct jobs in Atlantis (Green Cape, 2019: 3). Beyond its potentially transformative local impact, the SEZ also seeks to integrate itself in the wider regional economy, through the development of value chains (this is a central element of the AfCFTA). SADC structures including the SAPP, the Regional Energy Regulators' Association (RERA) and the SADC Centre for Renewable Energy and Energy Efficiency (SACREEE) (Grant et al., 2019: 7) are at the forefront of driving growth and scaling renewables through a regional market.

South Africa's green (export) industries and capabilities are still confined to a niche and are at a nascent stage that will require supportive policies to compete on international markets and generate the mass jobs required locally. Despite this potential, the Atlantis SEZ is also an example of the challenges that accompany the expansion of green industries, including policy uncertainty regarding the REIPPPP and local content requirements on the one hand (Burger, 2021), and local concerns around the quality of jobs produced and the level of socially inclusivity, on the other. Growth in the Western Cape province is still driven by non-green sectors given the durability of South Africa's existing production regime (Grant et al., 2019: 9) which is entrenched in the minerals-energy complex (Fine and Rustomjee, 2000). The DCD Towers in the Coega Industrial Development Zone – the first upstream wind turbine manufacturer, which began production in 2014 – is an example of a local manufacturing and engineering company 'transporting' its capabilities (in mining and rail) to other sectors to support industrialisation linked to green energy investments. However, DCD Towers stopped operating in 2019 due to Eskom's delays in signing purchasing power agreements. This meant there was no commercial guarantee of independently produced power and therefore no market for DCD's products (Fekisi, 2019).

There is a delicate balancing required between a just green transition, social transformation and international competitiveness. The new regional governance and trade framework under the AfCFTA is gaining traction within this changing context of industrial development, and South Africa's industrial policy will need to be embedded within this paradigm. In essence, a new energy system should be the cornerstone of South Africa's industrial policy and industrialis ation, with explicit and deliberate energy policies intended to drive structural change. Moreover, as a long-term endeavour, an inclusive transition requires a transformational shift from traditional policy making and political settlements (Montmasson-Clair, 2020), including at a regional level. As alluded to above, patterns of integration between South Africa and its regional trading and investment partners have often not been based on industrialisation capabilities (Langa et al., 2018: 41). Within the framework of a new energy economy, building regional capabilities must be a key component of South Africa's industrialisation strategy.

As Nkhonjera and Roberts (2020: 155) argue:

> A nationalist approach is incompatible with the [regional] requirements of deepening integration. Moving into the 2020s, the demands of regional industrialisation require regional cooperation in policy making and implementation to build value chains and industrial clusters across borders. This requires facing the trade-off between a narrowly framed industrial policy

for South African industry with properly resourced policies and institutions for industrialisation at the regional level.

To maximise the benefits of the energy transition, South Africa's energy mix must be altered to scale the uptake of renewables in a way that will align with its objectives of sustainable industrial development. Policies for an energy transition will need to be built on green jobs with a framework for reskilling workers from the phasing out of 'old energy' industries (Semelane et al., 2020); support for the development of local manufacturing through the localisation of targeted components; diffusion of new green technologies; diversifying supply chains; and scaling existing projects and programmes (IRENA, 2020: 96–113). The inclusion and targeting of socially and economically disadvantaged groups is critical for South Africa's energy transition. There is huge potential for South Africa to attract private and public investment into renewable projects, linked to industrial development and labour-absorbing sectors (Bulbuilia, 2021), as has been done in Morocco and other countries. Morocco provides a good framework for building linkages between energy and industrial policies (Box 6.2). This has expanded the market for renewables and the development of local capabilities (Altenburg and Assmann, 2017: 163).

Box 6.2: Green energy policies in the Middle East and North Africa: Lessons from Morocco

The Middle East and North Africa (MENA) region recognised the vital role that renewable energy technologies could play in driving inclusive industrial growth. In 2011, Morocco met over 90 per cent of its energy needs through fossil fuel imports. Today, 33 per cent of its energy mix is from renewable sources. Green industrial policy was viewed as a necessity for Morocco's economy, which was characterised by high youth unemployment, a lack of economic diversification and uncompetitive industrial sectors.

Morocco's government committed to diversifying its energy mix and 'linking solar and wind electricity generation projects to industrial development, employment creation and competitiveness'

(Altenburg and Assmann, 2017: 154). Not only did the country deploy renewable technologies; it also leveraged them to create new sectors and develop skills. Morocco's green industrial policy consisted of three key elements: market creation, supply side measures and an integrated strategy for industrial development.

Regarding market creation, a favourable legal framework (specifically a solar energy strategy) was critical for creating a market for renewable energy. This was supported with a commitment of substantial state resources and the establishment of a separate implementing agency responsible for coordinating bidding processes for solar projects.

Supply-side measures focused on developing industrial development opportunities from investments in renewables. Because existing capabilities in solar technologies were low, policies were required to build linkages between industry, technology providers, and local universities. Furthermore, cooperation with international agencies facilitated the establishment of solar industrial clusters. Lead firms were leveraged to drive supplier development programmes and knowledge transfer, in support of small and medium enterprises.

The success of Morocco's green industrial policies was underpinned by an integrated strategy for industrial development. This not only required a 'multi-stakeholder' governance process but the streamlining and coordination of various initiatives towards a national vision of industrial and energy development. Notably, Morocco prioritised a bottom-up approach which served to maximise the impact on its local economy.

Source: Altenburg and Assmann, 2017

South Africa is well positioned to leverage its existing socio-economic structures, historic industries and strong technological capabilities built in legacy industries such as mining, metals and machinery (Kaziboni et al., 2019: 1) to localise socio-economic development and build export-oriented industries. Industrial policies will need to support the development of production ecosystems of shared value where lead firms facilitate SME value chain upgrading around renewable energy technologies (Creamer, 2021c). As described, there is also potential for lateral migration of technological capabilities into new energy sectors and value chains.

Industrial policies will have to reflect the transformative dynamics of a new energy sector. A new industrial policy framework will encompass new policies and instruments. It will channel funds towards innovation in new green sectors (Hochstetler, 2020: 79) and create new efficient production systems and technologies that stimulate demand for cleaner products and services. South Africa's industrial policy will also need to pay more attention to greening existing activities irrespective of the nature of the sector or location (Mwangi, 2021). This will demand value chain-specific policies (in agriculture, for example). As a major polluter, Sasol, for instance, is committed to reaching net zero by 2050 (in line with the global energy targets). Its decarbonisation targets include a 30 per cent reduction in GHG emissions for its energy and international chemicals businesses by 2030, as well as increasing renewables in its energy mix (Sasol, 2021: 1). Sectoral initiatives will need to be accompanied by effective monitoring systems that track clean energy progress and hold organisations to account.

CONCLUSION

This chapter unpacked the potential linkage between energy and industrial policy as a mechanism to transition from the minerals energy complex towards an industrial framework based on clean energy and production, decent work, and increasing productivity and value addition.

The energy transition is an opportunity to re-energise debates on sustainable development. This must be fully supported by decisive policies and strategies that are integrated with a broader structural transformation agenda because low carbon power will form the foundation of South Africa's future industrial development path. An integrated strategy for industrial development will require coherent policies that 'target both the creation of a sizeable market for renewables and the development of a local industry' (Altenburg and

Assmann, 2017: 162).

Leveraging South Africa's natural resource capital to leapfrog to a new development path requires complementary investments, an enabling regulatory environment, targeted policies and decisive efforts to localise solutions that are inclusive. The very notion of a just transition considers measures that diversify economies, maximises jobs and ensures the protection and inclusion of socially vulnerable groups (Just Transition Centre, 2020: 13). Emphasis must be placed on the type of jobs advocated for by unions, which are about decent, quality jobs in the context of a green economy. For an industry that is both labour intensive and highly scalable in terms of energy access, the development of renewables will need to be informed by a unified message on a green economy that meets climate change commitments and socio-economic transformation.

Capturing the benefits of an energy transition will require far greater policy coordination at various levels (energy, economics, environmental, industrial and trade). It will also require an alignment of local, provincial and national government strategies for implementing a renewable energy-based industrialisation. The consequences of policy incoherence can be seen in the implementation of the REIPPPP, and the rather weak linkages created with industrial ecosystems. A policy that is truly comprehensive in terms of its co-objectives of clean energy and industrialisation will also consider the way supply chains are organised. This would entail unpacking what and how minerals are extracted and used; what new production regimes can be established; what market opportunities can be exploited; and what value-adding employment opportunities can be created from these processes.

The low level of power system integration on the continent can be enhanced through the Continental Free Trade Area and environment-friendly renewable technologies. The AfCFTA provides scope to pursue regional strategies and a more efficient allocation of energy resources, which create a conducive environment for investment and trade in energy across Africa's markets (Papaefstratiou, 2019; Energy Capital & Power, 2020). South Africa is strategically positioned to maximise the considerable socio-economic benefits of an energy transition, based on a new energy system. Drawing on renewable energy resources at a continental level will go a long way towards addressing deficits in energy generation and distribution, and unmet demand across Africa's economies. Green industrial policies offer clear opportunities for the energy economy and for the harnessing of industrial development opportunities.

South Africa's ability (or inability) to leverage renewable energy as a way of fueling sustainable growth will depend on how well it articulates the link between renewable energy policies and industrial development plans at national, sub-regional and continental levels. With that said, this paper argues that South Africa's energy transition and industrialisation agenda needs to pay special attention to underlying political economy dynamics, both in terms of entrenched domestic socio-economic structures and in cooperation with the rest of the continent. Any efforts at real transformation will need to capture the deep and complex social, political and economic context within which the energy transition is located. A multi-stakeholder governance process (that prioritises building coalitions with industry, research and civil society) adds a layer of complexity to this context, due to what has been characterised as the fragmentation of the South African state (Kaziboni et al., 2019: 36).

Research to further deepen our understanding of the political economy of regional (energy) integration in the context of green growth is essential. Although South Africa, and the continent at large, share the same need to diversify their energy systems and economies, politics and national interests tend to limit the scope and potential for integrated markets. This, in turn, reduces policy space and results in policy implementation gaps and missed opportunities for true regionalism.

REFERENCES

Adeniran, A. and Onyekwena, C. 2020. 'Accelerating green energy transition in Africa through regional integration'. South African Institute of International Affairs, Policy Brief 216.

Adeniran, A., Onyekwena, C., Osakwe, S. and Iheonu, C. 26 April 2021. 'How can the AfCFTA improve energy efficiency and access in Africa'. International Institute for Sustainable Development (IISD), https://sdg.

iisd.org/commentary/guest-articles/how-can-the-afcfta-improve-energy-efficiency-and-access-in-africa/, accessed 20 April 2021.

African Development Bank (AfDB). 2019. 'Light up and power Africa'. https://www.afdb.org/sites/default/files/2019/07/05/high_5_light_up_africa.pdf, accessed 5 May 2021.

Altenburg, T. and Assmann, C. (eds). 2017. 'Green industrial policy: Concept, policies, country experiences'. Partnership for Action on Green Economy (PAGE), Geneva, Bonn: UN Environment; German Development Institute / Deutsches Institut für Entwicklungspolitk (DIE).

Andreoni, A. and Tregenna, F. 2018. 'Stuck in the middle: Premature industrialisation and industrial policy'. Centre for Competition, Regulation and Economic Development and the SARChI Chair in Industrial Development, Working Paper 11/2018, Johannesburg.

Anthony, C. 30 October 2018. 'Forging a new energy path', in *The Future of Energy: The difficult path to a growing economy built on clean power,* 8–10, https://www.intellidex.co.za/wp-content/uploads/2018/11/ENERGY-PaGES_2018-410x275_WEB.pdf, accessed 30 May 2021.

Aiginger, K. and Rodrik, D. 2020. 'Rebirth of industrial policy and an agenda for the twenty-first century'. *Journal of Industry, Competition and Trade*, 20, 189–207.

Ashman, S., Fine, B. and Newman, S. 2013. 'Systems of accumulation and the evolving South African MEC', in Fine, B., Saraswati, J. and Tavasci, D. (eds), *Beyond the Developmental State: Industrial policy in the twenty-first century*. London: Pluto Press, 245–267.

Baigrie, B. 5 July 2021. 'Power struggle: The 100MW exemption is likely to be a monumental step towards privatisation–not necessarily for the good'. *Daily Maverick*, https://www.dailymaverick.co.za/article/2021-07-05-power-struggle-the-100mw-exemption-is-likely-to-be-a-monumental-step-towards-privatisation-not-necessarily-for-the-good/, accessed 20 July 2021.

Baker, L., Newell, P. and Phillips, J. 2014. 'The political economy of energy transitions: The case of South Africa.' *New Political Economy,* 19(6), 791–818.

Bazilian, M., Cuming, V. and Kenyon, T. 2020. 'Local content rules for renewables projects don't always work'. *Energy Strategy Reviews*, 32, 1–10.

Bell, J., Goga, S., Mondliwa, P. and Roberts, S. 2018. 'Structural transformation in South Africa: Moving towards a smart, open economy'. Centre for Competition, Regulation and Economic Development Working Paper No. 9/2018, Johannesburg.

Benoit, P. 21 June 2021. 'The Grand Inga Project: Green hydrogen, equity and ethics'. ESI Africa, https://www.esi-africa.com/industry-sectors/future-energy/the-grand-inga-project-green-hydrogen-equity-and-ethics/, accessed 9 October 2021.

Blumenschein, F., Brandi, C., Kraemer, A., Carin, B., Flores, R. et al. 21 March 2017. 'Green shift to sustainability: Co-benefits and Impacts of energy transformation on resource industries, trade, growth, and taxes.' G20 Insights, https://www.g20-insights.org/wp-content/uploads/2017/04/G20_T20Insight_Resources_170424-1.pdf, accessed 1 May 2021.

Bordoff, J. 15 March 2021. 'The time for green industrial policy is now'. Center on Global Energy Policy, https://www.energypolicy.columbia.edu/research/op-ed/time-green-industrial-policy-now, accessed 4 June 2021.

Bulbulia, T. 3 June 2021. 'South Africa's just transition must accommodate myriad of considerations'. *Engineering News*, https://www.engineeringnews.co.za/article/south-africas-just-transition-must-accommodate-myriad-of-considerations-2021-06-03, accessed 4 June 2021.

Burger, S. 11 June 2021. 'DTIC says to resolve ASEZ challenges'. *Engineering News*, https://www.engineeringnews.co.za/article/dtic-says-to-resolve-atlantis-sez-challenges-2021-06-11, accessed 20 July 2021.

Calitz, J. and Wright, J. 2019. 'Statistics of utility-scale solar PV, wind and CSP in South Africa in 2018'. CSIR Energy Centre, Pretoria.

Creamer, T. 2020.'Green hydrogen study integrating SADC ahead of trillion dollar market emergency'. https://www.engineeringnews.co.za/article/green-hydrogen-study-integrating-sadc-ahead-of-trillion-dollar-market-emergence-2020-09-23, accessed 04 May 2021.

Creamer, T. 1 March 2021a. 'De Ruyter urges greater industrial policy integration with renewables roll-out.' *Mining Weekly*, https://www.miningweekly.com/article/de-ruyter-urges-greater-industrial-policy-integration-with-renewables-roll-out-2021-03-01, accessed 30 April 2021.

Creamer, T. 8 April 2021b. 'Local content rules for PV modules posing challenges for emergency solar projects'. Engineering News, https://www.engineeringnews.co.za/article/local-content-rules-for-pv-modules-posing-challenges-for-emergency-solar-projects-2021-04-08, accessed 20 July 2021.

Creamer, T. 8 June 2021c. 'Masterplan to position South Africa as globally significant renewables manufacturer'. *Engineering News*, https://www.engineeringnews.co.za/article/masterplan-to-position-south-africa-as-globally-significant-renewables-manufacturer-2021-06-08, accessed 28 July 2021.

Dell'Aquila, M., Atzori, D. and Stroe, O.R. 2020. 'The role of policy design and market forces to achieve an effective energy transition: A comparative analysis between the UK and Chinese models', in Hafner, M. and Tagliapietra, S. (eds), *The Geopolitics of the Global Energy Transition*. Switzerland: Springer, 227–257.

Department of Energy (DoE). 2015. 'State of renewable energy in South Africa'. http://www.energy.gov.za/files/media/Pub/State-of-Renewable-

Energy-in-South-Africa.pdf, accessed 23 October 2021.

Department of Environmental Affairs (DEA). 2012. 'National Climate Change Response White Paper'. https://www.gov.za/sites/default/files/gcis_document/201409/nationalclimatechangeresponsewhitepaper0.pdf, accessed 10 August 2021.

Department of Mineral Resources and Energy (DMRE). 2019. 'Integrated Resource Plan 2019'. http://www.energy.gov.za/IRP/2019/IRP-2019.pdf, accessed 13 August 2021.

Department of Mineral Resources and Energy (DMRE). 2018. 'White Paper on Energy Policy'. https://www.gov.za/sites/default/files/gcis_document/201409/whitepaperenergypolicy19980.pdf, accessed 20 May 2021.

Department of Mineral Resources and Energy (DMRE). 2003. 'White Paper on Renewable Energy Policy'. https://www.gov.za/sites/default/files/gcis_document/201409/261691.pdf, accessed 1 October 2021.

Department of Trade, Industry and Competition (DTIC). 2018. 'Industrial Policy Action Plan 2018/19-2020/21: Economic sectors, employment and infrastructure development cluster'. https://www.gov.za/sites/default/files/gcis_document/201805/industrial-policy-action-plan.pdf, accessed 15 August 2021.

Department of Trade, Industry and Competition (DTIC). Undated. 'Green industries'. http://www.thedtic.gov.za/sectors-and-services-2/industrial-development/green-industries/, accessed 4 June 2021.

Eberhard, A. and Naude, R. 2017. 'The South African Renewable Energy IPP Procurement Programme: Review, lessons learned and proposals to reduce transaction costs'. Graduate School of Business, University of Cape Town, https://www.gsb.uct.ac.za/files/EberhardNaude_REIPPPPReview_2017_1_1.pdf, accessed 23 October 2021.

EE Publishers. 16 July 2020. 'SA Renewable Energy Masterplan (SAREM)'. https://www.ee.co.za/wp-content/uploads/2020/07/SAREM.pdf, accessed 29 July 2021.

Economic Consulting Associates. 2009. 'The Potential of Regional Power Sector Integration: South African Power Pool Transmission and Trading Case Study'. Energy Sector Management Assistance Program (ESMAP) brief note 004/10. World Bank, Washington, DC.

Economic Consulting Associates. 2009. 'The Potential of Regional Power Sector Integration: Cahora Bassa Generation Case Study'. Energy Sector Management Assistance Program (ESMAP), London.

Energy Capital & Power. 20 October 2020. 'Here's to a modern Africa of Continental Free Trade and Energy Access'. https://energycapitalpower.com/heres-to-a-modern-africa-of-continental-free-trade-and-energy-access/, accessed 8 May 2021.

ESI Africa. 30 July 2020. 'The benefits of cross-border renewable energy trading.'

ESI Africa, https://www.esi-africa.com/industry-sectors/transmission-and-distribution/the-benefits-of-cross-border-renewable-energy-trading/, accessed 30 May 2021.

Fine, B. and Rustomjee, Z. 2000. 'The political economy of South Africa: From minerals energy complex to industrialisation'. *Journal of the International African Institute*, 70(1), 161–162.

Fekisi, L. 19 April 2019. 'Uncertainty over renewable energy results in job losses at wind turbine company'. *SABC*, https://www.sabcnews.com/sabcnews/uncertainty-over-renewable-energy-results-in-job-losses-at-wind-turbine-company/, accessed 9 October 2021.

Flatabo, N., Doorman, G., Grande, O., Randen, H. and Wangensteen, I. 2003. 'Experience with the Nord Pool Design and Implementation'. *IEEE Transactions on Power Systems*, 18(2), 541–547.

Govender, N. 9 November 2020. 'Renewable energy's role in rebuilding our economy'. *Engineering News*, https://www.engineeringnews.co.za/article/renewable-energys-role-in-rebuilding-our-economy-2020-11-09/rep_id:4136, accessed 8 May 2021.

Grant, R., Carmody, P. and Murphy, J. 2019. 'South Africa's green transition? The case of Atlantis Greentech Special Zone'. *The Journal of Modern African Studies*, 58(2), 189–211. doi:10.1017/S0022278X20000208.

Green Cape. 2020. 'Background to the South African Renewable Energy Masterplan'. Green Cape, Cape Town.

Green Cape. 2019. 'Atlantis Special Economic Zone for Green Technologies Annual Report 2018/19'. https://www.greencape.co.za/assets/Atlantis_SEZ_single_FA_web1.pdf, accessed 19 July 2021.

Hochstetler, K. 2020. 'States, markets and energy transition: Good industrial policy?' in Hochstetler, K. (ed.), *Political Economies of Energy Transition: Wind and solar power in Brazil and South Africa*. Cambridge: Cambridge University Press, 79–131.

Ighbor, K. 2016. 'A green path to industrialisation: The only viable option for Africa's continued development'. *Africa Renewal*, https://www.un.org/africarenewal/magazine/august-2016/green-path-industrialization, accessed 8 May 2021.

International Energy Agency (IEA). 2019. Africa Energy Outlook 2019. https://iea.blob.core.windows.net/assets/2f7b6170-d616-4dd7-a7ca-a65a3a332fc1/Africa_Energy_Outlook_2019.pdf, accessed 13 April 2021.

International Renewable Energy Agency (IRENA). 2021. *World Energy Transitions Outlook: 1.5 °C Pathway*. Abu Dhabi: International Renewable Energy Agency. https://www.irena.org/publications/2021/Jun//media/E39E2962B96D489BBBB65DB5112DA1F2.ashx, accessed 12 October 2021.

International Renewable Energy Agency (IRENA). 2020. *The Post-COVID Recovery: An agenda for resilience, development and equality*. Abu Dhabi: International Renewable Energy Agency. https://www.irena.org/

publications/2020/Jun/Post-COVID-Recovery, accessed 23 October 21.

ITC Trademap. 2021. 'List of products exported by South Africa,' ITC Trademap website, https://www.trademap.org/Index.aspx, accessed 23 October 2021.

Just Transition Centre. 2020. 'Just transition in the international development cooperation context'. Just Transition Centre, Brussels.

Kaziboni, L. and Stern, M. 2021. 'The impact of local content policies on South Africa: Drawing lessons from foreign investors experience of the PPPFA and REIP4'. Paper for the TIPS Forum 2021, 2–3 August.

Kaziboni, L., Mondliwa, P. and Nkhonjera, M. 2019. 'The role of lead firms in the development of production ecosystems in process equipment and aerospace'. Centre for Competition, Regulation and Economic Development Working Paper 7/2019.

Komane, N. 2020. 'South African Trade and the African Continental Free Trade Agreement (AfCFTA)'. Institute for Global Dialogue, https://www.igd.org.za/infocus/12122-south-african-trade-and-the-african-continental-free-trade-agreement-afcfta, accessed 21 October 2021.

Kraemer, A., Carin, B., Gruenig, M., Blumenschein, F., Flores, R. et al. 21 March 2017. 'Green shift to sustainability: Co-benefits & impacts of energy transformation on resource industries, trade, growth, and taxes'. G20 Insights, https://www.g20-insights.org/wp-content/uploads/2017/04/G20_T20Insight_Resources_170424-1.pdf, accessed 1 May 2021.

Langa, E, Mondliwa, P. and Nkhonjera, M. 2018. 'Maintaining and building capabilities in capital equipment and related industries in Mozambique and South Africa'. Centre for Competition, Regulation and Economic Development Working Paper 1/2018.

Louw-Vaudran, L. 2019. 'Power and influence: Identifying champions of change in SADC'. Institute for Security Studies, Policy Brief 124.

Mathews, J. 9 December 2015. 'New renewables can now play important role in industrial development'. *Energy Post*, https://energypost.eu/new-renewables-can-now-play-important-role-industrial-development/, accessed 30 April 2021.

Medinilla, A., Buyiers, B. and Karaki, K. 2019. 'African power pools: Regional energy, national power'. Political economy dynamics of regional organisations in Africa (PEDRO), Discussion Paper No. 244.

Merten, M. 10 June 2021. 'Increase to 100MW embedded generation threshold will give "oomph" to South African economy, says Ramaphosa'. *Daily Maverick*, https://www.dailymaverick.co.za/article/2021-06-10-increase-to-100mw-embedded-generation-threshold-will-give-oomph-to-south-african-economy-says-ramaphosa/, accessed 19 July 2021.

Mkhabela, V. 20 April 2021. 'African Continental Free Trade Area needs an action plan to advance transformative industrialisation'. *Daily Maverick*, https://www.dailymaverick.co.za/opinionista/2021-04-20-african-continental-free-trade-area-needs-an-action-plan-to-advance-transformative-industrialisation/, accessed 30 April 2021.

Montmasson-Clair, G. 31 August 2020. 'Switching to green economy a holistic shift across entire society: A just transition must be at the core of the process and sustainability embedded in the state's industrial policy'. *Business Live*, https://www.businesslive.co.za/bd/opinion/2020-08-31-switching-to-green-economy-a-holistic-shift-across-entire-society/, accessed 30 May 2021.

Mwangi, C. 22 April 2021. 'Africa's green future: Rethinking industrial policy post COVID-19 pandemic'. Future Africa Forum, https://futureafricaforum.org/2021/04/22/africas-green-future-re-thinking-industrial-policy-post-covid-19-pandemic/, accessed 30 April 2021.

Nkhonjera, M. and Roberts, S. 2020. 'Regional integration and industrial development in Southern Africa: Where does South Africa stand?', in Bradlow, D. and Sidiropolous, E. (eds). *Values, Interests and Power: South African foreign policy in uncertain times*. Pretoria: PULP, 140–159.

Nomjana, L. 18 February 2020. 'REIPPP comes of age'. Future Growth, https://futuregrowth.co.za/insights/reippp-comes-of-age/, accessed 1 May 2021.

Papaefstratiou, D. 27 August 2019. 'What the AfCFTA means for the energy sector'. *Mining Review Africa*, https://www.miningreview.com/energy/african-continental-free-trade-area-energy-sector/, accessed 1 May 2021.

Power Futures South Africa. 2019. 'Information Brief: South Africa's Integrated Resource Plan'. *Power Futures*, https://www.powerfutures.org, accessed 30 May 2021.

Ratshomo, K. and Nembahe, R. 2019. 'The South African Energy Sector Report'. Department of Energy (DoE), Pretoria.

Rodrik, D. and Sabel, K. 2019. 'Building a good jobs economy'. Harvard Kennedy School Working Paper.

Sasol. 2021. 'Climate change report for the year ended 30 June 2021.' Sasol Limited.

Sasol. 6 October 2021. 'Sasol announces lead role in feasibility study for the Boegoebaai green hydrogen project'. https://www.sasol.com/media-centre/media-releases/sasol-announces-lead-role-feasibility-study-boegoebaai-green-hydrogen, accessed 9 October 2021.

Schepper, S. 2020. 'The Eskom Transmission Development Plan (TDP) 2021–2030'. www.eskom.co.za/news/Pages/2020Oct20.aspx, accessed 8 October 2021.

Semelane, S., Mkhwebane, E., Synman, A., Letete, T., Nhlapo, Z. et al. 2020. 'A just energy transition in South Africa: Socio-economic needs and the positive impacts of a future low-carbon economy'. RES4Africa Foundation, Rome.

Slater, D. 23 February 2021. 'Just energy transition remains priority to ensure sustainable future'. *Engineering News*, https://www.engineeringnews.co.za/article/just-energy-transition-remains-priority-to-ensure-sustainable-future-2021-02-23/rep_id:4136, accessed 28 April 2021.

Söderholm, P. 2020. 'The green economy transition: The challenges of technological change for sustainability'. *Sustainable Earth*, 3(1), 1–11.

Southern African Power Pool (SAPP). 2019. 'Annual report 2019/20'. http://www.sapp.co.zw/sites/default/files/SAPP%20ANNUAL%20REPORT%202019.pdf, accessed 7 October 2021.

Tena, N. 30 April 2021. 'New study in support of South Africa's energy reform'. *ESI Africa*, https://www.esi-africa.com/industry sectors/research-and-development/new-study-in-support-of-south-africas-energy-reform/, accessed 1 May 2021.

Tralac. 2019. 'Summary of intra-Africa trade 2019'. https://www.tralac.org/documents/publications/trade-data-analysis/3982-summary-intra-africa-trade2019/file.html#:~:text=Of%20the%20US%241.8%20billion,from%20non%2DECOWAS%20African%20countries.&text=South%20Africa%3A%20Between%202018%20and,4%25%20and%2012%25%20respectively, accessed 19 July 2010.

Tregenna, F., Ewinyu, A, Oqubay, A and Valodia, I. 2021. 'Challenges and complexities of the South African economy'. SARChI Industrial Development Working Paper 2021-02.

United Nations Economic Commission for Africa (UNECA). 10 December 2020. 'How AfCFTA can help solar power penetration in Africa'. https://www.uneca.org/, accessed 1 May 2021.

United Nations Economic Commission for Africa (UNECA). 2016. 'Greening Africa's industrialisation: Economic Report on Africa'. United Nations Economic Commission for Africa, Addis Ababa.

World Bank. 2020. World Bank World Development Indicators. https://data.worldbank.org/indicator/NV.IND.MANF.ZS?locations=ZA&year_high_desc=true, accessed 15 May 2021.

Yelland, C. 17 December 2020. 'Energy policy in South Africa: Are changes finally coming?'. *ESI Africa,* https://www.esi-africa.com/industry-sectors/generation/energy-policy-in-south-africa-are-changes-finally-coming/, accessed 8 May 2021.

Zalk, N. 23 April 2021. 'How Africa should approach trade and industrialisation'. Project Syndicate, https://www.project-syndicate.org/commentary/african-free-trade-area-ignores-limited-capacity-by-nimrod-zalk-1-2021-04?barrier=accesspaylog, accessed 30 April 2021.

SEVEN

South Africa's smoke signals for financing the just energy transition

CHANTAL NAIDOO

INTRODUCTION

IMPLEMENTING THE PARIS AGREEMENT (2015) implies a critical but inconvenient truth: the global economy requires simultaneous creative and disruptive processes to shift total consumption and production systems towards low emission and climate-resilient development. Such reality is evident in the urgent calls for energy and transport systems to turn away from fossil fuels towards cleaner options. For example, the 2020 edition of the World Economic Situation and Prospects Report acknowledges that meeting growing energy demands can only be achieved through 'a dramatic shift in the energy mix', which reduces harmful greenhouse gas emissions (Holland, 2020: 68). The creative and disruptive forces necessary to bring about such systemic shifts represent a volatile and unpredictable context, particularly for the financial community – as it generates a financing context where uncertainty is the only certainty. Transitions challenge the traditional way finance engages (Naidoo, 2019; Levin and Lowitt, 2021).

As governments around the world adopt policies to practically achieve the goals of the Paris Agreement, such uncertainty and disruptive effects become unavoidable. Implementing countries' Nationally Determined Contributions (NDC), adaptation strategies and more recent shifts towards net zero targets by over 137 countries between 2040 and 2060 all signal the onset of significant social, economic and environmental disruptions over the next decade. The changes are inevitable, based on the sombre evidence in the 6th Assessment Report of the Intergovernmental Panel on Climate Change (IPCC). The report warns that 'it is unequivocal that human influence has warmed the atmosphere, ocean and land. Widespread and rapid changes in the atmosphere, ocean and cryosphere and biosphere have occurred' (IPCC, 2021: 6). The scientific evidence adds to the chilling social and economic vulnerabilities laid bare by the COVID-19 pandemic, particularly the limited resilience of global systems and leadership to absorb systemic shocks since March 2020 (Allen et al., 2020).

Global public and private climate finance flow for 2019 ranged between US$608–622 billion, and is still deemed wholly inadequate to address major systemic shifts. Studies show that energy systems require over US$1.6 – 3.8 trillion through to 2050; transport systems require US$467 billion per year; and critical adaptation investment requires US$180 billion per year of climate finance flow (Macquarie et al., 2020). These estimates may be under-represented, particularly for developing country needs, as the amounts mainly relate to new investment costs with limited consideration of the social, policy and transition costs. Developing country parties to the UN climate negotiations are calling for a new goal for climate finance, to make available US$500 billion between 2020 and 2024 (V-20, 2021).

South Africa joins its developing country peers in publicly expressing its need for higher levels of climate finance to support its energy transition. Eskom requires at least US$11 billion (R140 billion) in concessional finance, over the next five years (2021–2025), to accelerate decarbonisation (Joubert, 2019). These levels of demand for specifically 'concessional' international climate finance are significantly higher than the US$2 billion per year currently accessed by South

Africa (DFFE, 2021).

The chapter reflects on the phenomena of climate finance as offered by multilateral development agencies, specialist climate funds and bilateral development agencies, and their potential role in supporting South Africa's aspiration for a just and inclusive energy transition. This chapter first engages on the nexus of climate, sustainability and finance; then the impacts of COVID-19 on climate finance, and finally explores South Africa's recent aspirations for climate finance to support a just energy transition. The chapter concludes by reflecting on policy and practice-related considerations relating to the strategic use of international climate finance.

NEXUS OF FINANCE WITH SUSTAINABILITY AND CLIMATE CHANGE

The seeds for what we now call 'climate finance' trace back to the sustainable finance movement triggered by the Brundtland Commission in the late 1980s. The Commission was sponsored by the United Nations and was set up to explore the connections between social equity, economic growth and environmental problems. It first introduced the concept of 'sustainable development' and proposed how public and private finance interact in the pursuit of such development objectives. But the story of finance and environment begins several years earlier with the 1972 Stockholm Declaration, which suggested that developed countries contribute towards the additional costs of tending to environmental considerations in developing countries (based on the 'polluter pays' principle). This principle is taken further in the 1987 Brundtland Commission report which states that since environmental issues add to development costs, public finance should offer private finance rewards for the additional risk they have to assume to implement environmental goals (WCED, 1987).

The 1987 Brundtland Commission report specifically distinguished between quantity and quality of finance that flows to developing countries (WCED, 1987: 29). The Brundtland Commission refers to the quantity of finance in terms of the amount of finance mobilised from public and private sources and a particular role for making finance available through the multilateral banks and the International Monetary Fund. Its references to the quality of finance provided to developing countries to support a transition to sustainability relates to forms of financial innovation; adjusting lending rates; integrating trade, economic and finance sectors; and ensuring that development interventions have sustainable development features. Integrating environmental and social concerns directly into economic development agendas was thus an important concept introduced in the early framings of finance, development and environment (Levashova, 2011; De Carvalho Ferreira et al., 2016).

Since the Brundtland Commission established finance in sustainable development, over 11 different terms now link finance with sustainability. The list grows even longer as new issues emerge such as the financing of just transitions and nature-based solutions (dealing with biodiversity systems). Two observations are evident from the terms (see Table 7.1). The first reflects growing innovations relative to financing dimensions of sustainability broadly, and climate change specifically. The second observation is that the growing list also reflects fragmented finance approaches that often compete for legitimacy, prevent coherent approaches to financing sustainability and separate from mainstream finance theory (Foxon, 2015; Diaz-Rainey et al., 2017; Naidoo, 2020).

Diaz-Rainey et al. (2017) classify such fragmentation and incoherent approaches to finance and sustainability as 'stranded research'. Thus,

Table 7.1: Different terms and year of emergence associated with finance, sustainability and climate

1988–1998	2000–2010	2010–present
Social finance Environmental finance Responsible investment Socially responsible investment Sustainable investment Sustainable finance Green finance	Impact finance Carbon finance Climate finance Adaptation finance Mitigation finance	Impact investing Transition finance Regenerative finance Transformative finance Nature-based finance

Source: Adapted from Anthony (2018: 8).

while further categorisations for financing, for example, just transitions and nature-based solutions, offer focused attention to the issues, they could be viewed as scaffolding for mainstreaming concerns into the incentives and investment practices of capital providers. However, the proliferation of terms suggests that the scaffolding never falls away, and we fail to transition the financial ecosystem towards a new development trajectory.

The early framings of how finance relates to the environment, the respective roles of, and mutual expectations between, private and public finance in support of environmental action were incorporated into the United Nations Framework Convention on Climate Change (UNFCCC), which was formed in 1992. The UNFCCC places primary responsibility upon the developed countries to provide new and additional resources to cover developing countries' incremental costs of responding to climate action. It extends this commitment by creating a dependency relationship. Developing countries are expected to implement climate measures to the extent that developed countries offer appropriate financial assistance and technology support (Gichira et al., 2014).

The Fourth (2020) Biennial Assessment and Overview of Climate Finance Flows (UNFCCC, 2021: 24) operationally defines climate finance as:

> Flows whose expected effect is aimed at reducing emissions or enhancing sinks of greenhouse gases and reducing the vulnerability of and maintaining and increasing the resilience of human and ecological systems to negative climate change impacts.

Climate finance flows from public sources are mainly channelled through funding instruments such as the UNFCCC's financial mechanisms; the Global Environment Facility (established in 1992); the Adaptation Fund (established in 2005), and the Green Climate Fund (established in 2011). The obligations of developed countries are largely channelled through these funds. Developed countries also deploy through their allocations to multilateral development banks such as the World Bank, and the African Development Bank. The third channel for public climate finance is through bilateral development agencies, such as the Agencie Française de Developpment, and KfW Development Bank.

The reality of climate finance architecture is not as simplified as depicted in Figure 7.1. In truth, new multilateral and bilateral climate funds have emerged creating a complex web of funds over the past 30 years, which in practice has added further administrative and accessibility barriers for developing countries (Thwaites and Amerasinghe, 2017). The determining factor for creating additional climate funds appears to be largely responses to relieving political and negotiation tensions. These lead to innovations such as the Climate Investment Funds (2008) provided by the multilateral funds to pave the way for a global fund on climate change. This was followed by 'fast-start finance' to catalyse climate investment ahead of the Green Climate Fund (2011) – intended as the premier global fund on climate change (2011).

Aside from public finance sources, private capital also supports climate action which speaks to the broader way the term 'climate finance' is understood in practice. Private finance providers control staggering finance flows through, for example, based on 2018 figures, equity (US$75 trillion), bond (US$102.8 trillion), real estate, infrastructure and venture capital (US$5 trillion) (Carter, 2020).

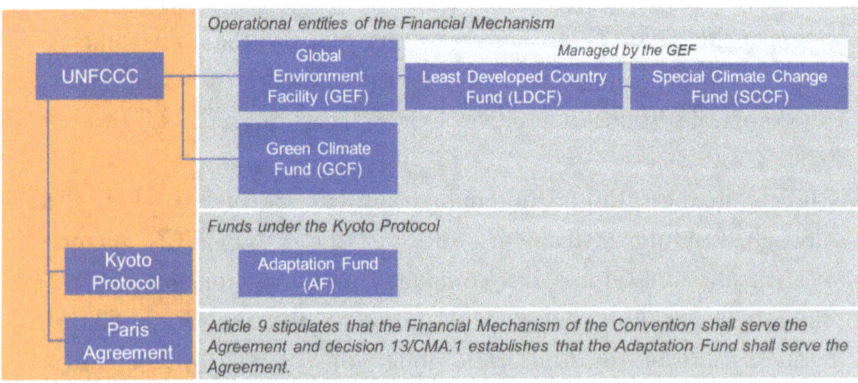

Figure 7.1: Climate funds under the UNFCCC

Source: UNFCCC (2021: 40).

Carter argues that unlocking the full might of private finance requires policymakers and other stakeholders to first recognise explicitly that all private investments – including climate – must deliver commercial investment rates of return (2020). Carter's observation harks back to the 1987 Brundtland Commission framing which positions the role of public finance as mainly compensating private capital for risks they assume, particularly when commercial rates of return are not achievable.

The UNFCCC's climate funds rely on developed countries' capital contributions and offer concessional finance to developing countries. Whereas, private finance offers commercial finance, as depicted in Figure 7.2, public and private capital providers typically engage in climate action opportunistically, so a project would have both components. The Green Climate Fund's Private Sector Facility and its support to public finance institutions are prime examples of such relationships. Public and private finance co-finance projects and allocate risk based on their respective risk absorption mandates.

Standard financing instruments, such as debt and equity, combined with de-risking and catalytic instruments such as guarantees, grants, and result-based incentives, are largely available for climate-related investment per Figure 7.3. The imperative of commercial returns by the private sector is typically achieved through combining public and private finance sources based on the type of capital that each offers, via a combination of the investment modalities and financial instruments depicted in Figure 7.3.

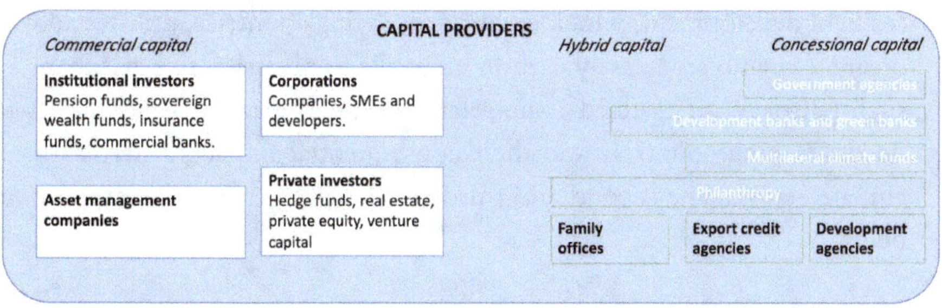

Figure 7.2: Capital providers to climate finance

Source: Carter (2020: 10).

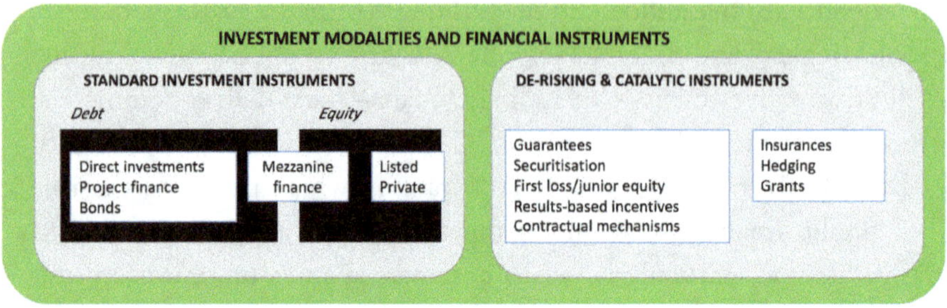

Figure 7.3: Investment modalities and instruments

Source: Carter (2020: 10)..

The UNFCCC climate funds have largely evolved in a reactionary rather than an anticipatory manner, despite signals that current structures do not fully address developing countries' needs. As countries begin implementing their climate strategies, new financing realities emerge, and existing issues are not fully accommodated in the offering by existing UNFCCC climate funds.

The first signal is the longstanding issue of the unfunded provision for financing loss and damage established by the Warsaw International Mechanism for Loss and Damage in 2013 (UNFCCC, 2013). This declaration concerns the compensation, technical support and assistance for the physical losses and damages experienced by Least Developed Countries (LDCs) and Small Island States (SIDS) (WWF, 2021). This critical financing signal is not elaborated on further in this chapter, though its importance is recognised. A second issue relates to financing the transition towards low emission and climate resilient development, which entails supporting countries, utilities and businesses who are heavily carbon intensive to diversify and exit from such pathways. The third issue relates to the impact of COVID-19 on developing countries and their consequential financing needs for climate action. The second and third issues are further elaborated on below.

FINANCING JUST TRANSITIONS

The second signal is a new process under the 26th Presidency of the Conference of the Parties to the United Nations Framework on Climate Change (COP26) held by the UK government: a new Energy Transition Council seeks to create financing facilities to support heavily fossil-fuel dependent countries such as South Africa, Indonesia and India to accelerate their clean energy transition (UK, 2021). Financing energy transitions is a key focus for the UNFCCC negotiations that will be presided over by the UK government this year. The Energy Transition Council aims to drive the shift to clean energy in developing countries, given that at least 50 countries are still building new fossil-fired power plants.[1] The Energy Transition Council promises ambitious climate finance to support the decarbonisation agenda of developing countries with high dependencies on fossil fuels. Countries such as India, Indonesia and South Africa are high contenders for such funding, to support technological shifts and rapid reduction in carbon emissions. For example, accelerating the retirement of, and replacing, current coal capacity in the Asian region is underway, though realising this goal will be difficult because these power plants are relatively new and likely to operate for some time (BBC, 2021).

Some argue that international climate finance differs from transition finance, and therefore requires different processes or additional mandates under the UNFCCC to incorporate transition-specific consequences (Meridian Economics, 2020). Some also differentiate climate finance as being for decarbonisation, while transition finance is for the socio-economic effects of transition due to decarbonisation (Lowitt, 2021a). An alternate view is that climate finance is a response measure to climate change, recognised as one of three primary means of implementation in UNFCCC processes (the others being technical assistance and technology transfer). Thus, climate finance is intended to meet the evolving financing needs of developing countries as they unfold when implementing the Paris Agreement, with transition effects being one such evolution with no additional need for new categories or framings.

[1] Based on data from Sustainable Energy for All as of 23 September 2020 (SEforALL, 2020).

The finance provisions in the Paris Agreement relating to developing countries (Article 9), for example, affirm that developing countries require financial support to transition their economies onto a low emission and climate-resilient pathway. The preamble to the Paris Agreement recognises impacts on livelihoods, and the need for decent jobs; hence, the need for a just transition (UNFCCC, 2021). The concept of a 'just transition' specifically draws attention to the need for equity and justice for those currently without access to reliable energy supply, those living in energy poverty and those whose livelihoods would be most affected by a shift away from a fossil fuel-based economy (Newell and Mulvaney, 2013).

Article 2.1c of the Paris Agreement offers further support for coupling the financing of climate and the process of transition. Its objective is to 'make finance flows consistent with a pathway to low greenhouse gas emission and climate resilient development'. As finance flows become consistent with the Paris Agreement, this should ideally negate the need for further categorisations of finance (see Table 7.2) as has evolved since the 1987 Brundtland Commission. These categories should only ever have been scaffolding to insert sustainability and climate into the essence of finance, working towards the long-term objective of mainstreaming and embedding.

COVID-19 AND CLIMATE FINANCE

The third signal relates to COVID-19, which makes responding to climate change immensely challenging for developing countries, especially those depending on significant international support.

COVID-19 brings the feasibility of increased climate finance from public finance sources into question.

According to the OECD (2020), COVID-19 is significantly altering economic activity and consumption and is predicted to reduce the tax base of middle-income countries. Developed countries may be under pressure to support domestic investment, and therefore may attach preconditions or even reduce their contributions to international climate funds. For example, a study predicts that overall international climate financing will fall by 7.1 per cent in 2021 and by an additional

11.8 per cent due to the COVID-19 pandemic (Quevedo et al., 2020). On the other hand, movements such as the United States government and other G7 countries' Build Back Better World (B3W) Partnership aim to respond to the strife exacted by Covid-19 by targeting the infrastructure needs of low- to middle-income countries (White House, 2021). The B3W Partnership aims to mobilise US$40 trillion of investment by focusing on trade and development, the Sustainable Development Goals (SDGs) and climate emergency, emphasising gender equity and equality.

COVID-19 allows reflection on how climate finance is being engaged with, as the economic, social and broader sustainable development impacts of the pandemic draw attention to the existing indebtedness of developing countries. These issues, first mentioned in the 1987 Brundtland Commission relating to the existing indebtedness of LDCs and other developing countries, are now assuming heightened importance. Coming more prominently to the fore now are issues related to the affordability of finance, cost of capital, foreign currency denominations and demands of the recipient countries' governments to international funding, such as providing sovereign guarantees.

The COVID-19 pandemic brings issues such as debt forgiveness and building economic and social resilience through greener economic recovery packages[2] to the forefront of international development and climate finance. The United Nations emphasises explicitly that international funders such as the World Bank and International Monetary Fund should consider a moratorium on debt payments, targeted debt relief and lead reforms to international debt architecture. The consequences are stark. A COVID-19-related global economic collapse places at least US$600 billion of developing countries' debt service payments at risk of default over the next five years. If developing countries cannot service existing debt, they cannot invest in domestic economic recovery and resilience (Guterres, 2021). Given that climate interventions are mainly funded through concessional or other debt mechanisms, responding to climate disasters in the future

[2] Various international finance entities offer COVID-19 debt relief to countries (e.g., IMF Financing and Debt Service Relief packages, the World Bank's Debt Suspension Initiative).

will be profoundly challenging, especially for those already heavily indebted (Sengupta, 2021).

Lower-income developing countries generally face severe economic and social consequences due to climate change, made even worse by COVID-19 responses. Yet, these same countries receive adaptation, recovery and redevelopment loans (Bassetti, 2019). For example, when Cyclone Idai struck Mozambique, a US$118 million loan was rapidly approved by the International Monetary Fund and the World Bank. The IMF and World Bank were deemed complicit in perpetuating the indebtedness of the world's poorest countries given that the losses suffered suggested that non-debt support is more appropriate, thus creating so-called climate debt traps (BrettonWoods, 2019). Funding the rebuilding of infrastructure purely on a debt basis is unsustainable and unjust, especially for the most vulnerable who face funding needs of at least US$300 billion per year due to loss and damage from climate-related events (Bassetti, 2019).

Climate finance potentially bridges the funding of COVID-19 and other vulnerabilities while contributing to greener recoveries, based on the type of projects it can finance (Dickman and Pitta, 2020). The challenge remains, however, that debt is the primary funding on offer. In contrast, access to grants remains limited or available only under preconditions that may benefit third parties in developed countries. Thus, greater attention and specific guidance to the UNFCCC climate funds and the multilateral development institutions such as the World Bank is essential in order to engage them on the qualitative aspects of climate finance provided, i.e., cost of finance, impact, co-financing and fiscal demands that attach to climate finance deployed by the UNFCCC climate funds.

At present, developing countries negotiate on a case-by-case basis with the climate funds without climate financing principles that can guide such negotiations. A financing protocol, for example, that allows developing countries to hold international funders to account may be valuable for negotiating better funding terms and conditions. For the moment, the scales favour the UNFCCC climate funds and private sector funders as the onus falls on developing countries to demonstrate evidence of their funding needs, prove 'bankability', and engage within terms and conditions primarily established by the protocols of these funds. Despite the IPCC demonstrating the necessity for urgent climate interventions and support to vulnerable countries, all of these asks are an injustice to developing countries.

There are calls for international climate finance to be transformed into a transformative and regenerative force for developing countries, thus realising the potential first seeded in the 1987 Brundtland Commission, and later in the 1992 UNFCCC founding statements. Since the Paris Agreement was adopted in 2015, a new paradigm for climate finance has unfolded as the implementation realities of climate goals compete with national development priorities and severe economic and social systemic shocks due to COVID-19. The climate science further warns that severe climate and biodiversity collapse await humanity in the next decade.

With this context in mind, South Africa's use of international climate finance to date is considered below.

SOUTH AFRICA'S ENCOUNTERS WITH CLIMATE FINANCE

South Africa invests approximately US$240 million per year of its public budget in national climate actions. It capitalised on a national Green Fund between 2012 and 2014 (US$60 million) to advance its transition towards a low-emission climate resilient development path (DFFE, 2020). International climate finance does not feature prominently as a funding source for climate interventions in South Africa, as 79 per cent of the R62.2 billion climate-related flows (tracked between 2017–2018) was domestically sourced (Cassim et al., 2020). The financial instruments offered by international climate finance are mainly loans for mitigation efforts (DFFE, 2020). The bilateral lenders are primarily Germany, France, United Kingdom and Italy. The evidence shows that adaptation is consistently underfunded by international climate funders (DFFE, 2020; Cassim et al., 2020; Winkler et al., 2021).

International climate funds such as the Global Environment Facility (GEF), Green Climate Fund (GCF) and the Adaptation Fund channel funding through the Development Bank of Southern Africa (DBSA) and the South African National Biodiversity Institute (SANBI). Access to these funding mechanisms allows DBSA and SANBI, in turn, to develop projects, submit funding proposals, and then manage and on-lend or on-grant as needed. In theory, funding from the international funds is on concessional terms (i.e., lower than market lending rates). During 2018–2019, the GCF supported South Africa through a US$543-million loan for energy efficiency projects, waste management and related projects. Also, a consortium of multilateral banks allocated funding to Eskom to support their developing 100MW wind farms (DFFE, 2020).

International climate finance visibility, access, allocation, and terms and conditions are inadequate. This applies to funding by both public and private finance institutions in South Africa. This presents two issues. The first is that the extent of promised benefits and concessions from these funds is not disclosed, thus there is no way of independently assessing their contribution to the country's climate response. Secondly, there is no disclosure of how national institutions pass concessional benefits to project developers, or whether the concessional finance is used to supplement institutional costs.

A recent paper by Winkler et al. (2021) comprehensively records the policy evolution of climate finance in South Africa, beginning in 2011 with early recommendations on climate finance embedded in the National Climate Change Response Policy White Paper (2011). The study traces the evolution of climate policy over time up to June 2021. It raises important questions on several persistent issues, such as the longstanding incoherence of climate policy and lack of coordination across government departments. It also notes limited understanding of South Africa's financing needs for mitigation and adaptation efforts and methodological differences where estimates do exist. The paper finds that public finance institutions are relatively more transparent about their climate interventions than private finance institutions.

Winkler et al. (2021) record the important strides made over the prior two years in South Africa regarding climate policy and embedding sustainability into the economy. Notably, the newly formed Presidential Climate Commission's mandate is to guide the country towards a just transition, National Treasury's work on sustainable finance, and the increased pressure for private finance on climate disclosures and taxonomies. Further example are the advances made by securing direct access to international climate finance as 'accredited entities' via the Development Bank of Southern Africa and South African National Biodiversity Institute, which complements the country's Green Fund and Climate Finance Facility (both hosted at the DBSA).

Within the private sector, the Johannesburg Stock Exchange (JSE) is developing market standards for green and sustainability bonds, sustainability-linked and transition debt securities (JSE, 2021). These standards are important catalysts to promote innovation among financial actors to finance climate interventions, especially as they reclassify the listed debt instruments based on their proceeds (categorised as either for sustainability or transition purposes). In particular, the standards relating to transition debt securities are an important innovation, as they recognise that 'issuers [need] to raise capital to enable their transition strategy and commitments with internationally established de-carbonisation pathways' (JSE, 2021: 3). The release of these market standards responds to the growing investors' interest in environmental, social and governance (ESG) investments, based on the selected examples of recent issuances by four of South Africa's major banks in Table 7.2.

Table 7.2: Examples of sustainability-linked securities issued by South African banks

Nedbank	Standard Bank	Investec	ABSA	RMB
Structuring and arrangement of R2 billion of Tier 2 green subordinated capital instruments (SDG-linked bonds) that were listed on the green segment of the JSE with the African Development Bank as sole investor (June 2020)	R1.6 billion sustainability-linked facility agreement comprising of two R800 million tranches. The interest rate is linked to Equities achievement of certain pre-agreed ESG performance targets	US$600 000 000 Syndicated Term Loan Facility for Investec Bank Limited linked to sustainability outcomes (March 2021)	IFC US$150 million certified loan for on lending to green projects. (May 2021)	Arranged a sustainability linked bond for Redefine properties, for renewable energy, and water efficiency performance targets

Source: Adapted from Anthony (2018: 8).

The interest in sustainability by South African banks is also aided by the pressure applied by South African civil society. For example, environmental justice groups initiated precedent-setting court cases relating to the environmental approvals for the Thabametsi and Khanyisa coal plants, where the judgment was that climate assessments should be mandatory in future (Humbly, 2018). In parallel, shareholder activism led major banks in South Africa to be challenged to re-evaluate their financing commitments to these plants and adopt policies to reconsider their investment in new coal and fossil fuel assets (Naidoo, 2019). Shareholder activism and social justice movements in South Africa like Just Share, Groundwork, Earthlife Africa and the Center for Environmental Rights, to name a few, are generating the societal tensions necessary in processes of change. They play an important role in promoting transparency and integrity to ensure the financial sector and businesses responsibly deploy finance relative to the climate and social risks and realities South Africa faces (Davies, 2021).

International climate finance, if deployed strategically, can be a powerful force to address risks that South African private and development finance institutions find difficult to assume, or offer at scale e.g., project and programme development support, and credit enhancement. However, the Presidential Climate Commission signals an important cautionary note in its consultations on the NDC regarding climate finance. It highlights that South Africa needs to develop a unifying climate finance strategy that requires complementary investment by national financial actors to climate-related investments (PCC, 2021). Such a climate finance strategy should direct financial actors in enhancing the capabilities of the national finance system to catalyse the transformation of the South African economy towards clean energy and climate resilience.

The PCC's call for long-term finance strategy supports the policy recommendations by Winkler et al. (2021), which was a recommendation first made 10 years ago in Naidoo (2011). The now Department of Forests, Fisheries and Environment (DFFE) has conducted initial work around such a strategy. In 2011, Naidoo (2011: 17) argued that [government should conceptualise]:

> A bold and comprehensive climate finance package or strategy to immediately enable South Africa to begin its transition towards climate resilience. This strategy should transcend the debates of development, mitigation or adaptation, and be underpinned by clear signals from the government of South Africa.

Naidoo further emphasised the need for the government to set the investment direction by developing a transition plan that allows other non-state finance actors to engage as per their risk absorption levels. The growing momentum among South African banks and the active engagement by civil society and interest in climate finance reflects the catalytic role a transition plan could potentially play, especially as the realities of implementing the Paris Agreement become more apparent.

SIGNALLING FINANCE NEEDS FOR SOUTH AFRICA'S JUST ENERGY TRANSITION

South Africa's need for comprehensive financial resources to transition is evident in the country's earliest framing of its climate response, where the 2011 National Climate Change Response Policy White Paper specifically classifies climate finance as (DEA, 2011; DFFE, 2020):

> ... all resources that finance the cost of South Africa's transition to a lower-carbon and climate resilient economy and society. This covers both climate-specific and climate-relevant financial resources, public and private, domestic, and international. This includes financial resources that go towards reducing emissions and enhancing sinks of greenhouse gases; reducing vulnerability, maintaining, and increasing the resilience of human and ecological systems to negative climate change impacts; climate-resilient and low-emission strategies, plans and policies; climate research and climate monitoring systems; as well as climate change capacity-building and technology.

More recently, South Africa has been sending strong signals to secure predictable, concessional and long-term climate finance to meet the substantial financial and social costs of a just energy transition process. Notably, at least US$10 billion of 'highly' concessional climate finance over the next five years would be needed to accelerate the country's decarbonisation (PCC, 2021; Renaud et al., 2021; Creamer, 2021a).

Various options are being tabled for how South Africa may utilise such climate finance (see Table 7.3), also expressed as 'transition finance':

- Just transition transaction (Steyn et al., 2021)
- sustainability-linked loan facility linked to performance targets (Creamer, 2021b)
- debt for climate initiatives (swaps) (Tyler et al., 2021; Sguazzin, 2021a; 2021b)

The options range from singular to more plural approaches. The sustainability-linked loan facility singularly pursues new renewable energy capacities for Eskom. Its management is not optimistic that concessional finance could address the utility's debt challenges in the short term (Creamer, 2021b). While the calls for just transition transaction and debt-for-climate address broader, more plural dimensions.

The three options are likely being considered by the same pool of international climate funders, but it is unclear whether the range of options are framed as part of South Africa's longer term financing plan for its energy transition. What is the theory of change underpinning the finance South Africa is seeking? Such vision is unclear for how South Africawn sponsors are presently framing individual options. There is also lack of clarity on the investments components related to the 'just' energy transition – what is new technology and what relates to justice? All options are also relatively silent on a precise role for South Africa's public and private finance institutions. How will international climate finance strengthen and expand national lending capacities?

The propositions in Table 7.3 do, however, recognise Eskom's existing debt levels at R483.6 billion (Eskom, 2020: 85) as a critical barrier to remove before accelerating South Africa's decarbonisation aspirations. By alleviating Eskom debt situation (depending on how this is structured), the company's capital structure (debt to equity ratio) and constrained cash flow has the potential to improve. Eskom is an inconvenient but necessary driver of South Africa's decarbonisation plan, considering its coal fleet, and the assets and value chains it both influences and controls. Presently, Eskom receives ongoing and longstanding support from the South African government through guarantees on its direct lending and payment guarantees related to the country's independent renewable energy procurement. The availability

Table 7.3: Components of South Africa's just energy transition proposals

	Just transition transaction	Sustainability linked loan facility	Debt for climate initiatives (swaps)
Primary borrower	South African government	Eskom (utility)	South African government
Proposed lenders	Development finance institutions	Development finance institutions	Existing / new lender portfolio
Description	Develop a 'Just Transition Transaction' component in National Treasury's existing borrowing programme	Develop a bilateral/ multilateral financing facility that is based on performance targets	Swap existing debt or issue new debt in exchange for certain climate commitments by South African government
Just components	Early ideas contained option for new Just Transition Fund	Based on components of Eskom's repurposing project portfolio	Unspecified
Primary use of proceeds	Alleviate Eskom debt Invest in renewables	New renewable energy generation, transmission & distribution capacity	Debt relief for Eskom Reduce fiscal impact
Preconditions proposed by South African sponsors	Adherence to an accelerated mitigation pathway	Adherence to performance targets attached to Eskom's decarbonisation schedule	Adherence to climate commitments, primarily accelerated decarbonisation
Financial request	Concessional finance Carbon credits	Concessional finance Grant component	New debt structure
Status	Concept socialised with government & others	In discussions on Framework Agreement	Early
Funder conditions	Unclear	Under negotiation	Unclear

Source: Author analysis of reports and media.

period for government support to Eskom's capital expenditure programmes will be up for consideration in 2022, as its expiry date approaches (31 March 2023). With Eskom positioned as a financially sound and strengthened institution, the need for ongoing government support has the potential to reduce.

Eskom's singularly focused sustainability-linked loan proposal to build new renewable energy plants represents the first financing domino to fall in South Africa's energy sector. This decision has major implications across the coal value chain and for the many businesses and livelihoods, municipalities and communities reliant upon Eskom in both positive and challenging ways. A longer-term finance strategy would therefore be helpful to show what are the knock-on effects of the Eskom domino falling, such that South African's transition needs are better forecast.

Though the financing options aim to enable a 'just' energy transition, the theory of change around the justice component is inadequately articulated across all options. The just transition transaction and sustainability linked loan options reference livelihoods and job losses in affected communities. South Africa has precedent for creating purpose-driven funds (such as the Green Fund, Infrastructure Fund, Jobs Fund), and COVID-19 enabled a private and public sector initiative around the Solidarity Fund. An earlier conception of the just transition transaction suggested a Just Transition Fund, which is since not evident in any of the options under consideration. To avoid such a fund being a 'tag-on' to securing international climate finance support or bilateral facilities, it is essential that any finance facility promoting justice and equity be co-created with the intended beneficiaries. The feasibility, efficacy and form of any 'just' purpose-driven fund for the social aspects of the just energy transition should make the case for a whole economy approach towards processes of change within the affected communities, and South Africa at large. The design features for such a fund should achieve targeted systemic, transformative and regenerative reforms. This means that though individual projects may appear less impactful, through a just transition investment portfolio (with multiple projects and programmes) all projects collectively contribute to deep economic, social and environmental shifts.

Lowitt (2021a) argues that the financing needs of a just transition depend on the spectrum of ambition in achieving social outcomes. The logic is that projects with higher finance needs, but with lower social justice ambitions, have better access to funding than projects with high social justice ambitions and lower funding sizes. This important observation recognises the dominant approach the financial sector applies to evaluating investments is to focus first on the investment amount (funding size) required by a project, and determine their engagement based on such 'transaction volumes'. This approach disadvantages smaller projects as in the case of the low investment in the Smalls programme of South Africa's renewable energy procurement programme, where the banks argued that the smaller transaction sizes carried same if not higher transaction (Naidoo, 2020).

An alternative to focusing on individual projects is essential for financing South Africa's just transition, one that recognises a 'just transition investment portfolio' (which is a series of interdependent projects) (Naidoo, 2020). A proactive co-creative approach to creating such a portfolio is essential, as most purpose-driven or specialist funding facilities generally rely on project developers approaching the lender with structured projects. A portfolio approach will also require new investment and risk assessment and financial innovations that prioritise their purpose-driven outcomes, in balance with financial returns. A portfolio approach will also require funding facilities that strengthen the risk absorption capabilities of public and private funders, are focused on the 'transition context' (e.g., specific challenge being faced by affected persons), thematic (broad scope not only energy) and set the pace of investment with defined investment milestones achieved over the short, medium and long term.

Defining the granularity of constituencies to be supported by the financing options through any just transition financing mechanism/ facilities is also essential, where parties directly and indirectly affected by decarbonisation are mapped out; with finance being tangibly accessible closest to the impact of Eskom's decarbonisation commitments. For now, only two primary recipients of funding are envisaged – national government and Eskom – and the funding will likely be centralised and utilised at this level. An integrated, more plural approach to finance would ensure that those parties affected directly and indirectly have urgent and immediate access to finance to also transition. This is an essential component of a just transition to ensure adequate, predictable and accessible access to funding for the most vulnerable and affected. For example, finance should be made available across the electricity supply industry to actors such as municipalities, service providers, employees and complementary industries. The consequence of Eskom's decarbonisation agenda requires, simultaneously, locating specialist finance facilities at public institutions such as the Development Bank of Southern Africa, the Industrial Development Corporation and South Africa's four major banks to aid those impacted to also begin to transition. Affected parties may then responsibly plan their exit and build capabilities to diversify as needed.

Considering the extent to which the financing options either open or close down options for other sectors in a need to transition is essential. Sectors such as agriculture also face the impending risk of EU border tax adjustments for South African exports (due for adoption in 2023). Over 137 countries have signed up for the Race to Zero Partner Initiative, which sets fully decarbonised economic targets between 2040 and 2050. These include some of South Africa's key trading partners such as China, Germany and United Kingdom – any mismatches with 'net zero' scheduling and target setting are likely to impact on South Africa's key agricultural-related exports (sugar, wool, fruits and vegetables). The broader scope of financing needs for South Africa's just transition is not yet being fully engaged or costed. The present focus for financing South Africa's just transition focuses primarily on Eskom and the Mpumalanga region, with limited inclusion of the broader work of the National Planning Commission.

A broader scope for South Africa's financing of just transitions must extend beyond energy, which further supports the need for a longer-term financing plan and coherent approach across the finance sector more generally. The 2011 National Climate Change Response Policy, for example, recommended that a task force be set up between the National Treasury, now DFFE and then Economic Development Department. Such a task force would convene national financial stakeholders to ensure the South African financial sector supports the transition process across all sectors and short-, medium- and long-term timeframes (DEA, 2011). No action to date towards creating such a task force has ever been taken, though the Presidential Climate Commission has been reflecting on the financing options for South Africa's energy transition. The absence of a strategic approach to financing South Africa's climate and just transition visions is notable in that the options in Table 7.3 are relatively silent about a precise contribution and role for the South African finance sector.

South Africa's past encounters with climate finance have raised around US$2 billion per year. Making the step change to much higher access levels to international climate finance raises questions about institutional capabilities to absorb such funding. An early version of the NDC suggested that South Africa would target US$4 billion per year to 2025 and raise US$8 billion per year to 2030. International climate finance can be channelled into a developing country through multilateral and bilateral arrangements and may be direct to the project or through accredited intermediaries such as the Development Bank of South Africa and SANBI. Raising the target for accessing climate finance poses several questions, whether South Africa's intermediaries for the GCF and others have the institutional capabilities and mandate to immediately absorb the additional funding, and on the terms and conditions required by climate funders. A recent complication presents that the Development Bank of South Africa's renewal for accreditation under the Green Climate Fund may require a precondition for the DBSA to decarbonise (Farand, 2021).

The alternative for accessing large sums of international climate finance is that multilateral and bilateral development finance institutions directly manage these finance flows for South Africa. This is less than ideal as the principle of 'country-ownership' is a key tenet in the provision of climate finance to developing countries. The risk of unforeseen trade-offs always exists where a developing country is not in direct control of the international climate finance flows through its own institutions. There could also be positive spin-offs, but this depends on how South Africa's negotiates funding terms and conditions and governance arrangements.

International climate finance providers are likely to make specific demands on the South African government in exchange for any funding facilities under consideration, such as requiring government guarantees on any debt provided. This will be challenging given South Africa's constrained fiscal space, which is due to longstanding issues around inequality, unemployment, corruption and slower economic growth even before COVID-19. Since March 2021, South Africa was downgraded to below investment grade credit rating which affects its cost of finance in international capital markets. The country has experienced various forms of protest due to poverty and unemployment. The development demands on government are intense. As potential recipients of international climate finance, South Africa must carefully scrutinise the terms and conditions of any future funding so it does not further burden the country's ability to deliver on its national development priorities.

CLIMATE FINANCE AS A RAGING FIRE?

Developing countries such as South Africa should critically evaluate whether international climate finance benefits manifest. This is especially important because South Africa has a well-developed finance sector, and a substantial finance asset base of about R6 200 billion (Winkler et al., 2021). As seen in Table 7.1, the financial sector in South Africa is already issuing green-, transition- and climate-related financing instruments to support investment. Regulatory instruments relating to climate risk and sustainable finance are under consideration by the National Treasury, among others. South Africa's track record in large renewable energy investment is robust. For example, 76 per cent of the R200 billion invested in South Africa's renewable energy procurement programme was from national banks and pension funds, and only 24 per cent by international funders (IPP, 2019).

Precise screening criteria in mobilising and deploying international climate finance may be useful to assess the quality, efficacy and impacts offered to South Africa, such as:

- What demands are made of the South African government in exchange for such funding?
- Which risks is such funding absorbing beyond the capacity of national institutions?
- How soon can such funds be deployed in support of NDC timeframes (e.g., 2025–2030)?
- How much of funding benefits are passed on to programme and project developers?
- How does the international climate finance strengthen the country's ability to implement?

These questions may contribute to precise decisions on how best to programme and apply international climate finance from, say, the Green Climate Fund or specialist facilities like the Climate Investment Funds managed by the World Bank and the African Development Bank. Developing countries must begin to lead the financing negotiations more precisely with developed countries' international climate funds. 'Leading' implies clear articulation of needs and proposing precise key financing terms and conditions.

South Africa as a fossil-fuel dependent country is racing against time to significantly reduce its greenhouse gas emissions. Eskom's focus on immediate build and decommissioning will be a valuable contribution to meeting the 2025 and 2030 NDC targets by the South African government – which sets clear time-based targets to reduce emissions by 112 $MtCO_2$ equivalent in 2025 70 $MtCO_2$ equivalent in 2030. But the elephant in the room is how soon international climate finance can tangibly contribute to South Africa's energy transition. Negotiating funding terms takes some time: e.g., the Clean Technology Fund loan to Eskom agreed in 2008 took two years before any financing tangibly materialised (Naidoo, 2014). Unless the negotiations accelerate towards a mutual agreement, and funding flows within the next 12 months to Eskom, a real risk exists that the NDC 2025 and 2030 emission reduction targets will not be achievable.

Deep engagement among policymakers, project developers and financiers are, however, essential. There are limitations to leaving financial innovation on social justice issues entirely up to the imagination of financiers. For example, in the case of the Renewable Energy Independent Power Producers Procurement Programme (REI4P), financiers and policymakers extensively engaged before the programme's launch on its various dimensions. Policymakers were not prescriptive on the social outcomes of the REI4P. Rather, they left project developers and financiers to largely apply existing precedents on equity participation and enterprise development for participation by broad-based Black Economic Empowerment groups. South Africa's innovative financial instruments rapidly evolved as the technological and commercial project risks reduced. Whereas policymakers expressed frustration that old equity-based models (three-year funding horizon) were used to finance equity participation in 20-year funding arrangements (Naidoo, 2019). By necessity, the emergent innovations on financing structures to support a just transition require guiding principles to inform the direction, pace and impact of financial innovation by financiers.

BEYOND SMOKE SIGNALS TO RAGING FIRE: ARTICULATING SOUTH AFRICA'S DEMANDS FOR FINANCE

South Africa's energy transition process offers important context for the type of financing innovations that are necessary. Perez (2002) and O'Sullivan (2005) argued that the characteristics of the innovation process should inform the type of financial innovations that unfold.

Applying the same logic to just energy transitions, South Africa has distinct transition characteristics that require a particular response from international climate funds and the national finance sector. Firstly, South Africa's transition requires deliberate shifts in direction (government policy, investment preferences, technology choices) that move away from fossil-fuel energy sources towards clean energy. Secondly, South Africa's energy transition is not yet generating the effect systematically of building up greener industries or clean energy, while aiding in phasing out harmful industries or practices. Climate finance needs to generate such simultaneous duality.

Thirdly, the processes of contestation around the country's

energy transition means that incumbents compete with new change makers such as youth, rural communities and civil society – many of whom refute the need for shifting towards sustainable modes of development. The just transition is a process of contestation as quality of life is compromised for those most affected through job losses and displacement. Climate finance has to regenerate new livelihoods for geographic regions across energy and other sectors. Fourthly, financing South Africa's energy transition is inherently experimental, where climate finance needs to go beyond individual projects and support constructing diverse portfolios of just transition interventions.

Finally, South Africa's energy transition is time-based with urgent science, social and economic threats – aided by the challenge of the pace set by the 2025 and 2030 goals in the updated NDC. There is urgency to regenerating and building resilience of South Africa's affected communities as deepening social and economic losses may be evident, and as trading partners impose fossil fuel-related import restrictions (e.g., border tax adjustments). Added to this reality is the growing vulnerability to climate change as more volatile climate events unfold, affecting biodiversity systems, which will affect food and water security.

This chapter covers the origins and evolving narratives of climate finance. It argues that international climate finance, as conceived by the UNFCCC and the Paris Agreement specifically, should recognise that climate finance needs to incorporate the transition-related impacts of meeting developing country implementation needs.

The chapter also considers South Africa's options under development for its just energy transition and offers reflections thereon. The three options are very useful and important beginnings; however, in aggregate, they do not reflect a long-term financing strategy powerful enough to drive transformative system change in South Africa's energy sector. In addition, the exclusive focus on financing the energy sector's transition risks deprioritising other sectors, which are also in urgent need of funding.

South Africa has sent clear smoke signals for international climate finance to finance its just energy transition. This is an important first step but the transformative potential of international climate finance complemented with national resources is not yet evident. South Africa needs a raging fire to finance its just transition – one that meets the pace, depth and breadth of investment and institutional commitment and behavioural shifts necessary for a just and inclusive transition. International climate finance can complement the contributions of every financial actor in South Africa. This can only manifest if South African finance actors develop transformative and regenerative approaches to financing the just transition, and so prevent piecemeal measures from proliferating.

REFERENCES

Allen, J.R., Burns, N., Garrett, L., Haass, R.N., Ikenberry, G.J. et al., 20 March 2020. 'Analysis: How the world will look after the Coronavirus pandemic'. *Foreign Policy*, https://foreignpolicy.com/2020/03/20/world-order-after-coroanvirus-pandemic/, accessed June 2021.

Bassetti, F. 29 October 2019. 'Migrations and inequalities: The cruel irony of climate debt'. *Climate Foresight*, https://www.climateforesight.eu/migrations-inequalities/the-cruel-irony-of-climate-debt/, accessed June 2021.

BBC. 3 August 2021. 'Finance firms plan to close coal plants in Asia'. *BBC News*. https://www.bbc.com/news/business-58066660, accessed August 2021.

BrettonWoods. 30 July 2019. 'IMF and World Bank complicit in "climate debt trap" following Mozambique cyclones'. BrettonWoods Project, New York, https://www.brettonwoodsproject.org/2019/07/imf-and-world-bank-complicit-in-climate-debt-trap-following-mozambique-cyclones/, accessed June 2021.

Carter, L. 2020. 'The ecosystem of private investment in climate action'. Invest4Climate Knowledge Series. United Nations Development Programme, New York, https://www.undp.org/sites/g/files/zskgke326/files/publications/53154%20-%20Invest4Climate%20Document%202%20-%20web_1.pdf, accessed June 2021.

Cassim A., Radmore, J., Dinham, N. and McCallum, S. 2020. 'South African climate finance landscape 2020'. Climate Policy Initiative, https://www.climatepolicyinitiative.org/wp-content/uploads/2021/01/South-African-Climate-Finance-Landscape-January-2021.pdf, accessed June 2021.

Creamer, T. 3 May 2021a. 'French financier pledges support for Eskom's just energy transition strategy'. *Engineering News*, https://www.engineeringnews.co.za/article/french-financier-pledges-support-for-eskoms-just-energy-transition-strategy-2021-05-03, accessed June 2021.

Creamer, T. 5 October 2021b. 'De Ruyter says "substantial" concessional finance is available to support just energy transition'. *Engineering News.* https://www.engineeringnews.co.za/article/de-ruyter-says-substantial-concessional-finance-available-to-support-just-energy-transition-2021-10-05, accessed October 2021.

Davies, T. 13 July 2021. 'More balance, less boasting'. *Financial Mail,* https://justshare.org.za/media/news/more-balance-less-boasting, accessed October 2021.

De Carvalho Ferreira, M.C., Sobreiro, V.A., Kimura, H. and De Moraes Barboza, F.L. 2016. 'A systematic review of literature about finance and sustainability'. *Journal of Sustainable Finance and Investment*, 6(2), 112–147.

Department of Environment (DEA). 2011. 'National Climate Change Response Policy White Paper'. https://www.gov.za/sites/default/files/gcis_document/201409/nationalclimatechangeresponsewhitepaper0.pdf, accessed October 2021.

Department of Forests, Fisheries and Environment (DFFE). 2020. 'South Africa's 4th biennial update report to the United Nations Framework Convention on Climate Change'. https://www.environment.gov.za/sites/default/files/reports/biennialupdatereport04tounfccc_zeroorderdraft.pdf, accessed June 2021.

Diaz-Rainey, I., Robertson, B. and Wilson, C. 2017. 'Stranded research? Leading finance journals are silent on climate change'. *Climatic Change*, 143(1–2), 243–260.

Dickman, J. and Pitta, E. 2020. 'How can climate finance support COVID-19 recoveries?'. Climate Investment Funds, New York. https://www.climateinvestmentfunds.org/sites/cif_enc/files/knowledge-documents/how_can_climate_finance_support_covid-19_recoveries_cif_lessons_0.pdf, accessed June 2021.

Eskom, 2020. Annual financial statements for the year ended 31 March 2021. https://www.eskom.co.za/wp-content/uploads/2021/08/AFS2021.pdf, accessed September 2021.

Farand, C. 2021. 'Dispute grips Green Climate Fund over net zero condition for accessing finance'. *Climate Change News*, https://www.climatechangenews.com/2021/10/08/dispute-grips-green-climate-fund-net-zero-condition-accessing-finance/, accessed October 2021.

Foxon, T.J., 2015. 'Rationale for policy interventions in sustainability transitions'. Conference paper for 6th International Sustainability Transitions Conference, Science Policy Research Unit, University of Sussex.

Gichira, P.S., Agwata, J.F. and Muigua, K.D. 2014. 'Climate finance: Fears and hopes for developing countries'. *Journal of Law, Policy and Globalisation*, 22, 1–7.

Guterres, A. 29 March 2021. 'Press Conference by Secretary-General Antonio

Guterres at United Nations Headquarters'. United Nations, https://www.un.org/press/en/2021/sgsm20659.doc.htm, accessed June 2021.

Holland, D. 2020. 'World Economic Situation and Social Prospects 2020'. United Nations Department of Economic and Social Affairs and United Nations Conference on Trade and Development, New York. https://www.un.org/development/desa/dpad/wp-content/uploads/sites/45/WESP2020_FullReport.pdf, accessed June 2021.

Humbly, T. 2018. 'The Thabametsi Case: Case No 65662/16 Earthlife Africa Johannesburg v Minister of Environmental Affairs'. Journal of Environmental Law, 30, 145–155. https://doi.org/10.1093/jel/eqy007, accessed June 2021.

Intergovernmental Panel on Climate Change (IPCC). 2021. 'Climate Change 2021. The physical science basis'. https://www.ipcc.ch/report/ar6/wg1/downloads/report/IPCC_AR6_WGI_Full_Report_smaller.pdf, accessed October 2021.

Investec. 2021. 'Investec plc closes USD600m sustainability-linked syndicated loan'. https://www.investec.com/en_gb/welcome-to-investec/press/investec-closes-600m-sustainability-loan.html, accessed June 2021.

IPP office, 2019: Independent Power Producers Procurement Programme (IPPPP): An overview, as at 31 March. https://www.ipp-projects.co.za/Publications/GetPublicationFile?fileid=b9781ba8-6588-e911-94aa-2c59e59ac9cd&fileName=20190522_IPP%20Office%20Q4_2018-19%20Overview.pdf.pdf, accessed June 2021.

Joubert, L. 21 October 2019. 'South Africa's energy crisis team unveils finance plan that could bring a just transition'. *Energy Transition*, https://energytransition.org/2019/10/south-africas-energy-crisis-team-unveils-finance-plan-that-could-bring-a-just-transition/, accessed June 2021.

Johannesburg Stock Exchange (JSE). 2021. 'Amendments to the JSE Debt Listings Requirements'. https://www.jse.co.za/sites/default/files/media/documents/regulation/Explanatory%20Memorandum%20DLR%2014%20June%202021.pdf, accessed June 2021.

Levashova, Y. 2011. 'Role of sustainable development in bilateral investment treaties: Recent trends and developments'. *Journal of Sustainable Finance and Investment*, 1(3–4), 222–229.

Levin, S. and Lowitt, S. 2021. 'Financing a just transition to a low-carbon, resilient economy'. *Business Day*, https://www.businesslive.co.za/bd/opinion/2021-01-26-financing-a-just-transition-to-a-low-carbon-resilient-economy/, accessed September 2021.

Lowitt, S. 2021a. 'Finance and the just transition. Draft policy brief for the Presidential Climate Commission'. Trade and Industrial Policy Strategies. https://a9322a19-efe3-4459-9a6c-ab806fededa3.filesusr.com/ugd/1eb85a_26395defa03049628aa3f712fda18bf3.pdf, accessed October 2021.

Lowitt, S., 2021b. 'Toward a contribution to a just transition finance roadmap in South Africa'. Trade and Industrial Policy Strategies, https://www.tips.org.za/research-archive/sustainable-growth/green-economy-2/item/4178-toward-a-contribution-to-a-just-transition-finance-roadmap-in-south-africa, accessed October 2021.

Macquarie, R., Naran, B., Rosane, P., Solomon, M. and Wetherbee, C., 2020. 'Updated view of the global landscape of climate finance 2019'. Climate Policy Initiative, https://www.climatepolicyinitiative.org/wp-content/uploads/2020/12/Updated-View-on-the-2019-Global-Landscape-of-Climate-Finance.pdf, accessed June 2021.

Meridian Economics. 18 May 2020. 'The role of transition finance for climate mitigation'. https://meridianeconomics.co.za/wp-content/uploads/2020/06/SA-Just-Transition-Transaction-proof-of-concept_Meridian-Economics_18062020.pdf, accessed October 2021.

Naidoo, C. 2014. 'Case study of the Clean Technology Fund in South Africa'. Master's thesis, University of Witwatersrand, Johannesburg.

Naidoo, C. 2011. 'Financing climate change'. Department of Environmental Affairs, https://www.environment.gov.za/sites/default/files/docs/financing_climate_change.pdf, accessed October 2021.

Naidoo, C.P. 2020. 'Relating financial systems to sustainability transitions: Challenges, demands and design features'. *Environmental Innovation and Societal Transitions*, 36, 279–290. https://econ.columbia.edu/wp-content/uploads/sites/41/2021/01/Relating-financial-systems_compressed.pdf, accessed May 2021.

Naidoo, C.P. 2019. 'Transcending the interregnum: Exploring the role of financial systems in sustainability transition processes'. University of Sussex, Brighton. http://sro.sussex.ac.uk/id/eprint/92245/, accessed May 2021.

Newell, P. and Mulvaney, D., 2013. 'The political economy of the "just transition"'. *The Geographical Journal*, https://www.researchgate.net/profile/Dustin-Mulvaney/publication/259043435_The_Political_Economy_of_the_Just_Transition/links/59e3a090a6fdcc7154dbadd7/The-Political-Economy-of-the-Just-Transition.pdf, accessed June 2021.

Organisation for Economic Co-operation and Development (OECD). 2020. 'Revenue Statistics 2020'. https://www.oecd-ilibrary.org/sites/8625f8e5-en/index.html?itemId=/content/publication/8625f8e5-en, accessed June 2021.

O'Sullivan, M. 2005. 'Finance and innovation', in Fagerberg, J., Mowery, D. and Nelson, R.R. (eds), *The Oxford Handbook of Innovation*. Oxford: Oxford University Press.

Perez, C., 2002. *Technological Revolutions and Financial Capital: The dynamics of bubbles and golden ages*. Cheltenham, UK: Edward Elgar.

Presidential Climate Commission (PCC). 2021. 'First Report: Recommendations on South Africa's draft updated Nationally Determined

Contribution'. The Presidential Climate Commission, Pretoria, https://www.climatecommission.org.za/ndc, accessed June 2021.

Quevedo, A., Peters, K. and Cao, Y. 2020. 'The impact of COVID-19 on climate change and disaster resilience funding: Trends and signals'. Overseas Development Institute, London, https://cdn.odi.org/media/documents/The_impact_of_Covid-19_on_climate_change_and_disaster_resilience_funding_trends.pdf, accessed June 2021.

Renaud, C., Tyler, E. and Mgoduso, L. 2021. 'The just transition transaction: Motivating climate finance support for accelerated coal phase-down'. Meridian Economics, Cape Town, https://meridianeconomics.co.za/wp-content/uploads/2021/05/JTT-Motivating-climate-finance-for-accelerated-coal-phase-down.pdf, accessed June 2021.

Sengupta, S. 2021. 'How debt and climate change pose "systemic risk" to world economy'. *New York Times*, https://www.nytimes.com/2021/04/07/climate/debt-climate-change.html, accessed June 2021.

Sguazzin, A. 30 July 2021a. 'South Africa's power giant lays out plan to move away from coal'. *Bloomberg News*, https://www.bloomberg.com/news/articles/2021-07-30/eskom-proposes-multi-lender-facility-to-fund-energy-transition, accessed June 2021.

Sguazzin, A. 8 September 2021b. 'Masondo proposes R146bn in government debt be forgiven – in exchange for climate targets'. *News24*, https://www.news24.com/fin24/economy/south-africa/masondo-proposes-r146bn-in-govt-debt-be-forgiven-in-exchange-for-climate-targets-20210908#:~:text=Under%20Masondo's%20proposal%2C%20which%20he,by%20new%20or%20existing%20creditors, accessed October 2021.

Steyn, G., Tyler, E., Roff, A., Renaud, C. and Mgoduso, L. 2021. 'The just transition transaction: A developing country coal power retirement mechanism'. Meridian Economics, Cape Town, https://meridianeconomics.co.za/wp-content/uploads/2021/09/2021-09-28_What-is-the-JTT_Final-Report.pdf, accessed October 2021.

Sustainable Energy for All (SEforALL). 23 September 2020. 'New COP26 Energy Transition Council to be co-chaired by UK government and SEforALL launched at CEM 11, https://www.seforall.org/news/new-cop26-energy-transitions-council, accessed October 2021.

Thwaites, J. and Amerasinghe, N. 27 March 2017. 'The climate finance architecture the world needs'. *Greenbiz*, https://www.greenbiz.com/article/climate-finance-architecture-world-needs, accessed June 2021.

Tyler, E., Renaud, C. and Roff, A., 2021. 'Debt for climate opportunities in South Africa. The role of concessional finance in unlocking the country's energy transition'. Heinrich Böll Foundation, University of London and Boston University, https://www.boell.de/sites/default/files/2021-03/Background%20Paper%20_5.pdf, accessed October 2021.

United Kingdom (UK). 2021. 'UK convenes key ministers to unlock investment for energy transition ahead of COP26'. https://www.gov.uk/government/news/uk-convenes-key-ministers-to-unlock-investment-for-energy-transition-ahead-of-cop26, accessed October 2021.

United Nations Framework Convention on Climate Change (UNFCCC). 2021. Fourth (2020) Biennial Assessment and Overview of Climate Finance Flows. UNFCCC Standing Committee on Finance.

United Nations Framework Convention on Climate Change (UNFCCC). 2015. 'The Paris Agreement'. https://unfccc.int/process-and-meetings/the-paris-agreement/the-paris-agreement, accessed October 2021.

United Nations Framework Convention on Climate Change (UNFCCC). 2013. 'Report of the Conference of the Parties on its nineteenth session, held in Warsaw from 11 to 23 November 2013'. https://unfccc.int/sites/default/files/resource/docs/2013/cop19/eng/10a01.pdf, accessed October 2021.

Vulnerable 20 (V-20). 2020. 'V20 calls on IMF and developed countries to develop practical steps to deliver climate finance commitment'. Climate Vulnerable Forum, https://www.v-20.org/our-voice/news/press-releases/v20-calls-on-imf-and-developed-countries-to-develop-practical-steps-to-deliver-climate-finance-commitment, accessed September 2021.

White House. 2021. 'Fact Sheet: President Biden and G7 leaders launch Build Back Better World (B3W) Partnership'. https://www.whitehouse.gov/briefing-room/statements-releases/2021/06/12/fact-sheet-president-biden-and-g7-leaders-launch-build-back-better-world-b3w-partnership/, accessed October 2021.

Winkler, H., Keen, S. and Marquard, A., 2021. 'South Africa: Policy approaches to guide finance flows for effective climate action in South Africa'. University of Cape Town, https://www.diw.de/documents/dokumentenarchiv/17/diw_01.c.821391.de/snapfi_financial_flows_sa_09072021.pdf, accessed October 2021.

World Commission on Environment and Development (WCED), 1987. *Our Common Future*. Oslo: World Commission on Environment and Development.

World Wildlife Fund (WWF). 2021. 'Expectations on loss and damage at COP26'. https://wwfint.awsassets.panda.org/downloads/wwf_expectations_on_loss___damage_at_cop26.pdf, accessed October 2021.

SECTION 3

Technology pathways for a just transition

EIGHT

Steering the South African energy sector towards a low carbon economy

The role of a well-managed energy transition

Nqobile Xaba and Zamanzima Mazibuko-Makena

INTRODUCTION

The provision of clean energy is central to achieving the climate goals outlined in the Paris Agreement which South Africa signed. If South Africa's energy system transitions away from fossil fuels towards a renewable energy-dominant system, this will enable the country to meet the Nationally Determined Contributions (NDCs) targets; these are currently that South Africa's greenhouse gas (GHG) emissions will range from 398–440 Mt CO_2-eq in 2030 (DFFE, 2021). There has been increasing pressure for South Africa to diversify from coal, decrease GHG emissions and improve the reliability of its electricity generation for some time. This culminated in the implementation of an Integrated

Resource Plan (IRP) through a Renewable Energy Independent Power Producer Procurement Programme (REIPPP) that had a few limited successes (DoE, 2015; DoE, 2019; Ting and Byrne, 2020). Although South Africa has experienced a swift introduction of renewables into the grid, the country still has widespread electricity challenges and high GHG emissions, evident in relentless load shedding and an NDC rating of 'highly insufficient' (CAT, 2021). Nonetheless, within the current electricity and climate crisis are opportunities for a sustainable energy transition in the country's energy system.

The production of energy through clean and efficient methods is one of the major undertakings for engineers and scientists (Stambouli, 2011). Sustainable energy is generated and consumed using processes that uphold human development and are not detrimental to the environment. The urgency for addressing sustainability issues and the interconnectedness of the social, environmental and economic goals for sustainable development have necessitated the use of the term 'just transition' to describe the pressing need for systemic changes in the energy sector (Geels and Schot, 2010). The current structure of the South African economy, however, is dominated by the energy (electricity), mining and petrochemicals sector. This structure leaves very little room for sustainability. A just transition requires policies concerning energy transitions to be equitable and sustainable and to entail purposeful engagement with all stakeholders, including communities, at the commencement of policy development (Ciplet and Harrison, 2020).

While renewable energy-based energy generation systems have huge potential to decentralise the energy sector, reducing GHG emissions will require an effort across all industries, and thus the adoption of a low carbon economy. Renewable energy offers opportunities for democratic processes and decision making through the REIPPP, and a move away from the current mineral-energy complex (MEC) paradigm and its vast reliance on fossil fuels. Hydrogen, an energy carrier that can decarbonise many sectors (including energy, agriculture, chemicals, steel and transport), can accelerate the adoption and impact of renewable energy. A hydrogen economy in South Africa will be critical in facilitating the country's full transition to a low carbon economy. Furthermore, using green hydrogen to advance the adoption of renewable energy presents a sustainable solution to the climate change crisis. The hydrogen economy can be developed using the notion of a sustainable transition by implementing systemic changes.

This chapter begins with a description of the properties and characteristics of hydrogen, and how these make hydrogen suitable as an energy carrier. These descriptions are intended to shed light on whether hydrogen can be used to help the South African economy transition towards a low carbon economy. The chapter goes on to assess the state of hydrogen and fuel cell technology, and evaluate how the country can position itself to fully exploit the transition and existing opportunities. The notion of a sustainable energy transition is also used to explore how the hydrogen economy can support a sustainable transition in South Africa. The chapter concludes with an assessment of which developments are required to create a thriving hydrogen economy, and with policy recommendations for such a development.

HYDROGEN

The hydrogen debate has evolved over the years from hydrogen being considered an energy carrier to discussion about the potential it presents for the decarbonisation agenda. Scientific and industrial interest in hydrogen technologies peaked for the first time in the 1970s during the oil crisis (Mazloomi and Gomez, 2012; Dawood et al., 2020). At that time, the global community had a shortage of oil and it was becoming more conscious of environmental problems such as acid rain and air pollution. Subsequently, in the 1990s and 2000s, climate change concerns emerged in bolder relief. However, the decline in oil prices and the financial crisis limited considerations of the potential use of hydrogen technologies. The priority given to the climate agenda in today's economy has resulted in hydrogen being one of the emerging technologies.

Hydrogen properties

The chemical element hydrogen is the third most abundant on earth, with silicon and oxygen in the second and first place, respectively (Mazloomi and Gomez, 2012; Felseghi et al., 2019; Sazali, 2020; Singla et al., 2021). The pure form of hydrogen is not freely available. As a result, hydrogen is not an energy source but an energy carrier (Rissman et al., 2020). Therefore, hydrogen needs to be produced from other hydrogen-containing compounds. Hydrogen is colourless, odourless and an element with a very small, lightweight molecular structure. It has three isotopes: protium (1H), deuterium (2H), and tritium (3H), which are formed when neutron bombards hydrocarbons. The most important property of hydrogen is its large gravimetric energy density, when compared to all other fuels, of 141.8 MJ kg^{1}: three times higher than that of liquid fuels at a higher heating value. Other advantages of hydrogen as a fuel include being environmentally friendly, the highest energy reserve factor and the largest conversion factor into electricity. As an energy vector, hydrogen is more attractive because it is non-toxic. It also has numerous other advantages: it can be generated from various compounds using different energy sources and processes; it can be transported remotely; it can be stored for a longer period compared to heat or electricity; and it can be used in a wide range of applications. The two main drawbacks of hydrogen are that it has a very low density (0.0838 kg m-^{3} at normal temperature and pressure, 20°C and 1 atmosphere) and needs to be compressed to increase its density. Secondly, it is not available in a naturally separate form, it is bound to carbon or oxygen. Liquifying and generating hydrogen are therefore both energy-consuming processes.

Hydrogen generation, storage and distribution

Hydrogen is a feedstock to various industrial processes including the production of ammonia and methanol. Fossil fuels have primarily been used in hydrogen production processes and these processes have long been established. Hydrogen production methods are well covered in the literature and include steam methane reforming (SMR); autothermal reforming (ATR); pyrolysis; electrolysis and gasification (Carrette et al., 2001; Sazali, 2020). The growing interest in clean hydrogen technologies has necessitated a classification system to differentiate between types of hydrogen, based on the source of hydrogen (Noussan et al., 2021). A colour coding system is used to label the type of hydrogen as follows: (i) grey or brown or black hydrogen is derived from fossil fuels causing carbon dioxide emissions; (ii) blue hydrogen is produced from natural gas either by steam methane reforming or auto thermal reforming but the CO_2 is captured and stored; (iii) green hydrogen is derived from electrolysers supplied with renewable energy and in some instances from biomethane reforming or solid mass gasification; (iv) yellow or purple hydrogen is derived from electrolysers supplied with nuclear energy This colour coding system is illustrated in Figure 8.1.

The distribution and storage of hydrogen is an important step in the hydrogen value chain. Hydrogen can be stored in liquid, gaseous or solid form (Carrette et al., 2001). Hydrogen gas has low energy density; it therefore requires a storage method that can increase the energy density. Hydrogen gas can be stored in high-pressure tanks as compressed hydrogen (Singla et al., 2021). Compressed hydrogen is time and cost efficient and provides an easy-to-use source for

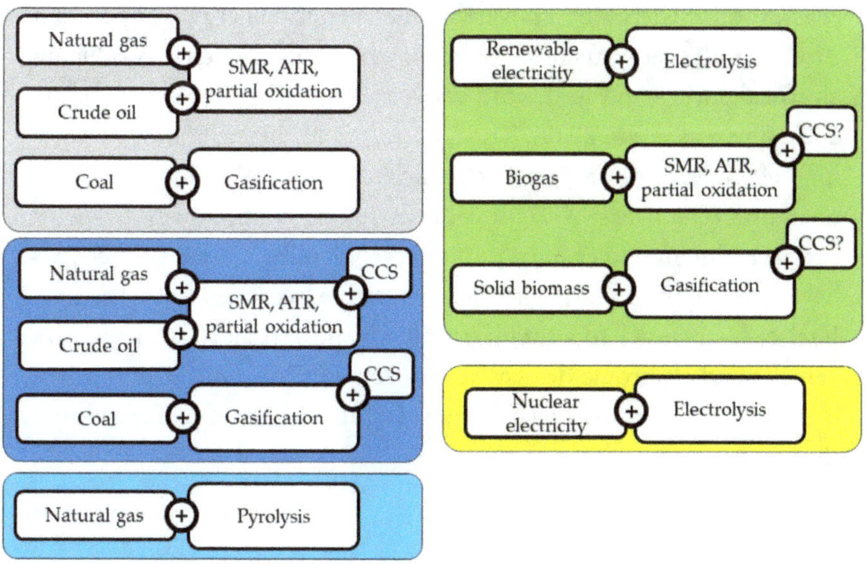

Figure 8.1: Hydrogen production pathways classified by colour

Source: Noussan et al. (2021: 3).

consumers (Mazloomi and Gomes, 2012). Hydrogen gas is cooled to -253°C to convert it to liquid hydrogen, which can also be stored in tanks. Liquid hydrogen storage must be limited to hydrogen already in liquid form to reduce energy consumption. Storage of hydrogen through other chemicals is beneficial as these chemicals can be easily handled and transported through existing infrastructure. Ammonia and LOHCs can store hydrogen in liquid state and atmospheric pressure. Pure hydrogen can also be stored underground in aquifers, depleted oil and gas reservoirs, and salt cravens (Noussan et al., 2021). Hydrogen can be stored in solid form as chemical compounds, and these are metal hydrides, activated carbon and composite porous materials.

Hydrogen application: Fuel cells

Increasing concerns over carbon dioxide emissions, energy security and efficiency have resulted in renewed interest in fuel cells, and in a focus on fuel cell technology to deliver efficient and clean energy. Fuel cells were commercialised globally in 2007, when Proton-Exchange Membrane Fuel Cells (PEMFC) and Direct Methanol Fuel Cells (DMFC) were commercially available for transport and portable electronics. Fuel cells produce energy by converting the chemical energy of hydrogen to electrical energy using a series of chemical reactions, producing electrical energy and heat, with water as by-products (Carrette et al., 2001; Thomas et al., 2020). The advantages of fuel cells include their high efficiency (40–85 per cent), quick start-up, reliability and silent operation (Demirbas, 2007). Fuel cells can be continuously fed with fuel to maintain power output indefinitely, unlike batteries. Fuel cells have a zero carbon footprint when renewable hydrogen is used as fuel. Fuel cells are used to provide stationary power, and also to power vehicles and electronic devices as illustrated in Table 8.1. The synergy between hydrogen and fuel cells must be fully exploited to decarbonise the transport and energy sector.

Table 8.1: Fuel cell applications

Sector	Application	Type of fuel cell	Reference
Stationery power	Back-up power, generating power in remote locations, standalone power supplies, distributed generation for buildings and cogeneration	PEMFC, solid oxide fuel cell, phosphoric acid fuel cell, molten carbon fuel cell	Singla et al., 2021; Carrette el al., 2001
Transport	Fuel cell vehicles (FCVHs): cars, buses, trucks, forklifts, ships, locomotives and aeroplanes	PEMFC	Ma et al., 2021; Singla et al., 2021; Sazali, 2020
Electronics	Phones, laptops and camcorders	PEMFC, DMFC	Ong et al., 2017; Fadzillah et al., 2019
Status	Concept socialised with government & others	In discussions on Framework Agreement	Early
Funder conditions	Unclear	Under negotiation	Unclear

Challenges and barriers for production and deployment of green hydrogen

The ultimate challenge for achieving a hydrogen economy is producing cost-competitive green hydrogen in large quantities. Hydrogen is produced through steam reforming of methane cheaply. Hydrogen and fuel cell technologies will not be fully implemented until green hydrogen can be produced competitively or more cheaply than grey hydrogen. The cost of renewables is already beginning to fall, making green hydrogen a more viable option (Thomas et al., 2020). The electricity used by electrolysers needs to be produced from renewables to produce green hydrogen, highlighting that renewable electricity is critical in achieving a green hydrogen economy. Progress towards improving the efficiency of electrolysers will ensure that they can compete with other hydrogen generation technologies. Electrolysers consume nine litres of fresh deionised water per kg of hydrogen produced per reaction stoichiometry, and this is a challenge as water scarcity will increase as climate change effects get worse (Noussan et al., 2021). Desalinisation and wastewater recovery technologies need to be developed to mitigate this problem.

Other barriers to overcome include: hydrogen storage in liquid form is difficult; infrastructure for hydrogen transport and distribution is expensive; and there is a lack of logistics for getting green hydrogen to consumers (Felseghi et al., 2019). Long-distance hydrogen transport requires seaborne hydrogen transport as pipeline transport costs increase with distance. Transportation of hydrogen on ships must ensure the highest density possible to minimise costs, and this means hydrogen must be in liquid form. Maintaining the cryogenic temperature necessary to keep pure hydrogen in liquid form consumes a lot of energy. The conversion of hydrogen to chemicals such as ammonia or liquid organic hydrocarbons (LOHC) is also energy intensive. Liquid hydrogen also evaporates at 2–3 per cent per day, causing the pressure in the tanks to increase, which creates a safety concern. Solutions include vacuum insulation, additional refrigeration systems and liquid nitrogen cooling. Storage of hydrogen as ammonia for global trade is the most viable option.

It is quite clear that certain shifts are required in order to fully exploit hydrogen and fuel cell technology: infrastructure for renewable energy sources must be developed to lower their cost. In addition, if green hydrogen is to be competitively priced or to replace grey hydrogen then the infrastructure for hydrogen storage and distribution must also be developed.

POSITIONING SOUTH AFRICA IN THE CURRENT GLOBAL TRANSITION USING HYDROGEN AND FUEL CELL TECHNOLOGIES

PGM beneficiation through fuel cell and electrolyser catalysts

South Africa is the leading producer of platinum group metals (PGMs) with more than 75 per cent of the world's known PGM reserves. This gives the country a strategic edge over others in efforts to advance fuel cell and hydrogen technology (Pollet et al., 2014). PGMs are used as catalysts for both fuel cells and electrolysers. Platinum, ruthenium and palladium are catalysts for fuel cells, and the efficiency and performance of the fuel cell is determined by these catalysts (Thomas et al., 2020; Bai et al., 2019). Platinum and iridium, however, are used as catalysts in electrolysers, utilised in the production of hydrogen (Creamer, 2021a). PGMs are mined in South Africa and exported to other regions where value addition occurs. South Africa has a unique opportunity to add value to the mined PGMs by developing and producing these PGM-based catalysts for fuel cell and electrolyser components. The mining of PGMs is a major part of the PGM value chain and threatens the transition to a low carbon economy. Sustainable mining practices will ensure that the net zero carbon target is achieved for PGMs. Fuel cells can play a critical role in decarbonising the mining sector through fuel cell-powered trucks used in mines. Anglo American has reported plans to have only fuel cell trucks in their mines (Anglo American, 2021). There is also an opportunity to use fuel cells to power underground mining trucks, loaders and machinery that uses diesel engines. The limitation for this application lies in managing the risks of delivering and storing hydrogen safely in confined spaces. Hydrogen South Africa (HySA) Infrastructure is running a facility to evaluate the risks of hydrogen storage technologies underground to make this feasible in South Africa (HySA Infrastructure, 2019).

Advancement of green hydrogen and power fuels

Green hydrogen can be produced from water, using electrolysis combined with power supplied by renewable energy sources such as photovoltaic, solar heat and wind energy (Singla et al., 2021; Noussan et al., 2021). Green hydrogen production can be used to store the excess electricity generated from renewables in a form of hydrogen. A system combining renewables, electrolysers and fuel cells can provide uninterrupted power, and so the combination of these offers the best possible option for achieving zero carbon electricity. The renewables provide electricity during peak times while excess electricity is deployed to electrolysers to produce hydrogen. This hydrogen then provides the energy required for fuel cells to provide power off peak. Fuel cells and electrolysers can be deployed anywhere, thus enabling clean energy to become accessible to a wider population. Compared with Europe and

Asia, South Africa has better conditions in terms of sunlight and wind to sustain the production of solar and wind renewables. Green hydrogen is the one energy vector that can decarbonise many sectors through power fuels. Power fuels are synthetic gas or liquid fuels produced from green hydrogen including pure hydrogen, hydrocarbons and ammonia (Roos and Wright, 2021). Many sectors can be decarbonised using power fuels including the chemicals, the transport (road, rail, aviation, shipping, heavy road vehicles), manufacturing (green steel) and the agricultural sector (fertilizer). Green hydrogen can be used to replace coal in the production of steel, using a mixture of hydrogen and carbon monoxide as reducing agents (IEA, 2019; IRENA, 2019). This route accounts for 7 per cent of global steel production. Steel is primarily produced using blast furnace basic oxygen furnace route at 90 per cent globally and this emits grey hydrogen mixed with other gases including carbon monoxide. The production of one tonne of steel emits 1.4 tonnes of CO_2 on average. Technological developments are looking into using carbon capture utilisation and storage (CCUS) to lower the CO_2 emissions, and CO_2 avoidance pathways where low carbon energy sources and reduction using hydrogen are used.

Beneficiation of green hydrogen

Africa's abundance of wind and sun present South Africa with an opportunity to export green hydrogen, either in its pure form or as an energy-intensive commodity, to countries without the same abundance of these natural resources. South Africa can competitively produce green hydrogen at US$1.8–2/kg H_2 (Roos and Wright, 2021). Europe and Japan have committed to bulk hydrogen import. Japan's climate obligations came into effect when they signed the Tokyo Protocol in 1998. They released a hydrogen roadmap and fuel cell strategy in 2014 that aims to decarbonise their transport, commercial and power sector using hydrogen (Japan, 2020). Europe is set to decarbonise the transport sector through its renewable energy directive and recently the ambitious European Green Deal (European Commission, 2019). Germany also drafted its national hydrogen strategy which identifies the country's requirement for between 90–110 TWh annual hydrogen volume. Germany will not be able to meet this demand through domestic generation and it will therefore seek to import hydrogen (Fuhrmann, 2020). The Netherlands also published its hydrogen strategy in 2020 with the aim of being 100 per cent climate neutral by 2050 (The Netherlands Government Hydrogen Strategy, 2020). The Netherlands can act as the energy hub in the green hydrogen supply chain due to its location, ports (Port of Rotterdam) and extensive gas grid and storage capacity. In Belgium, the port of Antwerp has a 613-km hydrogen pipeline by Air Liquide and is planning on becoming the hub for hydrogen production, transport and distribution. Currently, the Port of Antwerp produces 10–15 per cent of European Union's hydrogen (Roos and Wright, 2021).

South Africa currently has a €160 billion market potential in various green hydrogen beneficiation projects including green ammonia, sustainable aviation fuel and green steel. Green ammonia made from nitrogen and green hydrogen can be used as fertilizer, as fuel for ships and in ammonia fuel cells (Bischof-Niemz, 2021; Gallucci, 2021). Ammonia can be traded as a commodity for the forementioned applications, as ammonia cracking to release hydrogen is not efficient. Sustainable aviation fuel made from green hydrogen and carbon can decarbonise the aviation industry. Sasol is partnering with Linde, Enertrag and Navitas to bid for sustainable aviation fuel production (Sasol, 2021b).

Green steel is another commodity that can revolutionise the steel manufacturing industry. South Africa already mines and exports iron ore. If it does produce green hydrogen, then it can use this to produce reduced iron ore. This reduced iron ore can then be traded as a commodity which can be used to help decarbonise steel and other industries (IEA, 2019). In this way, value has been added in the country while reducing CO_2 emissions globally. Iron and steel currently produce 2.5Gt of CO_2 emissions and the RDI technology can reduce this by 0.8Gt. Green hydrogen can be traded as a commodity in liquid or compressed form or encapsulated in energy carriers, through existing natural gas infrastructure. This section has established that there is a market for green hydrogen export that South Africa needs to tap into. The success of this concept depends on infrastructure and policy development.

THE STATE OF SA'S FUEL CELL AND HYDROGEN TECHNOLOGIES

The inception of the South African hydrogen development strategy

South African has not been immune to the global transition trends in which hydrogen is receiving unprecedented attention as the fuel of the future. President Cyril Ramaphosa has announced the country's intention to move from research and development towards manufacturing and commercialisation. South Africa has developed strategies for, and invested in, the hydrogen economy; its plans for this are outlined in the research, development and innovation strategies developed by the Department of Science and Innovation (DSI) in 2007 (HySA Systems, 2014; Pollet et al., 2014; MISTRA, 2020). These were rebranded as Hydrogen South Africa (HySA).

HySA was established to ensure that South Africa participated in the fuel cell and hydrogen technology space considering the country's PGM endowment. It was envisioned that the HySA Programme would increase economic growth and enhance the country's skills. It was also envisaged that the programme would be South Africa's response and contribution to the global climate change challenge and thus allow the country to avoid any future carbon-related penalties on exports. HySA is comprised of three Centres of Competence with their own mandates, namely, HySA Infrastructure, HySA Systems and HySA Catalysis. The Centres of Competence were strategically placed at various institutions across the country. HySA Infrastructure's (North-West University-NWU) mandate is to develop novel technologies for hydrogen production, storage and distribution. HySA Systems' (University of the Western Cape-UWC) objectives are to develop hydrogen and fuel cell systems, produce prototypes and products, validate and verify these technologies, and conduct research on materials for combined heat and power (CHP) and fuel cell vehicles (FCVHs) systems. HySA Catalysis (University of Cape Town-UCT & MINTEK) focuses on portable power, through the development of membrane electrode assemblies (MEAs) and catalysts for fuel cells. The HySA Programme was projected to be a 15-year initiative to run in three phases. The programme has made great strides in generating capacity, knowledge and skills through publications and student/ human resource training. The programme was also key in developing prototypes and developing systems to support fuel cell and hydrogen activities in the country.

The HySA Programme

The programme has demonstrated the ability of hydrogen and fuel cell technology to provide clean energy in isolated regions. HySA installed a 2.5kW fuel cell power system to provide power for 500 pupils in Poelano Secondary School in Ventersdorp (HySA, 2018; HySA infrastructure, 2019). A 5kW solar PV system was installed to provide electricity used in electrolysers to generate hydrogen and a bore hole was installed to provide the water needed for electrolysis. Furthermore, a fuel cell system was installed at Windsor clinic in Randburg for continuous power supply during power cuts (HySA 2018; MISTRA 2020). Three schools in Cofimvaba in the Eastern Cape had fuel cell systems installed to meet their basic energy needs (HySA, 2018). These demonstrations are evidence of the important role that the deployment of fuel cell and hydrogen technologies will play in energy access, security and equity.

The HySA Programme must feed into existing value chains for economic stimulation. There need to be partnerships with the private sector to commercialise the prototypes and products from the HySA Programme. HyPlat is one example of a company specialising in MEA production in partnership with HySA, MINTEK, DSI, Amplats and others (GIZ, 2016). HySA Infrastructure is conducting research on the use of fuel cells and hydrogen technology for underground mining instead of diesel-powered machines and vehicles (McKay, 2019; HySA infrastructure, 2019). The test facility for assessing the feasibility of using hydrogen in underground confined spaces is based in NWU. The success of this project could revolutionise the mining sector. The HySA Programme has resulted in development of the South African hydrogen roadmap and in the establishment of a so-called 'platinum valley' in South Africa – an industrial cluster bringing together various hydrogen applications – as the next phase of the hydrogen economy (MISTRA, 2020).

South African industry transitions towards a hydrogen economy

There is a notable shift towards embracing the hydrogen economy in South Africa as large corporations are taking up the challenge to participate in the low carbon transition. Toyota South Africa Motors (TSAM) is partnering with Sasol to develop the hydrogen mobility ecosystem (Sasol, 2021a; Kirby, 2021; Takouleu, 2021). TSAM plans to manufacture the first fuel cell car in South Africa with a demonstration planned for 2021 (Kirby, 2021; Patel, 2021), in addition to the Toyota Mirai which is commercially available and is produced abroad, but TSAM is planning to also start manufacturing this FCVH in South Africa. Sasol, for its part, is a major producer of grey hydrogen and it brings expertise in the production, utilisation and marketing of grey hydrogen, as well as their ambitions of leading the establishment of a green hydrogen economy.

South Africa exported 63.9 per cent of the total vehicles it manufactured in 2020 to a range of countries, including the UK, Japan, Germany, France, Australia and others. Three out of every four vehicles exported were destined for Europe (DTIC, 2021). The European Union (EU) has implemented stricter legislation through the EU Green Deal; South African manufacturing needs to transition towards supplying zero emission vehicles. TSAM manufacturing FCVH will play a critical role in ensuring that our export revenue is secured in this sector. However, the country must also work towards ensuring that these FCVHs enter the domestic market. South Africa will need to develop a hydrogen mobility value chain with infrastructure investments in hydrogen generation, production, storage, transportation and fuelling sites. The TSAM and Sasol's hydrogen roadmap will address concerns related to infrastructure, regulation, technology, demand, cost competitiveness, skills, competence and time to market. Ultimately, partnerships and collaboration between government, the public and industry will enable the full realisation of hydrogen mobility economy in South Africa. TSAM, in partnership with other stakeholders, is investigating the pilot of other FCVH, including the bus already available in the European market by Caetano, and the heavy-duty truck by Hino that is only at a prototype stage (Kirby, 2021; Takouleu, 2021). Fuel cell vehicles, like trucks, are more suited to long-distance transport than battery electric vehicles (BEVs) since the former have a range of 500–600km on a full hydrogen tank, while BEVs have 200–300km on a single charge (Metcalfe et al., 2020). FCVHs are more fuel efficient and refuelling hydrogen is similar to diesel refuelling, both quicker than charging a battery. South African national roads are flooded with trucks for goods transportation; replacing these diesel-powered trucks with hydrogen fuel cell-powered trucks would be an efficient way to decarbonise the logistics industry. TSAM and Sasol are planning on implementing this along the N3 route as part of the hydrogen mobility pilot (Takouleu, 2021).

Sasol is also taking a stance on the transition to the green economy and has declared plans to take a leading role in the hydrogen economy since it has the capacity, infrastructure and technology to transition towards green fuels production (Sasol, 2021b; Grobler, 2021). The rapid development of power to liquids and high value chemicals (PtX) presents an opportunity for Sasol to leverage their Fischer-Tropsch (FT) technology. Sasol is partnering with Linde, Enertrag and Navitas to bid for sustainable aviation fuel production. They are developing an FT-based PtX process to produce power fuels, including carbon neutral kerosene for jet fuel, using Sasol's proprietary FT technology and technology from partners.

Sustainable aviation fuel is the most likely winner in power fuels as aviation is the industry that is hardest to decarbonise. Power fuels must be used in instances where they are the only option to avoid competing for resources and finance (IRENA, 2019). For example, there is no need to invest in green diesel when an option is investment in FCHV as the most radical and progressive technology. However, green aviation fuel is the only option to decarbonise the aviation industry. Green ammonia and methanol for the agriculture and chemicals industry are a more viable route for power fuels as they are the hardest to abate.

The mobile company Vodacom uses 300 fuel cells to power its network in South Africa and these fuel cells were imported from a Taiwanese company, CHEM energy (Patel, 2021). The Department of Trade, Industry and Competition (DTIC) secured an agreement with CHEM energy that saw the Taiwanese company building a US$200 million fuel cell manufacturing facility at the Dube Trade port in KwaZulu-Natal (Patel, 2021; FuelCellWorks, 2020). This facility has a capacity for production of 1500PEMFCs per annum. This establishment helps to attract investments to beneficiate South Africa's PGMs locally and job creation.

Mining sector contribution to hydrogen and fuel cells technology development and deployment

The primary contribution of mining in the green economy is through the production of PGMs, which are critical components for fuel cell and electrolysers. However, mining is a large consumer of Eskom's electricity, consuming 15 per cent per annum (Eskom, 2010). The industrial sector (includes mining) contributed 27 per cent of South Africa's GHG emissions in 2015 (DEA, 2020). There needs to be a change in the mining of minerals to achieve a zero net carbon. Anglo American has invested in a hydrogen-powered truck fleet for their Mogalakwena PGM mine to reduce their carbon footprint (Creamer, 2020). They are partnering with the energy company ENGIE to provide a 3.5MW alkaline electrolyser to produce green hydrogen to fuel the trucks. This project needs to invest in renewable energy to provide electricity to power the electrolyser for a net zero carbon emission. This will reduce the heavy reliance of South African mining on the Eskom grid and the use of diesel. Anglo American is also partnering with DSI, ENGIE, South African National Development Institute (SANEDI) and Bambili Energy to conduct a feasibility study on the hydrogen valley in PGM-rich regions as part of the initiatives to establish the hydrogen roadmap (Anglo American, 2021; Bambili Energy, 2021). These partnerships are all evidence of mining companies' investments in fuel cell technology development and deployment. Implats has invested R6 million in HySA Systems to develop a fuel cell prototype for mining applications and provides HySA Catalysis with platinum to be used for research into fuel cell catalysts (Patel, 2020). Implats also launched a fuel cell forklift to be used in their mines to reduce their mining GHG emissions, as part of its fuel cell strategy (Implats, no date; Creamer, 2021b). The future of mining in South Africa lies in the industry's ability to innovate and take part in the green economy transition.

Cities adopting the hydrogen economy

The eThekwini municipality is the first in South Africa to publish an integrated resource plan, titled the eThekwini Integrated Resource Plan (EIRP) (EIRP, 2020; Creamer, 2021c; Mkhabela, 2021). It includes plans to procure 40 per cent of the municipality's energy from renewable energy sources by 2030 and to contract its first independent power producer in 2022. This is in response to developments in the hydrogen economy as the city plans to position itself as an exporter of green hydrogen. The city acknowledges that renewable hydrogen will play an important role in the decarbonisation of the energy sector. The coastal cities all enjoy a competitive benefit as a hydrogen export hubs. The port of Coega in Port Elizabeth has also been identified as a potential hydrogen export site due to its proximity to the Petro-SA plant that is running out of gas and can be repurposed for hydrogen production. The Eastern Cape has abundant renewable energy (wind and solar) already installed with 1209MW of total wind and solar capacity (Roos and Wright, 2021; Gxasheka et al., 2018). The city of Johannesburg plans to obtain 35 per cent of its energy from renewables by 2030 to reduce reliance on Eskom. Hydrogen fuel cells are amongst the options being proposed and the city has consulted with Mitochondria Energy, a fuel cell company (Bloomberg, 2021). South African cities will play a major role in decentralising energy in order to facilitate energy security for its citizens and the meeting of climate goals. The role of municipalities will be to facilitate third-party access to the grid for green energy trade, and to maintain the grid for those without access to renewables. Policies and frameworks for these initiatives are required to ensure energy access for all.

SUSTAINABLE TRANSITION IN SOUTH AFRICA AND THE HYDROGEN ECONOMY

Sustainable transitions require an integrated approach, one that does not only aim to safeguard the environment but also to ensure sustainable energy for all, and the inclusion of all in opportunities presented by the transition. The new technological systems introduced by the hydrogen economy open up opportunities such as local production and ownership of new technologies. Furthermore, there are prospects of reducing energy poverty and increasing access to energy – a fundamental aspect of a sustainable or just transition to a low carbon economy (Janikowska and Kulczycka, 2021). The establishment of a hydrogen economy in South Africa in support of a low carbon transition should, essentially, not negatively impact the poor and disadvantaged; rather, they should participate in its growth and development. This participation includes women, who have reportedly been unable to leverage all opportunities available in the energy sector due to restrictions and culture that hinder their progression (ENERGIA, 2020; Lieu et al., 2020). Gender mainstreaming of energy policies and strategies should ensure women's entry into the renewable energy sector and the hydrogen economy, and so be at the core of planning a sustainable transition.

The protection of jobs (or mitigation of the impact of job losses) and livelihoods with the transition from fossil fuels is also crucial. Some countries, albeit in the Global North, put in place mitigation strategies for the impact of a low carbon transition. Included in these strategies were early retirement packages for workers who were approaching retirement age and reskilling younger workers to enter the renewable energy market, or to branch out into other industries and sectors (Daniel, 2020). These programmes were not infallible as not all the workers got absorbed into the labour market, but they were a step in the right direction. Therefore, upskilling and reskilling (and a sustainable plan for older workers) should be an integral part of developing a hydrogen economy in South Africa.

South Africa has formulated various policies and frameworks that promote a just transition (Mohlakoana and Wolpe, 2021). However, it has no actual, established just transition policy. This is an important consideration in the development of a hydrogen economy and a policy, regulatory and capacity environment which can support this economy as part of a sustainable transition. Sustainability should be at the centre of the development of a hydrogen economy, ensuring future energy security and creating sustainable employment. What is required is strong governance, political will and enabling policies.

Systems required for a sustainable transition to a hydrogen economy

There is no doubt that many opportunities lie within the hydrogen economy, particularly for South Africa. With the increasing effects of climate change and the worsening of the state of the economy because of COVID-19, applying a long-term recovery strategy that focuses on cleaner and more sustainable forms of energy is even more urgent. However, the country needs to be strategic and nimble in formulating and implementing a systematic plan to ensure it benefits from these prospects. HySA has been driving the development of a hydrogen roadmap for South Africa with the aim of establishing an inclusive hydrogen society. The roadmap is intended to be an enabler for a compact between industry, labour, communities and government.

This compact would perhaps also address the coal-driven mineral energy complex (MEC) that South Africa is locked into and help take forward a just transition that is driven by renewable energy and the hydrogen economy. A well-thought-out and systematic strategy would also prevent green hydrogen initiatives in South Africa's electricity sector being integrated into a high-carbon and electricity-intensive industrial infrastructure. This infrastructure would offer highly unequal access, and only limited benefits for labour and the energy poor (Baker, 2015). This is what was seen with the introduction of renewable energy, in a situation in which the MEC was still a key driver of policy decisions in electricity, and still represented an integral relationship between the state, private capital, and core mining and energy activities. This was the case despite the emergence of new players and evolving institutions and technologies in the energy sector. South Africa should aim for a strategy that facilitates the introduction of low carbon jobs, and enables a transition to a low carbon economy, which breaks away from South Africa's dependence on the MEC (in its current form).

Various other systems need to be in place to ensure that South Africa is able to leverage the opportunities.

Policy development and a regulatory framework

Coherent government policy will be necessary to support a sufficiently rapid rate of hydrogen development and provide adequate incentives for the transition towards green hydrogen. At the Green Economy Summit, the government used a 'supportive regulatory framework' to frame a 'green economy' pathway (South African Planning Institute, 2010). This pathway is aimed at forming green industries through sector action plans and market instruments that will offer incentives for the development and implementation of low carbon initiatives. Other issues were explored including: (i) greater localisation of manufacturing of materials (solar, nuclear, wind, hydro power and electronics industries); (ii) the expansion of green jobs opportunities through public works programmes; and (iii) acceleration of programmes supported by the Clean Technology Fund ($500 million from the World Bank) to meet renewable energy targets.

Various government institutions have all been charged with supporting the low carbon economy. They include the departments of Science and Innovation; Trade, Industry and Competition; Mineral Resources and Energy; and Public Works (Green Economy Summit, 2010). The Department of Forestry, Fisheries and the Environment is charged with leading these initiative. A regulatory framework for a low carbon economy needs to be extended to include the hydrogen economy too.

Progress is being made in the South African hydrogen space; however more steps need to be taken for South Africa to fully realise the benefits of the hydrogen economy. These include:

- Finalising the South Africa hydrogen strategy and roadmap and implementing a monitoring and evaluation system, including a compact between relevant stakeholders;
- Having a central coordinator of all the activities in the hydrogen economy;
- Providing clarity on which government ministry and department will be the main champion for a hydrogen economy;
- Striking a balance between regulation and providing an enabling environment for a competitive market;
- Accelerating renewable energy licensing needed for hydrogen production; and

- Capacity building and skills development for the entire hydrogen economy value-chain.

South Africa needs to commit to a systematic, transparent, accountable and enabling policy environment for hydrogen in order for the country to leverage the opportunities provided by the hydrogen economy for the benefit of all.

Education and skills development

The prospects of the hydrogen economy being a driver of increased employment is certainly an important addition to the already compelling list of advantages. It has been repeatedly reported that the majority of the jobs that will be created by the hydrogen economy, however, are expected to be high-tech and classified as skilled, requiring either university education or vocational training. A report by the Department of Energy in the US found that existing and emerging fuel cell applications hold large job growth potential and that as various fuel cell applications gain market share, the industry is expected to undergo significant growth. According to the report (US Department of Energy, 2016):

> As market demand for hydrogen and fuel cell technologies increases across sectors of the economy, there will be an increasing need for trained and experienced personnel and accompanying services such as qualified maintenance technicians, installers, manufacturing professionals, trainers, insurers, and educators.

Furthermore, another study in the US found that the hydrogen and fuel cell industries require numerous types of occupations, experience and skills (Bezdek, 2019). Many occupations in these industries will have educational requirements ranging from apprenticeships, matric qualifications and on-the-job training to more advanced qualifications such as undergraduate and postgraduate university degrees. Occupations will include scientists, engineers, chemists, managers and technicians. Average salaries for these emerging jobs vary significantly, from approximately US$23 000 for technicians to nearly US$140 000 for a director of hydrogen development (Bezdek, 2019). The study also included a position for a fuel cell engineering intern with an average salary of US$6 800. In South Africa, it is estimated that one-third of Technical and Vocational Education and Training (TVET) graduates are unemployed; there is therefore undoubtedly a critical skills gap between industry demands and what tertiary education is supplying. It is crucial that the country's tertiary education system – including university and TVET college systems – are aligned with industry needs and with opportunities to improve labour absorption in a future low carbon economy. Specifically, these institutions need to offer the right qualifications, and turn out enough graduates, for every hydrogen fuel cell technology application and sector-specific skills requirement.

Investment and creation of markets

Hydrogen and fuel cell technologies offer South Africa an opportunity to develop the local market for PGMs. This is particularly important in the wake of the local PGM industry enduring a decreased demand for platinum. Furthermore, as previously stated, there is a billion-dollar export market for green hydrogen that South Africa can exploit, which requires an investment in infrastructure and policy development. Market formation in the hydrogen economy speaks to the need for government to intervene to develop a market for new emerging technology. The formation of a fully fledged hydrogen and fuel cell industry can be achieved through government leading financial investment into the hydrogen economy, and the private sector co-funding and leading the piloting and demonstrations of new hydrogen technologies in collaboration with the Department of Science and Innovation (DSI), Department of Mineral Resources and Energy (DMRE) and Department of Trade, Industry and Competition (DTIC).

The government's extensive procurement processes which have, for example, worked for the Renewable Energy Public Procurement Programme, can be used to create a market for hydrogen. Therefore, the government can create markets by designing its procurement programmes in a way that will enable the development of the sector or will alter costs for existing players. The government can also provide incentives for fossil fuel companies to provide funding for alternative markets through tax rebates, or through a reasonable carbon tax.

Furthermore, beyond education and skills development in the hydrogen economy, the government and private sector can commit to investing in national hydrogen research and providing financial support for the existing HySA Programme. It would also be valuable to attract leading scientists to enhance current research efforts and to create a coordinating council for public and private sector hydrogen related research,. The government should, in addition, provide support for international collaboration.

CONCLUSION

This chapter has provided an analysis of the state of South Africa's hydrogen economy and PGM fuel cell technology sector, in the context of renewed interest in hydrogen and its potential to help the South African economy to transition to a low carbon one. The properties and characteristics of hydrogen, and how they make the mineral suitable as an energy carrier, were reported on and explored including hydrogen generation, storage and distribution. Furthermore, hydrogen's utility in fuel cell technology is highlighted and the role of platinum group metals, which South Africa is highly endowed with, is emphasised. The chapter points to the opportunities that lie in the hydrogen economy and how South Africa can position itself to take advantage of the transition to a hydrogen economy. With a €160 billion market potential, embracing and investing in the hydrogen economy is crucial for South Africa's economic growth as well as the creation of employment opportunities.

It was noted that there is a considerable shift by large corporations in South Africa, such as Toyota and Sasol, towards adopting the hydrogen economy and contributing to the low carbon transition. Additionally, the mining sector, whose key role in the hydrogen economy is through the production of PGMs that are critical components for fuel cells and electrolysers, is also investing in fuel cell technology development and deployment. Major cities in the country have also embarked on promoting the hydrogen economy and acknowledging its role in decarbonisation.

However, the chapter also argues that a transition to a low carbon economy, facilitated by the hydrogen economy, needs to be sustainable and just. Using a sustainable energy transition concept, the chapter highlights some of the core requirements of a just transition which will ensure that the development of a hydrogen economy is inclusive (particularly of disadvantaged groups), and also addresses issues of unemployment, skills development and energy security for all. The hydrogen economy must enable an inclusive contribution to the country's economic development and should not only create (local) jobs and ownership, but also address gender disparities. An integrated approach should therefore be incorporated into all just transition planning and strategies, including in the establishment of a hydrogen economy.

The chapter also explores some of the requirements for launching a hydrogen economy in South Africa and provides recommendations for an economy in which hydrogen is successfully deployed. Various systems, regulatory frameworks and enabling policies need to be in place to support the hydrogen economy, including ensuring there is human capacity for the employment opportunities created by this transition. Moreover, the creation of markets is central to the development of the hydrogen economy as there needs to be demand for these technologies. Essentially, all stakeholders, such as practitioners, independent power producers, academics, government and international partners, need to collaborate in the transition process to ensure that it produces desired outcomes.

REFERENCES

Anglo American. 2021. 'Anglo American collaboration on feasibility study for South Africa's hydrogen valley'. https://www.angloamerican.com/media/press releases/2021/31-03-2021, accessed 8 May 2021.

Anglo American. 2019. 'How hydrogen fuel cells work to power the future'. https://www.angloamerican.com/futuresmart/stories/our-industry/technology/how-hydrogen-fuel-cells-work, accessed 15 April 2019.

Bai, J., Liu, D., Yang, J. and Chen, Y. 2019. 'Nanocatalysts for electrocatalytic oxidation of ethanol'. *ChemSusChem*, 12(10), 2117–2132.

Baker, L. 2015. 'Renewable energy in South Africa's minerals-energy complex: A "low carbon' transition?'. *Review of African Political Economy*, 42(144), 245–261.

Bambili Energy. 2021. 'Anglo American collaboration on feasibility study for South Africa's hydrogen valley'. https://www.bambilienergy.com/anglo-american-collaboration-on-feasibility-study-for-south-africa-s-hydrogen-valley, accessed 22 April 2021.

Bezdek, R.H. 2019. 'The hydrogen economy and jobs of the future'. *Renewable Energy and Environmental Sustainability*, 4, 1.

Bischof-Niemz, T, 2021. 'Green hydrogen export opportunity for South Africa'. Renewable hydrogen and green powerfuel opportunities for South Africa webinar, 9 February 2021.

Bloomberg. 20 May 2021. 'Joburg plans move away from Eskom's grid, targeting renewable power'. https://businesstech.co.za/news/energy/491993/joburg-plans-move-away-from-eskoms-grid-targeting-renewable-power/, accessed 20 May 2021.

Carrette, L., Friedrich, K.A. and Stimming, U. 2001. 'Fuel cells-fundamentals and applications'. *Fuel Cells*, 1(1), 5–39.

Ciplet, D. and Harrison, J. L. 2020. 'Transition tensions: Mapping conflicts in movements for a just and sustainable transition'. *Environmental Politics*, 29(3), 435–456.

Climate Action Tracker (CAT). 2021. CAT Climate Target Update Tracker: South Africa. https://climateactiontracker.org/climate-target-update-tracker/south-africa/, accessed 24 August 2021.

Creamer, M. 7 April 2021a. 'Value of iridium in electrolysis could top R90bn mark in years ahead – HySA'. Engineering News, https://www.engineeringnews.co.za/article/value-of-iridium-in-electrolysis-could-top-r90bn-mark-in-years-ahead-hysa-2021-04-07/rep_id:4136, accessed 14 April 2021

Creamer M. 29 March 2021b. 'South African-developed fuel cell passing tests at Implats Refinery'. *Engineering News*, https://www.engineeringnews.co.za/article/south-african-developed-fuel-cell-passing-tests-at-implats-refinery-2021-03-27, accessed 19 May 2021.

Creamer T. 29 April 2021c. 'eThekwini aiming to conclude first IPP contract in 2022 as city mulls hydrogen role'. *Engineering News*, https://www.engineeringnews.co.za/article/ethekwini-aiming-to-conclude-first-ipp-contract-in-2022-as-city-mulls-hydrogen-role-2021-04-29, accessed 15 April 2021.

Creamer, M. 2020. 'Anglo praised for blazing decarbonised mining trail with hydrogen truck project'. *Mining Weekly*, https://www.miningweekly.com/article/anglo-american-praised-for-blazing-decarbonised-mining-trail-with-hydrogen-truck-project-2020-11-25, accessed 7 April 2021.

Daniel, M, 2020. 'Defining a just transition for Sub-Saharan energy workers:

A discussion paper of the Sub-Sahara Africa Energy Network (SSAEN)'. Labour Research Service, http://library.fes.de/pdf-files/bueros/suedafrika/16973.pdf, accessed 20 September 2021.

Dawood, F., Anda, M. and Shafiullah, G.M. 2020. 'Hydrogen production for energy: An overview'. *International Journal of Hydrogen Energy*, 45, 3847–3869.

Demirbas, A. 2007. 'Fuel cells as clean energy converters'. *Energy Sources*, Part A, 29, 185–191.

Department of Energy (DoE). 2015. 'State of renewable energy in South Africa'. http://www.energy.gov.za/files/media/Pub/State-of-Renewable-Energy-in-South-Africa.pdf, accessed 3 August 2021.

Department of Energy (DoE). 2019. 'Integrated Resources Plan (IRP)'. http://www.energy.gov.za/IRP/2019/IRP-2019.pdf, accessed 3 August 2021.

Department of Environmental Affairs (DEA). 2020. 'South Africa's Low-Emission Development Strategy 2050'.https://www.environment.gov.za/sites/default/files/docs/2020lowemission_developmentstrategy.pdf, accessed 9 September 2021.

Department of Forestry, Fisheries and the Environment (DFFE), 2021. 'South Africa's First Nationally Determined Contribution under the Paris Agreement'. https://www.environment.gov.za/sites/default/files/reports/draftnationalydeterminedcontributions_2021updated.pdf, accessed 26 May 2021.

Department of Trade, Industry, and Competition (DTIC). 2021. 'The South African Road to Production of Electric Vehicles (The Roadmap)'. http://www.thedtic.gov.za/wp-content/uploads/EV_Green_Paper.pdf, accessed 18 May 2021.

Deutsche Gesellschaft für Internationale Zusammenarbeit (GIZ) GmbH. 2016. 'Hydrogen research activities in South Africa: A review'. https://www.energypartnership.org.za/fileadmin/user_upload/southafrica/media_elements/GIZ_Raventech_2016_-_Hydrogen_Research_Activities_in_SA_Digital_low-res.pdf, accessed 18 May 2021.

ENERGIA. 2020. 'The ENERGIA Gender and Energy Research Programme: A Short Overview of the Results'. *International Network on Gender and Sustainable Energy*, www.hivos.org, accessed 17 September 2021.

Eskom. 2010. 'The energy efficiency series: Towards an energy efficient mining sector'. https://www.eskom.co.za/sites/idm/Documents/121040ESKD_Mining_Brochure_paths.pdf, accessed 9 September 2021.

eThekwini Integrated Resource Plan (EIRP). 2020. http://www.durban.gov.za/Resource_Centre/public_notices/Energy%20policy%20for%20public/Documents/eThekwiniDraftIntegratedResourcePlan01.pdf, accessed 15 April 2021.

European Commission. 2019. 'The European Green Deal'. https://eur-lex.europa.eu/resource.html?uri=cellar:b828d165-1c22-11ea-8c1f-

01aa75ed71a1.0002.02/DOC_1&format=PDF, accessed 6 August 2021.

Fadzillah, D.M., Kamarudin, S.K., Zainoodin, M.A. and Masdar, M.S. 2019. 'Critical challenges in the system development of direct alcohol fuel cells as portable power supplies: An overview'. *International Journal of Hydrogen Energy,* 44(5), 3031–3054.

Felseghi, R.A., Carcadea, E., Raboaca, M.S., Trufin, C.N. and Filote, C. 2019. 'Hydrogen fuel cell technology for the sustainable future of stationary applications'. *Energies*, 12(23), 4593.

Fuel cell today. (no date). 'History of fuel cells', Fuel Cell Works, https://fuelcellsworks.com/knowledge/history/#:~:text=The%20term%20fuel%20cell%20was,the%20technology%20generally%20remained%20obscure, accessed 5 March 2021.

FuelCellWorks. 7 September 2020. 'CHEM Corporation completes its $200 million fuel cell production factory in South Africa's Dube TradePort Special Economic Zone'. https://fuelcellsworks.com/news/chem-corporation-completes-its-200-million-fuel-cell-production-factory-in-south-africas-dube-tradeport-special-economic-zone/, accessed 18 May 2021.

Fuhrmann, M. 2020. 'Serious efforts to realize a decarbonized society; development of green hydrogen supply infrastructure is the challenge'. *Mitsui & Co. Global Strategic Studies Institute Monthly Report*, https://www.mitsui.com/mgssi/en/report/detail/__icsFiles/afieldfile/2021/02/19/2012_fuhrmann_e.pdf, accessed 6 August 2021.

Gallucci, M. 2021. 'Why the shipping industry Is betting big on ammonia: Ammonia engines and fuel cells could slash carbon emissions'. IEE Spectrum, https://spectrum.ieee.org/transportation/marine/why-the-shipping-industry-is-betting-big-on-ammonia, accessed 29 April 2021.

Geels, F.W. and Schot, J. 2010. 'The dynamics of transitions', in Grin, J., Rotmans, J. and Schot J. (eds), *Transitions to Sustainable Development: New Directions in the Study of Long Term Transformative Change*. New York: Taylor & Francis Group.

Green Economic Summit. 2010. 'SA Green Economy Summit'. http://www.sagreeneconomysummit.co.za/2about.html, accessed 5 September 2021.

Grobler F. 2021. 'Sasol's role in unlocking hydrogen's significant potential to contribute to energy security and trade'. 2nd Renewable Hydrogen and Green Powerfuels Webinar, 13 April.

Gxasheka, A., Ndlovu, N., Mokoena, R., Moroeng, M., Mogatusi, P., Kgopa, M.. 2018. 'Monitoring Renewable Energy Performance of Power Plants'. https://www.nersa.org.za/wp-content/uploads/2021/05/Monitoring-of-Renewable-Energy-Performance-of-Power-Plants-%e2%80%93-Performance-of-Power-Plants-in-2020.pdf, accessed 1 September 2021.

Hydrogen South Africa (HySA). 2018. 'HySA project installs fuel cell power for rural school in S Africa'. Fuel Cells Bulletin, 5, 6–7.

Hydrogen South Africa Infrastructure (HySA Infrastructure). 2019. 'CleanMIning Platform'. https://hysainfrastructure.com/clean-mining-platform/, accessed 14 April 2021.

Hydrogen South Africa Systems (HySA Systems). 2014. 'About HySA'. https://www.hysasystems.com/index.php/about-hysa, accessed 14 April 2021

International Energy Agency (IEA). 'The future of hydrogen: Seizing today's opportunities', Report prepared by the IEA for the G20, Japan, 2019. https://iea.blob.core.windows.net/assets/9e3a3493-b9a6-4b7d-b499-7ca48e357561/The_Future_of_Hydrogen.pdf, accessed 15 May 2021.

Implats. (no date). 'Fuel cell roadmap'. https://www.implats.co.za/pdf/fact-sheets/implats-cell-fuel-road-map.pdf, accessed 19 May 2021.

International Renewable Energy Agency (IRENA). 2019. 'Hydrogen: A renewable energy perspective'. International Renewable Energy Agency, Abu Dhabi.

Janikowska, O. and Kulczycka, J. 2021. 'Just transition as a tool for preventing energy poverty among women in mining areas: A case study of the Silesia Region, Poland'. Energies, 14(12), 3372.

Japan. 2020. 'The Strategic Road Map for Hydrogen and Fuel Cells'. https://www.meti.go.jp/english/press/2019/pdf/0312_002a.pdf, accessed 9 September 2021.

Kendall, C. and Doctor, D.H. 2003. 'Stable isotope applications in hydrologic studies'. *Treatise on Geochemistry*, 5, 605.

Kirby, A. 2021. 'Hydrogen for mobility in South Africa', 2nd Renewable Hydrogen and Green Powerfuels Webinar, 13 April.

Lieu, J., Sorman, A.H., Johnson, O.W., Virla, L.D. and Resurrección, B.P. 2020. 'Three sides to every story: Gender perspectives in energy transition pathways in Canada, Kenya and Spain'. *Energy Research and Social Science*, 68, 101550.

Mazloomi, K. and Gomes, C. 2012. 'Hydrogen as an energy carrier: Prospects and challenges'. *Renewable and Sustainable Energy Reviews*, 16, 3024.

Ma, S., Lin, M., Lin, T. E., Lan, T., Liao, X. et al. 2021. 'Fuel cell-battery hybrid systems for mobility and off-grid applications: A review'. *Renewable and Sustainable Energy Reviews*, 135, 110119.

Mckay, C. 2019. 'Industry keen on cleaner, fuel cell-based ventilation'. https://www.miningweekly.com/article/industry-keen-on-cleaner-hydrogen-fuel-cell-based-ventilation-2019-11-05/rep_id:3650, accessed 20 April 2021.

Metcalfe, J., Burger, L., and Mackay, J. 2020. 'Unlocking South Africa's Hydrogen Potential'. PriceWaterhouse Coopers, https://www.pwc.co.za/en/assets/pdf/unlocking-south-africas-hydrogen-potential.pdf, accessed 4 April 2021.

MISTRA. 2020. 'Partnerships for PGM Beneficiation Through the Hydrogen

Economy: A report on MISTRA's annual roundtables 2016–2019'. Mapungubwe Institute for Strategic Reflection, Johannesburg.

Mkhabela, N. 24 November 2021. 'Public encouraged to comment on Draft Energy Policy'. eThekwini Municipality, http://www.durban.gov.za/Resource_Centre/new2/Pages/Public-encouraged-to-comment-on-Draft-Energy-Policy-.aspx, accessed 15 April 2021.

Mohlakoana, N. and Wolpe, P. 2021. 'A just energy transition to facilitate household energy access and alleviate energy poverty'. Trade & Industrial Policy Strategies (TIPS), https://www.tips.org.za/policy-briefs/item/4199-a-just-energy-transition-to-facilitate-household-energy-access-and-alleviate-energy-poverty, accessed 15 September 2021.

Noussan, M., Raimondi, P.P., Scita, R. and Hafner, M. 2021. 'The role of green and blue hydrogen in the energy transition: A technological and geopolitical perspective'. *Sustainability*, 13, 298.

Ong, B.C., Kamarudin, S.K. and Basri, S. 2017. 'Direct liquid fuel cells: A review'. *International Journal of Hydrogen Energy*, 42, 10142–10157.

Patel, E. 2021. 'Address by Trade, Industry and Competition Minister Ebrahim Patel', 2nd Renewable Hydrogen and Green Powerfuels Webinar for South Africa, Johannesburg, 13 April.

Patel, M. 2020. 'Green hydrogen: A potential export commodity in a new global marketplace'. Trade and Industrial Policy Strategies (TIPS), https://www.tips.org.za/images/TIPS_Green_hydrogen_A_potential_export_commodity_in_a_new_global_marketplace.pdf, accessed 5 March 2021.

Pollet, B.G., Pasupathi, S., Swart, G., Mouton, K., Lototskyy, M., et al. 2014. 'Hydrogen South Africa (HySA) systems competence centre: mission, objectives, technological achievements and breakthroughs'. *International Journal of Hydrogen Energy*, 39, 3577.

Rissman, J., Bataille, C., Masanet, E., Aden, N., Morrow III, W.R. et al. 2020. 'Technologies and policies to decarbonize global industry: Review and assessment of mitigation drivers through 2070'. *Applied Energy*, 266, 114848.

Roos, T. and Wright, J. 2021. 'Powerfuels and green hydrogen'. https://www.euchamber.co.za/wp-content/uploads/2021/02/Powerfuels-Final-Report-South-Africa-EU-SA_Partners-for-Growth-Final-28-Jan-2021.pdf, accessed 12 February 2021.

Sasol. 14 April 2021a. 'Sasol And Toyota South Africa Motors form green hydrogen mobility partnership', https://www.sasol.com/media-centre/media-releases/sasol-and-toyota-south-africa-motors-form-green-hydrogen-mobility, accessed 25 April 2021.

Sasol. 14 April 2021b. 'Sasol to explore potential of cleaner aviation fuels with world-class partners'. https://www.sasol.com/media-centre/media-releases/sasol-explore-potential-cleaner-aviation-fuels-world-class-partners, accessed 22 April 2021.

Sazali, N. 2020. 'Emerging technologies by hydrogen: A review'. *International Journal of Hydrogen Energy*, 45(38), 18753–18771

South African Planning Institute. 2010. 'Draft statement of conclusion'. http://www.sapi.org.za/index.php?option=com_content&view=article&id=39%3Adraft-statement-of-conclusion-green-economysummit&Itemid=23, accessed 9 May 2021.

Singla, M.K., Nijhawan, P. and Oberoi, A.S. 2021. 'Hydrogen fuel and fuel cell technology for a cleaner future: a review'. *Environmental Science and Pollution Research*, 28, 15607–15626.

Thomas, J.M., Edwards, P.P., Dobson, P.J., and Owen, G.P. 2020. 'Decarbonising energy: The developing international activity in hydrogen technologies and fuel cells'. *Journal of Energy Chemistry*, 51, 405–415.

Takouleu, J.M. 20 April 2021. 'South Africa: An alliance between Sasol and Toyota for green hydrogen transport'. iAfrik 21, https://www.afrik21.africa/en/south-africa-an-alliance-between-sasol-and-toyota-for-green-hydrogen-transport/, accessed 14 May 2021.

Ting, M.B. and Byrne, R. 2020. 'Eskom and the rise of renewables: Regime resistance, crisis and the strategy of incumbency in South Africa's electricity system'. *Energy Research & Social Science*, 60, 101333.

The Netherlands Government Hydrogen Strategy. 2020. 'Government strategy on hydrogen'. https://www.government.nl/documents/publications/2020/04/06/government-strategy-on-hydrogen, accessed 1 September 2021.

Stambouli, B. 2011. 'Promotion of renewable energies in Algeria: Strategies and perspectives'. *Renewable and Sustainable Energy Reviews*, 15(2), 1169–1181.

United States Department of Energy (USDOE). 'Hydrogen production: Biomass gasification'. https://www.energy.gov/eere/fuelcells/hydrogen-production-biomass-gasification#:~:text=Biomass%20gasification%20is%20a%20mature,and%20other%20products%2C%20without%20combustion, accessed 25 March 2021.

NINE

Shaping the low carbon energy transformation for just urban transitions in South Africa

LAUREN HERMANUS

INTRODUCTION AND CONTEXT

THE JUST TRANSITION, internationally and in South Africa, often misses the urban scale of policy and planning. As a policy response to the complex socio-technical transformation of the energy system over time, the just transition must deal with the vulnerabilities and inequities that arise from this system in its current form, as well as in its transformed and reconfigured forms. In South Africa, several key actors have acknowledged the procedural and distributional disparities that characterise our power sector. There is potential for procedural, distributional and restorative justice as we move towards a low carbon, renewable energy-based electricity system. To date, the national just transition discourse has been primarily focused on transforming the coal-dependent power system, with Eskom at its core. The most prominent public and political debates have turned on the utility's future, dim as it often appears, and decommissioning coal power to meet climate change policy ambitions. The debates have therefore primarily considered the power system at the aggregate level only. Less attention has been paid to the legacy challenges, and the potential opportunities emerging at a local scale. Particular interfaces between local finances, economies and urban energy governance have often been marginal to national policy framing and responses to Eskom's problems, spanning 'load shedding', its burgeoning debt and the complex process of its restructuring. Just transition planning and implementation, however, are inherently multi-scale, multi-stakeholder processes.

In the South African context, local municipalities, particularly those that function as distribution utilities, mediate the relationship between people and the energy system, shaping the system's procedural dynamics and distributional outcomes. Municipal governments supply 40 per cent of the electricity distributed nationally to households, businesses and other organisations within their geographical jurisdictions (DNT, 2019). Additionally, the nation's electricity system is embedded in local systems, which function as critical interfaces between the energy system and the rest of the economy, through fiscal (including redistributive), service delivery (electricity, water, sanitation) and local economic development channels, as well as public participation processes. These interfaces have significant consequences for developmental ambitions and social justice outcomes for local governments and the people and businesses they serve. As the broader energy and electricity systems transform, so do capacities and capabilities at the urban scale to enable procedural, distributional and restorative justice.

There are risks and opportunities for urban energy governance actors in national sustainable energy transitions. Internationally, the increased investment in renewable energy, ranging from household solar installations to sizeable utility-scale wind and solar power plants, has been said to herald a necessary process of decentralisation of governance and a subsequent elevation of local government, cities and towns as 'an essential element of low carbon transition' (Goldthau, 2014). This process presents a significant change for the South African context. The power sector has a long history of high levels of centralisation, large-scale coal infrastructure, and highly concentrated networks of political and private actors shaping the rules of the game.

Despite a dearth of policy clarity for local energy governance actors at the national level, the past decade has seen significant work being undertaken by local government across the country's nine larger cities (metropolitan municipalities), better-capacitated secondary cities and towns (local municipalities), as well as district municipalities and provincial governments. There are also many advisory organisations focused on supporting urban energy transitions. In line with international trends, in 2021, the 'rules of the game' do indeed appear to be shifting in favour of a more decentralised socio-technical configuration. Most recently, in June 2021, President Cyril Ramaphosa announced that independent power generation projects up to 100MW could proceed unencumbered with national licencing requirements. This announcement comes after more than a decade of municipal governments simultaneously sounding alarms and announcing opportunities related to the renewable energy transition, particularly the uptake of rooftop solar photovoltaics (PV). It is a clear signal of transition; the system is changing. The nature and consequences of that change are evolving. Within the just transition policy agenda, the critical question is whether these dynamics are tending towards more-or-less just processes and outcomes and how justice can be facilitated.

This chapter does not provide a definitive answer to these questions. Instead, it aims to foreground the work, risks and opportunities for municipal governments and other local energy governance actors within South African's just transition. It speaks to the policy vacuum at a national level, which results in inadequate consideration of local risks and opportunities in planning and implementation. To assist in the implementation of a just transition in South Africa, this chapter begins by proposing the idea of 'just urban transitions' as a policy response 'through which a low carbon transition in an urban context is managed to bring about fair and equitable outcomes through representative and inclusive processes' (Hermanus, 2021: 1.)[1]

[1] This policy agenda brings together work on urban energy transitions, urban climate work, and discourse on urban justice and the 'just city' (Hughes and Hoffmann, 2020).

This chapter begins by locating the just transition within local sustainable energy transitions. It does so by applying multi-level perspective on socio-technical transitions[2] to trace aspects of the transition across different domains of change. These include (i) technology and infrastructure innovations, (ii) actors and institutions, (iii) policy and regulations, and (iv) goals and norms that inform the sector. The promulgation of renewable energy and related technologies is the focus of this analysis. Without overprescribing the meaning of justice in a contested and dynamic debate, this chapter raises key questions regarding whether and how socio-technological shifts shaping South Africa's urban energy transitions could deepen or ameliorate existing socio-economic inequalities and patterns of exclusion and marginalisation arising specifically from the energy system. This includes: issues of the (re)distribution of political and economic power (procedural justice); the (re)distribution of risks and benefits, such as energy access and energy poverty arising from the energy system (distributional justice); and managing historical and future social and ecological externalities of power generation (restorative justice). This chapter traces the South African energy transition as it manifests at the urban scale. Once characterised, it is possible to see how the de/centralisation has played out within this transition over the last 20 years. Finally, a few concluding reflections point towards a multi-scale approach to just transition planning by facilitating bottom-up, localised, cross-contextual problem definition, learning, and planning and investment.

[2] There is a well-developed body of work applying socio-technical transitions approaches to understanding energy systems (see, for example, Adil and Ko, 2016; Burke and Stephens, 2017; Geels et al., 2017; David and Schönborn, 2018; Jenkins et al., 2018; Sareen and Haarstad, 2018; Sorrell, 2018).

CONCEPTUALISING JUST URBAN TRANSITIONS FOR SOUTH AFRICA

Just urban transitions are local-level policy responses 'through which a low carbon transition in an urban context is managed to bring about fair and equitable outcomes through representative and inclusive processes' (Hermanus, 2021: 1). One can conceptualise just transitions as coherent policy responses that manage the procedural, distributional and restorative aspects of energy systems, their transformation and possible future configurations at the national aggregate level. As with all national policies, it must be asked: how does this policy look (and vary) in particular locations across the country?; who is affected, and how?; which actors are involved in the governance of this process, and how?; how do actions in one location impact on responses in other locations? In other words, the just transition becomes a local process as soon as concrete planning and implementation commence.[3] Despite the apparent significance of local context for defining, scoping and implementing just transition policy and investment packages, it is not particularly well investigated and conceptualised at the urban scale (Hughes and Hoffmann, 2020). This is also true of the South African context, even though significant city-led work exists to address climate mitigation and adaptation, energy access, energy efficiency, transport and a green economy. A range of equity and equality-related systems interface with these issues, such as housing, water and sanitation services, and the fiscal system on which service delivery depends.

Internationally, local governments are positioning cities and towns as critical sites of the global sustainable energy transition, and city governments as critical actors in this process (Droege, 2008; Westphal et al., 2017; Huang and Castán Broto, 2018; IPCC, 2018). To understand how the country's just transition lands at the urban scale, it is helpful to isolate those components of the sustainable energy transition that most immediately impact on cities, towns and

[3] South Africa's coal-to-power value chain, its operational social-ecological externalities, and the risks arising from its scheduled decommissioning are largely concentrated in four local municipalities in Mpumalanga Province (Hermanus and Montmasson-Clair, 2021).

their governments from other aggregate-level concerns. As renewable energy technologies displace current and future demand for fossil fuels, these technologies are also disrupting the entrenched centralised planning and investment, and concentrated networks of public and private actors, that have typically directed large fossil fuel (and nuclear) investments (Aklin and Urpelainen, 2013; Sareen and Haarstad, 2018). The proliferation of renewable energy technologies is now broadly understood to have particular implications for urban environments and the energy governance actors that steward local energy systems changing (Goldthau, 2014).

Renewable energy generation infrastructure, particularly solar photovoltaics (PV), can be financially and technically viable at different scales, from partially powering a single household, business or community up to utility-scale infrastructure that can power hundreds of thousands of homes and businesses. This flexibility allows for a configuration of energy generation distributed among many small, medium and large generators, with a proportion of generation feeding directly into local distribution grids (IRENA, 2019). This systemic reconfiguration enables and requires more localised responses in energy planning, operation, maintenance, governance and policymaking. This results in the decentralisation of political power and influence, and the augmentation of the distribution grid to facilitate distributed energy feed-in and associated trading. On the one hand, the proliferation of small-scale infrastructure presents a transformation in the system that creates risks for grid stability, system costs and financing, which must be managed. On the other, this same infrastructure reconfiguration creates opportunities for cities to drive local agendas such as climate mitigation and adaptation, energy access, local security of supply, and local economic development and job creation. To scope the issues relevant to South Africa's just urban transition and related concepts of energy justice and energy democracy, it is necessary first to scope the emergent socio-technological processes that result from the renewable energy transition, as shown in Table 9.1.

Although the transition is catalysed by a technological transformation over time, the implications, as indicated above, are clearly multi-dimensional. This transition is structuring an opportunity

Table 9.1: A summary characterisation of urban-scale dynamics of contemporary renewable energy transitions[4]

Domain	Selected developments impacting urban contexts	International examples of local governance responses
Technology and innovation	• An increasing share of distributed small-scale renewable energy and storage technologies; • Integration of smart grids to enable bidirectional communication, automation and electricity feed; buying and selling of self-generated electricity by energy users ('prosuming').	• New models for utilities, including distribution utilities, electricity planning, infrastructure finance, and operation; • Examples of dynamic energy 'prosuming' facilitated by local energy governance actors, such as local governments or local electricity utilities.
Policy and law	• The role of cities in mitigating and adapting to climate change through local policies is defined through platforms like the Intergovernmental Panel on Climate Change (IPCC); • Regulations to enable distributed small-scale embedded energy generation (SSEG) and off-grid energy generation in place at national levels.	• Local governments take the lead on climate and energy policies, plans, and regulations independently and through national and international forums.
Actors and institutions	• Energy markets allow for the entry of new, smaller players in energy sectors, including local governments, small businesses, communities, households and small businesses; • New, distributed, international renewable energy supply chains have emerged.	• Cities expand their scope of planning and investments related to climate and energy, including the municipalisation or re-municipalisation (ownership) of energy systems; • Local businesses, households, communities and municipal governments invest in energy; • Proactive local economic development facilitated related to local energy services.
Goals and principles	• International alignment of energy investment to sustainable development outcomes (e.g. Sustainable Development Goals (SDGs)) such as reduced environmental and social harm; • Greater emphasis on equitable energy access and shared benefit through 'energy justice' and 'energy democracy', driven through multi-stakeholder advocacy and theoretical development.	• Realignment of infrastructure investments to local climate resilience and local economic development (LED) needs; • Lobbying for energy democracy, to transfer the political and economic power in energy systems to a greater number of diverse actors through increased political participation and new forms of ownership, such as community-owned energy; • Multilateral energy access programmes for poor and marginalised communities.

Source: Hermanus (2021: 1).

[4] This table is adapted from a previous publication and grounded in a socio-technical transition-based approach (Hermanus, 2021).

for local energy governance actors to redefine the system's goals and use different means to achieve these outcomes. New, idealised, future infrastructure configurations are informing policies and plans. These speculative visions of dynamic local smart grids with multiple, distributed actors buying and selling electricity as required are often characterised as 'transactive' or 'fractal' (Retière et al., 2017; Thomas et al., 2019). There is tremendous enthusiasm regarding the potential of material infrastructural changes to shift the system's dynamics to facilitate more just processes and outcomes in energy systems at both local and national scales. These ideals interact with new ideas about the intersection between energy systems and social justice, namely, just transition, energy justice and energy democracy. Energy justice and energy democracy, respectively, have conceptualised renewable energy as a potentially transformative infrastructure (see Goldthau and Sovacool, 2012; Sovacool and Dworkin, 2015; Heffron and McCauley, 2018; McCauley et al., 2019). Drawing on these frameworks, we can assess the justness of the transition at the urban scale with respect to its impact on (re)distribution of political and economic power (procedural justice); the (re)distribution of risks and benefits, such as energy access; energy poverty arising from the energy system (distributional justice); and managing historical and future social and ecological externalities of power generation (restorative justice).

As with national planning and implementation, the particular concerns relevant to the facilitation of just urban transitions depend on local processes being adequately defined. Indeed, in South Africa, just urban transitions should be assessed in terms of the following questions, at a minimum:

- Are local public participation processes enabling effective representation of various affected communities, including the most vulnerable and marginalised, in policy, planning and investment?
- Are municipalities managing local energy systems to enable adequate levels of affordable electricity access for all households, businesses, and other organisations and to support resilient public infrastructure and services?

- Are energy-related local economic development mechanisms geared to address poverty, unemployment and inequality?
- Are energy-related developments supporting local climate change adaptation and mitigation strategies, as well as other ecological risk management plans?

As the country's sustainable energy transition progresses, it can only approach 'justness' in urban contexts if it leads to affordable energy access for all residents across diverse households and businesses in the formal and informal economies that support people's livelihoods. The externalities of the energy system must be appropriately managed, whether those accrue locally or elsewhere. Additionally, the solutions that allow for just processes and outcomes in one city or town cannot be implemented to the detriment of other cities and towns or the system overall. Just urban transitions cannot, then, be ignorant of their embeddedness and impacts in larger systems. South Africa's just urban transitions are local and national policy matters.

TRANSFORMING SOUTH AFRICA'S URBAN ENERGY SYSTEMS BETWEEN 1994 AND 2021

South Africa's energy system, and the power system at its centre, are highly centralised and ill-prepared for the coming socio-technical transformation arising from the sustainable energy transition. The infrastructure, policy and actors have been highly concentrated within an elite and shielded from democratic participation, a legacy of apartheid-era governance. The municipal role in this system was marginal to the overall direction that the system would take, as led by the Department of Minerals and Energy (DME), which would later morph into the Department of Energy (DoE), and then the Department of Mineral Resources and Energy (DMRE), and regulated by the National Energy Regulator of South African (NERSA).

Aligned to South Africa's highly centralised power system, national just energy transition planning has been necessarily concerned with aggregate trends of overall demand, supply, system costs, greenhouse gas emissions and local economic development. Most obviously, national energy investment plans – notably the Department of Mineral Resources and Energy's (DMRE) Integrated Resource Plan (IRP) – have historically grossly underestimated the scale and relevance of bottom-up, distributed generation (SALGA, 2017).[5] The 2021 presidential pronouncement of the relaxation of licencing rules is anticipated to accelerate the material fragmentation of this infrastructure system. The question is, do the existing conditions suggest that this reconfiguration will lead to fractal or fragmented outcomes over time, given the social systems in which the infrastructure is embedded?

Since the country's political transition in 1994, municipal governments have had defined and autonomous roles in South Africa's political system. The Constitution of the Republic of South Africa, Section 215 (1) and Section 229 (1), empowers municipalities with executive authority over electricity reticulation, which the Electricity Regulation Act (4 of 2016), as amended in 2017, defines as 'trading or distribution of electricity and includes services associated therewith' (Plaatjies et al., 2018). It includes the distribution of fully and partially subsidised energy to qualifying lower-income households under the Free Basic Electricity Policy (2003), as well as local policies (DME,

[5] SALGA's comments included the following (SALGA, 2018):

I. The response questioned whether the IRP 2018 was indeed least-cost (as claimed) from a municipal perspective, particularly noting the lack of consideration of Energy Efficiency and Demand Side Management (EEDSM) planning and the lack of integration of local energy planning in top-down processes.

II. The response noted that the policy process does not reflect the way that energy systems are transforming. This, therefore, creates the need and opportunity for localised planning and infrastructure investment and a redefining of roles for subnational governments. The IRP 2018 allocation for small-scale, embedded generation was not reflective of the real demand for planned installations.

III. The submission highlighted the impact that Eskom's internal governance, operational and financial failures (e.g., escalating tariffs, load shedding and spiralling debt) have on local economic development planning and service delivery, constitutional mandates of local government.

IV. The submission also highlighted the tension between local climate change mitigation, adaptation plans and national planning, including new coal-fired power station investments through IPPs.

2003). The policy and institutional landscape is complex, with unclear powers and functions; inadequate local policy development and integration processes; financial constraints; grid maintenance backlogs; lacklustre economic performance; endemic multi-dimensional poverty (including energy poverty); and the most severe income inequality in the world. Of the country's 257 municipalities,[6] 165 actually undertake this electricity reticulation function. Eskom serves the remainder, as well as operating in particular areas within the jurisdiction of municipal distribution business. The distribution function, as executed by 165 local governments, is embedded in local governments' revenue models. In practice, this function has at times been tightly circumscribed and hotly contested. Surcharges on this function are one of the few autonomous revenue generation mechanisms available to municipalities. This means that decisions to advance an energy policy direction have broad implications for municipal functions beyond electricity reticulation.

From 1997, a range of sweeping power system reforms was proposed that aimed to change the role of the private sector, restructure Eskom, and consolidate the country's electricity distribution industry (EDI), all of which would have consequences for municipal distribution functions. Following a Cabinet-approved proposal, the 1998 White Paper on Energy, the 2003 White Paper on Renewable Energy, and in 2006, the Energy Regulation Act (2006) (hereafter ERA) provided the parameters for a hotly contested national policy discourse, for and against renewables, and for and against privatisation, among other issues. ERA Schedule 2 would be of central importance for municipal governments, opening a small door for decentralised energy generation, exempting off-grid energy generation for own use from national licensing requirements. The distribution reforms, which tabled regional electricity distributors (REDs), were advanced again in 2009 and finally and successfully challenged on constitutional grounds in 2010. Still, national energy and electricity planning was undertaken centrally, through the national regulator, and then the DOE, which

[6] Local governments are divided into metropolitan (large city), local (secondary cities and towns) and district (a layer of government that performs a set of functions on behalf of a region comprised of several towns) governments.

published the country's first participatory Integrated Resource Plan (IRP) 2010–2030 in 2011 (DoE, 2011). This detailed plan for electricity infrastructure development acknowledged issues relating to distribution and the potential of distributed renewable energy generation.[7] Despite their constitutional mandate, municipalities made public submissions for this process, alongside all other stakeholders.

Municipalities were already being impacted by Eskom's rolling blackouts, which, from 2008, would regularly rise as a major issue and widely recognised barrier to local development ambitions. Additionally, municipalities were sensitised to climate change policy. While South Africa's national formal commitments on climate change would be rather ambitious, in practice, renewable energy was often positioned as counter-development, given the centrality of fossil fuels to the country's industrialisation path. Municipalities, however, were picking up their climate change adaption and mitigation work. In parallel, from 2008, municipalities worked with National Treasury and NERSA to unpack the potential for and impact of small-scale embedded generation (SSEG), particularly commercial solar PV embedded in municipal distribution networks. SSEG was gradually proposed as a way of driving local energy security for cities and decarbonising local infrastructure (Fakir, 2015). To wit, the Western Cape Infrastructure Framework from 2013 states: 'The energy focus in the province is on lowering the carbon footprint, with an emphasis on renewable and locally generated energy' (Palmer and Graham, 2013: 3).

Municipalities took the issue of distributed energy generation, as well as ideas for municipal-owned utility-scale renewable energy generation infrastructure, to NERSA and into collective learning

[7] The IRP 2010–2030 states in Section 7.2: 'The growth of distributed generation has a bearing on the development and operations of the network (predominantly the distribution network), especially if some, if not most, of the distributed generation is variable technology. The development opportunity of smart(er) grids and storage solutions – which can help in integrating variable renewable technologies – should also be considered, alongside the system's balancing capability (and ancillary services).' (DoE, 2011). And in Section 7.3: 'Off-grid activities should be considered especially as there is an impact on the potential future demand (through 'suppressed demand' which has occurred as a result of lack of grid access for a number of potential consumers)' (DoE, 2011).

processes. SSEG was recognised as being both a threat to current system configurations as well as representing a niche opportunity to facilitate improved arrangements for an electricity system that better served economic and human development goals within a green economic framework. Municipal governments variably resisted and explored this niche, with a growing appreciation for the bottom-up transformation of electricity systems, demonstrated in international cases. As Eskom's load shedding and price increases continued, municipalities were concerned about grid defection by paying customers, both commercial and residential, whose tariffs cross-subsidised electricity and other service delivery for lower-income households.

NERSA was not unresponsive. Eskom's challenges, together with the technology and finance dimensions of SSEG, continued to improve and drive interest from private investors. NERSA appeared to recognise the inevitability of investment in SSEG. These installations, at the time still expensive compared to Eskom-supplied electricity, covered single solar home systems as well as solar micro-grids, which could potentially meet commercial power needs, or community needs. In the same year that the DOE launched the national Renewable Energy Independent Power Producers Procurement Programme (REIPPPP), NERSA published the Standard Conditions for Embedded Generation within Municipal Boundaries (hereafter 'Standard Conditions') in 2011, in an attempt to provide the regulatory clarity for, and institutionalisation of, electricity system transformation that municipal (particularly city) governments were pushing for. The Standard Conditions gave municipal governments the power to enable SSEG up to 100kW (0.1MW) by registering and connecting these installations to their distribution grids (NERSA, 2011). While the regulations did go some way to legalising the buying and selling of distributed energy, they also created much confusion. The regulations acknowledged and opened a space for local governance to take on a degree of local planning. However, they still operated with a firm commitment to centralised planning and investment. Municipal governments' own power plants were not addressed, nor were community microgrids and larger commercial installations, with this size of infrastructure managed through REIPPPP. With Eskom as the sole purchaser of REIPPPP-generated power, municipalities kept driving regulatory development from the local level. When the IRP was updated in 2013, it recognised that flexible renewable energy infrastructure could present a 'path of least regret' compared to longer-term massive nuclear or coal investments (DoE, 2013). This document was, however, never ratified.

In 2013, NERSA awarded a private company, PowerX (then Amatola Green Power), an energy trader license. This license allows PowerX to buy electricity from IPPs and sell it to energy users under a 15-year wheeling agreement with Nelson Mandela Bay Municipality (NMBM) (ICLEI, 2015). The practice was limited to just this one municipality, however, given a lack of clarity on its general legality and other implications. It would set a precedent that would take a few years to be pushed forward. Renewable energy within municipal boundaries, advanced in parallel, is using solar PV to meet the needs of households that cannot access networked infrastructure because they do not, for practical or legal reasons, have formal electricity connections. There are examples of for-profit and non-profit companies facilitating these new business models and even securing subsidisation from municipalities for this service.

In 2015, NERSA itself conceded that the Standard Conditions framework 'was approved without due public consultations and is not clear to most stakeholders' (NERSA, 2015). In the ensuing years, the Standard Conditions were largely unimplemented and seen as unworkable. In 2015, NERSA published a consultation paper, 'Small-Scale Embedded Energy Regulatory Rules' for energy systems up to 1MVA (equal to 1MW) (hereafter 'Small-Scale Regulations'). This consultation paper's legal status was fuzzy. However, in principle, it did start to cover gaps: it created national standards for municipalities to register small-scale energy generators up to 1MW to feed surplus energy into local distribution grids, with guidelines for associated fees and compensation (NERSA, 2015). The small-scale regulations addressed technical issues regarding network capacity and smart metering and also created a process to track cumulative generation capacity to feed into national planning. In this evolving policy context, the realities of distribution grid maintenance backlogs and demands for upgrading to include advanced sensing, communication and automation ('smart' grids) for a new energy system were also well recognised.

NERSA's work, although responsive to municipalities' concerns, still viewed distributed generation as marginal to planned, centralised Eskom-led energy investments, and additional coal and renewable IPPs. Municipal tariff restructuring was also covered. The regulations appeared to be an attempt to make minor adjustments to the current system without fully comprehending the pace and scale of the transition, and related potential material decentralisation of the physical infrastructure, in that system. The Small-Scale Regulations proposed to create an intermediary body, a Central Power Purchasing Agency, to oversee and govern SSEG and transactions associated with feeding electricity into distribution grids (NERSA, 2015). This entity was meant to mitigate any revenue losses that municipal governments might incur, which would have knock-on impacts on pro-poor redistributive mechanisms. Within this ambiguous context, municipal governments forged ahead with local-level policy and regulatory development. At the same time, however, national policy and Eskom, embroiled in allegations of state capture, shut down the national policy to enable SSEG. They favoured instead plans to pursue a contentious nuclear deal with Russian state actors, validated in the 'Integrated Resource Plan Update' (hereafter Draft IRP 2016) and updated IEP (Joemat-Petersson, 2016; DoE, 2016).

Against a background of challenges against the infamous nuclear deal, municipalities continued to work at a local scale to facilitate private and state investment in residential and commercial solar PV, albeit in an uncoordinated manner. Municipalities were legitimately concerned about which customers were likely to invest in solar PV, incentivised by Eskom's increasing costs, growing dysfunction and load shedding. Given that electricity tariffs are tied to consumption, less consumption by high-income, higher-consuming households and businesses means less money into the system to cover distribution system costs, and to cross-subsidise electricity to lower-income households. It also means lower demand on Eskom, so less money into the national system. Currently, in 2021, support exists for municipalities to restructure these tariffs to offset this effect, to an extent aiming to be 'revenue-neutral'. In 2016, with Eskom blocking renewable energy IPPs from connecting approved projects or planning further investment, municipalities saw another opportunity. The Mayor of the City of Cape Town announced that the city would be making a legal challenge against the Ministry of Energy over the right to procure energy directly from IPPs, circumventing Eskom, as well as energy traders (Evans, 2016).

By the end of 2016, NERSA announced that its processes to regulate SSEG were officially on hold. The DoE was planning on amending ERA Schedule 2, which pertains to conditions for the licensing of energy generation. It was not until 2018 that further policy development was undertaken. The Draft Integrated Resource Plan (IRP) 2018 was developed and published for public comment. It was much better received than the 2016 update and was scheduled for finalisation in 2019. The South African Local Government Association (SALGA) developed considerable criticism of the document along with some other municipal governments who also made individual submissions to Parliament on the matter. Of particular concern was the IRP's low and arbitrary limit on local embedded generation. As national policies were contested, municipal governments used local regulations to process SSEG applications, as well as investing in their own solar PV installations and waste-to-energy plants. In 2019, the updated IRP did take some of the municipal concerns into account. Additionally, the DMRE released an update to the Electricity Regulation Act Schedule 2 (finally gazetted in 2021), which removed the need for NERSA licensing for any off-grid energy generation, and embedded generation up to 10MW complying with applicable regulations and codes. It also allows municipalities to contract with IPPs through service delivery agreements and to develop their own energy generation infrastructure. While there was much to be clarified in terms of implementation, the update was welcomed by municipal governments and by the business community. This framework allows for new roles, currently being trialled and institutionalised at a local level (see, for example, Montmasson-Clair et al., 2017; SALGA, 2018). Metropolitan, district and local municipal governments have been increasingly concerned with new possibilities for this role (summarised in Table 9.2).

There are several options currently being explored by better capacitated municipal governments (see Table 9.3). Between 2020

Table 9.2: Summary of new roles for municipalities in the electricity system[8]

Municipal role		Local energy infrastructure option
	Playing an aggregating / trading role	1. Buying from commercial, industrial, agricultural small-scale embedded generators and reselling at a premium
		2. Buying from residential rooftop embedded PV
	Wheeling	3. Community-owned microgrids (small-scale)
	Providing energy services	4. PPA with utility-scale IPP (under REIPPPP)
	Operating embedded storage	5. Installation and maintenance
		6. Invest in storage to store surplus energy and distribute when needed (supplementary investment to 1, 2, 3)
Procurement	Buying electricity for own-use or selling	7. Procuring energy from embedded generators (1, 2, 3) for own use or sale
	Buying electricity for own-use or selling	8. Procuring energy from IPPs for own use or sale
Direct Investment	Building, owning, operating infrastructure	9. Standalone utility-scale infrastructure
	Building, owning, operating infrastructure	10. Municipal rooftop embedded generation rooftop solar for government subsidy housing

and 2021, several municipalities announced plans to invest in local renewable energy, even going so far as declaring an intention to be independent of Eskom. Some municipal governments, like the Garden Route District Municipality, have published or are drafting their own energy masterplan, for example, the City of Cape Town and the Ekurhuleni Municipality[9] energy infrastructure procurement plans, the latter aiming for 680MW of solar PV and waste-to-energy power generation. The Municipal Energy Resilience Project (MERP) aims to support Western Cape municipalities in procuring power under the new regulatory regime, with six municipalities already signed up.

[8] This table draws on a review of regulation and draws on a 2017 review of municipal energy business models (Montmasson-Clair, et al., 2017).

[9] There have, however, also been limited examples of cities owning and operating energy generation infrastructure, notably Kelvin Power Station, a coal-fired power station in Ekurhuleni Municipality in Gauteng Province.

While SSEG was initially seen as a driver of grid defection by paying customers, the use of distributed infrastructure, particularly solar home systems and micro-grids, has been reframed as possible solutions to persistent energy poverty. This is particularly the case for enabling energy access in informal settlements. A recent study also suggests there is scope for potentially job-rich manufacturing development potential associated with distributed solar PV in South Africa (Fourie, 2021).

DECENTRALISATION AND JUST TRANSITION

Eskom's monopoly on energy supply is being challenged through this decentralised planning. The president's announcement of the Schedule 2 Amendment set to lift the threshold for licensing by NERSA to 100MW further disrupts Eskom's monopoly. It is not clear who will invest or how this will impact on local and national planning processes, system costs and energy access in specific locations and the national system overall. Running in parallel to the material fragmentation and reconfiguration of infrastructure, i.e. local energy transitions, is a clear process of transferring system governance from the national to the local sphere. Innovations in technology have implications for urban electricity service delivery (see Table 9.3). Decentralisation is a definite feature of the South African narrative.

It is necessary, in the South African context, to interrogate the social relevance and impacts of low carbon technologies. On the surface, there appears to be a good rationale for the continued decentralisation of the electricity system. There is, however, also a strong case for tracking and managing it from the bottom up and across regions. Decentralisation in the context of inequality within and between cities and towns, variable local government capacities and fiscal constraints could compromise existing mechanisms. These are important for the redistribution of resources within the broader energy system and local subsystems. Without any coordination or planning, the early fears of municipalities could be realised as businesses, higher-income households or better-prepared cities opt out of the national system. As noted above, because energy policy and decision-making happen in a complex multi-level environment, decisions taken by one actor

Table 9.3: A summary characterisation of urban-scale dynamics in South Africa

Domain	South African developments
Technology and innovation	• Legal and illegal SSEG installations • SSEG and off-grid infrastructure being implemented in underserved informal settlements • SSEG and off-grid targeting low-income communities in formal and informal settlements, who are unserved or underserved by national networked infrastructure • Waste to energy technology implemented by municipal governments • Distribution grids are being improved, beginning with improvements to metering • Limited examples of local manufacturing of renewable energy components
Policy and law	• National energy regulations amended to allow license-exempted energy generation up to 10MW, and possibly up to 100MW, pending implementation of the president's June 2021 announcement • Local policies developed for energy planning and climate change mitigation and adaptation • Municipal SSEG regulations • Electricity tariff redesign to reduce revenue losses related to decreased electricity demand from residential and commercial customers • Wheeling policies and tariffs in place
Actors and institutions	• New private and public investment in embedded and off-grid renewable energy generation
Goals and principles	• Local energy security in the context of Eskom's disfunction has become an important political ambition, linked to local economic development and job creation • Climate change is an important policy framing for pursuing local renewable energy generation • Energy democracy and community narratives are emerging, mostly driven from within the labour movement, but with implications for local government

have consequences for other actors, which need to be adequately understood. In a context in which not all municipalities are equally capacitated to undertake this work, developments are likely to be problematically uneven. Without management, there will be knock-on effects, such as increased central system costs and inequitable outcomes within or between municipalities.

The challenge is to understand under what conditions new renewables-based infrastructure configurations might support more just political and economic processes and outcomes for cities and towns. To this end, it is useful to return to and rephrase the just transition framing questions:

- How can local public participation processes enable effective representation of various affected communities, including the most vulnerable and marginalised, in policy, planning and investment, and how should national planning processes support this?
- Under what conditions (for example, innovative financing or alternative ownership models) do increased SSEG and off-grid solar PV enable adequate levels of affordable electricity access for households, businesses and other organisations, and support resilient public infrastructure and services?
- Under what conditions can local energy investments address poverty, unemployment and inequality in the formal and informal sectors through, for example, small, medium and micro-enterprise development, and through support for larger manufacturing investments?
- Are climate resilience and developmental benefits from an increased share of renewable energy fairly distributed within and between different cities and towns?

Any rational policy process must start from the basis of adequately answering these questions to determine optimal levels of decentralisation within the electricity system as a whole. The question for South Africa as it engages in the urban scale of just transition planning is whether this new decentralised future is fractal. Does it allow for justice-oriented flows of resources, benefits and costs within the system, or does it deepen the entrenched inequalities that shape our cities and towns?

CONCLUSION

It is now broadly accepted that South Africa's sustainable energy transition must be actively managed to ensure that its processes and outcomes tend to bring about more equal distribution of risks, costs, opportunities and benefits. The transition must also bring about increased levels of participation, a voice for stakeholders, and awareness of the impacts of the energy system, and the electricity system dominant within it. What is patently clear, as covered above, is that the sustainable energy transition, particularly the increase of renewable energy technologies within the system, is having specific impacts on the urban scale. Over time, however, municipalities have experimented, with intermittent support from NERSA and other actors, with new infrastructure configurations to support their service delivery and local economic development obligations. The highly centralised electricity system configuration that has characterised South Africa's energy landscape for so long has been slowly and consistently challenged from the ground up. South African city administrations are aware of the risks the energy system produces, and the profound effects of energy-driven uncertainty on their developmental policies and plans. This applies to the dysfunctional coal-fired power system in its current configuration, as well as to the transition risks associated with the increased and distributed uptake of renewables in the country. In 2021, these policy decisions and technology experiments have culminated in bold energy strategies, with some local governments even going so far as to seek relative independence from centralised energy planning.

Certainly, there are opportunities to reimagine the role of urban areas and urban energy governance in South Africa. This work is now well underway. However, it is not sufficiently connected to national planning processes, neither through energy planning, nor through political processes aimed at charting the country's just transition. Without this integration, the likelihood of fractured governance and infrastructure over the idealised fractal alternative configuration increases. It is necessary to embed national planning processes at a local scale and to integrate these local transition developments into emergent planning processes and platforms, such as the newly formed Presidential Climate Change Coordination C0ommission (PCCCC) and the District Development Model which seeks to align national and sub-national planning and implementation.

To achieve this technological and governance integration across scales, stakeholders must be able to facilitate robust dialogue about new possibilities for the locus of control and the distribution of political power within the electricity system and the roles of public and private sector actors within this configuration. These possible configurations must be linked to clear goals and ambitions for the country's electricity system. Ideas about the historical meaning and significance of the energy system appear to limit scope to reimagine its future, even as South Africa's technological base, ecological context and social pressures are seeding change from the ground up. While there is ongoing work underway, there are still significant knowledge gaps regarding how cities and towns can optimally navigate just urban transitions for individual and country-wide resilience. There are lessons to be learned from developed and developing country contexts, however, there is no defined template for the outcomes or the process of this profound socio-technical transformation. Renewable energy infrastructure has a clear climate mitigation benefit, but other possible benefits to enable energy justice and energy democracy, across urban and national scales, are policy choices that have yet to be entrenched in national just transition policy.

REFERENCES

Adil, A.M. and Ko, Y. 2016. 'Socio-technical evolution of decentralized energy systems: A critical review and implications for urban planning and policy'. *Renewable and Sustainable Energy Reviews*, 57, 1025–1037. doi: 10.1016/j.rser.2015.12.079.

Aklin, M. and Urpelainen, J. 2013. 'Political competition, path dependence, and the strategy of sustainable energy transitions'. *American Journal of Political Science*, 57(3), 643–658. doi: 10.1111/ajps.12002.

Burke, M.J. and Stephens, J.C. 2017. 'Energy democracy: Goals and policy instruments for socio-technical transitions'. *Energy Research and Social Science*, 33(September), 35–48. doi: 10.1016/j.erss.2017.09.024.

Congress of South African Trade Unions (COSATU). 2020. 'COSATU Submission: Eskom Social Compact Proposal'. Johannesburg.

David, M. and Schönborn, S. 2018. 'Bottom-up energy transition narratives: Linking the global with the local? A comparison of three German renewable co-ops'. *Sustainability*, 10(4). doi: 10.3390/su10040924.

Department of Energy (DoE). 2016. 'Integrated Resource Plan Update: Assumptions, Base Case Results and Observations, Revision 1'. http://www.energy.gov.za/IRP/2016/Draft-IRP-2016-Assumptions-Base-Case-and-Observations-Revision1.pdf, accessed 1 April 2021.

Department of Energy (DoE). 2013. 'Integrated Resource Plan for Electricity 2010-2030 Update Report'. http://www.energy.gov.za/IRP/2019/IRP-2019.pdf, accessed 10 April 2021.

Department of Energy (DoE). 2011. 'Integrated Resource Plan for Electricity 2010–2030'. http://www.energy.gov.za/files/irp_overview.html, accessed 4 May 2021.

Department of Minerals and Energy (DME). 2003. 'Electricity Basic Support Tariff (Free Basic Electricity) Policy'. https://www.gov.za/sites/default/files/gcis_document/201409/250880.pdf, accessed 5 June 2021.

Department of National Treasury-Republic of South Africa (DNT-RSA). 2019. '2019 Budget Speech of Tito Titus Mboweni, Minister of Finance'. http://www.treasury.gov.za/documents/national%20budget/2019/speech/speech.pdf, accessed 9 May 2021.

Droege, P. (ed.) 2008. *Urban Energy transition: From fossil fuels to renewable power*. First Edit. Elsevier.

Evans, J. 2016. 'Cape Town draws battle lines over the right to buy alternative energy from IPPs'. *News24*, 26 January, http://www.news24.com/SouthAfrica/News/cape-town-draws-battle-lines-over-right-to-buy-alternative-energy-from-ipps-20170126, accessed 26 January 2017.

Fakir, S. 2015. 'Localised energy generation is the solution to the Eskom crisis, but we need managed localism'. http://sacsis.org.za/site/article/2401, accessed 1 April 2016.

Fourie, R. 2021. 'Solar PV Industry Jobs Report'. https://www.sapvia.co.za/wp-content/uploads/2021/05/SAPVIA-PV-Industry-Jobs-Study-Report-COMBINED.pdf.

Geels, F.W., Sovacool, B.K., Schwanem, T. and Sorrel, S. 2017. 'The socio-technical dynamics of low-carbon transitions'. *Joule*, 1(3), 463–479. doi: 10.1016/j.joule.2017.09.018.

Goldthau, A. 2014. 'Rethinking the governance of energy infrastructure: Scale, decentralisation and polycentrism'. *Energy Research and Social Science*, 1, 134–140. doi: 10.1016/j.erss.2014.02.009.

Goldthau, A. and Sovacool, B.K. 2012. 'The uniqueness of the energy security, justice, and governance problem'. *Energy Policy*, 41, 232–240. doi: 10.1016/j.enpol.2011.10.042.

Heffron, R. J. and McCauley, D. 2018. 'What is the "Just Transition"?'. *Geoforum*, 88, 74–77. doi: 10.1016/j.geoforum.2017.11.016.

Hermanus, L. 2021. 'South Africa's Just Urban Transitions'. https://justurbantransitions.com/wp-content/uploads/2021/03/Just-Urban-Transitions_PolicyNote1.pdf, accessed 13 June 2021.

Hermanus, L. and Montmasson-Clair, G. 2021. '*Making sense of jobs in South Africa's just energy transition: Managing the impact of a coal transition on employment*'. TIPS, https://www.tips.org.za/policy-briefs/item/4111-making-sense-of-jobs-in-south-africa-s-just-energy-transition-managing-the-impact-of-a-coal-transition-on-employment, accessed 1 June 2021.

Huang, P. and Castán Broto, V. 2018. 'Interdependence between urban processes and energy transitions: The urban energy transitions (DUET) framework'. *Environmental Innovation and Societal Transitions*, 28, 35–45. doi: 10.1016/j.eist.2018.03.004.

Hughes, S. and Hoffmann, M. 2020. 'Just urban transitions: Toward a research agenda'. *Wiley Interdisciplinary Reviews: Climate Change*, 11(3), 1–11. doi: 10.1002/wcc.640.

ICLEI (Local Government for Sustainability). 2015. 'Embedded energy generation experience in a South African metropolitan municipality'. ICLEI Case Studies, https://africa.iclei.org/wp-content/uploads/2020/02/2015_Case-study_Urban-LEDS_Nelson-Mandela-bay-municipality.pdf, accessed 3 August 2021.

Intergovernmental Panel on Climate change (IPCC). 2018. 'What the IPCC special report on global warming of 1.5°C means for cities urban policy makers, Global Warming of 1.5°C. An IPCC Special Report on the impacts of global warming of 1.5°C above pre-industrial levels and related global greenhouse gas emission pathways, in the context of strengthening the global response to the threat of climate change'. doi: 10.24943/SCPM.2018.

International Renewable Energy Agency (IRENA). 2019. *Global Energy Transformation: A roadmap to 2050 (2019 Edition)*. Abu Dhabi: International Renewable Energy Agency.

Jenkins, K., Sovacool, B.K. and McCauley, D. 2018. 'Humanising socio-technical transitions through energy justice: An ethical framework for global transformative change'. *Energy Policy*, 117, 66–74. doi: 10.1016/j.enpol.2018.02.036.

Joemat-Petersson, T. 2016. 'Media Briefing on the IEP and IRP 22 November 2016 By Honourable Tina Joemat-Pettersson, MP: Minister of Energy'. Ministry of Energy, 1–4.

McCauley, D., Ramasar, V., Heffron, R.J., Sovacool, B.K., Mebratu, D. et al. 2019. 'Energy justice in the transition to low carbon energy systems: Exploring key themes in interdisciplinary research'. *Applied Energy*, 233/234, 916–921. doi: 10.1016/j.apenergy.2018.10.005.

Montmasson-Clair, G., Kritzinger, K., Scholtz, L., Gulati, M. 2017. 'New Roles for South African Municipalities in Renewable Energy. A Review of Business Models', (March), pp. 1–52. http://www.crses.sun.ac.za/files/research/publications/technical-reports/New roles for SA municipalities in RE - Discussion Paper - June 2017_final.pdf, accessed 5 August 2021.

National Energy Regulator of South Africa (NERSA). 2011. 'Standard Conditions for Embedded Generation within Municipal Boundaries'. https://www.cityenergy.org.za/wp-content/uploads/2021/02/resource_27.pdf, accessed 10 August 2021.

National Energy Regulator of South Africa (NERSA). 2015. 'Small-

Scale Embedded Generation: Regulatory Rules Consultation Paper', 27 February, https://www.sseg.org.za/wp-content/uploads/2019/03/Consultation-Paper-Small-Scale-Embedded-Gx-Regulatory-Rules.pdf, accessed 10 August 2021.

Palmer, I. and Graham, N. 2013. *Western Cape Infrastructure Framework*. https://www.westerncape.gov.za/assets/departments/transport-public-works/Documents/western_cape_infrastructure_framework.pdf, accessed 13 August 2021.

Plaatjies, D., De Beers, W., Baleni, P., Xulu, S., Letsatsi, K. et al. 2018. *Report by IMTT Advisory Panel: Electricity Reticulation and Distribution*. Pretoria.

Retière, N. Muratore, G., Kariniotakis, G., Michiorri, A., Frankhauser, P. et al. 2017. 'Fractal Grid – Towards the Future Smart Grid', in *CIRED 2017 – 24th International Conference on Electricity Distribution*. Glasgow: HAL. https://hal.archives-ouvertes.fr/hal-01518413, accessed 10 August 2021.

South African Local Government Association (SALGA). 2017. 'SALGA comments: IRP base case Submission – Executive summary March 2017' https://www.cityenergy.org.za/wp-content/uploads/2021/02/resource_466.pdf, accessed 12 August 2021.

South African Local Government Association (SALGA). 2018. 'SALGA Submission: Detailed Analysis on the Draft Integrated Resource Plan 2018', 26 October, Pretoria. https://static.pmg.org.za/181026SALGA.pdf, accessed 20 August 2021.

Sareen, S. and Haarstad, H. 2018. 'Bridging socio-technical and justice aspects of sustainable energy transitions'. *Applied Energy*, 228, 624–632. doi: 10.1016/j.apenergy.2018.06.104.

Sorrell, S. 2018. 'Explaining socio-technical transitions: A critical realist perspective'. *Research Policy*, 47(7), 1267–1282. doi: 10.1016/j.respol.2018.04.008.

Sovacool, B.K. and Dworkin, M.H. 2015. 'Global energy justice: problems, principles and practices'. Energy, 81, 802–803. doi: 10.1016/j.energy.2014.12.066.

Thomas, S., Surampudy, M. and Knight, M. 2019. 'Transactive Energy: Real-world applications for the modern grid'. Smart Electric Power Alliance, https://sepapower.org/resource/transactive-energy-real-world-applications-for-the-grid/, accessed 10 May 2021.

Westphal, M.I., Martin, S., Zhou, L., and Satterthwaite, D. 2017. 'Powering Cities in the Global South: How Energy Access for All Benefits the Economy and the Environment Powering'. World Resources Report, https://files.wri.org/d8/s3fs-public/powering-cities-in-the-global-south.pdf, accessed 15 May 2021.

SECTION 4

Social factors of climate change and the just transition

TEN

Assessing options of an energy transition and alternative agriculture in Mpumalanga

Malik Dasoo and Stanley Semelane

INTRODUCTION

South Africa is endowed with natural resources such as gold, diamonds, platinum and coal (Dou et al., 2020). As a result, the South African economic development set-up was configured to leverage mining resources through the minerals energy complex (MEC). This means that South Africa has been dependent on mining sector development for many years. Critically important to note is that electricity generation plays a central role in enabling economic development. For this reason, coal mining has been used as a backbone for electricity production since the 1900s (Malan, 1975). The apartheid government embarked on electricity infrastructure development as a major driver for economic growth. Table 10.1 lists South African coal power plants and the dates on which they were operational, ending in the 1990s.

Table 10.1: Commissioning dates of Eskom coal power stations

Power station	Date of commercial service (first–last unit)	Total nominal capacity (MW)
Arnot	1971–1975	2232
Camden	1966–1969	1481
Duvha	1980–1984	3450
Grootvlei	1969–1977	1120
Hendrina	1970–1977	1793
Kendal	1988–1993	3840
Komati	1958–1966	904
Kriel	1976–1979	2850
Lethabo	1985–1990	3558
Majuba	1992–2001	3843
Matimba	1987–1991	3690
Matla	1979–1983	3450
Tutuka	1984–1990	3510

Source: Eskom (2015; 2013).

Some of these power plants have reached their end of life although they are still operational. Many of them have not been maintained appropriately and are thus underperforming. Additionally, even the recently built Kusile and Medupi stations are underperforming.

Furthermore, South Africa's Nationally Determined Contributions (NDCs) as laid out in the Paris Agreement have recently been revised to cover our fair share of global emissions, and to reflect the government's commitment to the Paris Agreement. Meeting international obligations for emissions reduction and providing adaptation pathways will require the closure of South Africa's coal power plants and mines. Without sufficient transition strategies, and what is largely regarded as the inevitable closure of coal plants, South Africa's deep-rooted inequality, poverty and unemployment may be exacerbated.

This paper, which is divided into two sections, thus provides possible solutions for transitioning from a coal-intensive economy to a low carbon economy. The first part of this paper unpacks South

Africa's just energy transition gaps and potential indicators for a just energy transition, as well as potential renewable energy deployment options, coal phase-out and prospects for infrastructure repurposing. The second part of the paper positions regenerative agriculture as an option for a transition plan in coal areas, particularly in Mpumalanga. It questions the extent to which regenerative agriculture offers a feasible alternative to coal mining in Mpumalanga. In this section, regenerative agriculture is analysed to understand how well suited it is to respond to the principles of a just transition, and which policy options are available to support the uptake of regenerative agriculture.

SECTION ONE

ENERGY TRANSITIONS: OPTIONS FOR REPURPOSING COAL INFRASTRUCTURE

In the absence of a just energy transition policy, we are likely to witness negative economic impacts in regions that are dependent on the coal economy. The impact of coal-powered electricity on climate change needs to be reduced. This means that coal power plants that are reaching the end of their lifespans will need to be shut down. This would have implications for the employment opportunities created by the coal economy. Moreover, many development finance institutions have reduced funding for unsustainable infrastructure investments. Figure 10.1 shows the average age of South African coal fleets which will decommission between 2021 and 2030.

According to Climate Justice Alliance (2020),

> Just Transition is a vision-led, unifying and place-based set of principles, processes, and practices that build economic and political power to shift from an extractive economy to a regenerative economy. This means approaching production and consumption cycles holistically and waste-free. The transition itself must be just and equitable, redressing past harms and creating new relationships of power for the future through reparations. If the process of transition is not just, the outcome

will never be. Just Transition describes both where we are going and how we get there.

Winkler (2005) shows that the White Paper of 1999 set the path for the energy transition in South Africa. South Africa's over-dependence on the coal economy made it a complex challenge to transition the South African energy system on to a low carbon trajectory. Moreover, in 2009, South Africa boasted of being among the top five countries in the global coal exports market (Eberhard, 2011). This means that the coal sector contributes to the country's balance of payment.

Furthermore, at the end of 2008, South Africa encountered power cuts (i.e. load shedding) for the first time (Büscher, 2009). According to Büscher (2009), major power interruptions in 2008 forced the national energy utility, Eskom, to consort to load shedding. These energy cuts resulted in debate about electricity in South Africa and this dialogue will continue to remain intense until we have sufficient electricity supply from both Eskom and independent power producers (Büscher, 2009). Load shedding brings to the fore uneven access to reliable energy within South Africa (Büscher, 2009). However, what hardly features in the energy crisis debate is the political-economic basis on which important policy issues such as energy inequality and distributed energy supply for the poor should be considered. In this context, there is a need to diversify the country's energy supply system.

The independent power producers (IPPs) were introduced to implement a mix of energy technologies, mainly with the hope of

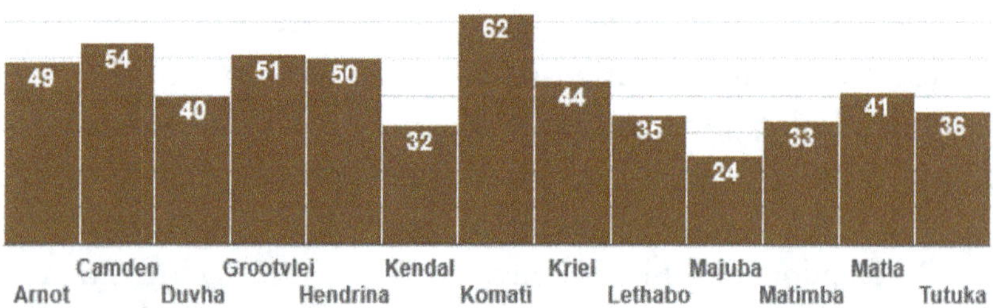

Figure 10.1: Period of existence

Source: Eskom (2013: 40; 2015).

reducing over-dependence on the coal economy. The key driver for introducing the IPPs was climate change commitments, as well as the need to moderate a power system dominated by monopolies. After the power cuts of 2008 and 2009, South Africa adopted the 2010 Integrated Resource Plan (IRP), which is a policy instrument that would enable the adoption of sustainable energy technologies and contribute towards creating a low carbon economy pathway (Department of Energy, 2011). This was followed by the launch of the Renewable Energy Independent Power Producer Procurement Programme (REIPPP), which enabled the procurement of South Africa's first renewable energy utility scale projects (DoE, 2018). At the time, South African coal power plants were experiencing increased challenges which prompted an acceleration in the adoption of renewable energy technologies.

In 2019, South Africa gazetted the 2019 IRP, which says that South Africa will phase out approximately 11017MW of coal power plants (Semelane et al., 2021a). These power plants will be replaced in the main by technologies such as wind, solar PV, gas and energy storage (DoE, 2019: 42). It is important to ensure that this energy transition complies with just transition principles. There is currently no policy in South Africa that will guarantee energy and economic justice as we embark on the low carbon path. Countries that have phased out coal economies have invested in initiatives such as a social protection plan for ensuring that those exposed to economic losses from phase-out are protected.

COAL INFRASTRUCTURE REPURPOSING OPTIONS

According to Chattopadhyay et al. (2021), there is global capacity for generation of 2000GW of coal power. This means that the shift to low carbon technologies is likely to result in stranded coal assets; available options for repurposing and repowering therefore need to be evaluated. Moreover, 20 per cent of existing coal power plants are inefficient and costly when compared with wind and solar power plants. Nonetheless, there is still a need to manage the socio-economic impact associated with the phase out of coal assets. Lessons could be drawn from initiatives such as the Climate Investment Fund of the

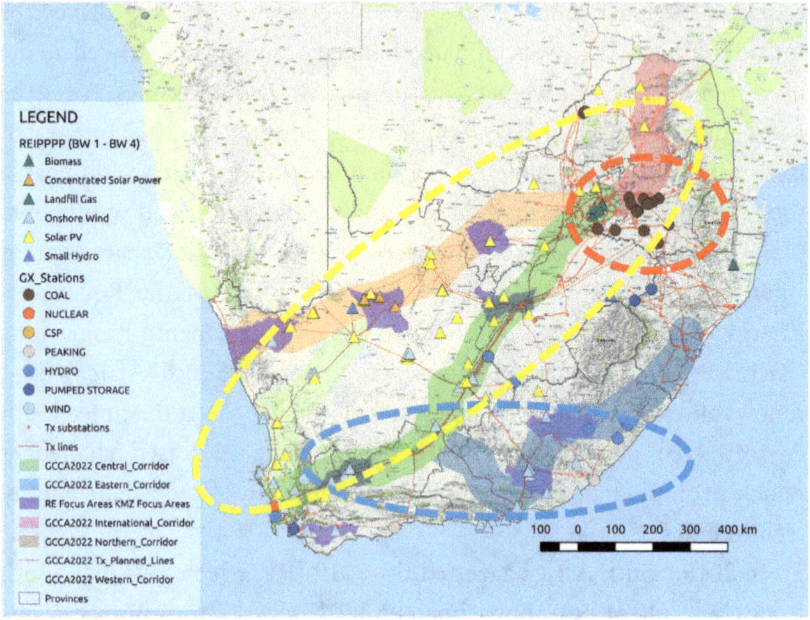

Figure 10.2: Location of coal power fleet and the renewable energy development zones

Source: Semelane et al. (2021b).

World Bank which enables investment in coal repurposing options. Decommissioning coal power plants can cost up to U$200 million, however, repurposing and repowering costs are site-specific and dependent on individual investors (Chattopadhyay et al., 2021). Therefore, consideration of costs for retrofitting and re-utilisation of coal assets and associated infrastructure is critically important. Figure 10.2 shows the deployment of coal, wind and solar energy in regions across South Africa. However, the country's IRP shows that most of the coal power fleet would shut down in the anticipated energy transition. This provides an opportunity for re-utilisation of the coal assets that might be left stranded.

In South Africa, all the ageing coal power plants are in Mpumalanga province, which is approximately 160km away from the country's economic hub, Johannesburg. South Africa's highest concentration of solar radiation is in the Northern Cape region, consequently most of its utility scale solar power plants are situated in the Northern Cape.

However, Semelane et al., (2021b) show that the grid infrastructure that exists in coal regions, together with available solar resources, mean that the coal phase-out regions are suitable for solar power plants (see illustration in Figure 10.2). The solar energy resources in the South African coal region are estimated to be 5.61kWh/m^2/day (Semelane et al, 2021b). This is an excellent resource which should be utilised to generate renewable energy power plants. Furthermore, excess power that could be derived from renewable energy deployment in the coal phase-out region might also be used for land rehabilitation purposes in former coal mining areas.

Many countries have repurposed their existing coal infrastructure using economically viable approaches. This process includes repowering (i.e, electricity generation) and repurposing the coal assets. Some of the initiatives that could be considered include fuel conversion, retrofit coal boilers to renewable energy generation and steam generation (Qvist et al., 2020). As has been witnessed elsewhere, the repurposing of coal power plants is a costly exercise (Shrimali and Jindal, 2020). Also, coal power plants can be repurposed to retain some of their functions thus mitigating against the potential negative socio-economic impacts associated with coal economy phasing out. Also, the repurposing and repowering options facilitate the early retirement of coal power stations (i.e., promote an accelerated decarbonisation agenda), which is urgently needed due to climate change risks (SA-NDC, 2021). These are possible viable options that can address environmental sustainability challenges while the coal assets are redirected and modified towards a sustainable pathway. Likewise, such options nullify the unbankable challenges that the coal sector investment have been confronted with lately (Burke et al., 2019).

According to Shrimali and Jindal (2020), several countries such as Canada, Germany, the United Kingdom, India, Australia and the United States of America have embarked on the coal power plants repurposing path, and the options illustrated in Table 10.2 cut across the repurposing and repowering opportunities that have been implemented in the aforementioned countries. These include:

- Conversion of coal power plants to solar
- Biomass, battery storage (demand response)
- Data centre for renewable energy power plants
- Pumped and salt thermal storage
- Tourism sites and museums in former coal mining sites

There are several costs associated with decommissioning coal power plants; however, the repurposing and repowering costs are inexpensive relative to a complete power plant retirement. This is because when coal power plants are repurposed, some of the initial investment in the plant can be saved, plus some jobs are created. This means that the

Table 10.2: Repurposed coal power station

No.	Plant name	Location	Country	End use	Status
1.	Nanticoke	Ontario	Canada	Solar	Completed
2.	Prosper Haniel	North Rhine Westphalia	Germany	Pumped storage, salt thermal storage	Completed
3.	Drax	North Yorkshire	United Kingdom	Biomass	Completed
4.	Beckjord	Ohio	United States	Battery storage	Completed
5.	Eastlake	Ohio	United States	Synchronous condenser	Completed
6.	Widows Creek	Alabama	United States	Data center	Completed
7.	Mount Tom	Massachusetts	United States	Solar and Battery storage	Completed
8.	Redbank	New South Wales	Australia	Solar, biomass	Proposed
9.	Liddell	New South Wales	Australia	Renewable energy (RE), battery storage, gas, demand response	Proposed
10	Guru Nanak Dev	Punjab	India	Solar	Proposed
11.	Brayton Point	New England	United States	Offshore wind	Proposed
12.	Komati power station	Middelburg	South Africa	Solar	Proposed

actual investment cost is mainly for retrofits. Other benefits include reduced pollution which has a positive correlation with social health benefits (Shrimali and Jindal, 2020). Table 10.2 shows some of the repurposing options that are available for South Africa to consider. Adoption of these available options is dependent on investment finance. The options shown in Table 10.2 are well established technologies that can form part of the repurposing and repowering options.

Figure 10.3 shows three scenarios that have been evaluated by (Shrimali and Jindal, 2020). It demonstrates that the repurposing of coal power stations represents least cost with maximum benefits. This is cheaper than continuing to operate or decommissioning coal power plants. Figure 10.3 shows that most benefits are in the retained ancillary services; reemployment opportunities; improved air quality; improved health; cheap electricity; re-utilisation of coal assets; and sunk investment cost benefits. Likewise, renewable energy technologies could be deployed for coal mining land rehabilitation, manufacturing and agricultural sector development. This means that the diversification of coal phase-out regional economies should not only include renewable energy technologies but rather other regional economic development initiatives as well, such as smart agriculture and deployment of decentralised renewable energy technologies for manufacturing purposes.

THE JUST ENERGY TRANSITION APPROACH

There is a need to ensure that the energy transition is just. According to Ramirez and Böhm (2021), energy and social science researchers have increasingly utilised the energy justice framework to investigate the connection between sustainable energy investments and justice. The South African energy transition has given rise to social concerns mainly due to sustainable economic development that excludes the majority of South Africans. There is also concern about the lack of a just energy transition policy framework which will ensure that long-lasting jobs are created as low carbon technologies are adopted. According to Henry et al. (2020), the energy justice framework prioritises harmless, affordable and sustainable energy technologies. However, in the South African context, internal colonialism, which Ramirez and Böhm (2021) define as a 'pattern of oppression, repression and violation within countries in the Global South', is perpetual and different from typical European colonialism. Instead, it emphasises how colonial forces are replicated within countries in the Global South by the overpowering of people and livelihoods. From the renewable energy standpoint, internal colonialism comprises the formation of structural economic and political power dynamics that enable 'low-carbon investments as a strategy for economic development and climate change mitigation' (Ramirez and Böhm, 2021). In the green growth neoliberal archetype, energy policies have been authorised to facilitate private sector investments in the renewable energy sector with limited participation of local communities and government (Devine and Baca, 2020).

The repurposing of coal assets could be a strategy for the just energy transition. This means that alternative options are pursued to ensure that the South African coal regions do not worsen the ailing economic conditions that have been experienced in the past years. As such, alternative investment options that will guarantee economic activities in coal phasing-out regions need to be addressed through thoughtful and inclusive policy design. Moreover, communities and stakeholders that have benefitted from the fossil fuels sector confronted with the inevitable phase-out need to be included in innovative low carbon investments opportunities. This will ensure that the energy transition is just, sound and acceptable. The labour movements and environmental justice groups provide several solutions for how a just energy transition path should unfold. These include tools, theories and models that should be adopted for an equitable energy transition (Henry et al., 2020). To understand the model for a just energy transition Henry and co-authors (2020) emphasise the need to recognise the principles of the just energy transition framework. The concept of a just transition originated with the US labour movement of the 1970s and broadened as labour organisations forged alliances with environmental justice groups starting in the 1990s. The South African just energy transition has been encouraged by the phase-out of ageing coal power plants. This means that the just energy transition will need to be integrated into South Africa's energy policy. The International Trade Union Confederation (ITUC) developed a climate justice framework that aims to ensure that new job opportunities are created through low carbon investments (International Trade Union Confederation, 2015). The repurposing of coal assets aligns well with the climate justice framework. The United Nations (Rio + 20) conference on sustainable development generated a resolution document termed 'The Future We Want'. The document outlines opportunities for green employment and sustainability for the

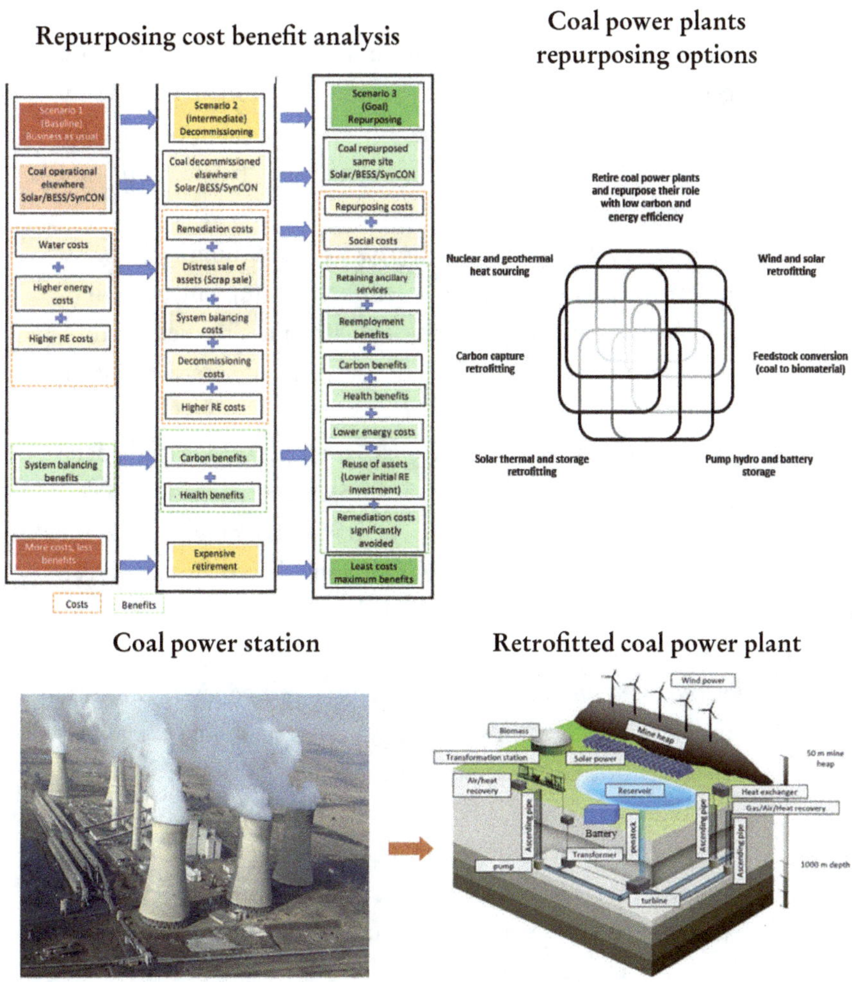

Figure 10.3: Repurposing options cost benefit analysis

Source: Redrawn by author based on analysis from Chattopadhyay et al. (2021) and Shrimali and Jindal (2020).

just transition (International Labour Organization, 2013). This means that the repurposing of coal assets to sustainable investment would contribute to a just transition. According to the Just Transition Centre (2018), the just transition should entail the vital steps outlined in points 1–3 below. The authors recommend the addition of steps 4–6 as key policy reforms which need to be adopted to achieve a just transition in South Africa.

1. *Consultation phase*: 'community goals development, economic development planning, creation of policies in support of transition efforts, the establishment of financial programs, economic impact analysis' (Just Transition Centre, 2018: 7)
2. *Project development execution phase*: 'retraining of workers, invest in economic development, scaled implementation of emissions reductions and investments in renewables, investment in community energy savings' (Just Transition Centre, 2018: 7)
3. *Just transition endorsement phase*: 'enact worker and social protections programs, implement wide-ranging apprenticeship and entrepreneurship training, repurpose and remediate properties, invest in regional green technology research and development' (Just Transition Centre, 2018: 7)
4. *Accelerated localisation of energy components*: increase the local manufacturing of energy components and create jobs
5. *Social protection packages phase*: develop compensation packages for those who might lose out in the transition (i.e., those who cannot be reskilled or re-employed elsewhere)
6. *Community ownership phase*: develop utility scale sustainable energy and distributed generation projects that are community-owned

Implementing the policy recommendation listed above would facilitate the adoption of a low carbon resilient future encompassed by all stakeholders. This would enhance the uptake of sustainable energy technologies, and would also generate increased tax revenue for the state. The recommended policy reforms will ensure that the energy transition is just and inclusive. The major indicators for the just energy transition are illustrated in Table 10.3. They should enable social, economic and environmental sustainability for coal phasing out regions.

CONCLUDING REMARKS

The coal phase-out will force the coal regions to rethink how they can enable economic development as the coal sector continues to decline. Repurposing and repowering were highlighted as key strategic options, which can ensure that sustained economic development is achieved in coal phasing-out regions. It is important to note that repurposing and repowering coal assets will not resolve all of South Africa's socio-economic challenges. This means that some of those that are dependent

Table 10.3: Just energy transition indicators proposed

Impact	Social	Economic	Environmental
Net increase in employment creation	•	•	
Tax revenue generation for the state	•	•	
Emissions reduction	•		•
Strong climate change adaptation options	•	•	•
Social protection and social inclusion (affected societies, NGOs and labour movements representation	•	•	•
Economic trade-offs that could be achieved from renewable energy development, tourism, agriculture, manufacturing, health benefits (air quality) and green transport as part of the Just Transition Framework	•	•	•
Repurposing existing coal infrastructure	•	•	•
Reskilling opportunities in the identified Just Transition key sectors	•	•	
Scalable energy technologies that could easily respond to economic growth and energy demand		•	

Source: Authors' analysis.

on the coal economy are likely to lose out from the energy transition. In South Africa, the key driver for coal phase-out is the advancement of sustainable development which enables accelerated adoption of cleaner energy technologies and emphasises the need for a net zero carbon future. They can be a major contribution to a framework that could be broadly adopted, and could involve other sectors.

Just transition investments should provide social, economic and environmental sustainability. This means that the transition should not be a formula for joblessness or worsen the inequalities in South Africa.

SECTION 2

REGENERATIVE AGRICULTURE: AN ALTERNATIVE ECONOMIC DEVELOPMENT PATHWAY

To meet international obligations for emissions reduction, the closure of coal power plants and mines will be required. Given that coal mining infrastructure is a critical part of the South African economy, sufficient transition strategies are required to ensure that South Africa's deep-rooted inequality, poverty and unemployment are not exacerbated. Alternative routes for economic development are required to meet the conditions of a just transition. Mpumalanga, a province in South Africa, contains the largest share of South Africa's coal mining infrastructure and will be a focal point for policy-makers in any transition strategy for a just transition.

In this section, we position and evaluate regenerative agriculture as one of the alternative options for Mpumalanga's transition plan. Regenerative agriculture is assessed on its ability to create employment and rehabilitate land. A literature review and subsequent case studies are used to assess the extent to which regenerative agriculture can mitigate the job losses incurred by the closure of coal plants.

Mpumalanga province has over 60 per cent of its surface area subject to mining rights or prospecting applications (Simpson et al., 2019). The economic and developmental context in Mpumalanga has favoured mining and electricity generation as main drivers of economic growth, above other sectors such as agriculture. This becomes evident from an evaluation of the water, energy and food nexus; it illustrates that food and water security are increasingly being threatened by the interests that serve the nation's energy needs (Simpson et al., 2019). In addition to this, 25 334 ha of commercial crop land cover and 22 885 ha of natural or semi-natural land cover was converted to mining between 1994–2014 (Stats SA, 2020b), which places major strains on the capacity of land to provide food and regulate the water cycle.

Despite the prioritisation of mining over other land uses, only 69 000 people were employed in the mining sector in Mpumalanga compared to the 86 000 people employed in agriculture (Stats SA, 2020a). Mpumalanga is important for the country's food production, with 46.4 per cent of the nation's high potential arable land situated within the province (BFAP, 2012) and 15.7 per cent and 0.8 per cent of the land cover being used for commercial and subsistence crop production respectively (Stats SA, 2020b). Mine closure is a necessary step in the lifecycle of mines due to mineral depletion or unsustainable financial viability. The process governing mine closure is, however, less resolute. As identified by multiple studies, the formal and successful closure of depleted mining complexes remains an elusive goal for firms and departments alike (Van Druten, 2017; Crous, 2020; Kauppila, 2021). Existing statutory and regulatory frameworks make provision for the closure of mines but are less flexible when mine closures are unexpected. This makes mine closure difficult in certain circumstances (Milaras et al., 2014; Crous, 2020; Perkins, 2020).

Environmental concerns about mine closure have mostly been attributed to acid mine drainage and its subsequent pollution of surface and groundwater (Naidoo, 2015). Other studies point to the dangerous air pollution caused by mining, especially coal mining, in the highveld of Mpumalanga (Gray, 2019).

Mining, however, contributes a significant proportion of jobs and GDP in the country (DMRE, 2019). The mining sector employs around 514 859 individuals (21 per cent in coal mining) (Stats SA, 2020) and contributes approximately 8 per cent towards national GDP (BFAP, 2021). It has also, however, been acknowledged that South Africa must relinquish its dependence on coal to contribute its part in addressing global climate targets (Stockholm Environment Institute, 2019; Climate

Investment Funds, 2020). This will, over time, entail mine closures (the process of ending the operation of a mine) and decommissioning (permanently ending mining operations and removing equipment and facilities not intended for future use) (Kaupilla, 2021). It also entails providing opportunities for alternative economic development and the rehabilitation of mine-owned land (Kauppila, 2021). One economic diversification route away from mining in Mpumalanga is agriculture. Regenerative agriculture in particular, as will be discussed later, has significant potential to rehabilitate land and provide opportunities for economic development. However, to meet the principles of the just transition, it is important that any alternative economic diversification route is discussed with stakeholders most affected by the transition strategy and include them in planning and decision-making processes. The following sections will detail the economic development and employment opportunities associated with regenerative agriculture. This is followed by an assessment of the rehabilitation potential of regenerative agriculture. Through this, we assess the economic and environmental opportunities associated with regenerative agriculture and position it as an alternative economic pathway to coal mining in Mpumalanga.

REGENERATIVE AGRICULTURE

Schreefal et al. (2020) define regenerative agriculture as an approach to farming that uses soil conservation as the entry point. The intention is to regenerate and contribute to multiple ecosystems with the objective of enhancing not only the environmental but also the social and economic dimensions of sustainable food production. It is a term that lacks universal scientific and legal agreement. Points of divergence and convergence often centre around the practices or objectives associated with regenerative agriculture. A common entry point for these practices and objectives is aligning with the aim of improving soil carbon and soil biodiversity. The activities associated with regenerative agriculture include no tillage/minimum tillage, using cover crops and manure to build soil fertility and employing crop rotations to ensure optimal use of soils. It can also include the integration of animals (domestic or wild) through methods like rotational grazing and silvopasture to stimulate plant growth (Regeneration International, 2021).

Regenerative agriculture is being widely acknowledged as a strategy to reduce the pressures that conventional agriculture has placed on the environment (climate change, land degradation and biodiversity loss) as well as improve the socio-economic conditions of our food system (improved nutrition standards and lower input costs) (Schreefel et al., 2020). It is an emerging trend in South African agricultural production with 48 farms identified as practising regenerative agriculture (RegenAg SA, 2021). It should be noted that this number presents a voluntary list of regenerative farmers in the country but is not a comprehensive total of all regenerative farmers in South Africa. It is also a concept that has recently been attracting interest from civil society and the private sector (Mhlatyana, 2021; Cullis, 2021; Malan, 2021; Grain SA, 2021). Lack of certification and standards are major obstacles to tracking the uptake of regenerative agriculture in South Africa. The next two sections evaluate the potential of regenerative agriculture to provide employment opportunities and rehabilitate land.

Employment in regenerative agriculture

Statistics of job creation in the regenerative agriculture value chain are currently anecdotal and region specific. There are few reports that have inventoried employment issues on 'green' agricultural practices. A seminal report released by Nemes (2009), for example, reviewed various methodologies to assess the impact of organic agriculture practices that are representative of green agriculture methods. The study found that 'the overwhelming majority of cases show that organic farms are more economically profitable, despite frequent yield decreases' (where such yield reductions may be encountered in the early years of organic implementation) (Nemes, 2009: 3). While organic agriculture and regenerative agriculture should not be conflated, the underlying reasons identified by the study provide encouraging insight into why regenerative agriculture may offer viable economic opportunities to farming. Overlaps between regenerative agriculture and organic agriculture include the reduction of production input costs; increased variety of total farm products and premium market prices were the main reasons why organic agriculture proved to be more economically viable than industrial agriculture (Herren, 2012). Regenerative agriculture is intended to reduce input costs, introduce greater on-farm diversity (crops and biodiversity) and is already signalling promising premium market prices (Lafave et al., 2021). Premiums for regenerative products are currently being seen in the European Union and the United States, with the former being South Africa's biggest export market. Economists are sceptical about whether the demand for more sustainable food is being driven by environmental concerns. The demand being driven by the possible health benefits associated with regenerative farming practices is, however, providing renewed optimism among economists and agronomists alike (Herren, 2012).

Twenty-six per cent of South Africans live in food-insecure circumstances and significant attention needs to be paid to domestic food demand to achieve the principle of a just transition of food sovereignty and food security in the country (Food and Agriculture Organization of the United Nations, 2016). Both South Africa's food and agricultural systems have been characterised by increasing concentration over the past decade (WWF SA, 2010). This means that farms are decreasing in number but are growing in size and productivity. Equally, fewer retailers and input suppliers are occupying higher market shares, creating oligopolies in the food system (Von Loeper, 2016). The switch from conventional agriculture to small-scale and regenerative farming practices is consistent with higher job creation (Herren, 2012). Industrial agriculture is often characterised by large areas of land being used for monocropping systems or large-scale livestock production with high inputs of synthetic fertilisers, pesticides and processed feed. In South Africa, industrial agriculture is being increasingly mechanised, meaning that on-farm labour is becoming more dispensable. Sales of farm machinery (especially tractors and harvesters) have increased year on year by 30 per cent and 4 per cent respectively (Sihlobo, 2021). In addition to this, pivot-irrigated commercial fields have increased in extent by more than 200 per cent since 1994, largely replacing rain-fed cultivated commercial fields and natural or semi-natural land (Statistics SA, 2020b). Besides the strain placed on surface and groundwater sources, these systems are associated with low labour requirements

(100 ha per field worker) (Jumman, 2021). A common counter argument to the narrative that mechanisation undermines employment is that it increases job creation by introducing new technologies that need operators (BBC, 2021). These counter arguments are often made by developed countries where high-skilled labour is common, and the introduction of new technologies is more accessible to producers. Realities in South Africa suggest that even though farmers are willing to employ new technologies on their farms, finance, insurance and a lack of skills are still common bottlenecks for the introduction to new technology (Von Loeper, 2016).

Regenerative agriculture, however, is largely consistent with traditional forms of agricultural production, which do not require technological on-farm advancements. It is also more conducive to the employment of people when compared to commercial farms (measured in person/hectare units) (Mishra, 2020). One regenerative agriculture farm (owned by Hendrik O'Neill) near Hammanskraal in Limpopo, for example, employs 12 people on a 40 ha plot of land (observed on a site visit in early September of 2021). This farm engages mainly in livestock production and has an employment ratio of 0.3 people/ha. Another farm, Afrikan Farms (a large-scale industrial livestock producer) employs 22 people on approximately 6000ha of land owing to an employment ratio of 0.0036 people/ha (approximately 83 times smaller than regenerative farms) (Dungmore, 2018). This example is anecdotal and has many variables influencing it (age of farm, money available for employment of labourers, economies of scale, etc.). It does, however, reflect a trend, which shows that the labour intensity of regenerative farms is significantly higher than those of industrial farms, a trend documented by Herren et al. (2012). As Delgado (1999: 165) stated, 'Smallholder agriculture is simply too important to employment, human welfare, and political stability in sub-Saharan Africa to be ignored'.

The central question is to what extent regenerative agriculture can absorb the job losses incurred by the closure of mining and power plant infrastructure. Recent employment figures in Mpumalanga's coal mining are difficult to qualify but Statistics South Africa estimated that around 69 000 people were employed in mining (13 800 in coal mining)

(Stats SA, 2019). Many of the mines responsible for these employment figures are found overwhelmingly in Mpumalanga (Bega, 2021). It is unlikely that regenerative agriculture alone will be able to compensate for job losses from mining in the province, given that the proportional extent of mining land cover in the province amounts to 1 per cent (Stats SA, 2020b). Regenerative agriculture offers a viable alternative to coal mining regarding employment given the high labour intensity required for the on-farm, off-farm and other activities associated with the rest of the supply chain. Ranching, composting, weeding (manual or limited mechanical intervention), crop monitoring, planting, animal husbandry and harvesting are among some of the on-farm activities required, as well as planning, administration and financial management of the farm. The rest of the supply chain that is created or used in the production of regenerative agriculture products will also contribute to the provision of jobs. These include hawkers, processors, distributors and retailers. A quantitative analysis of the labour absorption potential could provide valuable information towards this research. While the employment potential of regenerative agriculture may be insufficient to meet the labour deficit created by mining infrastructure closure, it is worth noting that there are other significant economic opportunities associated with regenerative agriculture. The first is that farmers require fewer costly inputs like fertilisers and pesticides; they manage their pests more effectively by promoting soil biology and organic matter, and biodiversity on their farms. Secondly, regenerative farms were found to be relatively more profitable than industrial farms in part because of how their products are marketed but also because of the potential to diversify their income (LaCanne and Lundgren, 2018).

It is worth noting that as part of the mine rehabilitation process, mine closure must involve the repurposing of land to a state that makes the land an asset to whoever takes ownership over it. The rehabilitation of the land has many associated opportunities for employment before agriculture even commences (limiting negative impacts of mining, restoring soil, improving and maintaining buildings for further use). Mpumalanga has already set a precedent of using mining land for agriculture but agriculture's rehabilitation potential is not well established.

LAND REHABILITATION THROUGH REGENERATIVE AGRICULTURE

Land use is widely considered a key driver in both climate change and biodiversity loss (Pörtner et al., 2021) and is, therefore, a topic which requires serious consideration in understanding land use practices that support the mitigation of and adaptation to climate change and biodiversity loss. Land use can be considered to be a series of terrestrial operations carried out by humans. This is not to be confused with land cover, which refers to the surface cover of the land (Coffey, 2021). Mining has a negative impact on the health of those who live around it. As recently brought to the fore through the Umoya Obulalayo (deadly air) case against the South African government, mining and coal power stations are facing increasing scrutiny for being implicated in dangerous living conditions in and around mining areas (Centre for Environmental Rights, 2021; Ncube, 2021). A study on air quality impacts and health effects in Mpumalanga's highveld region found that ambient pollution from 14 industrial facilities caused between 305–650 early deaths in the province (Gray, 2019). Of these 14 facilities, 12 were Eskom coal-fired power stations. Regenerative agriculture will have to ensure that land and water usage improve the conditions that mines have left through the restoration of mines to meet the conditions of the just transition. The Department of Mineral Resources and Energy's guidelines for the rehabilitation of mined land define mine rehabilitation as 'putting the land impacted by the mining activity back to a sustainable usable condition' (Chamber of Mines of South Africa/ COALTECH, 2007). This definition recognises that restoration of land to historical states is nearly impossible, and that rehabilitation focuses primarily on 'land capability' to meet community desires.

To meet this definition, the key assessment of this section is to test regenerative agriculture's capacity to rehabilitate previously mined land. There is unfortunately not a clear consensus on the viability of rehabilitating mined land for agricultural purposes. There are, however, examples in South Africa that point to success stories. Exxaro's land management goals for 2026, for example, include the transferring of 90 per cent of post-mining land to emerging farmers in local communities

(Arnoldi, 2021). A landmark study has documented the knowledge and gaps in the restoration of post-mining landscapes in Africa. It found that there has been substantial progress in identifying species that are suitable for phytoremediation (a process that uses plants to remove, transfer, stabilise or destroy contaminants in the soil and water) (Festin, 2019). It also identified successful stories of limestone quarries in South Africa. There is insufficient evidence to claim that regenerative agriculture can be used as an immediate land use on decommissioned coal mines to supply food security. The production of food without trace elements of pollutants needs to be tested further but processes such as phytostabilisation (reduction of the mobility of heavy metals in the soil) provides opportunities to improve land quality for regenerative agriculture. Fortunately, biochar production, one practice of phytostabilisation, is supported by regenerative agriculture. Biochar is a type of charcoal produced by the burning of biomass in the absence of oxygen (International Biochar Initiative, 2021). South Africa has vast experience in the production of biochar through the removal and use of alien invasive vegetation; the products can act as fertilisers and stabilisers of soil carbon. This process supports the stabilisation of pollutants from mines and offers a viable way of rehabilitating mined land.

Regenerative agriculture and its associated practices provide further opportunities to support the rehabilitation of mines. These include the practice of creation and use, composting, silvopasture and the introduction of indigenous plants into the relevant areas may support the rehabilitation of the land's soils (Gabriel, 2021). After the land has been suitably rehabilitated, many examples of regenerative agriculture suggest that soil health may be substantially improved over time (Lal, 2020; Soto et al., 2020; Ranganathan et al., 2020). No-till agriculture, for example, reduces soil erosion and encourages higher water infiltration and storage. The use of cover crops improves soil texture and mitigates water pollution. Diverse crop rotations can lower pesticide use and good grazing practices can increase vegetative cover (Ranganathan et al., 2020).

While regenerative agriculture alone is unlikely to compensate for the job losses incurred by the decommissioning and closure of mines, it does offer a better alternative than conventional agriculture in meeting the employment requirements of a just transition. Furthermore, there is substantial evidence to suggest that regenerative agriculture has significant potential to rehabilitate land but further work is required to assess the extent to which mining land needs to be rehabilitated before it is suitable for regenerative agriculture.

Policy requirements for regenerative agriculture to support a just transition

The relationship between land tenure and the willingness of farmers to invest in land improvement measures (like regenerative agriculture) is well established (Abdulai et al., 2011; Lovo, 2015; Ghebru and Lambrecht, 2017; Adnan et al., 2017; Nkomoki, 2018; Higgins et al., 2018; Infante-Amate et al., 2018). Given this, there must be renewed commitment towards land redistribution in Mpumalanga. This requires permanent land ownership to be allocated to communities living around mining areas. Carolan (2005) suggests that permanent land ownership is more likely to encourage the uptake of sustainable agriculture. Land reform will not only create a necessary base for the uptake of land reform but can provide an opportunity to transfer significant proportions of land from companies towards communities. It therefore offers a chance for individuals to address issues of racial and economic injustice. For instance, only 8 per cent of the agricultural land owned in Mpumalanga is owned by Africans (DRDLR, 2017). Currently, 15.7 per cent of the province's land cover is under commercial agriculture and 1 per cent is under mining land cover (the fourth and second highest in the country respectively) (Stats SA, 2020b). Both these land uses are regarded as drivers of land degradation and greenhouse gas emissions, thus providing additional incentive to transition to regenerative land uses.

The transition from these land practices will depend on existing ownership structures altering their land use practices, or transferring ownership to allow for new land use practices. Given the scope of this research, it is assumed that the decommissioning of mines and mine closure processes provide potential for the transfer of land ownership to new owners. Without using the constitutional mechanism of land reform, land ownership would be dependent on mining companies and applicants reaching an agreement on personal terms without the state as a mediator. The decommissioning of coal mining in the province, accompanied by land reform, provides a useful enabling environment for the uptake of regenerative agriculture by providing new owners with land.

Extension services must be a central part of the enabling environment to encourage the uptake of regenerative agriculture. Extension services refer to the informal educational process aimed at rural communities to provide technical and sometimes personal assistance to pursue agricultural enterprises. These are largely geared towards farmers to assist them in dealing with a range of problems (from financial to pest control) and are aimed at increasing farm efficiency (FAO, 2021). Manenzhe et al. (2016) undertook a random sampling assessment of the Bushbuckridge municipality to understand the sustainability of land reform projects in Mpumalanga. From the study, 83 per cent of key informants did not have farming skills (Manenzhe, 2016). While this is just one local municipality, anticipatory governance is needed to ensure that beneficiaries are well supported when they receive ownership of the land. This can be achieved in numerous ways such as through the provision of grants, capital and access to cooperative farming groups. A significant support mechanism can also be the provision of agricultural extension services. South Africa has a rich history in the development of its extension services dating as far back as 1924. In the 1980s, however, the knowledge institutions and the coordinating arms of the apartheid state became increasingly privatised and became inaccessible to black South Africans (Koch, 2013). At the advent of democracy, the government was unable to secure an effective rollout of extension services to most farmers given the increasingly privatised nature of experienced extension services. Given the historic success of extension services in achieving various mandates both in South Africa and abroad, it stands to reason that this is an effective tool in a land reform programme. It must be noted that historically extension services in the country have focused on improved efficiency, yield increases, access to markets and farmer profitability (Koch, 2013). Many extension services that meet their mandates are almost exclusively coordinated through commodity organisations (such as those for citrus, poultry, maize and sugar) (Liebenberg, 2015). These have invariably favoured industrial forms of agriculture that employ methods contrary to regenerative agriculture. The following conditions provide a starting point for the principles that should be incorporated into a regenerative agriculture extension programme:

1. Reducing and reversing soil erosion through effective livestock management, practising no tillage and rainwater harvesting through use of cover crops
2. Improving soil fertility through use of manure and composting
3. Improving soil texture through minimising disturbance of the soil, maximising organic matter incorporation into the soil through livestock rotation, using perennials and maximising soil cover
4. Improving soil and on farm biodiversity by minimising the use of synthetic pesticides and fertilisers, encouraging growth of indigenous flora and practicing intercropping
5. Enabling access to markets by identifying commodities demanding price premiums in domestic and export markets and their associated pathways; identifying products that contribute to local food security needs and training farmers in how to manage businesses

A state-coordinated rollout of extension services could incorporate universities, regenerative agriculture practitioners and the country's LandCare programme, which has extensive reach in every province (168 recorded projects nationally in 2019; 111 345 total beneficiaries and 151 033 ha of rehabilitated land) (LandCare Portfolio Committee, 2019).

CONCLUDING REMARKS

This section of the chapter has discussed regenerative agriculture's potential to meet the requirements of a just transition (employment and land rehabilitation). The high labour requirements for regenerative agriculture and the fact that converting mine-owned land to agricultural land is already taking place in Mpumalanga makes it a suitable alternative to mining in the province. Regenerative agriculture also provides opportunities to create financially viable systems that can support domestic food security. Food security is further supported by regenerative agriculture through the possible increase in nutrient-dense food due to the improvement of soil health.

To make regenerative agriculture a viable alternative to coal mining in Mpumalanga, it will have to match the interests of farmers, coal-affected communities, the labour sector, government, private sector and civil society. This means meeting productivity increases; market access for emerging and communal farmers; improved environmental outcomes; making South African products more competitive in domestic and international markets; and stimulating local demand for regenerative agriculture products. Pivotal to all of these are cross-cutting themes of gender equality, racial justice and the skills gap, especially in rural and peri-urban areas.

While it remains unclear to what extent mining-affected land can be regenerated sufficiently to produce food complying with safety standards, the activities associated with regenerative agriculture have significant potential to restore degraded landscapes. Given the employment opportunities and rehabilitation potential, regenerative agriculture offers a viable development pathway in the process of closing coal infrastructure. This will require a strong enabling environment to work at scale. For regenerative agriculture, land reform should be used to ensure effective transfer of ownership of the land. Supporting services, especially extension services focused on the principles of regenerative agriculture, should be rolled out at scale to support its uptake and provide land owners with the means to make the farms financially viable.

CHAPTER OVERVIEW

This chapter has demonstrated the significant potential that both regenerative agriculture and the repurposing of coal infrastructure have to meet the requirements of a just transition. Both activities are characterised by high levels of potential to create jobs and contribute to the wider economy. Regenerative agriculture also provides opportunities to create financially viable systems that can support domestic food security. Food security is further supported by regenerative agriculture through a possible increase in nutrient-dense food acquired through the improvement of soil health.

The repurposing of coal infrastructure and its associated benefits may provide significant benefits to the requirements of the just transition in the context of energy. The activities associated with the repurposing of coal infrastructure, such as retrofitting, provide potential for job creation and the mitigation of health and pollution events related to the maintenance of coal infrastructure. Furthermore, the activities associated with regenerative agriculture have potential to decrease total water demand on farms and improve the resilience of farms to cope with both flood and drought conditions. While it remains unclear whether food or feed produced from abandoned mines can be consumed safely, the activities associated with regenerative agriculture have significant potential to restore degraded landscapes.

Together, regenerative agriculture and the repurposing of coal infrastructure meet several of the requirements contained within different conceptualisations of the just transition. They both require a strong enabling environment to work at scale. For regenerative agriculture, land reform or private agreements should be used to ensure effective transfer of ownership of the land. Supporting services, especially extension services, should be rolled out at scale to support the uptake of regenerative agriculture and provide landowners with the means to make farms financially viable. To meet the requirements of a just transition in energy, consultations with communities, project development and execution, and a just transition endorsement phase will have to be part of the transition plan.

REFERENCES

Abdulai, A., Owusu, V. and Goetz, R. 2011. 'Land tenure differences and investment in land improvement measures: Theoretical and empirical analyses'. *Journal of Development Economics*, 96(1), 66–78.

Adnan, N., Nordin, S.M. and Bin Abu Bakar, Z. 2017. 'Understanding and facilitating sustainable agricultural practice: A comprehensive analysis of adoption behaviour among Malaysian paddy farmers'. *Land Use Policy*, 68, 372–382.

Arnoldi, M. 2021. 'Repurposing of mining land could help create farming jobs at scale'. *Engineering News*, https://www.engineeringnews.co.za/article/repurposing-of-mining-land-could-help-create-farming-jobs-at-scale-2020-09-25, accessed 11 May 2021.

BBC. 2021. 'The incredible farms being run from space'. *Follow the Food Series*, https://www.bbc.com/reel/video/p0997dt3/the-incredible-farms-being-run-from-space, accessed 21 May 2021.

Bega, S. 5 Jan 2021.'Sisulu: Third of audited mines violate conditions of water use licence'. *Mail & Guardian*, https://mg.co.za/environment/2021-01-05-sisulu-third-of-audited-mines-violate-water-use-licence-conditions/, accessed 30 July 2021.

Bureau for Food and Agricultural Policy (BFAP). 2021. 'BFAP baseline agricultural outlook 2021–2030'. https://www.sagis.org.za/BFAP-Baseline-2021.pdf, accessed 10 September 2021.

Bureau for Food and Agricultural Policy (BFAP). 2012. 'Evaluating the impact of coal mining on agriculture in the Delmas, Ogies and Leandra districts: A focus on Maize production'.

Bureau for Food and Agricultural Policy, https://libkey.io/10.22004/ag.econ.279783?utm_source=ideas, accessed 21 July 2021.

Burke, P.J., Best, R. and Jotzo, F. 2019. 'Closures of coal-fired power stations in Australia: Local unemployment effects'. *Australian Journal of Agricultural and Resource Economics*, 63, 142–165. https://doi.org/10.1111/1467-8489.12289.

Büscher, B. 2009. 'Connecting political economies of energy in South Africa'. *Energy Policy*, 37, 3951–3958. https://doi.org/10.1016/j.enpol.2009.04.041

Carolan, M. 2005. 'Barriers to the adoption of sustainable agriculture on rented land: An examination of contesting social fields'. *Journal of Rural Sociology*, 387–413.

Centre for Environmental Rights. 2021. 'Environmental groups take government to High Court over violation of Constitutional right to clean air'. Centre for Environmental Rights, https://cer.org.za/news/environmental-groups-take-government-to-high-court-over-violation-of-constitutional-right-to-clean-air, accessed 11 May 2021.

Chamber Of Mines of South Africa/Coaltech. 2007. 'Guidelines for the rehabilitation of mined land'. Chamber of Mines, Johannesburg.

Chattopadhyay, D., Bazilian, M.D., Handler, B. and Govindarajalu, C. 2021. 'Accelerating the coal transition'. Electricity Journal, 34(2), 106906. https://doi.org/10.1016/j.tej.2020.106906.

Climate Investment Funds. 2020. 'Supporting just transitions in South Africa'. https://www.climateinvestmentfunds.org/sites/cif_enc/files/knowledge-documents/supporting_just_transitions_in_south_africa.pdf, accessed 11

May 2021.

Climate Action Tracker (CAT). 2021. 'South Africa country summary'. https://climateactiontracker.org/countries/south-africa/, accessed 25 September 2021

Climate Justice Alliance. 2020. 'Just transition: A framework for change'. Just Transit, https://climatejusticealliance.org/just-transition/, accessed from 2 May 2020.

Coffey, R. 2021. 'The difference between "land use" and "land cover". Michigan State University, https://www.canr.msu.edu/news/the_difference_between_land_use_and_land_cover, accessed 30 May 2021.

Crous, C.O. 2020. 'Public disclosure of mine closures by listed South African mining companies'. *Corporate Social Responsibility and Environmental Management*, 1032–1042.

Cullis, C., 2021. 'Regenerative agriculture: An idea 12 000 years in the making'. Talk Radio 702, http://www.702.co.za/articles/399385/regenerative-agriculture-an-idea-12-000-years-in-the-making-bizun, accessed 29 July 2021.

Delgado, C. 1999. 'Sources of growth in smallholder agriculture in Sub-Saharan Africa: The role of vertical integration of smallholders with processors and marketers of high-value items'. *Agrekon*, 165–189.

Department of Energy (DoE). 2019. 'Integrated Resource Plan (IRP) 2019'. Government Gazette. Pretoria. https://doi.org/http://dx.doi.org/9771682584003-32963.

Department of Energy (DoE). 2018. Independent Power Producers Procurement Programme – An Overview. Annual Report. https://www.ipp-projects.co.za/Publications/GetPublicationFile?fileid=71515393-218c-e811-9489-2c59e59ac9cd&fileName=20180629_IPP%20Office%20Q4_2017-18%20Overview.pdf, accessed 21 May 2021.

Department of Energy (DoE). 2011. 'Integrated Resource Plan for electricity 2010–2030'. Department of Energy, Pretoria.

Department of Forestry; Fisheries and the Environment. 2021. 'Proposed updated Nationally Determined Contribution: South Africa's First Nationally Determined Contribution under the Paris Agreement'. Updated in 2021. Pretoria.

Department of Rural Development and Land Reform (DRDLR). 2017. 'Land Audit Report November 2017 Version 2'. https://www.gov.za/sites/default/files/gcis_document/201802/landauditreport13feb2018.pdf, accessed 23 August 2021.

Devine, J.A. and Baca, J.A., 2020. 'The political forest in the era of green neoliberalism'. *Antipode*, 52, 911–927. https://doi.org/10.1111/anti.12624.

Dou, S. Quan, Liu, J. yi, Xiao, J.Z., Pan, W., 2020. 'Economic feasibility valuing of deep mineral resources based on risk analysis: Songtao manganese ore - China case study'. *Resources Policy*, 66, 101612. https://doi.org/10.1016/j.

resourpol.2020.101612.

Dungmore, H., 2018. 'Khanyile's unstoppable Afrikan Farms'. https://heatherdugmore.co.za/khanyiles-unstoppable-afrikan-farms/, accessed 25 September 2021.

Eberhard, A. 2011. 'The Future of South African Coal: Market, Investment and Policy Challenges'. https://fsi-live.s3.us-west-1.amazonaws.com/s3fs-public/WP_100_Eberhard_Future_of_South_African_Coal.pdf, accessed 12 September 2021.

Eskom, 2013. 'A New Dawn Has Arrived 1923–2013 [WWW Document]'. http://www.eskom.co.za/sites/heritage/Documents/Mpumalanga90th.pdf, accessed 22 March 2021.

Eskom, 2015. 'List of fact sheets [WWW Document]'. http://www.eskom.co.za/OurCompany/SustainableDevelopment/Pages/CDM_Calculations.aspx, accessed 22 March 2021.

Food and Agriculture Organisation of the United Nations (FAO). 2021. 'Understanding extension'. https://www.fao.org/research-and-extension/en/, accessed 14 September 2021.

Festin, E.T. 2019. 'Progresses in restoration of post-mining landscape in Africa'. Journal of Forestry Research, 381–396.

Food and Agriculture Organisation of the United Nations. 2016. 'AQUASTAT Country Profile'. https://www.fao.org/aquastat/en/countries-and-basins/country-profiles, accessed 12 May 2021.

Gabriel, S. 2021. 'Six key principles for a successful silvopasture'. Cornell College of Agriculture and Life Sciences, https://smallfarms.cornell.edu/2018/06/six-key-principles-for-a-successful-silvopasture/, accessed 11 May 2021.

Ghebru, H. and Lambrecht, I. 2017. 'Drivers of perceived land tenure (in) security: Empirical evidence from Ghana'. *Land Use Policy,* 66, 293–303.

Grain SA. 2021. 'Farmer innovation programme: Conservation Agriculture Farmer Innovation Programme: Rationale and motivation'. *Grain SA*, https://www.grainsa.co.za/pages/grain-research/conservation-agriculture/farmer-innovation-programme, accessed 29 July 2021.

Gray, A.H. 2019. 'Air quality impacts and health effects due to large stationary source emissions in and around South Africa's Mpumalanga Highveld Priority Area (HPA)'. Centre for Environmental Rights, California, United States of America. https://cer.org.za/wp-content/uploads/2019/06/Andy-Gray-Report.pdf, accessed 20 July 2021.

Henry, M.S., Bazilian, M.D. and Markuson, C. 2020. 'Just transitions: Histories and futures in a post-COVID world'. *Energy Research & Social Science*, 68, 101668. https://doi.org/10.1016/j.erss.2020.101668.

Herren, H.B., Bassi, A. M., Tan, Z. and Binns, W.B. 2012. 'Green jobs for a revitalized food and agriculture sector'. FAO, https://www.fao.org/fileadmin/user_upload/suistainability/pdf/FAO_green_jobs_paper_

March_31.pdf, accessed 29 May 2021.

Higgins, D., Balint, T., Liversage, H. and Winters, P. 2018. 'Investigating the impacts of increased rural land tenure security: A systematic review of the evidence'. *Journal of Rural Studies*, 61, 34–62.

Infante-Amate, J., Aguilera, E., Palmeri, F., Guzmán, G., Soto, D. et al. 2018. 'Land embodied in Spain's biomass trade and consumption (1900–2008): Historical changes, drivers and impacts'. *Land Use Policy*, 78, 493–502.

International Biochar Initiative. 2021. 'BIOCHAR'. https://biochar-international.org/biochar/ , accessed 12 May 2021.

International Labour Organization (ILO). 2013. 'Resolution concerning sustainable development, decent work and green jobs', Geneva.

International Trade Union Confederation(ITUC). 2015. 'Climate Justice: There are no jobs on a dead planet'. https://www.ituc-csi.org/IMG/pdf/ituc_frontlines_climate_change_report_en.pdf, accessed 12 July 2021.

International Renewable Eenergy Agency (IRENA). 2016. 'The Power to Change: Solar and Wind Cost Reduction Potential to 2025'. https://www.irena.org/-/media/Files/IRENA/Agency/Publication/2016/IRENA_Power_to_Change_2016.pdf, accessed 24 May 2021.

Jumman, S. 2021. 'Information sheet: irrigation systems selection'. South African Sugarcane Research Institute, https://sasri.org.za/wp-content/uploads/Information_Sheets/IS_5.8-Irrigation-systems-selection.pdf, accessed 29 July 2021.

Just Transition Centre. 2018. 'Just transition: A business guide'. https://www.ituc-csi.org/IMG/pdf/just_transition_-_a_business_guide.pdf, accessed 29 July 2019.

Koch, B.H. 2013. 'An overview of agricultural extension in South Africa'. *South African Journal of Agricultural Extension*. 41, 107–117.

Kaupilla, T. 2021. 'Mine closure consists of decommissioning and mine site reclamation'. Mine Closure, https://mineclosure.gtk.fi/mine-closure-consists-of-decommissioning-and-mine-site-reclamation/, accessed 21 May 2021.

LaCanne, C.E. and Lundgren, J.G. 2018. 'Regenerative agriculture: Merging farming and natural resource conservation profitably'. *PeerJ: Life and Environment*, 6, 4428, DOI 10.7717/peerj.4428.

Lafave, C.H., Renton, C.A. and Sierks, K. 2020. 2021. 'Show me the money: Making a downstream market for diverse regenerative crops'. Conservation Finance Network, https://www.conservationfinancenetwork.org/2020/04/16/show-me-the-money-making-downstream-market-for-diverse-regenerative-crops, accessed 12 August 2021.

Lal, R. 2020. 'Regenerative agriculture for food and climate'. *Journal of Soil and Water Conservation*, 75, 5, 123A–124A.

LandCare Portfolio Committee. 2019. 'Landcare Programme Portfolio Committee presentation given to the Department of Agriculture, Forestry and Fisheries on 10 September 2019'.

Liebenberg, F. 2015. 'Agricultural advisory services in South Africa, extension and rural development'. Faculty of Natural and Agricultural Sciences, University of Pretoria.

Lovo, S. 2015. 'Tenure insecurity and investment in soil conservation: Evidence from Malawi'. *World Development*, 78, 219–229.

Malan, N. 14 August 2021. 'Regenerative agriculture can herald a new dawn for Mzansi farmers'. *Food for Mzansi*, https://www.foodformzansi.co.za/regenerative-agriculture-can-herald-a-new-dawn-for-mzansi-farmers/, accessed 29 July 2021.

Malan, T. 1975. 'The energy situation in South Africa'. *Africa Insight*, 5, 47–65.

Malzbender, D. 2005. 'Domestic electricity provision in the democratic South Africa'. African Water Issues Research Unit, University of Pretoria.

Manenzhe, T.D., Zwane, E. M. and Van Niekerk, J. A. 2016. 'Factors affecting sustainability of land reform projects in Ehlanzeni District Mpumalanga Province, South Africa'. *South African Journal of Agricultural Extension*, 44, 30–41.

Milaras, M., Ahmed, F. and McKay, T.J.M. 2014. 'Mine closure in South Africa: A survey of current professional thinking and practice'. Mine closure conference, 1–3 October, Johannesburg.

Mishra, N.K. 2020. 'Introduction', in Mishra N.K. (ed.), *Development Challenges of India After Twenty Five Years of Economic Reforms. India Studies in Business and Economics.* Springer, Singapore. https://doi.org/10.1007/978-981-15-8265-3_1.

Mhlatyana, U. 7 June 2021. 'Regenerative farming is vital to ensure food security'. *Mail & Guardian*. https://mg.co.za/opinion/2021-06-07-regenerative-farming-is-vital-to-ensure-food-security/, accessed 30 July 2021.

Naidoo, S. 2015. 'An assessment of the impacts of acid mine drainage on socio-economic development in the Witwatersrand: South Africa'. *Springer*, 17, 1045–1063.

Ncube, V. 11 May 2021. 'South Africa's "deadly air" case highlights health risks from coal'. Human Rights Watch, https://www.hrw.org/news/2021/05/14/south-africas-deadly-air-case-highlights-health-risks-coal, accessed 20 July 2021.

Nemes, N. 2009. 'Comparative analysis of organic and non-organic farming systems: A critical assessment of farm profitability'. Food and Agriculture Organization of the United Nations, Rome.

Nkomoki, W., Bavorová, M. and Banout, J. 2018. 'Adoption of sustainable agricultural practices and food security threats: Effects of land tenure in Zambia'. *Land Use Policy*, 78, 532–538.

Okharedia, A.A. 2019. 'A conceptual framework in promoting knowledge management in electricity industry in South Africa: The case of ESKOM'.

Journal of Business and Retail Management Research. 13, 269–281. https://doi.org/10.24052/jbrmr/v13is03/art-24.

Perkins, D.C. 2020. 'Mine closure and rehabilitation in South Africa activating coalitions of the willing for a just future'. WWF SA Briefing Paper.

Pörtner, H.O., Scholes, R.J., Agard, J., Archer, E., Arneth, A. et al. 2021. 'IPBES-IPCC co-sponsored workshop report on biodiversity and climate change', Intergovernmental Science-Policy Platform on Biodiversity and Ecosystem Services (IPBES) and Intergovernmental Panel on Climate Change (IPCC), https://ipbes.net/sites/default/files/2021-06/20210609_workshop_report_embargo_3pm_CEST_10_june_0.pdf, accessed 15 August 2021.

Qvist, S., Gładysz, P., Bartela, Ł. and Sowizdzał, A. 2020. 'Retrofit decarbonization of coal power plants: A case study for Poland'. *Energies*, 14, 120. https://doi.org/10.3390/en14010120.

Ranganathan, J., Waite, R., Searchinger, T. and Zionts, J. 2020. 'Regenerative Agriculture: Good for Soil Health, but Limited Potential to Mitigate Climate Change'. World Resources Institute, https://www.wri.org/insights/regenerative-agriculture-good-soil-health-limited-potential-mitigate-climate-change, accessed 21 May 2021.

Regeneration International. 2021. 'What is regenerative agriculture?'. *Regenerative Agriculture Initiative and the Carbon Underground*, https://regenerationinternational.org/wp-content/uploads/2017/02/Regen-Ag-Definition-2.23.17-1.pdf, accessed 29 July 2021.

RegenAg SA. 2021. 'RegenAg SA map'. https://www.regenagsa.org.za/regenag-sa-map/, accessed 29 July 2021.

Republic of South Africa (RSA). 2021. 'South Africa's First Nationally Determined Contribution under the Paris Agreement'. https://www.environment.gov.za/sites/default/files/reports/draftnationalydeterminedcontributions_2021updated.pdf, accessed 26 May 2021.

Ramirez, J. and Böhm, S. 2021. 'Transactional colonialism in wind energy investments: Energy injustices against vulnerable people in the Isthmus of Tehuantepec'. *Energy Research & Social Science*, 78, 102135. https://doi.org/10.1016/j.erss.2021.102135.

Schreefel, L., Schulte, O., De Boer, M., Pas Schrijver, A. and Van Zanten, H. 2020. 'Regenerative agriculture – the soil is the base'. *Global Food Security*, 26, https://doi.org/10.1016/j.gfs.2020.100404, accessed 15 September 2021.

Simpson, G.B., Badenhorst, J., Jewitt, G.P.W., Berchner, M. and Davies E. 2019. 'Competition for land: The water-energy-food nexus and coal mining in Mpumalanga province, South Africa'. *Frontiers in Environmental Science*, 7, 86. doi: 10.3389/fenvs.2019.00086.

Soto, R., Martínez-Mena, M., Padilla, M. and De Vente, J. 2020. 'Restoring soil quality of woody agroecosystems in Mediterranean drylands through regenerative agriculture'. *Agriculture, Ecosystems & Environment*, 306,

107191, https://doi.org/10.1016/j.agee.2020.107191.

Sihlobo, W. 2021. 'Will the positive trend of South Africa's agricultural machinery sales persist?'. *Harvest SA*, https://www.harvestsa.co.za/2021/04/16/will-the-positive-trend-of-south-africas-agricultural-machinery-sales-persist/, accessed 29 July 2021.

Semelane, S., Nwulu, N., Kambule, N. and Tazvinga, H. 2021a. 'Evaluating available solar photovoltaic business opportunities in coal phase-out regions – An energy transition case of Steve Tshwete local municipality in South Africa'. *Energy Policy*, 155, 112333. https://doi.org/10.1016/j.enpol.2021.112333.

Semelane, S., Nwulu, N., Kambule, N. and Tazvinga, H., 2021b. 'Evaluating economic impacts of utility scale solar photovoltaic localisation in South Africa'. *Energy Sources, Part B Economics. Planning and Policy*, 16, 324–344. https://doi.org/10.1080/15567249.2021.1894513

Shrimali, G. and Jindal, A. 2020. 'Cost-benefit analysis of coal-plant repurposing in developing countries'. Working paper, http://dx.doi.org/10.2139/ssrn.3646443, accessed 28 July 2021.

Statistics South Africa (Stats SA). 2020a. 'Quarterly Labour Force Survey Quarter 1: 2020'. Statistics South Africa.

Statistics South Africa (Stats SA). 2020b. 'Natural Capital 1: Land and Terrestrial Ecosystem Accounts, 1990 to 2014'. Discussion document D0401.1, produced in collaboration with the South African National Biodiversity Institute and the Department of Environment, Forestry and Fisheries. Statistics South Africa, Pretoria.

Statistics South Africa (Stats SA). 2019. 'Four facts about the mining industry 2019'. http://www.statssa.gov.za/?p=14682, accessed 25 September 2021.

Stockholm Environment Institute. 2019. 'The end of coal? Planning a "just transition" in South Africa'. SEI, Stockholm.

Van Druten, E. S. 2017. 'Towards an inclusive model to address unsuccessful mine closures in South Africa'. *Journal of the Southern African Institute of Mining and Metallurgy*, 117(5), 485–490.

Von Loeper, W.M. 2016. 'Analysing challenges facing smallholder farmers and conservation agriculture in South Africa: A system dynamics approach'. *South African Journal of Economic and Management Sciences*, 47, 773.

Walwyn, D.R., Brent, A.C., 2015. 'Renewable energy gathers steam in South Africa'. *Renew. Sustain. Energy Rev.*, 41, 390–401. https://doi.org/10.1016/j.rser.2014.08.049.

Winkler, H., 2005. 'Renewable energy policy in South Africa: Policy options for renewable electricity'. *Energy Policy*, 33, 27–38. https://doi.org/10.1016/S0301-4215(03)00195-2.

World Wildlife Fund South Africa. 2010. 'AGRICULTURE: FACTS & TRENDS South Africa'. WWF SA, http://awsassets.wwf.org.za/downloads/facts_brochure_mockup_04_b.pdf, accessed 11 May 2021.

ELEVEN

Democratising a just transition in South Africa

LEBOGANG MULAISI AND JACKLYN COCK

INTRODUCTION

THIS CHAPTER AIMS TO CONTRIBUTE to 'democratising' the concept of a just transition, by which we mean deep, transformative change that benefits the majority of our people. The chapter describes the international origins of the concept in the Global North and how it was radicalised in the process of translation in South Africa. The chapter demonstrates how, in the last 10 years, the concept of a just transition as a revolutionary idea containing the possibility of radical change to redistribute power and resources to create a more equal society has been appropriated. Powerful social forces have stripped much of this transformative content. The chapter describes how these social forces – particularly coal mining corporations – form a set of constraints on achieving a just transition. At the same time, new social forces are emerging from civil society to address the climate crisis and promoting the concept of climate justice. The chapter suggests that the

COSATU Policy Framework document of 2012 provides a basis on which the labour movement could mobilise different forms of power to address unemployment, poverty and inequality, as well as climate change. It provides the basis for a democratic, eco-socialist alternative future. The chapter emphasises that a process of 'democratisation' is necessary because in the present cacophony of voices addressing a just transition, those most affected, namely coal workers and people living in mining-affected communities, are seldom heard. It concludes that a just transition must be driven from below in an alliance led by labour.

When the concept was introduced into South Africa by COSATU, it was grounded in people's lived experience and aspirations; it was at the heart of a powerful narrative of hope for a better life. This chapter suggests that labour's present commitment to measures such as job protection, environment-friendly investment, comprehensive social security for displaced workers and skills development provides a basis for cooperation between labour and the initiatives around climate justice emerging in civil society. There is no single movement for a just transition in South Africa; no master frame encoded in any blueprint with a coherent centre and tidy margins. However, such an alliance has the potential to drive a mass-based movement for a just transition from our present dependence on coal.

INTERNATIONAL ORIGINS

COSATU radicalised the concept of a just transition that emerged from the international labour movement. This was led by the International Trade Union Confederation (ITUC) and the International Labour Organization (ILO) and involved a long struggle. But at the 2010 United Nations Framework Commission on Climate Change (UNFCCC) conference in Cancun, Mexico, organised labour successfully lobbied to include the concept of a just transition into the UNFCCC negotiations. The Paris Agreement of 2015 accepted the ILO guidelines for a just transition stating (Stevis and Felli, 2015: 34):

> ... the policies guiding the transition from fossil fuels to renewables must promote the creation of more decent jobs,

> anticipate the impact on employment, provide adequate social protection for job losses and displacement, skills development and social dialogue – including the effective exercise of the right to organise and bargain collectively.

However, the ITUC approach has been criticised as still 'trapped within the existing social democratic, sustainable development paradigm committed to a capitalist growth system' (Cottle, 2015: 3).

CONSTRAINTS ON ACHIEVING A JUST TRANSITION

South Africa signed the Paris Agreement, but it is significant that the word 'justice' only appears once and 'amounts to an explicit disavowal of the concept' (Ghosh, 2016: 158). Furthermore, energy discussions tend to have a narrow technical focus and 'rarely incorporate justice dimensions' (Healey and Barrow, 2017: 415). In South Africa, the neglect of justice is evident in how the transition unfolds without planning (Cock, 2019: 866). Eskom has a detailed decommissioning schedule for its existing coal generation. By 2040, only Majuba, Medupi and Kusile power plants will remain, but there is no plan for the workers affected. This has been an issue of contention within trade unions.

In arguing for a broader and inclusive movement for a just transition, we are aware of the obstacles involved. The power of the minerals energy complex (MEC), a system of accumulation that has dominated our history, is a significant obstacle (Baker, 2015; Fine and Rustomjee, 2018; Burton et al., 2018). Other obstacles include the drop in trade union membership; rising unemployment; increasing fragmentation (Bezuidenhout et.al., 2017: 5); differences between labour and environmentalists over the nature of ownership of renewable energy; the power of a state committed to extractives; and material dependence on coal which provides 90 per cent of our electricity and is a significant source of foreign exchange and employment. In addition, powerful social forces driven by strong thermal coal prices appropriate the concept of a just transition in defending coal.

An 'elite capture' means that recently growing numbers of coal mining corporations speak of a just transition, which is reduced to meaning only a shift to a new energy regime; a shift, which is slow, orderly, managed from above, neglects considerations of justice and does not threaten their profitability. They are powerfully organised in the Minerals Council (earlier called the Chamber of Mines), which has promoted the notion of coal mining and burning as the essential road to economic growth and stability. One report was deliberately aimed at countering 'negative public opinion about coal' and emphasises the role of coal in the creation of jobs, procurement spending and the 'adverse' effects of strict environmental laws (Council of Mining statement, 2018: 13). Only in 2019 did the Council call for 'rational and sombre debates on a just transition from coal' (Cloete, 2019). According to the CEO Roger Baxter, 'this concept around a just transition has to be very much part of a carefully thought-out transition from the older power stations to more efficient, newer generation of power stations like we have at Medupi and Kusile' (Baxter, 2020). This reduces the just transition to a purely technicist issue.

Generally, coal mining corporations fail to recognise the extent and urgency of the climate crisis. These companies respond to falling demand and to increasing pressure on banks and investment companies to stop financing coal. Big capital such as Glencoe, Anglo American and Exxaro is exiting coal. In some cases, local, mostly BEE capital, such as Mike Teke's Sereti, which took over South32's coal assets in June 2021, is moving in to replace them and defend coal. July Ndlovu, chair of the World Coal Association and CEO of Thungela Resources (the coal mining company spun off from Anglo American), has defended coal as an investment opportunity, promises 'cleaner coal' and urges a more holistic and nuanced debate on the transition that 'addresses energy poverty and ensures developing economies that depend on coal do not suffer irreparable damage from switching off fossil fuels' (cited by Joffe, 2021: 3).

Coal mining corporations are not the only forces defending coal. For many communities living near coal mines or coal-fired power stations in Mpumalanga, where 16 of Eskom's coal plants are situated, material dependence on coal creates an ambivalence (Cock, 2019: 15). These are spaces of displacement and exclusion, often deprived of access to essential services such as housing, electricity, water and, particularly, jobs (Mashaymombe, 2018: 12). Many people living near the Mabola Protected Area, for example, are supportive of Uthega Energy's plan to build a coal mine because they are desperate for employment. In the context of high structural unemployment and the nonexistence of a just transition plan that results in actual job creation, workers and community members cannot comprehend a future without coal. Furthermore, the National Union of Mineworkers has been active in defending coal – supporting the expansion of coal mining, protesting job losses from mine closures, and promoting controversial 'cleaner coal' technologies such as Carbon Capture and Storage.

Nevertheless, a process of transition is underway. The process is highly contested because 'a just transition is intensely political, not simply a technical matter' (Healy and Barry, 2017: 452). It has become embedded in 'contentious politics' involving competing claims and interests. This chapter follows the power resources approach, which emphasises worker agency in this contested process.

A QUESTION OF POWER

In the past few years, the labour movement has retreated into a defensive, reactive position, focused on protecting existing jobs in the energy sector. This protective stance is wholly understandable in the light of South Africa's unemployment rate of 42 per cent (Stats SA, 2021: 1) (one of the highest in the world), massive job losses in the mining industry (particularly gold and platinum) and high levels of poverty. The labour movement can potentially draw on several sources of power (Schmalz et al., 2018: 113). Examples are structural power which reflects its place in the economy and could involve disruptive power such as strikes and protests. Such strikes damage supply chains, institutional power involving the judicial system and structures such as Nedlac (Webster, 2020: 221).

A crucial question now is whether labour can draw from these powerful resources. Forging closer connections with other social forces in civil society, particularly environmental and climate justice organisations and initiatives, could reclaim the concept and drive a just transition. In doing so, labour could better manage the immediate tensions between promoting workers' long-term interests through supporting a just energy transition to reduce carbon emissions and protecting their short-term interests in the form of support for retrenched workers and coal-dependent communities.

INSIGHTS FROM LABOUR ON A JUST TRANSITION

Long before the Paris Agreement, COSATU warned about climate change and advocated for the just transition to ensure that workers and communities would not be left behind in the move to a low carbon economy. For example, the 2009 Congress resolution states that: 'climate change is one of the greatest threats to our planet and our people' (COSATU, 2011: 52). 'The congress further noted that unless the working class and its organisations take climate change seriously, all the talks about "green jobs" will amount to nothing except being another site of capitalist accumulation' (COSATU, 2011: 52). These warnings about climate change were a precursor to cooperation between labour and civil society. This collaboration was evident in the labour/civil society conference held in 2010. Over 300 delegates from civil society organisations collectively represented millions of South Africans committed to rebuilding a strong mass democratic movement to address critical problems that confront workers and communities. They also agreed to the concept of a social justice charter.

This event drew from South Africa's tradition of 'social movement unionism', meaning a form of unionism that goes beyond workplace issues and engages actively in political and community struggles. This blurred the distinction between unions as formal organisations and social movements as 'loosely structured networks of action' (Schmalz et al., 2018: 113). In South Africa and other countries in the Global South, this involved struggles over wages and working conditions and over living conditions and services in working-class communities (Seidman, 1994: 33–50; Webster, 1987: 174–196).

This chapter's argument for a labour-environment alliance to drive a just transition builds on the climate change reference group established by the research arm of COSATU in 2011. The reference group was an example of where environmentalists from civil society successfully collaborated with labour to engage in research, policy formulation and worker education on a just transition. Twenty-two affiliated unions of COSATU were represented as well as activists from environmental justice groupings in the project. The research culminated in the agreement on the 15 COSATU Climate Change policy principles. Endorsed by the COSATU Central Committee, this document linked sustainability and justice and was widely distributed.

THE COSATU CLIMATE CHANGE POLICY FRAMEWORK

This 'red-green' collaboration recognised that the expansionist logic of the capitalist system is at the centre of the ecological crisis. The first principle of the climate change policy framework stated that 'Capitalist accumulation is the underlying cause of excessive greenhouse gas emissions' (COSATU, 2011: 53). The argument that capitalism is the root cause of environmental degradation was also reflected in a joint organised labour (COSATU, National Council of Trade Unions – NACTU and the Federation of Unions of South Africa (FEDUSA)) submission in 2012 in response to the government's Green Paper on Climate Change.

The submission stated that (NACTU, 2010: 2):

> We are confident that any efforts to address the problems of climate change that does not fundamentally challenge the system of global capitalism is bound to fail, and to generate new, larger and more dangerous threats to human beings and our planet. Climate change is caused by the global private profit system of capitalism. Tackling greenhouse gas emissions is not just a technical problem. It requires a fundamental economic and social transformation to substantially change current production and consumption patterns.

The second principle in the COSATU policy document asserts that 'a new low-carbon development path is needed which addresses the need for decent jobs and the elimination of unemployment' (COSATU, 2011: 53). This means that economic activities must be altered in such a way that reduces carbon emissions. COSATU's growth path, published by the federation in 2011, presents solid arguments for redistributive growth that will result in the creation of decent jobs and drastically reduce inequality through the elimination of the existing wage gap.

Principle four states that 'All South Africans have the right to energy' (COSATU, 2011: 55). In South Africa, thousands of households lack access to energy, either due to the lack of infrastructure or unaffordable pre-paid meters. Justice demands affordable energy for all; linking justice and sustainability requires that energy is affordable, clean and safe, which means that renewable energy is socially owned and democratically controlled. South Africa's Renewable Energy Independent Power Producer Programme (REIPPP) relies heavily on the profit-driven private sector as the primary player and investor in renewable energy generation. There is debate as to whether this approach can reach emission reduction standards and protect workers (Sweeney and Treat, 2018). Trade unions, particularly South African Federation of Trade Unions (SAFTU), the National Union of Mineworkers (NUM) and National Union of Metalworkers of South Africa (NUMSA), have rejected this privatisation programme and call for publicly owned and democratically controlled renewable energy generation.

The labour movement's opposition to the REIPPP is also related to the perceived high technological costs associated with building renewable energy power plants. Most energy sources are expensive in the initial construction phase and become affordable as the technical costs stabilise. To address the issues of affordability and access, renewable energy must be distributed and controlled by the government.

COSATU's proposal on the turnaround of Eskom details labour's calls for the parastatal to begin renewable energy generation. Initially, the main focus was on a just transition for Eskom and the power sector. COSATU's plan has three key elements. First, COSATU proposes using state and worker pension funds to purchase part of Eskom's debt while giving workers equity in Eskom and board representation. This will maintain jobs in Eskom and its supply chain, strengthen efforts to clean up corruption and maladministration in Eskom and keep national ownership of this strategic sector. Second, COSATU proposes a mandate for Eskom to generate renewable energy and for private, municipal and community entities to be able to build renewable projects. This will accelerate the process of bringing down power sector emissions along with creating local jobs. Third, COSATU proposes negotiating a just transition and regional economic development plans for coal-dependent regions based on renewable energy and manufacturing jobs.

Principle eight of the COSATU policy document addresses both unemployment crises and ecological crises. 'There are few accurate statistics on the number of jobs that could be under threat in the transition to a low-carbon economy. Still, the number of new jobs created in a just transition could exceed any possible job losses' (Ashley and Rudin, 2016: 414). 'There are opportunities for local manufacturers. Production processes that are more environmentally friendly tend to be more labour intensive, using people rather than machines or chemicals to do the work' (COSATU, 2011: 56).

However, planning for jobs has lagged in the planning for a transition so far. Workers in the coal-fired power stations have not been prepared for alternative jobs after an announcement about the decommissioning of five of the older coal plants. The just transition to a low carbon economy cannot occur without workers and people living in mining communities. They are currently experiencing multiple impacts from climate change and will be most affected by a transition from coal. Such a change requires extensive planning (Strambo et al., 2019). The establishment of the Presidential Climate Change Coordinating Commission (PCCCC) is in the early stages of planning for a just transition, and working-class interests should be reflected.

The COSATU policy on climate change forms the basis on which we argue for a 'red-green alliance'. Taken together, the 15 principles form a solid basis on which many elements in civil society can agree.

INSIGHTS FROM CIVIL SOCIETY ON A JUST TRANSITION

There is a growing energy and commitment expressed in several different climate justice organisations and initiatives. These tend to be urban-based, with progressive intellectuals playing a prominent role and having different relations with coal workers and mining-affected communities, some tenuous and others deeply rooted. With some exceptions, they are focused on the principles informing a just transition rather than on material conditions and immediate social needs. However, they all mobilise considerable social power through their campaigns, demonstrations and use of social media.

Several organisations codify principles of a just transition in terms of 'charters'; charters have a rich history in South Africa. However, the emphasis on principles means they do not always provide strategic direction, and are not always the product of deep and extensive participatory processes. They are also often framed in abstract and inaccessible language and are therefore inaccessible to a wider public. However, they all offer ideas that could be building blocks for a just transition, such as climate justice, food sovereignty, a universal basic income grant and energy democracy.

An example of a civil society initiative that links labour and the environment is the Climate Jobs Campaign, driven by the Alternative Information and Development Centre. This was formed in 2011 by 40 different organisations including labour, which linked the climate crisis with the unemployment crisis. It engaged in extensive research and has identified over one million new, alternative 'climate jobs', specifically 'those that help reduce greenhouse gas emissions and build the resilience of communities to withstand the impact of climate change' (Ashley, 2016: 27). Examples include developing renewable energy plants, public transport and small-scale organic agriculture. COSATU's Central Committee endorsed the Million Climate Jobs Campaign in June 2011.

This is part of a growing swell of support for a Universal Basic Income transfer to all citizens. Both could be elements of a just transition. The idea of a basic income grant has a recent resurgence but a long history in South Africa. It was first raised in the 1997 White Paper on Social Welfare and then again in a discussion between COSATU and the government ahead of the Presidential Jobs Summit in 1998. Others have taken it up since then.

The Alternative Information and Development Centre (AIDC)'s strategic programme is focused on '[b]uilding alliances for a just transition to a wage-led, low carbon development path'. It is currently working with several trade unions on the restructuring of Eskom. AIDC, NUMSA and NUM produced the report 'Eskom transformation: Achieving a just energy transition' (AIDC, 2020). This promotes a model of Eskom remaining a public entity with conditions that it transitions to renewable energy and no workers are retrenched.

Several more civil society organisations are advancing a transformative just agenda, including the Coalition for Climate Justice. Their members include those with strong connections with the South African Federation of Trade Unions (SAFTU). However, it is not a community-based alliance. It may not always appeal to communities in mining-affected areas whose notion of justice prioritises immediate, concrete issues such as compensation to their homesteads from blasting, mining blocking access to a water source and local people's employment in the mines. Questions of gender are not neglected. WoMin has an explicit gendered agenda for a just transition and is mobilising for an African Feminist Just Transition Charter with grassroots women throughout Africa. A detailed charter for 'Climate justice and a deep just transition' was launched in Johannesburg in August 2020 and presented to parliament on 16 October, supported by a signature campaign that topped 100 at the launch event and has grown substantially to some 6 000. The intention is to have the charter adopted by parliament in terms of section 234 of the Constitution. The content of the charter is described as emerging from 'a participatory grassroots process'. This involved six roundtable discussions with various constituencies, including drought-affected communities, labour, youth and environmental and social justice organisations. The document stresses 'people's power' and unity, stating 'solidarity is central to the deep just transition and serves to unite all struggling for emancipation from oppression and for a post-carbon world' (Satgar, 2020).

The charter is a powerful document consisting of eight very broad principles: climate justice, social justice, eco-centric living, participatory democracy, socialised ownership, international solidarity, decoloniality and intergenerational justice. The document presents a comprehensive vision of an eco-socialist society. However, 'socialism' is not mentioned, and the language (especially the notion of 'decoloniality') is somewhat inaccessible to grassroots communities. Overall, the Climate Justice Charter Movement is mobilising extensive social power through the link to food sovereignty and widespread use of social media platforms.

The older environmental justice organisations have strong links with labour, though not all overtures have been reciprocated. Groundwork organised a 'coal exchange' in 2019, which came up with 12 points intended as 'starting points for a community-driven open agenda for a just transition. It is an open agenda because it is an invitation to explore proposals already identified by coal affected communities' (Hallowes and Munnik, 2019: 98). The agreed proposals included (Hallowes and Munnik, 2019: 120):

> Protecting incomes of retrenched workers; building a new energy system; rehabilitating individual mines and the mining region as a whole. This will restore and detoxify damaged land and ecosystems; making people's food gardens a first step towards creating a healthy food system under democratic control based on ecological agriculture and ensuring enough for all.

This was a very significant event. After the coal exchange, some laid-off mine workers joined environmental activists, local trade union officials from NUM, NUMSA and the Transport and Allied Workers Union (SATAWU) and Naledi to exchange views on a just transition. Groundwork hosted it to open on-the-ground dialogue for a just transition between workers, their organisations and community groups. There were 'Sharp differences on the future of coal and a NUM official stated, 'You green activists take delight in ending coal, but coal means jobs and life for us' (Hallowes and Munnik, 2019: 183).

Groundwork is part of a very active alliance called Life After Coal consisting of Groundwork, the Centre for Environmental Rights (CER) and Earthlife. Established 30 years ago, Earthlife is at the core of the environmental justice movement, reaching down into grassroots communities and up into policy arenas. The director Makoma Lekalakala (formerly a trade union organiser) maintains that 'a just transition in South Africa is overdue and is driven by poverty and inequality. What is needed is concrete actions which cannot be reduced to debate'. Among the concrete actions are 'small-scale, socially owned local production of renewable energy to promote energy democracy, a new food system to address food insecurity, a reliable transport system – all measures which would improve our lives'. Water and land also warrant attention. In a recent presentation, she gave content to the notion of a just transition and argued that 'we need a vision of all human beings living in a harmonious way' (Lekalakala, 2020a). On another occasion, she stressed that 'we need to learn from our own culture regarding our relationship with nature … ubuntu, caring for each other and nature is an example. Another is the traditional African notion which stresses the importance of learning from the past. Both philosophies can give us a vision for the future that includes ecological balance' (Lekalakala, 2020b). All these initiatives demonstrate strong social or symbolic power in their public protest events.

The Centre for Environmental Rights is the best example in South Africa of judicial activism. It is dedicated to advancing environmental justice through educating citizens on their constitutional rights and court action to hold corporate and state authorities accountable. This involves what Nielsen calls 'rightful resistance', which challenges the abuse of power by the powerful (Nielsen, 2010: 76). It illustrates high levels of institutional power, compared to the erosion of associational power as increasing numbers of workers are engaged in precarious jobs.

AREAS OF CONSENSUS AND CONVERGENCE

The links with labour need to be strengthened in all these formations. The main factors potentially holding a networked movement together are a blurring of the distinction between social and environmental justice. There has been a significant shift from the apartheid period when environmentalism operated mainly as a conservation strategy largely concerned with protecting threatened plants, animals and wilderness areas and neglected social issues. Furthermore, for many black South Africans, environmentalism was linked to dispossession. Thousands were forcibly removed to create national parks and, in the process, lost their land and livelihoods (Cock and Fig, 2000; Walker, 2008). The notion of environmental justice represents a dramatic shift away from this and puts the needs of the poor and the excluded at the centre of its concerns. The exposure to polluted air and water, degraded land, inadequate sanitation and housing, for example, are all social as well as environmental justice issues.

Secondly, carbon emissions continue to rise, and the climate crisis is deepening. There are more extreme weather events in the form of floods and droughts. The water crisis is impacting half of South Africa, and air pollution is decimating the health of thousands of coal workers in Mpumalanga and Limpopo. The planet is running out of time to reduce climate change before the damage is irrevocable. Thirdly, the debate about the form and pace of substantial change in the shape of a just transition is intensifying. There is a growing consensus globally and in South Africa that we have to reduce carbon emissions, and our historical dependence on coal. As Neva Makgetla writes, 'coal dependence is fuelling SA's interlinked electricity and climate crises… Yet the coal value chain produces just 5 per cent of the GDP and 1.5 per cent of formal jobs' (Makgetla, 2021: 8).

There is also consensus that there is a shift away from coal. As Mitchell (2013: 231) writes, 'We are entering the declining decades of the fossil fuel era, a brief episode of human time.' 'Coal-based technologies are less and less competitive, and demand for coal is shrinking at home and abroad. SA coal exports fell 8 per cent from 2012 to 2019, then another 14 per cent in the pandemic' (Makgetla, 2021: 8). In addition, there is a growing consensus that the savage poverty and inequality in our society, highlighted during the COVID-19 pandemic, must be addressed.

While the initiatives in civil society are fragmented and the concept of a just transition contested, there are grounds for a convergence of interests between labour and environmental justice activists. However, this convergence is not straightforward. Elements in the environmental movement have reduced the concept of a just transition to mean a shift to a new energy regime. For some, this could even take the form of privatised renewable energy, which is not labour intensive and is likely to mean higher energy prices that are not in the working class's interests. The labour movement is not against renewables but is increasingly defensive and adamant that the state's privatised renewable energy policy is a threat because it will involve job losses and higher energy prices. After all, private interests prioritise profit maximisation above the need to meet social needs. Labour – particularly NUMSA – has called for publicly owned and democratically controlled renewable energy largely made up of state-owned entities and community cooperatives. The environmental movement is increasingly adamant about the immediate closure of coal mines and coal-fired power stations. However, a shift to renewable energy (in whatever form) is essential to a just transition. The environmental movement does not acknowledge that a deep just transition requires changes in the sources of energy and who owns and controls various components of the energy system (Overy, 2018: 8). Recently tensions and animosities have surfaced on this issue, expressing the 'rancour and open hostility between labour and environmental activists at worst' in many countries (Uzzel and Ratzel, 2012: 1).

Labour has held the strong view that Eskom can generate renewable energy and connect it to the grid. COSATU's proposals towards Eskom's turnaround articulates this view. Labour's opposition to the REIPPP has been widely reported as a response to imported technologies, owned and controlled by private white foreign groups and individuals mainly from the North, and backed by national and politically connected elites.

A second major area of contestation is around the use of gas after the decommissioning of the coal-fired power stations. The economic recovery plan (2020) commits to implement the Integrated Resource Plan, which will ensure the diversification of energy sources. The government will continue to explore the conversion of old power stations to be decommissioned – with proximity to Mozambique and its natural gas reserves – for gas conversion. Labour has welcomed the gas conversion of coal power stations as an interim job-saving measure post the decommissioning of power stations.

Negative elements must be replaced by stronger connections between labour and environmental initiatives. This could be linked to extending the network to include other organisational groupings, for example, health workers concerned with the impact of coal on air quality. The debate on the future of work is also relevant to preparing for a world without coal. There is also the possibility of further connecting with global initiatives. The concern with deepening climate change can connect particular local and national struggles, generalise them and link them into a global project of transformation.

GLOBAL SOCIAL MOVEMENT AND THE JUST TRANSITION

Globally, climate change protests have been on the rise and instrumental in heightening calls for climate justice and legislative reform to address environmental degradation and pollution. The case of Germany illustrates the efficacy of mass mobilisation. The extinction rebellion that resulted in the closure of sections of London in 2019 and the 'Fridays for Futures' led by Swedish teen Greta Thunberg are examples of massive social power that have demanded decisive policies to reach net zero emissions by 2025. Even though helpful in highlighting pertinent issues of climate justice, the global social movement has previously been criticised as ineffective in realising actual policy change. This fits with the view of Srnicek and Williams (2015: 12) of social movement politics as politics transmitted into part-time activities and unable to effect the necessary policy change. Earlier waves of climate movements in the UK became ineffective in bringing about change because of fundamental differences around strategy, tactics and ideology among grassroots climate campaigners. The fundamental disagreement was about the conceptualisation of what should be done to resolve the crises.

Social movements in the global North have been frustrated by the slow progress in climate change negotiations and the lack of political will. 'Civil society coalitions recognise that joining forces with other social movements and labour is the only way to exert the necessary pressure on the policymakers and legislators' (Pettit, 2004: 102). To some extent, the Global North faces the same challenges of mobilisation that the Global South faces. These include civil society being completely focused on the environment and scientific solutions to greenhouse gas emissions, to the exclusion of interrelated issues of poverty trade and globalisation. These messages are only recently appearing in the northern development discourse. The big difference between the Global North and South is that the levels of poverty mean that survival is an immediate rather than a long term issue. Climate change is a multi-dimensional threat to society as well as environmental justice.

CONCLUSION: THE BASIS FOR THE MASS COALITION MOVEMENT ON THE JUST TRANSITION

The challenge is to build a mass-based social movement for a just transition led by a labour–environment alliance drawing on coalition power. The immediate task is a massive public education programme to explain the climate crisis and why the gradual closing of the coal mines and coal-fired power stations is necessary, and also to protect workers' immediate interests. These interests include income support, reskilling and job replacement. The longer-term task is organising for a deep transformation of the current economic system of production and consumption.

Too many civil society charters and manifestos are abstract and not grounded in grassroots participation. Their statements are largely principled and aspirational rather than agendas that provide strategic direction. But they do provide what could be building blocks for a transformative just transition driven from below: community-owned and controlled renewable energy plants; small-scale agroecology; communal kitchens and food gardens; a basic income grant; alternative forms of construction and transport, and other social forms that are infused with a sense of solidarity.

Labour's conceptual framing of the just transition can provide a basis for a mass coalition for the broader social movement. COSATU (2011: 3) states:

> The issues unions have been fighting for, and building (full employment, decent jobs and livelihoods, gender equality, clean water for all, food security, affordable access to health care, better education, decent housing in well-planned settlements with good affordable transport, people uniting to help each other, environmental sustainability, an economy which puts people before profits) are the same issues that will strengthen us to deal with climate change and usher in a just transition.

Labour's eight principles of a just transition are the basic blocks for the mass coalition campaign. These include (COSATU, 2011: 56):

> (1) Investment in environmentally friendly activities that create decent jobs, which offer a living wage, and which meet standards of health and safety, promote gender equity, and are secure; (2) Putting in place comprehensive social protection (pensions, unemployment insurance, etc.) to protect the most vulnerable; (3) Researching the impacts of climate change on employment and livelihoods to inform social policies better; (4) Skills development and retraining of workers to ensure that they can be part of the new low-carbon development model; (5) Ensure that the concept of a just transition is built into the final text of the international legally binding agreement that we are pushing for as international labour; (6) The International Labour Organisation (ILO) should be given the mandate to set recommendations to the UNFCCC on operationalising the just transition agenda. The ILO should also be mandated to monitor and report on progress in achieving a just transition; (7) Develop the Just Transition further to incorporate our commitment to a fundamentally transformed society fully. We need to embed it in all our local campaigning and negotiating on climate change; (8) We need to urgently educate our members on the shop floor so that they can identify issues for negotiation and join in the struggle for a very different future.

However, if capitalism continues, will there be a future for humanity?

The goal of a just transition is sometimes described as a form of a 'green capitalism' dependent on expanding markets and new technology, or as a 'green economy', 'which works to either obscure alternatives or make them seem unviable and irrational' (Brand and Wissen, 2015: 508). They suggest that 'the various strategies pursued under the green economy umbrella are in the process of establishing what may develop into a new capitalist formation, potentially taking the place of the crisis-ridden post-Fordist neoliberal formulation' they call 'green capitalism' (Brand and Wissen, 2015: 509). But Angus (2009: 232) warns that 'if capitalism (of whatever type) remains the dominant social order, the best we can expect is unbearable climate conditions, an intensification of social crises and the spread of the most barbaric forms of class rule'. Swilling (2019: 131) warns: 'there is a distinct danger that one direction is towards a decarbonised, ecologically unsustainable future which leaves existing inequalities intact.' The central principle of the COSATU 2012 policy on climate change is that capitalism is the cause of the climate crisis. It follows logically that capitalism must be dismantled. The notion of a just transition could unite labour and environmental activists in a struggle for survival in the form of eco-socialism.

Eco-socialism is a viable alternative if it demonstrates concrete examples of cooperative work and communal ownership of productive resources. For many people, socialism is discredited because its claims have been marred by a history of authoritarianism, productivism, human rights abuses and environmental destruction. But others argue for a new democratic, ecological and ethical socialism. The aim of the struggle for socialism is, in the first instance, to replace a society based on profit with one based on satisfying the needs of people (Kovel, 2007; Lowry, 2020). This would involve democratic planning instead of relying on markets; different forms of ownership and democratic control of productive resources; access to decent work; quality and affordable education, health care, public transport, housing and energy. At the core of a democratic eco-socialism is the link between the principles of sustainability and justice. To illustrate, in terms of ecological sustainability, the critical question is not limited to the protection of natural resources but rather that those resources are used to benefit all.

New social forms involving reciprocity, solidarity and cooperation emerge around these ideas, and they embody fragments of a vision of an alternative post-capitalist future. This vision also implies a new narrative of relations with nature, grounded in the acknowledgement that humans exist as part of an ecological community. It involves new social relations with the environment, which bolster trust, cooperation and reciprocity. An alliance between labour and the progressive elements in civil society could generate solidarity to achieve this future.

REFERENCES

United Nations (UN). December 2015. 'Paris agreement'. In Report of the Conference of the Parties to the United Nations Framework Convention on Climate Change.

Alternative Information and Development Centre (AIDC). 2020. 'Eskom Transformed: Achieving a just energy transition for South Africa'. https://www.tips.org.za/just-transition/item/download/2091_1503eaa0e1f2e5bfc45441c0d692a584, accessed 12 May 2021.

Angus, I. 2009. 'The politics of ecosocialism'. *Monthly Review*, 43.

Ashley, B. 2016 *One Million Climate Jobs*. Alternative Information and Advice Centre, accessed 12 May 2021.

Ashley, B. and Rudin, J. 2016. 'One Million Climate Jobs Campaign', in Swilling, M., Musango, J.K. and Wakeford, J. (eds), *Greening the South African Economy: Scoping the issues, challenges and opportunities*. Cape Town: UCT Press.

Baker, L. 2015. 'Renewable energy in South Africa's minerals-energy complex: A low carbon transition?'. *Review of African Political Economy*, 42(144), 245–261.

Baxter, R. 2020. 'More efficient power generation'. *Engineering News*, https://www.engineeringnews.co.za/article/minerals-council-south-africa-backs-just-transition-to-cleaner-energy-2020-02-04, accessed 4 May 2021.

Bezuidenhout, A., Tshoaedi, M. and Bischoff, C. (eds), 2017. *Labour Beyond COSATU: Mapping the rupture in South Africa's labour landscape*. Johannesburg: Wits University Press.

Brand, U. and Wissen, M. 2015. 'Strategies of a green economy, contours of a green capitalism', in Van der Pijl, K. (ed.), *Handbook of the International Political Economy of Production*. Cheltenham: Edward Elgar Publishing, 508–523.

Burton, J., Caetano, T. and McCall, B., 2018. 'Coal transitions in South Africa: Understanding the implications of a 2C-compatible coal phase-out plan for South Africa'. Energy Research Centre, University of Cape Town.

Cock, J., 2019. 'Resistance to coal inequalities and the possibilities of a just transition in South Africa'. *Development Southern Africa*, 36(4), 860–873.

Cock, J. and Fig, D. 2000. 'From colonial to community-based conservation: Environmental justice and the national parks of South Africa'. *Society in Transition*, 31(1), 22–35.

Congress of South African Trade Unions (COSATU). 2011. 'A Just Transition to a low-carbon and resilient economy'. COSATU policy framework on climate change, adopted by COSATU Central Executive Committee meeting, Johannesburg.

Congress of South African Trade Unions (COSATU). 2010. 'Declaration of the civil society'. Conference, Boksburg, 27–28 October, https://www.polity.org.za/article/cosatu-declaration-by-the-congress-of-south-african-trade-unions-on-the-civil-society-conference-28102010-2010-10-28, accessed 1 August 2021.

Cottle, E. 2015. 'The myth of a green economy and green jobs: What strategy for labour?'. Council of Mining Press statement, Council of Mining, Johannesburg.

Cloete, K. 2019. 'Minerals Council calls for rational debates on a just transition'. *Engineering News*, https://www.engineeringnews.co.za/article/minerals-council-calls-for-rational-debates-on-a-just-transition-2019-10-09, accessed 24 May 2021.

Department of Environmental Affairs (DEA). 2010. 'National Climate Change Response Green Paper'. Department of Environmental Affairs, Pretoria.

Fine, B. and Rustomjee, Z. 2018. *The Political Economy of South Africa: From minerals–energy complex to industrialisation*. New York: Routledge.

Ghosh, A. 2016. The Great Derangement. Climate change and the unthinkable. Chicago: University of Chicago Press.

Hallowes, D. and Munnik, V. 2019. *Down to Zero: The politics of just transition*. Pietermaritzburg: Groundwork.

Healy, N. and Barry, J. 2017. 'Politicizing energy justice and energy system transitions: Fossil fuel divestment and a "just transition"'. *Energy Policy*, 108, 451–459.

Galgóczi, B. 2018. 'Just transition towards environmentally sustainable economies and societies for all – ILO ACTRAV Policy Brief'. https://www.ilo.org/wcmsp5/groups/public/---ed_dialogue/---actrav/documents/publication/wcms_647648.pdf, accessed 25 May 2021.

Joffe, H. 9 May 2021. 'Coal mogul offers clean fossil options'. *Sunday Times*, https://www.timeslive.co.za/sunday-times/business/2021-05-09-coal-mogul-offers-clean-fossil-options/, accessed 27 September 2021.

Kovel, J. 2007. *The Enemy of Nature: The end of capitalism or the end of the world?*. London: Zed Books.

Lowry, M. 2020. 'The ecosocialist alternative', in Legun, K., Keller,

J., Bell, M. and Carolan, M. (eds), *The Cambridge Handbook of Environmental Sociology*. Cambridge University Press. https://doi.org/10.1017/9781108554510, accessed 8 July 2021.

Lekalakala, M. 2020b. 'Presentation at TIPS panel on Just Transition Stakeholder Perspectives', Johannesburg.

Lekalakala, M. 2020b. 'University of Johannesburg Roundtable on Action against Climate Change', Johannesburg.

Makgetla, N. 18 May 2021. 'SA will be compelled to kick its expensive coal habit'. *Business Day*, https://www.businesslive.co.za/bd/opinion/columnists/2021-05-17-neva-makgetla-sa-will-be-forced-to-kick-its-coal-habit/, accessed 30 September 2021.

Mashayamombe, J., 2018. 'Sanitised spaces: The spatial orders of post-apartheid mines in South Africa'. Doctoral thesis, Faculty of Humanities, University of Pretoria, South Africa.

National Council of Trade Unions (NACTU). 2010. 'Labour's Initial Response to the National Climate Change Green Paper', http://www.ilr.cornell.edu/globallaborinstitute/research/upload/Labours-Initial-Response-to-theClimate-Change-Green-Paper2-2.pdf, accessed 27 June 2021.

Nielsen, A.G. 2010. *Dispossession and Resistance in India: The river and the rage*. London: Routledge.

Mitchell, T. and Jaquet, C. 2013. 'Carbon Democracy: Political Power in the Age of Oil'. La Decouverte, France.

Overy, N. 2018. 'The role of ownership in a just energy transition'. *Project 90 by 2030*, https://90by2030.org.za/wp-content/uploads/2018/04/Just-Energy-Transition-The-Role-of-Ownership-in-a-Just-Energy-Transition.compressed.pdf, accessed 5 September 2021.

Pettit, J. 2004. 'Climate justice: A new social movement for atmospheric rights'. *IDS Bulletin Climate Change and Development*, 35, 102–106.

Republic of South Africa (RSA). 2020. *The South African Economic Reconstruction and Recovery Plan*. Pretoria: Government Publications.

Satgar, V. 2020. *Worsening Climate Crises and the Challenge of Red-Green Alliances for Labour: Introducing the Climate Justice Charter Alternative in South Africa* (No. 31). University of Kassel, Fachbereich Gesellschaftswissenschaften (Social Sciences), International Center for Development and Decent Work (ICDD).

Schmalz, S., Ludwig, C. and Webster, E. 2018. 'Power resources and global capitalism'. *Global Labour Journal*, 10, 84–90, https://doi.org/10.15173/glj.v10i1.3824.

Seidman, G.W. 1994. *Manufacturing Militance*. New York: University of California Press.

Srnicek, N. and Williams, A. 2015. *Inventing the Future: Postcapitalism and a world without work*. New York: Verso.

Statistics South Africa (Stats SA). 2021. 'Quarterly Labour Force Survey.

Statistical Release PO211'. http://www.statssa.gov.za/publications/P0211/P02111stQuarter2021.pdf, accessed 12 September 2021.

Stevis, D. and Felli, R. 2015. 'Global labour unions and just transition to a green economy'. *International Environmental Agreements: Politics, Law and Economics*, 15(1), 29–43.

Strambo, C., Burton, J. and Atteridge, A. 2019. 'The end of coal? Planning a "just transition" in South Africa', Stockholm Environment Institute, Stockholm.

Sweeney, S. and Treat, J. 2018. 'Trade unions and just transition. The search for a transformative politics'. Trade Unions for Energy Democracy.

Swilling, M. 2019 *The Age of Sustainability: Just transitions in a complex world*. London: Routledge.

Uzzel, D. and Ratzel, N. 2012. 'Mending the breach between nature and labour-environmental engagements of trade unions and the North-South divide'. *Interface: A Journal for and about Social Movements*, 4(2), 81–100.

Walker, C. 2008. *Landmarked*. Johannesburg: Jacana Media.

Webster, E., 2020. 'Building counter power in the workplace: South Africa's inequality paradox', in *Inequality Studies from the Global South*. New York: Routledge, 221–239.

Webster, E., 1987. 'The two faces of the black trade union movement in South Africa'. *Review of African Political Economy*, 14(39), 33–41.

TWELVE

Climate liberalism, the green deal and strategic competition

The geopolitics of decarbonisation

SALIEM FAKIR, FATEN AGGAD AND ELLEN DAVIS

INTRODUCTION

IN 1532, MACHIAVELLI WROTE that for a conqueror to maintain control he must do three things: 'the first is ruin them, the next is to reside there in person, and the third is to permit them to live under their own laws, drawing a tribute and establishing with it an oligarchy which will keep it friendly to you' (Machiavelli, 1532 at 44).

The War in Afghanistan arguably exemplifies the approach described by Machiavelli above. It has also raised important questions for global powers about how best to exert their influence in other parts of the world. In Africa, and elsewhere, they have used several tactics to bend sovereign powers towards their sphere of influence. In some instances, as in Libya, they have exerted hard military power to enforce compliance. In other cases, they have employed soft power tactics like economic diplomacy to influence and persuade.

The growing rivalry between the world's superpowers, the United States of America (USA) and China, is seeing the emergence of a new set of alliances that are beginning to reshape geopolitics. Brexit, the election of a new Chancellor in Germany and most recently the side-lining of France by the Aukus Deal (between the USA, the United Kingdom and Australia) are raising questions about the European Union's (EU) role in this new order. As global powers vie to secure dominance, new geopolitical and economic strategies are beginning to emerge, with the climate agenda becoming an increasingly important instrument. This is already beginning to have implications for the African continent.

Through the prism of green technologies, this paper will interrogate the increasing convergence of geopolitical interests and decarbonisation, and outline how climate diplomacy is being used as a tool to serve geopolitical ends. Section one will begin by sketching the genesis and nature of the growing tension between the US and China. Section two will outline China's dominance over green technologies and inputs and the threat this poses to other global powers. Section three will discuss the response to China's dominance in the green technology space, with a focus on the European Green Deal and emerging debates around gas. Section four will consider the implications for African countries and explore potential strategies for them to leverage these geopolitical battle lines to pursue their own interests. Section five will outline South Africa's potential role in shaping Africa's response and section six will conclude.

THE ASIA PIVOT: CHINA'S INCREASING THREAT TO WESTERN SUPREMACY

The Asia pivot, a foreign policy doctrine under the then Secretary of State Hilary Clinton and former President Barack Obama, has become a common feature of US foreign policy, irrespective of the political party in power (Goldberg, 2016; Klein, 2020). This was evident under the Trump administration and is also very much on the agenda of

President Biden. As US Secretary of State Antony Blinken noted, in a speech delivered in March 2021, China represents the most important geopolitical test for the US in the coming century – challenging all frontiers on which the US has to date enjoyed dominance (Blinken, 2021). Blinken's speech and Biden's position at the G7 Summit in June 2021 suggest that the stakes may be growing. Biden used the G7 event and accompanying state visits to push reluctant G7 members to adopt a more militant approach towards China (Behr, 2021).

The conflict with China is not merely economic. It is also a battle over alternative systems with both the US and China attempting to carve out spheres of influence for their competing political and ideological approaches. In many respects, China carries the mantle of Eurasianism – an alternative to Western liberalism – which until recently was propagated most strongly by Russia (Stronski, 2020). Instead of becoming the 'vassal' state that Jimmy Carter's foreign policy czar, Zbigniew Brzezinski, had hoped for, China is amassing its geopolitical clout as a bulwark against Western powers. It is doing this through its Eurasian strategy and in particular its Belt and Road Initiative (BRI), with maritime and digital Silk Road components. Drawing on Halford Mackinder (1904), this suggests that China, by, inter alia, occupying the largest landmass, and controlling a large population and important sea lanes, is well-positioned to become the next world power.

The threat to US hegemony is clearly not lost on the current US government. Blinken's speech in Washington in March 2021 set the tone for the Biden administration's foreign policy towards China with the mantra of 'Confront, Compete and Cooperate' successfully introduced into social discourse by the time of the Alaska talks a few weeks later. While the irony of this position is not lost – this position is precisely what China was criticised for in media commentaries and by Western policy think-tank monographs and missives – it is also not surprising (Kennedy, 2020). As the saying goes: 'He who controls the narrative also controls the people.' As China begins to match and even surpass Western dominance in information technology with massive strides being made in 5G technology, quantum computing, artificial intelligence (AI) and surveillance technologies (Ni, 2021), this commentary is becoming ever more strident.

China and the US are, of course, not the only players. For Europe and others' future positioning, China's economic might needs to be curtailed. The creation of an Indo-Pacific alliance largely shaped by the QUAD[1] and France has been strengthened by recent announcements that Europe is also developing its own Indo-Pacific strategy (Henderson and Rogers, 2020). This grand geopolitical strategy to tame, corner and suppress the rise of China by creating an economic, technological and military bloc is part of a neo containment policy akin to George Kennan's memo, which defined the USA's Cold War doctrine.[2] Climate diplomacy has also become part of the package. For example, the EU's announcement explicitly references the importance of this region and market for climate and green investments, and increased connectivity (an explicit push against China's BRI) (European Commission, 2021).

For proponents of international liberalism, the strategy has effectively been to bring China into the World Trade Organization (WTO) and the global economy so that the benefits of Chinese state-led capitalism and mutual interdependence can lure it away from Maoist socialism – and eventually give way to liberalism.[3] And for as long as liberal capitalism has benefitted from China acting as the world's factory, the mutual interdependence between advanced economies of the West and China has grown. But as China becomes more determined to stamp its own mark on this new wave of industrialism,[4] and the technological supremacy of the West is challenged, cooperation begins to give way to conflict. And so, new battlelines are being drawn – with

---

[1] The QUAD or the Quadrilateral Security Dialogue is an informal alliance between Japan, the USA, India and Australia said to focus on maritime cooperation in the Indo-Pacific.

[2] In 1947 George Kennan's anonymous contribution in the journal, Foreign Affairs, set out a policy of 'containment' for the US approach to the USSR. Kennon's suggestion of a strategy for 'long-term, patient but firm and vigilant containment of Russian expansive tendencies' was to become the basis for the US's Cold War approach. See United States Office of the Historian (no date) and Kennan (1947) for further detail.

[3] This was a thesis also promoted by Francis Fukuyama when he wrote his famous Foreign Affairs essay titled 'The End of History'.

[4] China is already leading in quantum physics and computing (see Kania and Costello 2018).

dominance over frontier technologies in clean energy and AI taking centre stage.

CHINA'S POSITIONING IN GREEN TECHNOLOGIES AND GREEN MINERALS: A GROWING THREAT TO WESTERN SUPREMACY

A big part of China's strategy has been to leverage its industrial strategy Made in China 2025 to assert leadership in a new set of technologies (Popper et al., 2020). Its massive investment in research and development (R&D) has played an important role in this regard. The latest available figures from 2017 estimate that China's contribution to global growth in R&D was around 44 per cent compared to 19.4 per cent from the US and 11 per cent from the EU (Cookson, 2021). The drive for innovation in China is also reflected in the number of patents registered by companies based in China. Approximately 81 per cent of registered patents in the renewable energy field between 2018–2019 were from Chinese-based companies (Geary, 2020) with the Chinese state-owned electric corporation, State Grid Corporation of China, emerging as an international leader by a significant margin (Ainscow, 2021). At the same time China is positioning its own flagship companies, themselves major investors in R&D. Chinese business's share of R&D expenditure represented more than 77 per cent of total business sector, compared to 71 per cent for the US (UNESCO database, 2018) – with Chinese companies expanding the global frontier in these new tech sectors. Simultaneously China has pursued prototyping, financing, manufacturing, public procurement and boosted domestic demand – all of which have enabled the mass production of new technologies – from solar panels to electric vehicles.

In essence, China has leapfrogged other global players in advanced technologies (Ding and Dafoe, 2021) and signalled its ability to compete directly with Western multinational and transnational companies for global markets and hegemony. The growing potential of China to capture renewable energy markets is borne out by the US's attempt to use other measures to curtail competition, including citing human rights violations as a basis to impose restrictions on Chinese polysilicon imports (Fickling, 2021).

With dominance over clean technologies becoming a new battleground, control over access to the minerals necessary for the green transition (IEA, 2021) has become equally important. As the European Commission (2019: 8) put it, '(a)ccess to resources is also a strategic security question for Europe's ambition to deliver the Green Deal'. The same minerals necessary for many green technologies are also increasingly critical for the military-industrial complex of major economies and their ambitions to weaponise space, making control over supply ever more important. Many of these minerals are also key inputs for hypersonic weapons and new nuclear weapons and warheads.

In terms of supply, China currently dominates the rare earth market – accounting for close to 60 per cent, if not more, of global supply. With the finicky, expensive and highly polluting nature of rare earth processing, China also holds a market advantage – making it difficult for new players to enter (Foss, 2021). China has effectively now positioned itself as the rare earth's OPEC (Bartekova, 2014) having shifted rare earth dominance from the West (Nakano, 2021). Copper is another crucial mineral for the green transition which Chinese firms, mainly based in Africa, also dominate. As the biggest consumer of globally refined copper – accounting for around 52 per cent of global demand – China invested significantly in securing supply. Between 2005 and 2020, it invested more than US$56 billion in copper assets, mostly in Africa and particularly in Zambia (Foss et al., 2020).

With the energy transition on the horizon, China has effectively captured the future market. For example, in the automobile sector alone, electric vehicles (EVs) cannot function without super magnets that are derived from rare earth minerals.[5] Globally, there are over 1.4 billion vehicles on the road with seven million being added each year. Achieving net zero targets in transport alone will take a Herculean effort with EVs occupying a substantial share of the market. Battery electric vehicles (BEVs) also require substantial amounts of copper – 30 000 BEVs would require a skyscraper worth of copper. Turning

[5] Super magnets rely, in particular, on the rare earth minerals neodymium and praseodymium (NdPr).

over one third of the global supply of BEVs would consume as much copper as the current annual copper supply – around 20 million tonnes. Control over the supply of these inputs clearly gives China a strategic advantage in the future automobile market.

Indeed, if one studies the history of critical minerals (see Pitron, 2020), a side of the climate debate that is hidden from the usual moral platitudes begins to emerge. For example, in 2010, China made a decision that would become a geo-economic landmark: it embargoed the export of rare earths to Japan over a dispute about the Senkuku Islands.[6] This move was a clear indication of China's power and willingness to use its monopoly over rare earths and with that control over the production of key telecommunications and other technologies that are essential for modern economies to pursue other interests (Pitron, 2020).

China's non-commercial and non-market mechanisms for supply chain security also favour its "at any cost" strategy. Compared to critical minerals acquisitions in the West, China's position is driven by the impetus of politics and control by state enterprises. This model, which would be difficult to replicate in the West, may serve it well if increased encirclement and containment under the Indo-Pacific alliance strategy starts to take shape (Bachhawat et al., 2020).

A conflict over rare earths is increasingly possible. In March 2021, the QUAD raised concerns over China's dominance of rare earth production and significant attention was paid to exploring alternatives for rare earth supplies. Australia, for example, is looking to capture a bigger share of rare earths mining and processing. But its current production, 17 000 tonnes in a facility in Malaysia, is a drop in the ocean compared to China's 140 000 tonnes. The EU, which now finds itself with limited access to these resources, has opted most recently to focus on standards creation (European Commission, 2020a).

Only naive moralism and sentimental logic would accept that these massive strides and structural shifts in decarbonisation are simply about the climate. The strategic alignment of geopolitics, climate norms, climate finance and climate technologies are part of the next wave of the technology revolution currently underway. These are

[6] The Senkuku Islands were seized by Japan following the occupation of Manchuria during the Second World War.

comingled with rapid developments taking place in AI, big data and digital technology (The White House, 2021b). As such, the realm of critical weapons and their diverse industrial uses are also beginning to overlap with the climate agenda – from electrolysers, to renewables, to small modular reactors and electric vehicles.

AS NEW BATTLE LINES ARE DRAWN, HOW ARE OTHER GLOBAL PLAYERS RESPONDING?

Naive climate liberalism and internationalism is being buried by a 'geopolitical bus' with the economic imperatives of global powers discreetly shaping the climate agenda. As China works to maintain dominance in clean technologies and minerals through initiatives like the greening of the BRI (the Green BRI) announced in 2017, other powers are looking at how they can displace China and secure market share.

After four lost years under Trump, the US is now gearing up for its own net zero push and fast aligning its infrastructure investment plan with a review of strategic supply chains to enable it to compete with China and Europe in AI, robotics, digital technologies and 5G (The White House, 2021a). As Biden candidly put it at the G7, these initiatives are being implemented to counter China's Belt and Road Initiative (BRI) (Aljazeera, 2021). The Pentagon is also interested in climate issues, not only because of the risk that extreme weather poses to military bases and installations, but also because access to critical minerals, which are now being used in multiple domains, can restrict supply or add to the cost of acquisition for the military. The US military is now investing considerably in AI and quantum computers with quantum technology, though China is currently leading this field.

As part of its COVID-19 response, Europe is seeking to rebalance its economy and introduce within its political domain a significant economic recovery package, with close to a trillion Euros in climate stimulus, under the auspices of the European Green Deal (EGD). While packaged as Europe exercising its global responsibility to the fight against climate change, the EGD's ties to a new European doctrine of strategic autonomy (Grajewski, 2021) in essence is just another way of saying 'Europe first' and then the rest of the world. The EGD effectively seeks to strengthen Europe's future position in the world and competitiveness in new sectors as it weans itself off fossil fuels and shapes a new 'ecological civilization' and industrial pathway (Lee-Makiyama, 2021). Not surprisingly, the EU's partnership model with Africa, China and other trading partners is increasingly being guided by this doctrine – despite its difficulties in selling the EGD to its own constituencies (as evidenced by the very limited ambition of its freshly renegotiated Common Agriculture Policy Framework) (De Lorenzo, 2021).

The debate around gas is also illustrative of the unfolding geopolitical landscape. The tension around Nord Stream II is a case in point. Gas is an important catalyst for the EU's Green Deal as a transition fuel for green hydrogen. Gas-based hydrogen is currently the most cost-effective option as the costs for fossil-based hydrogen (€1.5/kg) are currently much less than that of renewables (€2.5–5.5/kg) (European Commission, 2020b). To mitigate the risk of stranded assets, the EU intends to invest in at least 60 GW of renewable hydrogen electrolysers – at around €24–42 billion over the next 10 years – while retrofitting existing hydrogen plants with carbon capture and storage technologies. Thus, in the short-term, natural gas will act as an important bridge for the EU's green hydrogen plans (European Commission, 2020b). A steady supply of gas is thus critical.

Those who argued that Nord Stream II would increase European energy reliance on Russia and strengthen Russia's political power initially garnered support from both Barak Obama and Donald Trump. But as gas has become more important for the realisation of the EU's Green Deal, President Biden's willingness to lift sanctions on the company building the pipeline (with conditions that would allow the US and its EU allies to rein Russia in should the need arise) is a compromise that will favour the EGD in the short term.

At the same time, Russia is using the warmer Arctic conditions and icecap melt to exploit oil and gas reserves in the Arctic and lower its dependence on demand from Europe. It is investing in the North Sea Route, along Russia's Arctic border to service increased gas demand from Asia – and particularly from China. Global warming, paradoxically, is favouring more gas extraction in the Arctic. This is attracting the likes of Total – thereby also revealing (French President) Emmanuel Macron's 'forked tongue' approach to the Paris goals. Total appears to be free of any diplomatic restraint to explore frontier gas regions such as those in the Arctic or indeed in Southern Africa.[7] The same is true of the US's Anadarko and ExxonMobil, and China's China National Petroleum Corporation (CNPC) to name a few.

While the EGD looks benign from the outside, it has sharp teeth. The EU's Green Deal is Europe's Marshall Plan for the climate but not one intended to benefit everyone else. For one, it has significant financial clout that allows the EU to repurpose strategic economic sectors. Hard to abate sectors, i.e. sectors for which the transition is particularly challenging, will have to reach net zero targets and the EU wants to be the first in the new technology wave to achieve that – hydrogen is one of the key technology breakthroughs the EU wants to lead (European Commission, 2020b). Europe is investing significantly in R&D, with subsidies for flagship pioneer companies and incentivising market creation through the EU Emissions Trading System (ETS) and a carbon border tax adjustment which it argues is WTO compliant. The US, not wanting to be caught off guard due to Trump's anti-climate 'wrecking ball', is looking to push back on the EU's carbon border tax adjustments. And so, global powers are increasingly developing 'climate response' packages that serve to achieve other geoeconomic and political ends – in particular curtailing China and thereby securing future market share.

---

[7] USA Total, has a 20 per cent share in the Yamal LNG export terminal (see Rumer et al., 2021).

THE ROAD AHEAD FOR AFRICA: LEVERAGING THE NEW GEOPOLITICAL BATTLE LINES

Africa needs, as a matter of urgency, to put measures in place to enable it to benefit from the new technology wave that decarbonisation is bringing about. This is critical not only to enable it to build resilience against climate change impacts but also to position itself for future markets. In this regard, African countries need to ensure that they are not simply relegated to consumers of green technologies manufactured elsewhere but that they are also able to establish themselves as producers thereof. This is a difficult task that requires much more than mere climate populism – a lazy, faith-based approach to tackling problems on the continent underpinned by a heroic saviour mentality propagated by those from outside.

In this regard, the challenge in Africa is not renewables but models of development that continue to rely on the false promise that minerals and fossil fuel extraction result in greater well-being and opportunities for people. Precolonial features of the extractive industry continue to permeate post-colonial rule. Those that rely on African extractive exports are equally complicit in perpetuating these unbalanced forms of economic growth and development, rendering false the claim so often repeated on billboards and magazine covers that 'Africa is Rising'. It will only rise if more sustainable economies are built, and extractives become a fraction of total GDP and cease to crowd out developments in other sectors.

Major African fossil fuel exporting countries will need to – in the long-run – re-evaluate their dependence on fossil fuel exports and commodity dependence in general. These countries will need to pursue far greater economic diversification and investment with deeper economic inclusion. To avoid long-term stranded assets, they will need to ensure a seamless transition from fossil fuel dependency to alternative export opportunities by replacing fossil fuels with something better and more sustainable (the idea of displacement equivalence). These displacements will need to be rooted in strategies that enhance greater accountability and transparency over resource extraction, and extractive revenues must be used to deepen economic diversification and expand the fiscal space for social investments.

Given the immensity of the shifts that African countries will need to undertake, the question for Africa is how best to navigate brewing global tensions to secure its own long-term interest. This is a gamble that requires countries to effectively back a winner. One option is to rebalance some of the power asymmetry between itself and the West by backing China. In this regard, the first step would be to break the long-standing precolonial resource extraction model which the EGD is currently in danger of perpetuating. Another option is to build on its history (albeit a chequered one) with the West, and work on developing more favourable terms of engagement with the EU and US. A third option would be to take the middle ground and attempt to build favourable relations with both sides. However, given the nature of current tensions between China and the West and its escalation in recent months, sitting on the fence will likely become increasingly difficult.

All three of the crudely described options above carry risks. However, arguably the biggest risk is that irrespective of the strategy taken, African countries do not use their collective bargaining power and instead act alone. In this regard, the African Continental Free Trade Agreement (AfCFTA) becomes a very important tool for African countries. While primarily a free trade agreement, it is also a mechanism for regional economic integration and, if successful, a mechanism that strengthens Africa's collective bargaining power with the rest of the world. There is potential, for example, through the AfCFTA to ring-fence revenues in short- and long-run commodities trade. This revenue could be used to finance a regional superfund to support continent-wide economic diversification (Usman and Landry, 2021) and industrial development (Signé, 2018).

In this regard, an important metric for assessing what strategy to pursue with global powers will be the extent to which these powers either support or undermine mechanisms and institutions that seek to strengthen greater regional cooperation, like the AU and the AfCFTA. The EGD, for example, is taking place in a context where the EU is still seeking to secure long-term free trade agreements (FTAs) with different economic subregions within Africa. These not only undermine the current AfCFTA negotiations but will also make its eventual implementation far more difficult. At the same time, while European foreign aid is being used to support technical work on greening the AfCFTA, the EGD's approach towards Africa and the Africa-Europe partnership in general, has no in-built focus on industrial development on the African continent – an explicit objective of the African Union. This is perhaps because European negotiators share the same bias as European think tanks and experts, namely that industrial development in Africa is a lost cause – although the assertion that Africa is deindustrialising is now being challenged (Lopes and te Vrede, 2021). It is also possible that African industrialisation does not serve Europe's doctrine of strategic autonomy. For African countries, a stronger push for a wider industrial programme, through the AfCFTA, would be critical for driving clean energy investments and broader access to digital infrastructure. Roberto Unger (2019) argues this could enable developing countries to embed themselves at the frontier of the global knowledge economy. The extent to which the EU through its EGD enables or hinders this should shape the approach African countries as a collective take to their engagements with Europe.

While China, like Europe and indeed the US, does not engage with Africa for altruistic purposes, it arguably has a better track record on important questions like key infrastructure development and industrialisation. It is expected to continue to be a key player in Africa's power sector development, especially in the development of renewables (Ayele et al., 2021). With China being the largest financier of infrastructure on the continent (Benkerroum et al., 2021; Baker McKenzie, 2021) including green energy infrastructure (Shepard, 2021), there is potential for African countries to tap into more green infrastructure finance under the Green BRI. However, Africa faces competition from Southeast and Central Asia, which currently attracts the majority of Chinese investment in green energy. African countries will therefore need to move fast to create the enabling environment needed to attract more green funding from China. At the same time, African countries need to heed the warning of Ha Joon Chan, that as China cements its position as the world's industrial powerhouse, it 'kicks away the ladder' for other developing countries to follow suit.

As such, much like the EU, African countries will need to ensure that Chinese engagements do not undermine mechanisms like the AfCFTA, and that green industrialisation becomes an explicit objective of China-Africa relations.

The US's approach to Africa, under Biden, and indeed the success of the Build Back Better World Initiative (Biden's counter to the BRI initiative) is yet to be seen. The Build Back Better Bill is currently being delayed by Biden's own party who cannot agree on its priorities. Nevertheless, what is clear is that as the US and China continue to vie for global dominance, and China's relative importance on the African continent continues to grow, Africa will increasingly come into the US's radar. Much like with the EU and China, Africa's priority in its engagement with the US's Build Back Better World Initiative must be to ensure that it protects its policy space to drive localisation and green industrialisation on the continent.

While decision-makers navigate these new battle lines, Global South African activists and NGOs need to engage their Northern and Southern counterparts in a form of internationalism and climate justice solidarity. This must involve a critical engagement around how climate geopolitics are changing in advanced economies where political leaders 'speak green' yet pursue economic self-interest. Naive climate liberalism that perpetuates the idea of climate internationalism without geopolitical filters can hold dire consequences for countries and continents at the forefront of this new battleground. Ensuring that Africa benefits from the decarbonisation agenda will require those committed to the continent's development to move beyond mere climate populism and begin to actively engage with the real politic.

SOUTH AFRICA'S ROLE IN SECURING AFRICA'S FUTURE POSITIONING IN THE DECARBONISATION AGENDA

South Africa remains a powerful voice amongst its African counterparts. It carries influence not only with its neighbours but on the continent more broadly. As such, it needs to continue to play a leading role in fast-tracking the AfCFTA, regional integration and improving cooperation and coordination amongst AU member states. It also needs to play a leading role in supporting the capacity of the AU and other institutions to understand and engage the multitude of objectives behind the various 'green deals' – i.e., those objectives over and above decarbonisation – and the implications that these will have for the continent. As a fossil fuel dependant country, South Africa's ability to accelerate its own just transition to a low carbon economy will also have spill-over effects in other parts of the continent and can act as a model for other countries facing similar challenges.

Fast-tracking South Africa's just transition and the decarbonisation of its electricity sector will not be easy. It will, however, be critical for its future economic sustainability by, amongst other things, enabling it to avoid its exports being subject to the EU's Carbon Border Adjustment Mechanism. Realising a just transition, in South Africa, will require a multi-pronged approach that is able to address the peculiarities of its political economy. Within the formal economy, the highly financialised and digitised sectors will, to some degree, be able to transition to net zero relatively easily. However, the challenge will be in energy intensive sectors, which largely remain under government but in which the financial sector also plays an important enabling role, for example through the financing of extractives. A coordinated effort by government and finance will be key in redirecting investments to more sustainable sectors which can begin to displace South Africa's fossil fuel dependence and support diversification.

This effort needs to be replicated beyond South Africa's borders. South Africa's financial sector, with the support of the South African government, needs to move away from investing in resource extraction in other parts of the continent and direct its investment towards productive activities in the green economy space. This not only makes business sense, in terms of avoiding longer-term stranded assets, but is also important from a credibility point of view and will ensure that South Africa is not guilty of doing what others are critiqued for, namely exacerbating resource dependence in other African countries.

CONCLUDING REMARKS

Walter Scheidel (2019), in his seminal work on the Roman Empire, made the observation that the best thing Rome did as a single monopolistic hegemony over most of Europe and the rest of its empire, was to go away and never come back. One cannot help but wonder whether the same holds true for Africa's geopolitical partners, the Bretton Woods system, Official Development Assistance and outsider voices that continue to shape the discourse around development and economic sovereignty on the continent. The coded lingua franca of 'help and assistance' is laden with a paternalistic subtext that if Africa just adheres to the form and substance of models (including decarbonisation models) developed elsewhere, some sort of civilisation can emerge on the 'dark continent'. However, history has shown us that the mimetic impulses to draw on liberal economies' growth models, assistance and technology often do not align with African interests. Indeed, for Africa to reap the benefits of advances in modern technology, science and industrial development – these must be locally driven and locally owned.

Naive climate populism must be replaced by more grounded climate realism. This is not the task of foreign policy advocates and mouthpieces but must be homegrown. It must have a Southern tilt, voice and organic intellectual origins (to draw on Gramsci). Partly, this means not blindly accepting the climate promises of advanced economies but rather being mindful of the geopolitical arc in which climate policy is now intimately connected with other interests: military, geo-economic, industrial and trade. It is essentially to critically engage this intricate web and develop an analytical frame that moves beyond purely science-based approaches to climate debates or the Paris Agreement.

For the climate agenda to succeed on the African continent, energy transitions must be pursued as part of a broader developmental model. This will not be accomplished by non-Africans no matter how well meaning they are. To borrow from Pankaj Mishra's latest book, *Bland Fanatics* (2020) – the idea that free markets and democracy will simply triumph is symptomatic of a blind belief in the superiority of the model and a lack of critical engagement with its inherent contradictions. Net zero triumphalism has the hallmarks of this bland fanaticism. For green and net zero ambitions to succeed, they must be organically adopted at a pace and in a manner that enables countries on the continent to simultaneously pursue their climate objectives and their developmental needs.

REFERENCES

Ainscow, G. 3 March 2021. 'The future of renewable energy – Tracking the patent trends'. *Reddie & Grose*, https://www.reddie.co.uk/2021/03/03/the-future-of-renewable-energy-tracking-the-patent-trends/, accessed 21 June 2021.

Aljazeera. 26 March 2021. 'Biden suggests creating initiative to rival China's Belt and Road'. *Aljazeera*, https://www.aljazeera.com/economy/2021/3/26/biden-suggests-creating-initiative-to-rival-chinas-belt-and-road, accessed 19 June 2021.

Ayele, S., Shen, W., Chiyemura, F. and Gu, J. 25 March 2021. 'Enhancing China-Africa cooperation in the renewable energy sector'. Institute of Development Studies Policy Briefing (176), https://opendocs.ids.ac.uk/opendocs/handle/20.500.12413/16516, accessed 16 June 2021.

Bachhawat, A., Cave, D., Kand, J., Rajagopalan, R.P. and Ray, T. 15 October 2020. 'Critical technologies and the Indo-Pacific: A new India-Australia partnership'. Australian Strategic Policy Institute and Observer Research Foundation, https://www.aspi.org.au/report/critical-technologies-and-indo-pacific-new-india-australia-partnership, accessed 20 June 2021.

Baker McKenzie. 29 April 2021. 'New dynamics: Shifting patterns in Africa'. Baker McKenzie, https://www.bakermckenzie.com/en/insight/publications/2021/04/new-dynamics-patterns-of-change, accessed 18 June 2021.

Bartekova, E. 2014. 'Introduction to the economics of rare earths'. United Nations University-Maastricht Economic and Social Research Institute on Innovation and Technology (MERIT), https://www.researchgate.net/publication/279514600_An_Introduction_to_the_Economics_of_Rare_Earths, accessed 17 June 2021.

Behr, R. 8 June 2021. 'Joe Biden's mission at the G7 Summit: To recruit allies for the next Cold War'. *The Guardian*, https://www.theguardian.com/commentisfree/2021/jun/08/joe-biden-allies-g7-cold-war-summit-china-washington, accessed 26 June 2021.

Benkerroum, B., Liu, Y., Mabuza, P. and Omotilewa, O.J. 2021. 'China's infrastructure financing in Africa: Stylized facts and impact of COVID 19'. Africa Economic Brief of the AfDB, 12(8), https://www.afdb.org/en/documents/africa-economic-brief-chinas-infrastructure-financing-africa-stylized-facts-and-impact-covid-19-volume-12-issue-8, accessed 26 June 2021.

Blinken, A. 21 March 2021. 'A Foreign Policy for the American People'. Speech delivered on the 21 March 2021 at the White House, United States Department of State, https://www.state.gov/a-foreign-policy-for-the-american-people/, accessed 27 June 2021.

Cookson, C. 11 June 2021. 'Coronavirus has "energised" science spending, says Unesco'. *Financial Times*, https://www.ft.com/content/b83e9ae5-f769-4f6b-b7de-5a1d01f2d927, accessed 01 July 2021.

De Lorenzo, D. 26 June 2021. 'EU's common agricultural policy falls short of sustainability expectations'. *Forbes*, https://www.forbes.com/sites/danieladelorenzo/2021/06/26/eus-common-agricultural-policy-deal-still-doesnt-place-the-future-of-eu-farming-on-the-right-path-for-sustainable-transition/, accessed 29 June 2021.

Ding, J. and Dafoe, A. 2021. 'The logic of strategic assets: From oil to AI'. *Security Studies*, 30(2), https://www.tandfonline.com/doi/full/10.1080/09636412.2021.1915583, accessed 27 June 2021.

European Commission. 2021. 'The EU Strategy for cooperation in the Indo-Pacific'. Joint Communication to the European Parliament and the Council, https://eeas.europa.eu/sites/default/files/jointcommunication_2021_24_1_en.pdf, accessed 21 September 2021.

European Commission, 2020a. 'Joint Declaration on Processors and Semiconductor Technologies'. *Shaping Europe's Digital Future*, https://digital-strategy.ec.europa.eu/en/library/joint-declaration-processors-and-semiconductor-technologies, accessed 20 June 2021.

European Commission. 2020b. 'A Hydrogen Strategy for Climate-Neutral Europe'. Communication from the Commission to the European Parliament, the Council, the European Economic and Social Committee and the Committee of the Regions, https://eur-lex.europa.eu/legal-content/EN/TXT/PDF/?uri=CELEX:52020DC0301&from=EN, accessed 16 June 2021.

European Commission. 2020c. 'Circular Economy Action Plan: For a Cleaner and More Competitive Europe'. https://ec.europa.eu/environment/pdf/circular-economy/new_circular_economy_action_plan.pdf, accessed 29 June 2021.

European Commission. 2019. 'The European Green Deal'. Communication from the Commission to the European Parliament, the European Council, the Council, the European Economic and Social Committee and the Committee of the Regions, https://ec.europa.eu/info/sites/default/files/european-green-deal-communication_en.pdf, accessed 17 June 2021.

Fickling, D. 13 June 2021. 'The real solar-panel price crises hasn't begun yet'. *Bloomberg Opinion*, https://www.bloomberg.com/opinion/articles/2021-06-13/the-coming-solar-panel-crisis-could-be-less-about-price-and-more-about-xinjiang, accessed 27 June 2021.

Foss, M.M. 5 May 2021. 'Minerals and materials supply chains: Considerations for decarbonization of transport'. Testimony before the US House of Representatives Committee on Energy and Commerce, Hearing on 'The Clean Future Act: Driving Decarbonization of the Transportation Sector', https://www.bakerinstitute.org/media/files/files/159d50df/witness-testimony-foss-eng-2021-05-05.pdf, accessed 20 June 2021.

Foss, M.M., Moats, M.S. and Awuah-Offei, K. 2020. 'Framing energy and minerals for future pathways'. Policy Brief: Saudi Arabia 2020 Think, https://www.bakerinstitute.org/media/files/files/e974ed25/ces-g20-t20-minerals-100821.pdf, accessed 20 June 2021.

Geary, J. 31 January 2020. 'A Rise in "Green" Energy Patents Filed'. *EMW*, https://www.emwllp.com/latest/a-rise-in-green-energy-patents-filed/, accessed 20 June 2021.

Grajewski, M. 30 March 2021. 'The EU strategic autonomy debate'. *What Think Tanks are Thinking*, European Parliamentary Research Service, https://www.europarl.europa.eu/RegData/etudes/BRIE/2021/690532/EPRS_BRI(2021)690532_EN.pdf, accessed 20 June 2021.

Goldberg, J. 15 April 2016. 'The Obama Doctrine'. *The Atlantic*, https://www.theatlantic.com/magazine/archive/2016/04/the-obama-doctrine/471525/, accessed 27 June 2021.

Henderson, M. and Rogers, J. 8 April 2020. 'The Indo-Pacific: An enlarged perspective'. The Henry Jackson Society, https://henryjacksonsociety.org/publications/indo-pacific-an-enlarged-perspective/, accessed 20 June 2021.

International Energy Agency (IEA). May 2021. 'The role of critical minerals in clean Energy Transitions'. World Energy Outlook, https://www.iea.org/reports/the-role-of-critical-minerals-in-clean-energy-transitions, accessed 20 June 2021.

Kania, E.B. and Costello, J.K. September 2018. 'Quantam hegemony? China's ambitions and the challenge to US innovation leadership'. Center for New American Security, https://s3.amazonaws.com/files.cnas.org/documents/CNASReport-Quantum-Tech_FINAL.pdf?mtime=20180912133406, accessed 20 June 2021.

Kennan, G.J. July 1947. 'The sources of Soviet conduct'. *Foreign Affairs,* 566–582, https://www.cvce.eu/content/publication/1999/1/1/a0f03730-dde8-4f06-a6ed-d740770dc423/publishable_en.pdf, accessed 20 June 2021.

Kennedy, C. 27 July 2020. 'Washington's China policy has lost its Wei'. Center for Strategic & International Studies Briefs, https://www.csis.org/analysis/washingtons-china-policy-has-lost-its-wei, accessed 20 June 2021.

Klein, A.O. 23 April 2020. 'The U.S.-China race and the fate of transatlantic relations. Part II: Bridging differing geopolitical views'. Center for Strategic & International Studies, Washington, https://www.csis.org/analysis/us-china-race-and-fate-transatlantic-relations-0, accessed 27 June 2021.

Lee-Makiyama, H. February 2021. 'The EU Green Deal and its industrial and political significance'. *European Center for International Political Economy*, https://ecipe.org/publications/eu-green-deal/, accessed 21 June 2021.

Lopes, C. and te Vrede, D.W. 2021. 'Structural transformation, economic development and industrialization in post-Covid-19 Africa'. Institute for New Economic Thinking, https://www.ineteconomics.org/uploads/papers/Lopes-te-Velde-African-industrialisation.pdf, accessed 20 June 2021.

Machiavelli, N. 1532. *The Prince*. https://www.earlymoderntexts.com/assets/pdfs/machiavelli1532.pdf, accessed 10 March 2021.

Mackinder, H.J. 1904. 'The geographical pivot of history'. *The Geographical Journal,* XXIIL(4).

McGrath, M. 22 September 2020. Climate Change: China Aims for 'Carbon Neutrality by 2060'. BBC, https://www.bbc.com/news/science-environment-54256826, accessed 19 June 2021.

Mishra, P. 2020. *Bland Fanatics: Liberals, race and empire*. USA: Verso Books.

Ni, V. 1 May 2021. 'Failure to improve US-China relations "risks Cold War", warns Kissinger'. *The Guardian*, https://www.theguardian.com/us-news/2021/may/01/us-china-doomsday-threat-ramped-up-by-hi-tech-advances-says-kissinger, accessed 16 June 2021.

Nakano, J. 11 March 2021. 'The geopolitics of critical minerals supply chains'. Center for Strategic & International Studies, https://www.csis.org/analysis/geopolitics-critical-minerals-supply-chains, accessed 17 June 2021.

Pitron, G. 2020. The Rare Metals War: The dark side of green and digital technologies, translated by Bianca Jacobsohn. Australia: Scribe Publications.

Popper, S.W., Blumenthal, M.S., Han, E., Lilly, S., Morris, L.J. et al. 2020. 'China's propensity for innovation in the 21st century: Identifying indicators of future outcomes'. Rand Corporation, https://www.rand.org/pubs/research_reports/RRA208-1.html, accessed 26 June 2021.

Rumer, E., Sokolsky, R. and Stronski, P. 2021. 'Russia in the Arctic: A critical examination'. Carnegie Endowment for International Peace, https://carnegieendowment.org/2021/03/29/russia-in-arctic-critical-examination-pub-84181, accessed 16 June 2021.

Scheidel, W. 2019. *Escape from Rome: The failure of empire and the road to prosperity*. USA: Princeton University Press.

Shepard, C. 26 January 2021. 'China pours money into green belt and road projects'. *Financial Times*, https://www.ft.com/content/8ec30baf-69e9-4d73-aa25-13668dcb659f, accessed 26 June 2021.

Signé, L. September 2018. 'The potential of manufacturing and industrialization and strategies'. Brookings Africa Growth Initiative, https://media.

africaportal.org/documents/Manufacturing-and-Industrialization-in-Africa-Signe-20180921.pdf, accessed 21 June 2021.

Stronski, P. 2020. 'There goes the neighbourhood: The limits of Russian integration in Eurasia'. Carnegie Endowment for International Peace, https://carnegieendowment.org/2020/09/16/there-goes-neighborhood-limits-of-russian-integration-in-eurasia-pub-82693, accessed 20 June 2021.

The White House. 2021a. 'Fact sheet: President Biden sets 2030 greenhouse gas pollution reduction target aimed at creating good-paying union jobs and securing US leadership on clean energy technologies'. Statements and Releases, https://www.whitehouse.gov/briefing-room/statements-releases/2021/04/22/fact-sheet-president-biden-sets-2030-greenhouse-gas-pollution-reduction-target-aimed-at-creating-good-paying-union-jobs-and-securing-u-s-leadership-on-clean-energy-technologies/, accessed 20 June 2021.

The White House. 2021b. 'Building resilient supply chains, revitalizing American manufacturing, and fostering broad-based growth: 100-day reviews under executive rrder 14017'. https://www.whitehouse.gov/wp-content/uploads/2021/06/100-day-supply-chain-review-report.pdf?utm_source=sfmc%E2%80%8B&utm_medium=email%E2%80%8B&utm_campaign=20210610_Global_Manufacturing_Economic_Update_June_Members, accessed 27 June 2021.

UNESCO Institute for Statistics Database. 2018. 'How Much Does Your Country Invest in R&D?'. http://uis.unesco.org/apps/visualisations/research-and-development-spending, accessed 21 June 2021.

Unger, M.U. 2019. *The Knowledge Economy.* Verso, UK.

United States Office of the Historian. (no date). 'Kennan and Containment, 1947'. https://history.state.gov/milestones/1945-1952/kennan, accessed 28 June 2021.

Usman, Z. and Landry, D. 2021. 'Economic diversification in Africa: How and why it matters'. Carnegie Endowment for International Peace Working Paper, https://carnegieendowment.org/2021/04/30/economic-diversification-in-africa-how-and-why-it-matters-pub-84429, accessed 21 June 2021.

THIRTEEN

Reimagining skills planning for a low carbon and sustainable future

Conceptualising skills ecosystems

Presha Ramsarup and Najma Mohamed

INTRODUCTION AND BACKGROUND

Globally, the transition to low carbon economies and actions to limit greenhouse gas emissions could create 24 million jobs by 2030 according to the International Labour Organization (ILO, 2018). Other estimates are even higher. The International Renewable Energy Agency (IRENA), for instance, found that accelerated uptake of renewable energy and energy efficiency measures could boost total clean energy jobs globally, from 11 million at the end of 2018 to 100 million by 2050 (IRENA, 2020). In a 2020 report, the World Economic Forum (WEF) suggested that if businesses prioritise nature in investments, nature-positive solutions could create 350 million jobs by 2030 (World Economic Forum, 2020). Green jobs, the new jobs that are created as industries and sectors transform, are a core outcome of green transitions. The ILO and United Nations Environmental Programme (UNEP) found that at least half of the global workforce – the equivalent of 1.5 billion people – would be affected by the transition to a low carbon economy.

The creation of new green jobs, as well as the successful re-allocation and upskilling of workers, is dependent on access to training, capacity development and related policy measures. Knowledge and skills to adapt products, services and processes to climate change and attendant environmental requirements and regulations will be needed by all sectors and at all levels in the workforce.

This green economic restructuring will have a profound impact on the labour market and has precipitated rapid calls for skills development responses. As countries and regions plan, design and implement a just and inclusive transition to a green economy, skills development will play a role in reskilling, upskilling and more importantly enabling a real paradigm shift that focuses on the holistic integration of social, economic and environmental sustainability.

Skills are among the main drivers to achieve a just transition to a low carbon economy, yet skills mismatches and shortages are among the key obstacles to green transitions. For skills to become central in transitions – and in a green and just recovery from the global COVID-19 pandemic – the identification, anticipation and provision of green skills is crucial.

However, even with the growth in analytical models and approaches to assess the skills needs of green transitions, there are systemic challenges to promoting such skills. These include a lack of institutional structures to deal with green skills as a cross-cutting concern in the education and training landscape; and a lack of education and training opportunities and dated curricula in education and training institutions. Labour market analysis instruments do not capture green occupations and, for the most part, there is a discord between skills and environmental policies. Few countries have yet reoriented their skills systems in line with their green ambitions. An economy-wide transition will impact on how we produce and consume, live and work. And it will shift what we need to learn (and unlearn).

The chapter unpacks the nub of the dilemma in addressing the way skills policies and approaches have been located within a neoliberal paradigm. It argues that transitions to low carbon economies are contested and uneven, creating rapidly changing contexts which need a revitalised approach to how skills development can be conceptualised and implemented. In this chapter the salient literature on skills for a green and just transition is explored, in order to draw out some of the conceptual challenges. The chapter then argues that conceptualising skills for just transition requires a framework that moves beyond the individual, to organisations and systems as a systemic collective. This framework is needed to drive regime change and work against the lock-ins that keep us trapped in unsustainable practices within the skills ecosystem. Skills development that supports these transitions will only emerge where a mutually reciprocal relationship is developed between the state and social groups, including employers, workers communities and their representatives. The framing of skills ecosystems provided in this paper explores the skills needed for a just transition, conceptualising the role of skills within the ecosystem as an enabling factor between the vertical and the horizontal dimensions of the skills ecosystem. This conceptual framework is then applied to local case studies with emerging lessons on the role of skills highlighted, including how skills ecosystems can be planned and implemented.

Green skills: A meander through the literature

Significant transitions are required because of climate change, poverty and resource shortages in South Africa. These transitions are going to require new knowledge and skills within both existing and emerging sectors and occupations.

Skills development plays a crucial role in seizing opportunities and unlocking the potential for reimagining jobs and work in the just transition. Defining green skills has always been fuzzy and contentious. Some generally used definitions of green skills include the following:

- Green skills are the abilities, values and attitudes people need to build and support a sustainable and resource-efficient society (OECD, 2014).

- Green skills are the technical skills, knowledge, values and attitudes needed in the workforce to develop and support sustainable social, economic and environmental outcomes in business, industry and the community (Australian Green Skills Agreement, 2009).
- Green skills can be defined as the skills needed by the workforce, in all sectors and at all levels, in order to help the adaptation of the products, services and processes to the changes due to climate change and to environmental requirements and regulations (OECD, 2014).

These definitions illustrate that skills are multidimensional; they are not linked to technology only. Rather their purpose goes beyond improving productivity to include a strong social and public good goal, and they take account of the work, learning and community contexts.

As outlined by Kwauk and Casey (2021: 17), not only do these skills carry the key to unlocking renewable industries, but also the potential to promote equity and social inclusion in an alternative version of sustainable economic growth. This aligns strongly with the findings of the Green Economy Learning Assessment for South Africa (PAGE, 2016), which concluded that the green transition requires diverse competencies including technical, relational and so-called 'transformational' competencies, which in turn involve particular skills, knowledge and values, including a commitment to change.

Green skills constitute a socially constructed concept, intangible and often unobservable. A demand-led approach to green skills has not worked because employers are unable to effectively articulate their skills and training needs to skills delivery bodies. Furthermore, research has also shown that understanding green skills needs is complex and multi-levelled because the demand is latent (not visible now).

Green skills are also not homogeneous. This has methodological implications for how green skills research is designed and structured and for who constitute the central actors. To facilitate an understanding of what a green skills learning agenda could involve, Kwauk and Casey (2021) developed the framework shown in Figure 13.1:

Figure 13.1: Green skills continuum

Source: Kwauk and Casey (2021: 7)

The work of Kwauk and Casey (2021) has been useful in conceptualising green skills as a continuum because this helps to avoid a conflation of skills responses. Figure 13.1 illustrates that at one end of the continuum, green skills are understood as technical skills that are directly linked to jobs and occupations. As such, they are central to green jobs, the jobs at the core of transitioning the economy. At the other end of the continuum is more transformative skills and competencies, which are meant to be more disruptive of the status quo. The model also shows that nestled between these two ends are the generic life skills that are central to the transition.

Skills approaches within the green transition are often critiqued for being conceptualised as skills for green jobs, framed through 'skills gap' and 'skill deficit' arguments, reminiscent of human capital approaches. The critical challenge with this position is that it presents a linear relationship between education, skills and the economy. Its neoliberal framing defines the purpose and relevance of education and skills in terms of how they serve the market and hence locates skills within the traditional economic discourses. Moving beyond a narrow focus on the 'skills gaps' requires the assumption that skills should not be determined by business interests and concerns only. This would negate the importance of understanding worker needs, skills, career interests and aspirations, as well as the salience of specific community and socio-economic contexts in which skills are embedded.

Stroud et al. (2014) also argue that these economically framed skill responses place little emphasis on skills ecosystems holistically. Rather, skills development and training is left to private providers who operate on limited contracts that usually leave workers with few formally recognised transferable skills, thus limiting the extent to which regions can shift to a low carbon economy.

A further critique of these traditional conceptions of skills responses is the focus on the individual. This focus is a constraint in enabling transitions and contradicts the deep systemic co-evolution needed for a just transition. There is a need also to draw on the work of PAGE (2016) which shows that many diverse skills and competencies are needed for driving the transition to a low carbon economy. We use two crucial points that they make: first, the skills needed are technical, relational and transformational in nature; for example, the kind of modelling required for greening the economy would also have a transformative dimension (visioning, ethical valuing); and second, these competencies occur or are needed not necessarily in individuals, but in teams of people (distributed competencies) who have different roles and who need to work effectively with each other. For this, effective leadership is required.

This section traced some of the current skills approaches and tried to illustrate that while they have been useful on some levels, their instrumentalist framing in traditional economic discourses present a regime of truth that does not resonate with a just transition. Thus, drawing from these critiques, an attempt is made in the next section to conceptualise how skills development can be envisaged within a just transition.

Framework for looking at skills for a green and just transition

This section of the chapter attempts to develop an analytical framework for looking at skills for a just transition – one that takes cognisance of critiques of individualistic fallacy embedded in skills responses. The chapter discusses an approach that rather focuses on the 'distributed agency' that is needed across individuals, organisations and systems. The constructs of 'skills ecosystems' are accordingly introduced here. Skills ecosystems are defined as regional or sectoral social formations in which a skill is developed and deployed; they emphasise the importance of understanding the context within which skills are developed and used. Although the construct was originally used for productive purposes, today there are strong arguments for skills ecosystems that connect living, working and learning. In this chapter, the work of Spours (2019) and colleagues is drawn on to help frame the nature of skills ecosystems that are essential for the green transition. Their work on the social skills ecosystem foregrounds a more regional, place-based model for skills planning. Hodgson and Spours (2018) and Spours (2019) 'envisage bringing together of a wide range of social partners around the relationship between working, living and learning'. They place education practice/systems as important to '45-degree activity' with 45-degree activity referring to the connecting skills development activity that mediates between 'connecting horizontalities' and 'facilitating verticalities'. Spours (2019) further argues that socio-ecosystemic skills planning leadership should be place-based and should involve the capability to define the problem terrain, and the goal of inclusive sustainable social, economic and educational development (Lotz-Sisitka, 2020). Figure 13.2 illustrates the dimensions of the skills ecosystem model advocated by Spours (2019).

Drawing on the elements represented above, skills are framed as a continuum between the vertical and horizontal domains and seen as critical enablers of linking these distinctive elements of skills ecosystem. This helps to construct a framing that examines skills as the enabling factor between the vertical and the horizontal domains. Constructing the vertical domain involves policies, hierarchical structures and leadership structures that exist at different levels, and the ways in which they may shape activity at the local level. In constructing the horizontal domain, the relationships between actors are examined. These include the complex dynamic and multi-layered

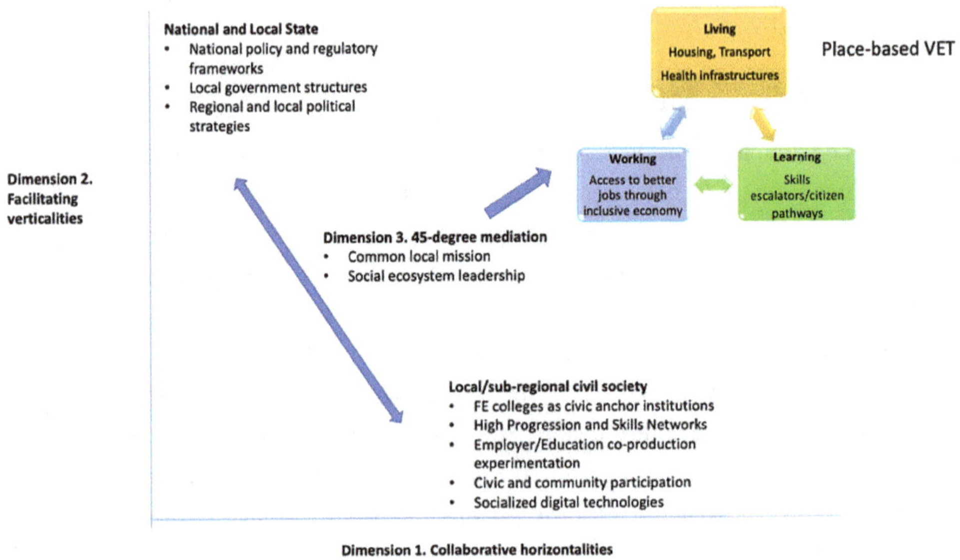

Figure 13.2: Social skills ecosystem

Source: Spours (2021).

relationships that may sit within and across various clusters as well as nested relationships associated with a particular case. Using this framing, some of the mediating factors between the vertical and the horizontal domains are explored as well as various emerging tensions between these two domains. This should provide lessons to help plan more resilient skills ecosystems.

In the next section this framework is applied to some local cases. To illustrate the skills dynamics that emerge, we trace the vertical and horizontal domains of the skills ecosystem and how they can assist in reframing skills planning.

UNPACKING CASE STUDY EXAMPLES TO DEPICT THE VERTICAL AND HORIZONTAL DIMENSIONS OF TWO SKILLS ECOSYSTEMS

In this section, local case studies are examined to determine how the framing described above enables a more systematic viewing of skills development. Working with the skills ecosystem more constructively, it examines skills as the mediator between the vertical and the horizontal domains.

CASE 1 – Skills ecosystem – The wood pellet value chain in the Expanded Public Works Programme

Invasive alien plants (IAPs) represent an integral opportunity to create green jobs through the clearing and harvesting of IAPs and transforming the feedstock into products to add value to the IAP supply chain. IAPs threaten not only South Africa's biological diversity, but also water security, the ecological functioning of natural systems and the productive use of land. A study conducted by Trade and Industrial Policy Strategies (TIPS) (Jenkin and Mudombi, 2018) explored how IAP clearance could be extended: wood pellets could be created from the IAPs removed, and these pellets could replace paraffin as a source of fuel in non-electrified homes, thus reducing paraffin-related deaths and illnesses. The study indicated that approximately 1 480 000 direct person day jobs could be created by 2028, which in turn could result in the clearance of an estimated 2.3 million Ha of IAPs, and 1 060 000 households converted from 'dirty' fuel use to wood pellets. An assessment of the types of jobs employed along the wood pellet manufacturing value chain suggests that the majority are low- to medium-skilled, with most allocated to harvesting and pellet manufacturing in rural areas (Pellet Manufacturer 1, 2017).

A study of the skills ecosystem that can support this initiative involved examining the facilitating verticalities comprising the ecosystem, as discussed below:

> A suite of national government strategies, e.g., the Biofuels Industrial Strategy of the Republic of South Africa (DMRE, 2007) and the Bioeconomy Strategy (DST, 2013), and programmes, e.g. the Department of Forestry, Fisheries and Environment's (DFFE) management of the environment sector component of the Expanded Public Works Programme (EPWP), have enabled the clearing of IAPs and biomass beneficiation. The EPWP has supported biodiversity-benefiting businesses over the past decade to enable innovation and job creation through the

> eradication of IAPs. This is part of the enterprise development approach, one of the delivery mechanisms of the EPWP that focuses on supporting emerging enterprises, including cooperatives, to leverage additional work opportunities. While these state-level enabling initiatives exist, government intervention is weak with institutional [policy] barriers (Petrie, 2014; Ward et al., 2017; Jenkin, 2020), and business models that focus on large-scale manufacturing sites and the export market rather than local economies and communities. This failure led to the mothballing of most wood pellet manufacturing sites by the end of 2017, creating financial and job losses. Most of the job opportunities through this initiative are realised through the government's public employment programme, the EPWP, in the harvesting and processing of IAPs. However, the EPWP funding model faces challenges, mainly through delayed contracts and payments resulting in job precariousness through contractors receiving delayed payments, with salaries not being paid, and employee dissatisfaction at a high level (Ward et al., 2017; Jenkin and Mudombi, 2018).

Some of the collaborative horizontalities that comprise the skills ecosystems that:

> At the local (horizontal element) of the associated system, collaboration is required to interpret, enable, implement and sustain the IAP wood pellet added value chain to ensure it is situated within local communities and networks. Currently the predominant dimension witnessed at the local level is that of the landowner (upon whose land IAPs are located), local civil society organisations, municipalities and businesses (e.g., saw mills) contracted by DFFE to implement the related programme activities (harvesting and product production), and to hire, train and pay the associated work force. This reflects a very disconnected, ad-hoc approach to skills development. Spours's (2019) approach would argue for a more localised approach that would make a stronger strategic contribution to

> the local economy, supporting a sense of local identity within the skills ecosystem. A notable gap in the actor network on the horizontal dimension is that of community and TVET colleges and broader co-ordinated civic and community participation, e.g., inclusion of the local community. Improved engagement with the communities and education providers in the localities in which the programme is initiated could significantly enhance relationship building, connectivity between 'infrastructural' opportunities (e.g., wood pellets to replace paraffin burners) and enhanced capability of the local workforce. This would hopefully, therefore, result in less precarious employment and improved rural livelihoods. In addition to the above, another horizontal infrastructure and actor absence within the skills ecosystem is that of small enterprises and small-scale technologies, especially in the cooking stove sector, with large-scale centralised solutions prevailing. Moreover, the green innovation landscape is littered with solutions that failed due to lack of local buy-in and uptake – involvement of local communities and technology users is essential for the design, uptake and even marketing of the solution.

Regarding the implications of national (vertical) financial and business model challenges, this is expressed in the horizontal through ecosystem leadership, which is therefore challenged to adequately support and implement the programme locally. Social ecosystem leadership should be supportive and strategic to enable implementation on the ground. Otherwise the common mission of the intervention and its significant transformative economic, social (job creation) and environment potential is hindered.

CASE 2 – Towards a resilient food ecosystem: Addressing food waste

The COVID-19 pandemic shone a light on the value and importance of food, and the inequalities and complexities of South Africa's food system. While it is known that in South Africa 55 per cent of the population lives below the poverty line (BusinessTech, 2019), the pandemic further exposed the flaws in the food system (Cramer,

2020; Mofokeng and Nyoni, 2020). As such, collective action between government, business and civil society was expedited, with the urgent need to develop and implement interventions to curtail growing food poverty (Vermeulen et al., 2020). The minimisation of food waste and distribution of surplus edible food are a vital component of these interventions, and a broader response to the complexities and failures of our food system.

South Africa generates an estimated 12.6 million tonnes of food waste per annum (a third of all food produced), of which approximately 80 per cent is edible (WWF South Africa, 2017). This happens in a context where 12 per cent of South Africa's population experience hunger (about 6.8 million people) (StatsSA, 2019). In addition, wasted food also equates to wasted water and energy, increased methane emissions from landfill, and impacts on natural resources and biodiversity (Parfitt and Jenkin, 2020).

With the launch of South Africa's food waste voluntary agreement in September 2020, there is commitment from government, industry and civil society to minimise food waste and to divert nutritious surplus to those in need. This is notable progress towards achieving the UN's Sustainable Development Goal 12.3 to halve global food waste by 2030 (United Nations, 2021). Skills and knowledge will be required to support the intended transition towards a resilient South African food system – and to meet the voluntary agreement's ambitions, with regard to current and future green jobs. This case explores this knowledge and skills dimension.

Facilitating verticalities within the skills ecosystem that emerged from this case

While COVID-19 forced actors within South Africa's broader food system to develop and implement interventions to curtail growing food poverty (Vermeulen et al., 2020), broader long-term verticalities are driving and enabling a transition to resilience within the skills ecosystem. In the case of food waste, some of the critical global, regional and national enablers include the following:

- SDG 12.3 to reduce food loss and waste (United Nations)
- South African food waste voluntary agreement (CGCSA, DFFE and DTI)
- Operation Phakisa Chemicals & Waste Economy (The Presidency, DFFE)
- Organic waste to landfill ban by 2027 (Western Cape Provincial Government)

All of these present a macro frame that shape and influence skill priorities, and the allocation of resources that ultimately shape the skills landscape and the actors within the ecosystem.

While both international and national policy and initiatives that address food waste exist, there are some recognised challenges, e.g., inhibitive legislation, lack of funding and national food system complexity. Legislation covering two different areas inhibits food waste minimisation and donation: the Consumer Protection Act imposes conditions and potential liabilities for passing on food, and there is also legislative confusion around date labelling, which relates to the disposing of food while still fit for consumption. Lack of both government and private support and investment to shift at scale and 'make things happen' is also prohibitive. For example, the DFFE's Operation Phakisa Chemicals and Waste has stakeholder-developed food waste interventions but is relying on public-private partnerships to enable implementation. Government does not have the ability to fund the initiative, as is often the case for similar international initiatives. The food waste voluntary agreement therefore currently relies on external international funding to maintain much needed implementation and momentum. The food system is also complex, with large-scale wastage and inefficiencies, and difficulties in coordination among the system actors, which would ensure that they could operate as a cohesive large-scale unit of change. The regional and local implications of this are explored further below.

Consultation about policies and strategies has been at the thought-leadership level, confined to those with high levels of skills. For example:

- Undertaking research to inform the food waste agreement's purpose, quantitative targets, reporting methodology, funding model, governance structure and implementation mechanisms;
- Facilitation and negotiation capabilities of the CGCSA, DTI and DFFE to ensure adequate cross-departmental engagement and agreement; provincial and local stakeholder engagement with the broad food system, and the ability to generate funding from international entities and partnerships.

With the platform for implementation now in place, the focus of activities is shifting from research and development to transformative implementation at scale. The current reliance on knowledge and capabilities of a few, including international 'experts', will have to shift to implementation knowledge, skills and capabilities at the local level.

Horizontalities (collaboration) that emerged

At the local level, the food system and activities around food security, food waste and distribution are dominated by regional nodes or intra-networks of activity and communities of practice. This can often lead to duplication or dominance of certain actors, or in the case of a crisis, such as COVID-19, the bringing together of various local communities of practice around a common local mission. A good example of this was witnessed in Cape Town, with those in positions of leadership in the broader city food system quickly setting up a network of actors:

- Government (e.g., City of Cape Town's Climate Resilience Unit, GreenCape, Department of the Premier);
- Industry and business (e.g., Consumer Goods Council of South Africa, retailers with their headquarters in the city, and food / waste consultants);
- Academia (e.g., University of the Western Cape's Centre of Excellence in Food Security and the University of Cape Town's African City for Cities); and
- Civil society/NGOs (e.g., WWF South Africa, GreenCape, Southern Africa Food Labe, Local

> Governments for Sustainability [ICLEI] and Food Forward [food donation charity]).

It could be suggested that the common local mission and drivers for the rapid response were the need to sustain local livelihoods (ensuring food did not go to waste, but could be sold or donated), and ensuring the continued health and wellbeing of those on the poverty line (e.g., food donations for feeding schemes, orphanages and old age homes). The ability to rapidly network and collaborate could be attributed to strong civic and community participation, leadership, local knowledge, skills and capabilities, which drew on local actor and knowledge access. One of the outcomes of this unintended response was a closer-knit local community of practice, which continues to engage on other food-related systemic matters.

THE INTERPLAY BETWEEN THE VERTICAL AND HORIZONTAL IN THE SKILLS ECOSYSTEMS

While policy exists and investments have been made in the manufacturing of wood pellets and technologies that can use wood pellets, there appears to be a disconnect between government, not-for-profit and private entities. This has prevented a collaborative systems approach to effectively introducing wood pellets into the South African market and thus creating permanent and decent green jobs and learning pathways, especially in rural areas. The vertical issues of inadequate and misaligned government policy and an ineffective business model has resulted in tensions with the horizontal domain of the skills ecosystem, which invariably impact on any skills development intervention. This in turn inhibits possibilities for localised, rural green job creation and collaboration with local educational institutions, land and business owners (including entrepreneurs) and households that could benefit from access to cleaner fuels. Hence skills development interventions that focus on enhanced coordination of the ecosystem collective (vertical and horizontal) would enable access to a diversity of vertical specialist and horizontal knowledge. This would allow for realisation of the opportunities presented by this technological shift and also ensure that local employability and demand are more stable, locally relevant and sustainable.

Collective skills within the system can be realised through the opportunities presented by IAP beneficiation, namely local manufacturing and maintenance of machinery, tools and systems to support the core IAP added-value chain. Vertical enablers can enhance the creation of entry level and technical employment in rural areas where the feedstock is readily available through community-based and/or localised and decentralised wood pellet manufacturing. In turn, local skill providers like TVET or community colleges can play a role in developing the skills required to implement the enhanced beneficiation of IAPs. Local skill providers play 'a particular role as local anchor institutions ... can facilitate "citizen pathways" to new jobs and sustainable living' (Hodgson and Spours, 2018: 3). This place-based approach can then facilitate the use of skills development to enable economic and social renewal in communities.

To mediate and enable the transformation envisaged, the added value system will require more than individual skills or competencies. Coordinated and collaborative skills and competencies would range from traditional technical measures – like machinery and tool operation, product and innovation design – to non-technical interventions – like policy development, actor engagement and negotiation, operation and project management, market research and skills training (Jenkin, 2020; Ward et al, 2017; PAGE, 2016). In addition, adopting a transformative greening skills systems approach as opposed to an individual skills or linear value chain approach would both enable significant adoption through the wood pellet added value programme, and bring additional benefits, notably local benefits. These would include improved health and safety through the reduced use of firewood and paraffin (Ecozoom, 2017; Petrie, 2014), and environmental benefits, such as lower GHG emissions (Viking Energy Development Africa, no date); a reduced dependency on fossil-based fuels (Ernsting, 2014), and a reduced reliance on trees for fire wood (Petrie, 2014; Sander et al., 2011).

It is evident that the vertical enablers, such as the international sustainable development goals and national waste and policy and interventions exist, with good stakeholder engagement and commitment. However, emerging tensions between these and the horizontal dimension of local implementation will require some form of mitigation and prioritisation to ensure scaled collective and effective transformation towards system resiliency and achievement of the voluntary agreements targets. This includes strengthened job permanency and sustained livelihoods throughout the system (whether formal or informal).

While vertical enablers have focused on the technicalities of achieving sustainability targets, these should also acknowledge and support the significant job creation and social renewal potential offered through interventions like food waste minimisation, beneficiation and food surplus diversion. To date, the majority of educational provision has been at university level, e.g., universities holding chairs in waste management and food security, or undertaking research to map actors in the system, calculate the magnitude of food waste or to better understand consumer food waste behaviours. The transition to implementation will require an emphasis and shift towards the provisioning of locally contextual and pragmatic knowledge and skills, from farm to fork, to reduce food waste on farms, in packhouses and manufacturing facilities, through to distribution and retail. Local community and TVET colleges, and existing civil society training, e.g., agriculture and entrepreneurial programmes, are perfectly placed to provide these skills.

By way of example, local colleges can enhance their offerings to support farmers who will require a skilled labour force to adopt optimal and sustainable farming practices to reduce yield loss, e.g., through improved harvesting practices. Food processing outfits will require skilled workers who understand how to reduce food waste during the preparation stage or where and how to divert non-edible food waste from landfill. Entrepreneurial and job creation opportunities will exist in the beneficiation of food waste, e.g., in biodegradable packaging or for identifying opportunities to trade and distribute surplus food from farms, manufacturers and retailers. These opportunities will require individuals with technical, innovation, business, negotiation and sales skills, amongst others. The strength of these collective skills can enable a significant transition towards achieving South Africa's food waste goals, with broader expanded benefits also being realised, e.g., more people in need having access to nutritious edible food that would have gone to waste.

The two cases highlight the roles played by a range of actors and institutions in the skills ecosystem and how these should ideally interact to facilitate place-based, socially just work opportunities that enhance living through working and learning. They clearly illustrate that a human capital approach that focuses on 'train the trainer' and short skill course cultures that reflect generic training 'delivered' in communities cannot enable viable skills for a just transition approach.

LESSONS ON SKILLS AND SKILLS ECOSYSTEMS

Through the two cases above an attempt was made to show that a just transition requires an approach to skills development that is a strongly constituted, place-based approach that can play a transformative role in local communities. Lotz Sisitka (2020) argues that a paradox exists between the top-down approach to training, and the primarily regional implementation platforms of, for example, EPWP job opportunities, skills and training, and their developmental intent. Seeking ways to reconcile this paradox, while giving attention to the intention of the skills development interventions, ecosystems skills research offers potential for a conceptual and theoretical framework for guiding skills research for a just transition.

In framing skills responses for a just transition, there is a need to be wary about the individualistic fallacy in the skills discourse (which dominates development responses), and which often assumes that people apply their skills and knowledge in decontextualised situations. Few if any individuals will have all the knowledge and skills required to undertake the complex and often drawn-out work required to advance the green economy in a particular context. Rosenberg et al. (2016) also found in investigating champions in government, that sustainability policy actions occurred in a distributed format among collectives of professionals and other practitioners. Instead, the abilities people need to respond to complex sustainability challenges and opportunities are called forth in relation to the specific, shared object at hand from groups of people who need to function together to be successful. That is, the competencies are distributed among groups of people, and never reside only in an individual, and are called forth in real-world situations that are almost always unique in their particular set of challenges. Hence, skills for a just transition need to facilitate distributed agency that is needed across individuals, organisations and systems to drive regime change and work against the lock-ins that hinder structural and systemic change. This has implications for how training is conceptualised, as learning networks or as 'training of individuals'.

The cases illustrate that context and community change is central; decontextualised notions of skills and training are not advisable and cannot facilitate local transitions. It further illustrates the role of networks and situating and conceptualising skills so that they facilitate and strengthen these networks. The cases also showed that local network building is critical to supporting institution building. The future stability of the social ecosystem will depend not only on networks and relationships, but also on robust, agile and inclusive anchor organisations like local skills providers that are core to the networks that form the foundations of and strengthen local institutions. However, any attempt to develop local educational and training institutions need to consider the community they are embedded in.

Regarding the implications of national (vertical) challenges, such as siloed operations or (top-down) research and development-led (R&D) innovation-focused support, this finds expression in the horizontal dimension through poor local implementation and/or insignificant benefits to rural economies. This notable gap also plays out in terms of the occupational, knowledge and skills required to significantly transform uptake of greening interventions and highlights the need for more 'on-the ground' pragmatic implementation. This will require more people to understand how to implement programmes at scale through decentralised rural development models and will need new ideas and solutions for implementation.

What the cases also show is that although fragmented green skills initiatives exist, they are not cohesive or coordinated. They are currently dominated by government, industry and academia, with little civil society and/or localised penetration or alignment. In addition, most of the occupational opportunities are associated with policy development and R&D, which gravitates and lends itself to preferring techno-economic specialisms and knowledge, thereby reducing the collective potential of various levels of knowledge and skills that could be brought to the system to realise significant uptake.

CONCLUSION

South Africa's transition to a low carbon economy has prompted some rapid, albeit naive, educational responses that are framed around individuals, not collectives. Limited, fragmented adaptive responses to skills – which reflect 'bolt on' approaches to existing education and training system and structures – will not enable a just transition though they may present short-term benefits.

Rather, what is required is building systems of skills research, planning and analysis that are relevant for communities and the labour market, and are reflective of the sustainability pathways and vision required in any particular place, industry or region. Skills can be one of the enabling factors for just and inclusive transitions to low carbon economies. It is also vital that we invest in education and training for a strong and sustainable recovery as we face the global challenge of skilling our economies for a greener future.

However, the envisaged transition is an ambitious one and will require a comprehensive policy mix. It will also necessitate transversal engagement across education and training systems, as sustainability practices are embedded in schooling, higher education and occupational training. This will further burden the currently overextended and inefficient skills development system.

Development to support a green transition in South Africa has been inadequate, ad hoc, fragmented, reactive and inefficient (Ramsarup, 2017). This has been the case despite expanding mandates, skills planning and provisioning for environmental skills.

To facilitate and enable the scale that is required to shift the country to meet its renewable energy ambitions, individuals within both government and beneficiary actor groups need to hold the appropriate skills, knowledge and capacity to do so. Occupational opportunities to leverage this significant shift will sit within policy development (ensuring cross-departmental alignment), development of financing mechanisms and models, negotiation, law, procurement and supply chain management, engineering, monitoring and evaluation, strategic stakeholder engagement, and management. Many of these occupations will require high levels of specialism or skill. At the local (horizontal) level it is collaboration with beneficiaries that is key, as well as local knowledge, skills and capacity.

Lotz-Sisitka (2020) further argue that traditional research orientations were not adequate for identifying green skills demand, transitioning, occupational analysis or green skills supply. This is because many of the green jobs are themselves still emerging, and because green skills are often 'latent' and not yet articulated in terms of green work, and the greening of work. Additionally, green skills transitioning between education levels and into work is complicated by the fact that the qualifications and workplace demands are poorly aligned as these are often 'new' or under-developed. Green skills occupations are poorly defined in the national system of occupations, as there is as yet under-developed understanding of the nature of green work, greening of work and green jobs. Hence the educational needs to support the transition have shown up some critical disjunctives in the skills supply systems and the need for the co-evolution of environmental policy systems together with education and training systems (Ramsarup, 2017; Rosenberg et al., 2020).

The chapter has argued that the enabling verticalities and government intervention critical for ensuring socio-economic benefits are realised through skills development. However, as indicated by the cases, the interface between the horizontalities and verticalities are weak through many skills development initiatives – through poor management and collaboration. This is further compounded by the precarious nature of many of the potentially significant vocational job opportunities. Consequently, the rural local livelihood benefits that could be sustained by large-scale initiatives may not be realised. In addition, and as is often the case with skills initiatives, much of the discourse and emphasis is on human capital – the number of jobs – with little detailed insight into the actual types of vocational occupations, and skills and knowledge provisioning that is required to support more sustainable living, working and learning.

REFERENCES

Australian Green Skills Agreement. 2009. 'Council of Australian Governments: Green Skills Agreement: An agreement between the Australian Government and the state and territory governments'. Council of Australian Governments, Barton, Australian Capital Territory.

BusinessTech. 1 August 2019. 'This is how much money the poorest are living on each month in South Africa'. https://businesstech.co.za/news/finance/332553/this-is-how-much-money-the-poorest-are-living-on-each-month-in-south-africa/, accessed 5 August 2021.

European Centre for the Development of Vocational Training (Cedefop). 2012. 'Green skills and environmental awareness in vocational education and training: Synthesis Report'. Research Paper, No. 24, Publications Office of the European Union, Luxembourg.

Cramer, C. 10 September 2020. 'The effect of Covid-19 on the food system: The cost of feeding a child increased by 5%'. Southern Africa Food Lab, https://www.southernafricafoodlab.org/the-effect-of-covid-19-on-the-food-system-the-cost-of-feeding-a-child-increased-by-5/, accessed 5 August 2021.

Department of Minerals and Energy (DMRE). 2007. 'Biofuels industrial strategy of the Republic of South Africa'. https://www.gov.za/documents/biofuels-industrial-strategy-republic-south-africa, accessed 5 August 2021.

Department of Science & Technology (DST). 2013. 'The bioeconomy strategy'. https://www.gov.za/sites/default/files/gcis_document/201409/bioeconomy-strategya.pdf, accessed 13 July 2021.

Ecozoom. 2017. 'Portable wood burning cook stoves'. www.ecozoomstove.com, accessed 12 July 2017.

Ernsting, A. 2014. 'A new look at land-grabs in the global South linked to EU biomass policies'. Biofuel Watch, https://www.biofuelwatch.org.uk/2014/biomass-landgrabbing-report/, accessed 10 May 2021.

Hodgson, A. and Spours, K. 2018. 'A social ecosystem model: Conceptualizing and connecting working, living and learning in London's "New East"'. ELVET Programme Research Briefing 3, Centre for Post-14 Education and Work, UCL Institute of Education.

International Labour Organization (ILO). 2018. 'Greening with Jobs: World Employment Social Outlook'. https://www.ilo.org/weso-greening/#Intro-2, accessed 5 August 2021.

International Renewable Energy Agency (IRENA). 2020. 'Measuring the socio-economics of transition: Focus on jobs', International Renewable Energy Agency, Abu Dhabi.

Jenkin, N. 2020. 'Collaboration in South Africa's Forestry-Products Biorefinery Innovation System: Examining the knowledge network of leverage professionals'. University of the Witwatersrand, Johannesburg.

Jenkin, N. and Mudombi, S. 2018. 'Unlocking and retaining jobs in the alien vegetation added value chain through industrial symbiosis: Case study on wood pellets'. World Wide Fund for Nature South Africa (WWF-SA) and Trade and Industrial Policy Strategies (TIPS).

Kwauk, C. and Casey, O. 2021. 'A new green learning agenda: Approaches to quality education for climate action'. Center for Universal Education at The Brookings Institution, https://www.brookings.edu/wp-content/uploads/2021/01/Brookings-Green-Learning-FINAL.pdf, accessed 3 May 2021.

Lotz-Sisitka, H. 2020. 'Probing the potential of social ecosystemic skills approaches for green skills planning', in Rosenberg, E., Ramsarup, P. and Lotz-Sisitka, H. (eds), *Green Skills Research in South Africa Models, Cases and Methods*. New York: Routledge, 113–127.

Mofokeng, N. and Nyoni, N. 2020. 'Report on the impact of Covid-19 on food systems in the Eastern and Southern African region'. Graca Machel Trust and FANRPAN. https://gracamacheltrust.org/wp-content/uploads/2020/05/REPORT-ON-THE-IMPACT-OF-COVID-19-ON-FOOD-SYSTEMS-IN-THE-EASTERN-AND-SOUTHERN-AFRICAN-REGION.pdf, accessed 5 August 2021.

OECD. 2014. 'Greener Skills and Jobs'. OECD Publishing, Paris. https://www.oecd-ilibrary.org/industry-and-services/greener-skills-and-jobs_9789264208704-en, accessed 5 August 2021.

Nahman, A. and De Lange, W. 2013. 'Costs of food waste along the value chain: Evidence from South Africa'. *Waste Management*, 33(11), 2493–2500.

Partnership for Action on Green Economy (PAGE). 2016. 'Green Economy Learning Assessment South Africa: Critical Competencies for Driving a Green Transition'. Partnership for Action on Green Economy, https://www.un-page.org/files/public/green_economy_learning_assessment_south_africa.pdf, accessed 4 August 2021.

Parfitt, J. and Jenkin, N. 2020. 'South Africa's food waste agreement: Implementation plan'. SA-EU Strategic Partnership, Consumer Goods Council of South Africa (CGCSA), and the Department of Trade & Industry (DTI).

Pellet Manufacturer 1. 17 October 2017. Interview with N. Jenkin, Cape Town.

Petrie, B. 2014. *South Africa: A case for biomass?* London: International Institute for Environment & Development.

Ramsarup, P. 2017. 'A critical realist dialectical understanding of learning pathways associated with two scarce skill environmental occupations within a transitioning systems frame', PhD thesis, Rhodes University.

Rosenberg, E., Ramsarup, P. and Lotz-Sisitka, H. 2020. *Green Skills Research in South Africa: Models, Cases and methods*. London: Routledge.

Sander, K., Haider, S. and Hyseni, B. 2011. 'Wood-based biomass energy development for Sub-Saharan Africa: Issues and approaches'. World Bank, https://documents.worldbank.org/en/publication/documents-reports/documentdetail/843941468009629566/wood-based-biomass-energy-development-for-sub-saharan-africa-issues-and-approaches, accessed 17 October 2017.

Spours, K. 2021. 'The dynamics of the Social Ecosystem Model (SEM) in cities – connecting working, living and learning'. https://www.kenspours.com/set-and-cities, accessed 5 October 2021.

Spours, K. 2019. 'Social ecosystems: A place-based and inclusive approach to working, living and learning'. Edge Foundation, Glasgow, United Kingdom.

Stroud, D., Fairbrother, P., Evans, C. and Blake, J. 2014. 'Skill development in the transition to a "green economy": A "varieties of capitalism" analysis'. *The Economic and Labour Relations Review*, 25(1), 10–27.

Statistics South Africa (StatsSA). 2019. 'Towards measuring the extent of food security in South Africa: An examination of hunger and food inadequacy'. http://www.statssa.gov.za/publications/03-00-14/03-00-142017.pdf, accessed 5 August 2021.

United Nations. 29 May 2021. 'Goal 12: Ensure sustainable consumption and production patterns'. https://www.un.org/sustainabledevelopment/sustainable-consumption-production/, accessed 5 August 2021.

Vermeulen, H., Muller, C. and Schonfeldt, H. 22 April 2020. 'Food aid parcels in South Africa could do with a better nutritional balance'. *The Conversation*, https://theconversation.com/food-aid-parcels-in-south-africa-could-do-with-a-better-nutritional-balance-136417 accessed on 5 August 2021.

Viking Energy Development Africa (VEDA). (no date). 'The value of biomass in alien eradication'. Viking Energy Development Africa.

Ward, M., McLean, D., Kraak, A., Jenkin, N., and Mushangai, D. 2017. 'The eco-furniture programme: An evaluative review'. Unpublished report, Department of Environmental Affairs, http://www.c-s-v.co.za/wp-content/uploads/2020/04/EFP-Evaluation-Final-171122.pdf, accessed 10 August 2021.

World Economic Forum (WEF). 14 July 2020. 'New Nature Economy Report II: The Future Of Nature, http://www3.weforum.org/docs/WEF_The_Future_Of_Nature_And_Business_2020.pdf.

WWF South Africa. 2017. 'Food loss and waste: Facts and futures: Taking steps towards a more sustainable food future'. https://wwfafrica.awsassets.panda.org/downloads/wwf_2017_food_loss_and_waste_facts_and_futures.pdf?21641/Food-Loss-and-Waste-Facts-and-Futures-Report, accessed 10 August 2021.

FOURTEEN

Conclusion

Insights and recommendations for building a just low carbon future in South Africa

Nqobile Xaba and Saliem Fakir

INTRODUCTION

The adoption of a just transition framework for South Africa's low carbon transitions provides an opportunity to plan for a variety of consequences as the world shifts to deeper decarbonisation strategies, such as net zero targets by 2050 (IEA, 2021), which will influence South Africa's own transitions and the burden of socio-economic issues that it will have to carry. However, South Africa's decarbonisation strategy faces a multitude of existing challenges including very high and growing unemployment, inequality and poverty. Therefore, while the just transition framework offers an opportunity to address these challenges, the just transition in South Africa still needs to define a clear and managed approach to decarbonisation transitions, also in light of the government's new ambitions in the National Determined Contributions (NDCs).

The book interrogates aspects of the just transition relevant to South Africa with the main question relating to how South Africa can decarbonise while providing economic opportunities for the most vulnerable and alleviating all forms of inequality. The book provides recommendations that can be factored into a strategy and incorporated into policies to fully realise a just transition in South Africa. The authors focus on the South African context and draw lessons from broader African and international cases. The book chapters showed specific gaps in current policies that need to be addressed. In the following sections, this chapter provides recommendations organised in specific themes, namely, social dialogue and cohesion for a just transition, just and inclusive economic growth, technological innovations for equitable energy access, strategy, capacity building and skills development for a capable workforce.

SOCIAL DIALOGUE AND COHESION FOR A JUST TRANSITION

The just transition process in South Africa, given the nature of South Africa's society, requires active engagement processes to attain consensus with key stakeholders that are key to economic and climate policy in the country. In early 2021 the President of South Africa established the Presidential Commission on Climate Change (PCC) to facilitate a multi-stakeholder dialogue and setting the framework for South Africa's just transition (The Presidency, 2020). The PCC is a path-breaking institution constituting of a 30-member body of commissioners and a secretariat; it is chaired by the president of South Africa and has an influential deputy chair, the former Minister of Environment. The PCC seeks to bring together technical and economic aspects of the transition, especially in the energy sector given South Africa high coal dependence, with a social compact between major stakeholders on the just transition (PCC, 2021). It will be formalised as a quasi-statutory body through the climate bill (DEA, 2018). Chapter 2 (Nzimande and Khambule) raises the importance of an independent, cross-sectoral and multi-disciplinary forum such as the PCC to provide the necessary locus for the climate and transition discussion.

The PCC also has an important policy facilitation role to ensure that the whole of government is aligned and has the capacity to deliver a transition as the public sector has a major role to play. The transition will still be an uncomfortable proposition for incumbents, such as those in the coal industry and the fast developing gas value chain in South Africa. The need for political infrastructure to manage this transition cannot be underestimated. The resistance to accelerating decommissioning of coal plants is growing and there is mounting resistance to lock in gas as a transition fuel in South Africa. The recent controversy around using emergency gas generators under the risk mitigation independent power producer procurement programme (RMIPPP) bid process and the selection of the Turkish power-ship Karpower legal challenge is a good case in point. Chapter 5 (Burton, Baker, Marquard, and Lehmann-Grube) argues that the political and industrial push for gas in South Africa as a bridge will only slow down the pace of coal phase-out, while there is global divergence on the future of gas in both global climate pathways and local energy systems.

The chapters cover a vast terrain from science, economics and civil society mobilisation to approaches to dealing with decarbonisation transitions. The role of civil society and labour is emphasised in chapter 11. Mulaisi and Cork argue that given that social justice and climate are intersectional issues, the green climate movement has to work closely and in alliance with the labour movement. The relationship has not always been easy, but the just transition debate is bringing the two groups a lot closer. The authors recommend further that the question of new types of social arrangements need to be interrogated beyond the usual capitalism versus socialism debate and where tactical issues are becoming far more important than just ideological positions.

Vulnerable communities, particularly those in coal areas, need to be included in the just transition debate and plans. Besides the impact of the transition, these communities in coal areas still lack basic services such as electricity, health and education, while they suffer from the effects of pollution daily from coal use. These communities also have high unemployment rates. Coal power plants have not necessarily provided employment opportunities to the most vulnerable. Chapter 10 by Dasoo and Semelane explores the energy and agricultural nexus that exists in coal areas, and it seeks to address the question of what will happen to the retired coal plants (repurposing options) and whether regenerative agriculture can be implemented for new types of economic investments. It must be emphasised that just transition dialogues must extend to all citizens. As underlined in chapter 2 (Nzimande and Khambule), democracy calls for involved citizens, engaged with the decisions that affect them; South Africa is a democratic country and democracy calls for involved and engaged citizens who have a say in the decisions that impact or affect them as stated in chapter 2 (Nzimande and Khambule).

Approaches to dealing with the transition challenges in coal mining areas require a different development vision for coal mining areas. While chapter 10 states the case, chapters 3 (Mohamed and Montmasson-Clair) and 13 (Ramsarup and Mohamed) provide a framework and insights into matters related to distributional issues, skills needs and training. Not all jobs can be created by new energy options and so while the coal sector is going to be affected the approaches to a just transition at a very localised level require strong community buy-in and a whole economy approach.

A 'JUST' INCLUSIVE ECONOMIC GROWTH

South Africa is faced with the enormous challenge of restructuring its current economy that has been characterised as the minerals energy complex (MEC) to transition to a low carbon economy. Energy-intensive sectors in South Africa, including mining, chemicals and manufacturing must develop alternative decarbonised energy sources. These sectors contribute immensely to the country's gross domestic product (GDP) and therefore their decarbonisation will affect the economy.

The restructuring of the national energy utility Eskom has become a necessity as a response to its current failure to provide sufficient power to the country and for renewable energy integration towards a decentralised power system. The renewable energy shift in South

Africa is not happening in the orderly manner and pace that it required. The 100MW concession of independent power procurement is being used to manage the crisis for the interim and at the non-utility scale while a positive policy shift for the entire energy services sector requires rethinking and structural reform. Chapter 4 (Creamer) explores the economic contribution new energy sources and policy reforms can bring to the South Africa economy, which has to both improve energy security and decarbonise the grid. Creamer also notes (as do Burton, Baker, Marquard and Lehmann-Grube in chapter 5, and Naidoo in chapter 7) that South Africa's energy transition – coupled with the unbundling of Eskom into three entities, namely, generation, distribution and transmission – can potentially attract global climate concessional finance that can seek to resolve Eskom's debt overhang and finance new clean energy infrastructure. South Africa is positioning itself to attract close to R4 billion worth of climate finance at COP 26 under the Just Energy Transition Transaction (JETT) as stated by Naidoo in chapter 7. This is a significant global development, though not without its challenges. The JETT deal can also be the basis for unlocking further and yet-to-tapped domestic sources of institutional and private finance. South Africa demonstrated this capacity for domestic finance participation through the REIPPP. Creamer further recommends that a supportive and well-designed industrial policy will help to maximise localisation, employment, and race and gender transformation objectives.

Nkhonjera in chapter 6 proposes a strategic opportunity for South Africa to use the African Continental Free Trade Agreement (AfCFTA) as part of a continental industrialisation process through renewables. Nkhonjera explores the potential of linkages between energy and industrial policy, as a mechanism to transition from the MEC towards an industrial framework based on renewable energy. Nearly half of Africa's population lacks electricity access; therefore, energy needs to be viewed as a tool for inclusive economic growth. A new energy system should be the cornerstone of Africa's industrial policy and industrialisation, accompanied by energy policies intended to drive structural change. AfCFTA is not only about trade policy; it is also a mechanism that can drive economic diversification and facilitate transformative industrialisation on the continent. The potential for regional energy integration within the AfCFTA, therefore, provides a greater incentive for the entry of private sector finance into the renewables market while strengthening the energy sector, the interconnection of power systems, the pooling of public and private resources and increasing cross-border power trade.

Nkhonjera recommends that South Africa must develop a policy that is truly comprehensive in terms of its co-objectives of clean energy and industrialisation that considers the way supply chains are organised. Further, how South Africa articulates the link between its energy policy and industrial development at the local, national and continental levels will determine whether renewable energy can fuel sustainable growth. Nkhonjera also emphasises that industrial policy will need to focus strongly on producing enough decent jobs. Mohamed and Montmasson-Clair in chapter 3 explore green technology, innovation and industrial development in a lot more detail and demonstrate that through the South African Renewable Energy Master Plan, South Africa's green technology and industrial policy landscape can shift significantly to deepen manufacturing and industrial development, which in the last decade has shown a steady decline. Existing industrial capacity in energy, automotive, hydrogen and other areas can be adapted to play a bigger role in green industrial development provided the policy landscape is backed by an ambitious long-term policy vision. Creamer, in chapter 4, for instance, estimates that about 38 000 direct jobs will be created between 2022–2030 from expanded wind and solar capacity projects.

The energy transition landscape is fast changing to include rapid developments in the hydrogen economy. The development of green hydrogen investments on the back of South Africa's long track record with platinum and fuel cell development can extend to green steel and aviation fuel, as well as ammonia and hydrogen itself as a store of energy and a thermal fuel. As more countries decarbonise, these initiatives will be critical to decarbonising hard-to-abate sectors based on the use of green hydrogen. They present a potentially large export market for South Africa. This is elaborated in chapter 8 (Xaba and Mazibuko-Makena) which provides an analysis of the socio-economic benefits that the green hydrogen economy presents for South Africa. Failure to comply with greenhouse gas emission standards places South Africa at risk of bearing a carbon abatement tax imposed by our trade partners. This will reduce South Africa's economic competitiveness.

Chapter 3 (Mohamed and Montmasson-Clair) also ties in well on how to link decarbonisation, energy security and growth in new investments with a redistributive framework. The authors provide some elegant conceptual hooks and introduce some novel framings to the current lacunae in literature and policy debates on the just transition. The chapter uses a normative framework that proposes key dimensions of a just transition and the variants of a just transition to access the industrial, employment and climate policy readiness for it. The key dimensions are procedural, distributive and restorative justice. These would faciliate the attainment of managerial reform, structural reform and overall transformation.

TECHNOLOGICAL INNOVATIONS FOR EQUITABLE ACCESS TO ENERGY

Technology is anticipated to be a key component of the accelerated decarbonisation and reaching net zero (IEA, 2021). However, the introduction of new technology comes with challenges that need to be addressed. Technological innovations must be used in a manner that addresses the socio-economic needs of South Africa.

Chapter 8 (Xaba and Mazibuko-Makena) uses a sustainable energy transition framework to analyse the role of hydrogen and fuel cell technologies in the low carbon transition. This framework is fitting since green hydrogen and fuel cells offer the cleanest form of energy. The chapter argues that these technologies must be used to bridge the existing energy gap to provide electricity to remote areas. Technology can be a tool to address energy equity. The main advantage of hydrogen and fuel cells is that they complement each other and other forms of renewable energy. However, there are systems that need to be put in place for South Africa to fully exploit this technology as recommended by the authors. For example, coherent government policy will be necessary to support the rate of hydrogen development and adequately incentivise the transition towards green hydrogen. South Africa needs to commit to a systematic, transparent, accountable and enabling policy environment for hydrogen, for the country to leverage the opportunities provided by the hydrogen economy for the benefit of all. The formation of a fully fledged hydrogen and fuel cell industry can be achieved, for example by government leading the financial investment into the hydrogen economy and the private sector co-funding and leading the piloting and demonstrations of new hydrogen technologies in collaboration with the Department of Science and Innovation (DSI); the Department of Environment, Forestry and Fisheries; the Department of Minerals Resources and Energy (DMRE) and the Department of Trade Industry and Competition (DTIC).

Technology will also play a critical role in renewable energy generation, distribution and uptake. Chapter 9 (Hermanus) looks closely at how scale in clean energy can be achieved through mobilising local authorities and metros around an enabling policy and infrastructure framework to support stronger decentralisation of energy provision. Municipalities, which have to align the needs of poorly serviced areas with sources of income from more affluent residents, are facing deeper and deeper shortfalls in revenue, given that electricity sales are core to the sustainability of municipal budgets. The chapter focuses on these challenges and the role that municipalities can play in the just transition. It argues that municipalities can play a stronger leadership role in the just transition space and should be far more active in both the clean energy transition as well as shaping the just transition outcomes at a local level. The chapter also brings into play the importance of the political economy and local politics as far as energy and just transitions go.

Decarbonisation also brings to the fore the relationship between climate imperatives and geoeconomics interests. While they are couched in the language of benign environmental endeavours, large-scale transformation transitions built into the vision of the European Green Deal (EUGD) have consequences for developing countries especially in Africa. These implications of the EUGD have to be studied carefully as they contain new standards, financial imperiatives, and technology innovation policy measures that will advantage those countries leading the frontier of decarbonisation, while not giving those countries lagging behind enough time to catch up. Decarbonisation in the EU, China or the US and other advanced countries will eventually crowd out carbon intense goods and services of exporting countries and create new markets for countries that decarbonise. Africa, and South Africa in particular, has to keep abreast of these developments and ensure there are neither losses nor are they left occupying the same status they currently enjoy: a continent valued only as a a home for new types of extractive industries. In chapter 12, Fakir, Aggad and Davis recommend that, for the climate agenda to succeed on the continent, the energy transition must be framed within a broader developmental model in Africa. The authors emphasise that South Africa must strive to reap the benefits of the advances of modern technology, science and industrial development. They also emphasise the need to shape a transition that is aligned not only to modernising Africa's energy systems but also localising the application of new clean energy technologies with stronger linkages to beneficiation and industrial development.

CAPACITY BUILDING AND SKILLS DEVELOPMENT FOR A CAPABLE WORKFORCE

The low carbon transition requires new knowledge and skills both within existing sectors and occupations and in emerging sectors. The just transition needs a capable workforce for the emerging new sectors. Therefore, skills development programmes to stimulate employment should be prioritised during the transition. Upskilling, and reskilling workers to meet the skills requirements for the transition will ensure that the transition does not exacerbate inequality, unemployment and poverty in already marginalised populations. Skills development will play a crucial role in seizing opportunities and unlocking the potential of reimagining jobs and work in the just transition.

The hydrogen economy, as an emerging sector, is expected to require high-tech and other skill sets that require either university education or post-school vocational training as stated by Xaba and Mazibuko-Makena (chapter 8). Aligning the country's tertiary education system (university and TVET college systems) with industry's needs and with opportunities to improve labour absorption in the future low carbon economy is crucial, specifically in offering the right qualifications and turning out enough graduates. These skills issues are relevant to all sectors of the green economy. The need for higher education institutions to align their curricula and qualifications with industry's requirements cannot be overemphasised. The HySA programme is a great example where, given the need to build South Africa's capacity in the hydrogen and fuel cell technology fields, the Department of Higher Education, Science and Innovation, institutions of higher learning and industries all demonstrated the value of collaboration to address the skills shortage in the country. The programme has produced skilled doctoral and master's graduates, technologists and other service providers, spin-off companies, and technology demonstrators. It represents a good example of how South Africa can respond to the skills shortage in the country.

A just low carbon transition requires a different approach to traditional skills development that South Africa is accustomed to. Chapter 13 (Ramsarup and Mohamed) recommends that South Africa considers a more holistic approach to skills development, where the conceptualisation of skills for the low carbon transition must look beyond the individual. The proposed approach requires a framing of skills that looks at individuals, organisations and systems as a coordinated system to drive change. Skills are multidimensional; green skills not only unlock renewable energy potential and productivity, but they have the potential to promote equity and social inclusion under an alternative version of sustainable economic growth (Kwauk and Casey, 2021). Skills development needs to shift from a narrow focus on the 'skills gap' towards an approach that considers worker needs, career interests and aspirations, community facilitation and social compacting skills as well as the socio-economic contexts in which the skills are embedded. The cases cited in this chapter show that currently green skills development is not well coordinated and does not take into account the transdisciplinary nature of the low carbon transition. The chapter thus emphasises building systems of skills research, planning and analysis relevant for the communities, the labour market and reflective of the sustainability pathways and vision of a particular place, industry or region to enable a just and inclusive low carbon economy.

The just transition cannot take place without finance. Climate finance is meant to be an obligation of advanced countries to support developing and emerging economies fund their NDCs and transitions. Chapter 7 (Naidoo) takes a closer look at the climate finance and just transition finance issues. The chapter provides a historical overview of the origins of climate finance and the role it can or cannot play. Naidoo presents the global picture and South Africa's place in this dynamic. The chapter traverses a broad range of issues related to climate finance and emergent new categories of finance such as transition finance and what they mean for South Africa. The key message of the chapter is that South Africa's needs for climate finance should not only pivot around energy transitions but also financing needs for other sectors that have to engage in deep decarbonisation strategies.

CONCLUDING REMARKS

The just transition has moved from a worker-centred framing to one that considers society and economy as a whole, with the chapters in this book coherently articulating this holistic vision. The fundamental argumens is that a just transition must be people-centred. The words 'people centred', 'society', 'most vulnerable', 'communities' and 'stakeholder' feature prominently in the chapters to signify 'the people' as the most important stakeholder in just transition processes. In this way, the just transition can be used to address challenges of poverty. Related to this is the need to ensure that planning for the just transition extends to a local level, and, at the same time, not only supplements the current energy shortages but promotes energy equity by addressing the inequalities that exist in the energy sector. A just transition to a low carbon economy in South Africa must be centred on the interests of all the people, especially the most vulnerable.

REFERENCES

Centre for Environmental Rights (CER). 2021. 'Environmental justice groups urge NERSA to deny Karpowership licences'. Centre for Environmental Rights, https://cer.org.za/news/environmental-justice-groups-urge-nersa-to-deny-karpowership-licences, accessed 2 October 2021.

Department of Environmental Affairs (DEA). 2018. 'Climate Change Bill'. Department of Environmental Affairs, https://www.environment.gov.za/sites/default/files/legislations/climatechangebill2018_gn41689.pdf, accessed 20 May 2021.

International Energy Agency (IEA). 2021. 'Net zero by 2050: A roadmap for the global energy sector'. https://iea.blob.core.windows.net/assets/beceb956-0dcf-4d73-89fe-1310e3046d68/NetZeroby2050-ARoadmapfortheGlobalEnergySector_CORR.pdf, accessed 24 July 2021.

Kwauk, C. and Casey, O. 2021. 'A new green learning agenda: Approaches to quality education for climate action'. Centre for Universal Education at The Brookings Institution.

Presidential Climate Commission (PCC). 2021. 'Presidential Climate Commission: Towards a just transition'. https://www.climatecommission.org.za/, accessed 20 August 2021

The Presidency. 2020. 'Presidential Climate Change Coordinating Commission appointed'. http://www.thepresidency.gov.za/press-statements/presidential-climate-change-coordinating-commission-appointed, accessed 25 July 2021.

United Nations (UN) 2020. 'The sustainable development goals report 2020'. https://unstats.un.org/sdgs/report/2020/The-Sustainable-Development-Goals-Report-2020.pdf, accessed 20 August 2021.

Index

www.ingramcontent.com/pod-product-compliance
Lightning Source LLC
LaVergne TN
LVHW052022200926
848481LV00005B/1553